On to Perfection

On to Perfection

Nels O. Westergreen and the
Swedish Methodist Church

Carol M. Norén

WIPF & STOCK · Eugene, Oregon

ON TO PERFECTION
Nels O. Westergreen and the Swedish Methodist Church

Wipf & Stock
An Imprint of Wipf and Stock Publishers
199 W. 8th Ave., Suite 3
Eugene, OR 97401

www.wipfandstock.com

PAPERBACK ISBN: 978-1-6667-1083-0
HARDCOVER ISBN: 978-1-6667-1084-7
EBOOK ISBN: 978-1-6667-1085-4

04/05/22

In memory of my immigrant grandparents,
Niels J. and Belle Larsen Creston,
Gustav E. P. and Selma Karlsson Norén

Contents

List of Illustrations

Preface

"ARE YOU GOING ON to perfection?" This question from the *Book of Discipline* has always been asked of candidates for ordination in the Methodist Church. It was a question taken to heart by Swedish immigrants: the largest foreign language group in the Methodist Episcopal Church in the nineteenth century. They had their own annual conferences, theological seminary, campmeetings, newspapers and book concern before being absorbed into the larger church in 1942. Their particular story has been given minimal attention in English language denominational and general American church histories in the last century. For example, Frederick Norwood's *The Story of American Methodism* (Abingdon, 1974) devotes only three pages to describing Scandinavian churches and annual conferences. J. Gordon Melton's *Log Cabins to Steeples: The United Methodist Way in Illinois* (Parthenon, 1974) does somewhat more, with about eight pages concerning Swedish Methodism. Two significant aspects of Swedish Methodism are not included in Norwood's and Melton's works: an analysis of the distinctive theological emphases of the movement, and "putting a face" to the challenges of itinerant ministry in an immigrant community. Henry Whyman addresses the second issue in *The Hedstroms and the Bethel Ship Saga* (SIU Press, 1992), but his book does not take the reader beyond 1876.

In the 1970s, several boxes of forgotten Swedish Methodist documents were discovered in the attic of a Kendall College building in Evanston, Illinois. They included the writings of Nels O. Westergreen, a Swedish immigrant who became Methodist after coming to the United States in 1852. As founder and first professor of the Swedish Methodist Theological Seminary, circuit rider, military chaplain during the Civil War, presiding elder, and one-time editor of the Swedish Methodist weekly newspaper, Westergreen was a key figure in the immigrant church. His papers, now housed in the Northern Illinois Conference Archives, include over six hundred sermons, theology and church history lectures, hymns and other poetry, a manuscript autobiography, and daily journals running from 1856, the year he began to preach, until two days before his death in 1919. His ministry spanned over sixty years, from the pioneer period until after World War I.

This is a biography of Westergreen as a leader in Swedish Methodism, but through his eyes it is also a view of denominational and national history. Better educated than most of his peers in Swedish Methodism, Westergreen understood and wrote about both cooperation and conflict with other immigrant religious groups. Perhaps most significant is the unique introduction to and wholehearted embrace of sanctification theology—both Wesleyan and non-Wesleyan—among early Swedish immigrants. The doctrine featured prominently in newspaper articles, debates, sermons, and campmeetings. Westergreen wrote a book about "true holiness" vs. counterfeit in 1885, and preached about sanctification regularly. His lifestyle, friendships, and journal entries document his personal and lifelong commitment to go "on to perfection."

All translations from Swedish are by the author, unless otherwise noted.

Acknowledgments

I AM INDEBTED TO many people who lent their assistance in research and preparation of this book. Among those who did not live to see the completed project are the following: Nils J. Anderson, professor of Scandinavian studies at Augustana College, who encouraged me to pursue further studies in the Swedish language; the Reverend Wesley Westerberg, who introduced me to the Nels Westergreen papers and urged me to "give him the full treatment"; the Reverend Dr. Paul Elmén of Seabury-Western Theological Seminary, who shared his reflections on the relationship between the Eric Janssonists and Methodism; Bishop Ole Borgen of the Methodist Church in Sweden, who provided materials from his personal library and through whom I gained access to the library at Överås, the Methodist Theological Seminary in Göteborg; Arthur Westergreen of Copley Township in Knox County, Illinois, who remembered his great-uncle Nels and shared photographs and letters, and, with his wife, Marion, showed me around the Swan Westergreen farm; Eda Trip of Minot, Maine, who provided contextual information and showed me the Washburn farm where Nels Westergreen worked when he was newly arrived in America, as well as the church where he worshiped.

I am also indebted to living members of Westergreen's extended family: Louise and Tom Mosher of Victoria, Illinois, for providing many photographs and documents of the Westergreen family; Robert Beekman, another descendant of Swan Westergreen, for additional perspective of Westergreen family dynamics.

I am grateful to others who provided research assistance: Carl-Axel Tholin did preliminary genealogical research and guided me through the county archives in Bromölla, Sweden; Mary-Carol Riehs, Lucy Cheo, Daniel Smith, and the library staff at Garrett-Evangelical Theological

Seminary; Kevin Leonard, archivist at Northwestern University; the Reverend Richard Wang, offering insights regarding Norwegian-Danish Methodism and its relationship to Swedish Methodism; Marilyn Steenwyk and the Reverend Dr. Daniel Swinson, fellow historians and archivists for the Northern Illinois Conference of the United Methodist Church; Dag Blanck and the staff at the Swenson Swedish Immigration Center at Augustana College, for research support; North Park Theological Seminary, which provided funding for research trips; Madeline Lund, who served as navigator on a trip to Westergreen's birthplace in Sweden; Dr. Alan M. Swanson, who shared his expertise about Eric Jansson and the Bishop Hill Colony; H. Constance Bonbrest, MD, who provided professional assessment of medical issues in the Westergreen family and read early drafts of chapters; the Reverend Arlene Christopherson, assistant to the bishop of the Northern Illinois Conference of the United Methodist Church, for her insights concerning present-day immigrant congregations.

Thanks are also due the clergy and laity at former Swedish Methodist and other churches in the Chicago area and western Illinois, who welcomed me at their worship services, allowed me free access to their archives and permitted me to take photographs. These include:

The Reverend Calvin Gipson of Church of the Living God (formerly Union Avenue); the Reverend Anthony Williams of Labor of Love Apostolic Church (formerly South Side/South Shore/Cheltenham); the Reverend Scort Christy of Emmanuel United Methodist Church (formerly Evanston); Elizabeth Stegner of Immanuel Lutheran Church, Evanston; the Reverend Dr. Larry Gaston of New Deliverance Church of God in Christ (formerly Austin); the Reverend William Owens of Waukegan United Methodist Church; the Reverend Ann Champion of Bishop Hill United Methodist Church; Helen and Edgar Bantz of First United Methodist Church of Galesburg; Karen Tate of Desplaines Methodist Campground.

Finally, I am grateful to DiAnne Walsh, Dr. William Flodin, Dr. Ann Boaden, Andrew Noren, Dr. Philip Anderson, and Dr. Klyne Snodgrass for providing the support and encouragement to see this project to completion.

1

Westergreen's Early Life in Sweden

1834 to 1852

Without being made holy, none can behold the Lord God on high.[1]

—J. O. WALLIN

SOUTHERNMOST SKÅNE AND BLEKINGE have some of the most fertile farmland in Sweden. The staple crops of rye, barley and oats flourished there in the first half the nineteenth century, but many farms also produced wheat, buckwheat, peas and beans. In the area around Näsum and Ägerum, fruit trees and berries were also plentiful, and the average farm family cultivated potatoes for its own consumption. The land lies close to Hanöbukten, a sandy bay along the coast that opens to the larger Baltic, and a landless peasant there might seek employment in agricultural, maritime, or other work. In Sweden, a *bondeman* (peasant) was a serf not bound to a particular manor, and a *torpare* (crofter) was a tenant farmer on a large estate.[2] Nels Westergreen's forebears were in the latter category. His paternal grandfather, Nils Nilsson, born 1760, took on the surname

---

1. See Wallin, "Ho är den för Herren träder" [Who shall come before the Lord], 294.

2. Patrick Svensson, "Peasants and Entrepreneurship," 3. Svensson uses the term peasant when talking about all non-gentry landowners. They "formed a specific social group with political representation in the then Swedish parliament and they therefore were separated socially from other farmers. . . . About ninety percent of all land in Sweden was managed by peasants, either as self-owners or as tenants."

Kaxe when he entered military service. He married a woman three years
his senior, named Sissa Persdotter, and they settled in Västanå in Näsum
parish, where they became tenant farmers. Sissa gave birth to two boys,
Lars and Nils, before a third son, named Ola (some records say Olaf), was
born in 1799. Ola was baptized when he was five days old at the parish
church, and one of the godparents was Petter Westergren, leaseholder of
a local paper mill. Ola and most of his family later adopted a variant of
this surname for their own.

Ola grew up in the Västanå area and, like his parents, supported
himself as a farmer leasing a plot of land. He married and was widowed
before he met Hanna Jacobdotter, almost ten years his junior. She spent
part of her youth in Karlshamn, and worked as a maid prior to their May
3, 1833, marriage in Gammalstorp parish church in nearby Blekinge.
They settled within that parish in Bjäraryd, near Ägerum. Hanna's widowed mother moved in with them. Their first son, Nels, was born July 25,
1834. Around the time of his eldest child's birth, a loaded cart of hay fell
on Ola, temporarily causing him to lose the use of one arm. The family
moved back to Västanå in Näsum parish, where presumably his parents
helped support them until Ola recovered. Hanna gave birth to six additional sons: Erik in 1837, Sven in 1839, Anders in 1842, Johan in 1844,
Olaf in 1847, and Thomas in 1849. The two youngest sons died a few
months apart in 1850.[3]

Both Ola and Hanna had a keen interest in education, as well as
being deeply religious. A paragraph in Nels Westergreen's manuscript
autobiography reflects the latter commitment:

> My parents were both so-called *läsare* or readers. They tried
> to live piously as they understood it, and although their piety
> was imperfect they still kept apart from the general crowd, and
> therefore were called scornful names such as readers, godly
> ones, holy, etc. This, in my opinion, was a title of honor rather
> than derision. My parents used to fall on their knees and have
> morning and evening prayers, and made us do the same. When
> we were too young to pray in our own words, they gave us
> prayers to memorize. Although this was only following a form,
> I shall nevertheless always be thankful for it. It was a long time
> before I could rest in the evening unless I had bowed my knees
> and said my prayers. Even after I gave up bowing the knees, I

3. After their arrival in America, Erik changed his name to Alex, Sven became Swan,
Anders became Andrew, and Johan became John. With the exception of Erik/Alex, who
used the surname Olsson, the entire family eventually took on the surname Westergreen.

could seldom close my eyes to sleep unless I first lifted up my supplications to God.[4]

Another aspect of the boys' religious upbringing was limiting contact with other children during their early years. They were not allowed to participate in most games with other children, and the resulting ostracism was sometimes difficult for them to bear. Card-playing, dancing, taking God's name in vain and using vulgar speech were strictly prohibited, as one might expect in a Pietist household. Ola and Hanna abstained from drinking anything containing alcohol: a truly countercultural practice, given that Sweden's per capita consumption of brännvin (distilled from grain and potatoes) at the time of Nels Westergreen's birth was estimated to be about forty-four liters per year, as opposed to two and a half liters per capita in 2015.[5] In spite of their parents' strictness, the boys were not lonely, because they had each other as playmates. At preschool age, Nels manifested an unusual capacity for reading and memorization, and soon became his father's protégé. Many of his parents' religious and vocational aspirations were projected onto him. When he was six years old, he suffered a mysterious illness that left him with "weak nerves," and which made it necessary for him to learn his letters all over again.[6] The next two sons, Erik and Sven, were not as intellectually precocious as their elder brother, but being born only eighteen months apart, they naturally teamed up in childhood escapades. There is little written about the early life of Anders and John, and nothing about Olaf or Thomas, almost as though Nels did not know them well. By the time the last two boys were born, his days were divided between farm labor and pursuing his education.

Both parents took an active role in teaching their sons, though their methods would be considered unnecessarily harsh today. Mistakes in arithmetic and other subjects were subject to corporal punishment, as though they reflected willful disobedience rather than a normal part of the learning process. As soon as Nels was deemed sufficiently recovered from his illness, his mother placed a copy of *A Short History of Religion* in his hands, and told him to read it aloud to his brothers. When he

4. Westergreen, *Levnads Anteckning* från *Min Barndom* [Life memorandum from my childhood], 4.

5. Scott, *Sweden: The Nation's History*, 354, and https://www.statista.com/statistics/562763/per-capita-consumption-of-spirits-in-sweden/.

6. Westergreen, *Lefnads Anteckning*, 6.

mispronounced the word "Israel," she got out a cane to strike him; however, her aim was faulty and instead she accidentally broke a window. The book was used to keep out the cold air until the pane could be replaced.[7]

Ola was restless and dissatisfied with life as a tenant farmer, and it was increasingly difficult to provide for his household, since at one point he had ten mouths to feed. In the late 1830s he began studying to become a schoolteacher, leaving their small plot of land for his wife and sons to work . He was tutored by a clergyman named Hjortsberg in Kiaby, between Brömolla and Kristianstad. His ambition was to take the examination for teachers and pastors in Lund, but for unknown reasons, he never went to Lund. Instead, he became an itinerant teacher, going to nearby towns to hold school for weeks or months at a time. Although the *riksdag* (parliament) passed a law in 1842 that every parish must establish a common school, it was many years before this was fully implemented.[8] Since Ola did not take the qualifying exam, his civil status did not change; in the parish register for 1844, the year Johan was born and baptized, he was still listed as a farmer. Meanwhile, Hanna stayed at home to raise their growing family, tend the crops, and care for her elderly mother. Once while he was away, the house was robbed of almost everything they owned, causing further hardship for the family. Hanna's mother died in 1842, which meant one less mouth to feed, but also less supervision for the children. As early as 1840 or 1841, young Nels began accompanying his father on his teaching sojourns: his first formal schooling.

His education was weighted in favor of theology and spiritual formation. The Westergreens were what C. Howard Smith would describe as conservative rather than radical Pietists.[9] Sweden had officially become Lutheran in 1544, four years after the church in Denmark was transformed into an official Lutheran state church. The state churches were intertwined with the government; clergy functioned as civil servants, taking the census and tax rolls as well as leading worship and instructing parishioners in matters of faith.[10] Although Lutheranism was monolithic until around 1850, there were regional theological and spiritual differences among clergy and laity.

7. This may have been *History of the Reformation*, by Johannes Sleidanus (1506–1556), the first volume of which was published in 1545.

8. Scott, *Sweden*, 352–53.

9. Smith, *Scandinavian Hymnody*, 93.

10. Granquist, *Scandinavian Pietists*, 4.

The *läsare* were already well-established in Sweden when Ola Westergreen was born, particularly in the south and southwest and in Hälsingland, north of Stockholm along the Baltic coast. This evangelical movement was sometimes perceived as subversive, and a potential threat to the authority of the state church, so the Swedish parliament passed the Conventicle Edict of 1726, prohibiting religious meetings in homes without the permission and possibly the participation of a state church clergyman. The *läsare* called for a renewal of preaching, conversion, and a godly lifestyle. The latter two in particular were facilitated by gathering for Bible study, extemporaneous prayer, and mutual support and accountability. Conservative or churchly *läsare* remained active in the parish church, while the more radical groups denounced those religious leaders whom they saw as unconverted, and met separately as a body of true believers.

A second formative religious influence, of which Ola and his family may not have been aware at the time, was the devotional legacy of the Moravians. Moravian spirituality found its way to Sweden in the eighteenth century, having originated in the early fifteenth century with Jan Hus in what is now the Czech Republic. It reorganized in the eighteenth century under Count Nikolas Ludwig von Zinzendorf in Herrnhut, a community outsider Berthelsdorf in eastern Germany. Mark Granquist describes Zinzendorf's theological orientation this way:

> Where the Lutheran Pietists tended toward an emphasis on moral introspection and penitence for sin, Moravian spirituality was more focused on the joy in the love of Jesus for the believers. Moravian spirituality also had the distinctive emphases of contemplation on the wounds and blood of the crucified Christ, and a piety that at times verged on the mystical.[11]

These themes and vocabulary found expression later in Nels Westergreen's life as a minister, and, it may be claimed, in much of Swedish Methodism in the United States. His journal regularly expressed sentiments such as, "I have not felt that same happy state of mind as I did yesterday, yet I trust in Jesus";[12] and "Bless the Lord, my soul is happy in trusting in my Savior's blood";[13] "I prayed for a little while and then looked up to Jesus by faith and was able to give over to him myself and

11. Granquist, *Scandinavian Pietists*, 7.

12. Westergreen, *Journals*, February 29, 1868.

13. Westergreen, *Journals*, August 28, 1873.

all, and a feeling of rest entered my heart."[14] However, Westergreen's spirituality and preaching differed from the Moravians in the latter's being an amalgamation of different (mainly German) Protestant groups without being bound to a particular confessional statement. While Westergreen was unusually ecumenical for his context, to the point that he was once invited to become pastor of a Lutheran congregation, his published works carefully delineate doctrinal differences between Wesleyan and Lutheran theology, the theology of the Eric Janssonists, and fanatical extremes that evolved out of the American Holiness Movement.

The Westergreens were more directly influenced by the work and legacy of the Reverend Henric Schartau (1757–1825), dean of the cathedral at Lund. Born in Malmö, he claimed to have been in a state of grace given at baptism until he was about ten years old. After his mother died, Schartau was sent to University of Lund at age fourteen, where he earned his MA at twenty-one. In describing his conversion experience, Schartau said it occurred during a worship service, where the Spirit and Word moved him in spite of slipshod leadership. Conviction, absolution and assurance occurred in a single day.[15] He was ordained a year later. Schartau was influenced by Moravians early in his ministry, but later reacted against their view of conversion as "resting in the blood and wounds of Christ," and, as Karl Olsson described it:

> He developed a doctrine of justification which implied an in-grafting into Christ according to an "order of faith." There are strong reminiscences in Schartau of the old Lutheran piety of Arndt and of Pietism. He insisted upon the necessity of conversion and a personal relationship with Christ which would result in a growth in grace. . . . The Schartauian form of piety still holds sway in parts of southwestern Sweden and is characterized by strong loyalty to the established church and an austere and legalistic attitude toward the Christian life.[16]

One might say that Schartau participated in "the quickening spirit of pietism, with its emphasis on the emotional and subjective aspects of Christian experience and the ethical and moral demands of sanctification," but he was critical of other aspects of pietism and insisted on using

14. Westergreen, *Journals*, March 13, 1894.

15. Hägglund, *Notes on Henric Schartau*, 15.

16. Olsson, *By One Spirit*, 658.

prescribed liturgical forms.[17] Furthermore, Schartau distinguished between assurance unto confession and assurance unto faith, stating that
the former is a special gift of grace, while the latter belongs to the normal
life of a believer.[18] His sermons and catechism were widely published and
used in parish churches. As a mentor to dozens of candidates for ordination, it would be difficult to overestimate Schartau's impact on the state
church, particularly in southern Sweden, in the first half the nineteenth
century. His personality has been described as having a heart aflame with
the love of Christ, but prone to be authoritative, stern, dignified. Even his
close associates addressed him as *prosten* (dean) rather than the more
familiar *du* (you).

There can be no doubt that the Schartauan revival touched the
Westergreen family. After all, Nels was required to memorize Schartau's
catechism when he reached the age of confirmation. The legalism of the
parents' *läsare* lifestyle and their tendency toward melancholy mirrored
Schartau's own orientation.[19] What is more, the logic and structure of
Schartau's sermons were sometimes echoed in Nels Westergreen's own
preaching, decades later. With or without a sermon title, Schartau began
by giving his text followed by a substantial introduction. The sermon
was then divided into major headings, with a separate application and
exhortation, addressing the listeners personally and inviting them, with
the help of the Holy Spirit, to receive and act on the Word proclaimed.

One additional religious influence on the Westergreens before their
emigration should be noted: the hymns and sermons of Johan Olof Wallin (1779–1839). Wallin, the son of a military officer in Dalarna, was a
Swedish minister who became Archbishop of Uppsala, but his lasting
legacy was his hymns and poetry. The 1819 *Psalmbok*, approved by the
king and used in the state church for over a century, was Wallin's project. It was also the hymnal used by the earliest Swedish immigrants in
the United States, both Lutheran and non-Lutheran. Of its five hundred
hymns, Wallin wrote 128, translated 23, and was involved in the revision

17. Arden, *Augustana Heritage*, 5.

18. Hägglund, *Notes on Henric Schartau*, 24.

19. There is evidence of clinical depression in the Westergreen family. Nels Westergreen's daily journals are punctuated with laments over his spiritual state and sporadic
discouragement about his effectiveness in ministry. During her latter years, Hanna
lived with Nels and suffered spells of melancholy and/or weeping that lasted for days.
And Anders/Andrew Westergreen was hospitalized for depression and a heart ailment
during his final year of life.

of another 178. The Wallin hymn most widely used today is "*Var hälsad, sköna morgonstund*," which has been translated to "All hail to you, O blessed morn." He was also responsible for the structural arrangement of the hymnal, which, unlike the more recent 1987 *Psalmbok*, had a section with the heading "sanctification." A stanza from one of Wallin's hymns in this section is as follows:

> Utan helgelse kan kan ingen
> Skåda Herren Gud i höjden,
> Minns det, själ, som lyfter vingen
> Trängtande till himlafröjden!
> Intet orent väg kan finna till lycksalighetens rike;
> Mänskan för att himlen vinna
> Måste bliva änglars like.[20]

> Without being made holy, none can
> behold the Lord God on high;
> Remember that, my soul, who lift your yearning wings
> to the joys of heaven!
> Nothing unclean can find the way to the realm of bliss;
> The human who would gain heaven
> must become as the angels.[21]

Wallin's writing was beloved by Swedes throughout the nineteenth century, and praised by intellectuals for its eloquence. Since Ola and his family attended their parish church, they would have been shaped by the theological emphases of Wallin's hymnody.

Ola's teaching method and curriculum reflected his faith and his desire to instill it in others, even as he sought a deeper religious experience for himself. On Saturday afternoons he would read the Sunday gospel to the children and then explain it to them, preparing them for worship in the parish church the next day. The first time Nels accompanied his father as he held school in a village about two Swedish miles from Näsum, he was initially allowed to play with the other children, but then Ola found other ways to keep him busy during the lunch hour. This may have been an extension of the segregation Ola and Hanna enforced when he was younger, though when they were at Liretorp, staying inside to study seemed to be motivated by a desire for his son to excel academically. Ola also took Nels

---

20. See Wallin, "Ho är den för Herren träder" [Who shall come before the Lord], 294.

21. Translation by the Reverend Tyler A. Strand.

with him to *läsare* gatherings while they stayed in Hällevik. Nels enjoyed the singing and the prayers, but thought their lifestyle was hard. In spite of this assessment, it appears Nels did not chafe against his parents' efforts to shape him religiously or intellectually. For example, in the summer of 1842 Ola was away, holding a school in Hörvik, and Hanna gave birth to Anders, her fourth baby. The older boys were left to their own devices. Nels wrote that they picked berries, climbed trees and engaged in other normal play, but he also began studying geography and the historical books of the Bible on his own, and started memorizing the catechism. He enjoyed the admiration of his knowledge by his parents' fellow *läsare*, as well as the measure of prestige it gave him with his brothers and other children. By contrast, his brothers demonstrated less aptitude, and Erik in particular was often caned by Hanna and Ola because he had difficulty learning to read. Nels himself was punished severely when he spilled some food on the Bible he was reading. The brothers sympathized with each other, but did not rebel openly against parental discipline.

For much of the 1840s, the family's arduous routine did not vary much. Ola held schools in various villages—usually in someone's home rather than a school building—leaving his wife and older sons to work their plot of land as best they could while he was away. He went alone to Hörvik and to Kulla and Lönshult in Jämshög parish, but Nels accompanied his father on other teaching ventures in Blekinge and Skåne, going several times in Liretorp, Klagstorp, and Hällevik. They boarded with different families, went to hear the local priest preach, and participated in conventicle meetings. Erik was deemed old enough to go with them twice. Nels continued to study Schartau's catechism and Hubner's Bible history. During their second sojourn in Liretorp, in 1847, they enjoyed a fine new schoolhouse that had been built. However, it was an awkward period for Nels; some of his former friends had already been confirmed, and others were married, so he was more socially isolated than before. His father maintained the practice of leading the school in prayer and song every morning and afternoon. For reasons not explained, Ola was once detained or called away, and ordered Nels, who was only thirteen years old, to teach in his place.[22] It did not go particularly well; his brother Erik did not want to listen to him, and thus set a bad example for the other pupils, though in general the children obeyed him better than he

22. Scott, *Sweden*, 353. This was perhaps a variation on "rotation teaching," in which more advanced pupils helped the younger while the trained teacher only supervised. Rotation teaching was legally abolished in 1864.

expected. He tried to follow his father's practice of leading prayer, but selected an unfamiliar one that the children had difficulty reading, leading to embarrassment and stifled snickering rather than an atmosphere of reverence and seriousness. And because Nels was so young, he went outside and played games with the other children during the dinner break. It was a relief when his father returned and took charge of the school again. Ola also held a school in their own home in Västanå before a school building was erected. Hanna was pregnant or nursing most of the 1840s. As a result of all these factors, the elder Westergreen sons received more attention and education than the younger ones, the land was not as productive as it might have been had a mature man worked it full-time, and the family's economic situation was precarious. There were periods when the boys stayed home from church because they did not have clothing deemed suitable.

Hanna and Ola continued their pursuit of holiness both at *läsare* gatherings and on their own. On one occasion, most likely in 1843, they left all their children with a neighbor to travel north to Kronobergs County to hear Pehr Nyman speak. Nyman (1794–1856) was considered one of the leading revivalist preachers in the first part of the nineteenth century. He went through a spiritual crisis after his ordination in the state church, and became a popular but controversial preacher. His blunt and dramatic oratory, along with theological clashes with authorities, led to a temporary suspension from his post, though at the time Ola and Hanna heard him, he was the parish priest at Stenbrohult. One of Nyman's fellow clergy described him as "a spouting volcano against sin, who could also pour balm into crushed hearts. He thundered from Sinai but comforted with sympathetic love from Golgotha." Nels had opportunity to hear him a few years later, and recalled the large crowds and their visible response to Nyman, but could remember nothing of the preaching itself. Writing years later, he characterized Nyman as "notorious." When his father was teaching in Hällevik, Nels often went to the parish church in Mjällby to hear the parish priest preach, but was not moved by his sermons. He found more meaning in the *läsare* meetings to which Ola took him and Erik, in part because he now understood better what was happening, and the adults spoke with him more than previously. With his father and by himself, Nels began to seek out evangelical preachers, both to evaluate their homiletical skills and to consider what their words might mean for his own soul. His seeking was reinforced by his mother, who on one occasion took him aside from his brothers, sang some spiritual songs and spoke to him about his religious state until he broke down weeping. He prayed earnestly for conversion but, he said, did not understand what it was and was disappointed when he did not feel moved or changed.

It is often difficult to distinguish between events as Nels experienced them at the time and as he interpreted them decades afterward in his autobiography. The theological significance attributed to major and mundane events brings to mind the famous Kierkegaard quote: "Life must be understood backwards, but it must be lived forwards."[23] Regarding the previously mentioned emotional scene with his mother, he concluded his anguish was evidence that even then, God's Spirit was already at work within him—i.e., prevenient grace. He recounted another occasion when he and his brothers brought berries they had picked to sell in nearby Sölvesborg. On their way home they encountered some drunken farmers, who invited the boys to take a turn driving their wagon. Nels gladly took the reins and let the horses go faster and faster, not understanding the danger it posed to themselves and the cargo. The runaway wagon came to no harm, but afterward he attributed the fact to "the Lord's patience and sustaining grace."[24] Still another time they were some distance from home, gathering birch bark to make baskets. Nels fell fifteen or twenty feet from the tree he had been climbing, landed on some blueberry bushes, and escaped with only a few abrasions. He noted:

> I see now clear evidence of the Lord's protection for unworthy me. If I had been killed [in that fall], I doubt if I would have been ready for heaven. The Lord saw this and therefore extended grace and lengthened my time to prepare for eternity, for which I owe him all glory and praise.[25]

When he returned home after this accident, his mother exhorted him to thank God for divine protection and take the event as a warning to make his preparation for eternity.

Concurrent with his private pilgrimage of faith, in 1849 Nels began preparing for his first Communion by enrolling in confirmation class. This meant walking nearly a Swedish mile every week to the minister's house in Jämshög. Nels excelled among his peers, since he had already memorized the necessary portions of Schartau's catechism. The pastor who taught them, E. M. Holst, also schooled them in the differences

23. Dru, *Journals of Soren Kierkegaard*, 167.

24. Westergreen, *Levnads Anteckning*, 32.

25. Westergreen, *Levnads Anteckning*, 35.

between Lutheran, Roman Catholic, and Reformed theology. In reminiscing about that phase of his life, Nels distinguished between outward appearance and inner experience, both in himself and the pastor. Of Holst he wrote:

> It was generally thought he was a spiritual man. His fear of God I cannot judge. I believe he meant well, but I don't believe he was sanctified, for he was very hot-tempered and too hasty to box a confirmation candidate's ears. I remember there was one young man who became sleepy during the question and answer time. The pastor ordered him to leave, but he didn't obey promptly, at which point the young man barely escaped getting a kick from the pastor's foot.[26]

Regarding himself, Nels said he enjoyed the admiration of the congregation on the Sunday the class members were questioned during the worship service. However, he could not recall being asked if he renounced sin and the devil's service and would covenant to serve the Lord instead, and reflected that if the question *had* been asked, he would have perjured himself. He had "touching and holy feelings" over the act of kneeling with the others at the altar and receiving Communion, but did not believe there had been any real change within. He was admonished to come to Jesus as he was, rather than trying to prepare himself, but it was not until sometime after he joined with the Methodists in America that he could "cast himself on Jesus' redemption with a simple faith."[27]

As noted earlier, Ola and Hanna were tenant farmers. The lease they had signed when Ola's arm injury healed was for a piece of land that turned out to be stony and difficult to cultivate. To make matters worse, around 1847 the family learned that the estate from which they leased their land had been heavily mortgaged, and was now being foreclosed. There were financial repercussions for all the crofters, and Ola had to go through a lengthy and complicated legal process to get compensation for his loss. The former owner was granted a lifetime tenancy on part of the land abutting the Westergreen farm, and he and his family proved to be very unpleasant neighbors, allowing their cattle to trespass on the crops. There were two sons who were older and larger than Nels and his brothers, and who took delight in insulting them and trying to pick a quarrel. The mother of the family, who was perhaps as fond of *brännvin* as her husband

---

26. Westergreen, *Levnads Anteckning*, 55.
27. Westergreen, *Levnads Anteckning*, 70.

was, would stand on the stone wall in front of their cottage and scream her complaints about them so loudly it could be heard across the river in the nearby village. On one occasion Ola and the neighbor and his sons got into an argument that escalated into a fistfight, and Ola got the worst of it. For the most part, the Westergreens tried to stay away from these quarrelsome people, but Erik, who tended to be short-tempered, had to been dissuaded from using his fists to get revenge on one of the sons.

With the coming of winter, the conflict seemed to subside. Nels and his father spent much of their time going into the nearby forest to cut firewood, which they would then carry home on their backs. On one such trip, a heavy load slipped from Nels's back and broke his arm. Unable to do manual labor for a time, he resumed his studies at home, and thought he would like to become a schoolteacher. When his arm healed, he expressed a wish to study at the parish school in Näsum. It was free, but for once Ola was reluctant for his son to pursue more education; he was needed to help put bread on the table at home. Hanna persuaded her husband to allow Nels to attend the next winter with two other crofters' sons. He excelled in his studies, but when spring came he had to leave in order to help work the land. At the parish school it appears he was introduced to biblical languages and geography; he never mentioned being taught these in Ola's schools. Nels was now sixteen years old, and believed his own education had come to an end. Soon afterward the schoolteacher at Västanå, their own village, left, and Nels took his place for a time. The pay was poor, but it helped feed the family. He then taught another school in a more prosperous settlement in the area, and his pay increased. There were discipline problems with a few of the children. One boy in particular resisted learning to read and made problems in the classroom, despite Nels's attempts to be patient but firm. Eventually he gave up hope of teaching him anything. In other respects, this period of teaching was pleasant, and he had some leisure time to attempt writing poetry. By the end of the term, however, he decided this was not his vocation, and returned home.

Late in the following summer, several events at the farm spurred the family to consider emigration seriously. The difficulties with neighbors had resumed. The root of these seemed to be over land ownership and usage. Ola was already in litigation with some of the crofters and awaiting a judgment in his favor. One afternoon he sent his eldest son on an errand pertaining to this suit, and on his way home, Nels passed by a garden belonging to one of the litigants. Without thinking, he stopped and picked a handful of the man's pears. This was an act he acknowledged was foolish, given that they had their own pear trees at home. One of the other farmers saw him and remarked to Nels that if the owner knew, he would bring action against him. Nels laughed it off, but the farmer repeated the warning the next time they encountered one another. The man made good on his threat, and Nels was summoned before a local council. The owner said he would drop the charge against Nels if Ola would drop his own suit. Several witnesses came forward and said Nels was one of the most upstanding young men in the parish, and an example to others. Arguments and negotiations went on for several hours. At the end of the day, they settled the matter, but the handful of stolen pears ended up costing Ola about ten *riksdalers*.[28]

This was not the end of trouble, however. Once again, the neighbor boys let the cattle onto the Westergreens' land, and when Erik and Sven tried to drive the animals out of the field, the older boys began hitting them. Nels came out and struck one of them on the side of the head. Retribution soon followed; while it was still dark enough to need candlelight, a few mornings later, one of the boys threw a large rock through the window of the kitchen where Hanna was working. Another time Hanna went outside to pick up firewood and the neighbor boy picked up a piece of wood and struck her on the head severely enough that she bled. Nels had a rock thrown at him, which struck his shoulder but did not cause serious injury. He began carrying a weapon if he went any distance from the house, half-hoping to meet one of his adversaries, but Hanna persuaded him to detour from his usual route so as to avoid another confrontation.

Why was there such animosity toward Ola and his family? There is nothing in the written account by Nels to explain the depth of hostility they endured. Yes, the Westergreens were *läsare*, but they were also regular communicants in the parish church. Ola and Nels had helped with the education of the children in the community. The legal difficulty seemed to have been settled, but strained relations continued. Ola declared himself ready to pack up and leave. Hanna had no great desire to stay, but she was worried about the family's debts and how they could manage to feed the family if they sold and moved. Nels described these few years as the darkest period in his life up to that point.

Finally a decision was made. They sold the lease on their land, but continued to live there and work as tenants until the way forward

---

28. Named after the German *Thaler*, this coin was the currency of Sweden from 1777 to 1873.

became clear. Ironically, persecution from the neighbors eased once this occurred. Shortly before the sale, a fellow *läsare* named Måns Jönsson came to their home and began to talk about America. He was a poor crofter, and perhaps he had heard about America through letters written to people back in Sweden; in any case, he spoke enthusiastically of how a poor person could achieve prosperity and enjoy religious freedom in the New World. Soon Ola had the atlas in his hands and began thinking about the possibility of emigrating. His interest wavered a bit when another *läsare* showed him a letter that painted America in less glowing colors. Other friends began to speak to him for and against emigration, and he was shown a letter by Pastor Esbjörn, describing the "false doctrines" being preached to some after they arrived in the United States. Hanna and Ola were attached to Lutheran teaching, and decided they must seek counsel from a sympathetic state church minister. They heard that the Reverend T. N. Hasselquist, whose church was about six miles away in Åkorp, was planning to go to America with some in his congregation, so they went to consult with him. While in Åkorp they stayed with the Rander family, who had relatives living in Knoxville, Illinois, and also made the acquaintance of others hoping to make the journey to western Illinois with Hasselquist. Ola hoped his own family could join the travel party, but as things unfolded, the farm auction was scheduled and the Westergreens had to vacate their home before Hasselquist was ready to leave. Others who lived closer to them expressed a wish to emigrate with them, but in the end, only one family from Näsum parish accompanied them. Nels acquired a language book in English from P. O. Welander and began studying it, but it was of limited value; when he tried to pronounce phrases from the book after his arrival in America, he reported that almost no one could understand him. They made their way to Göteborg by way of Åkorp to stay with Pastor Hasselquist and receive any parting advice from him and their new friends in his congregation, hoping to meet up with them again in the new land.

2

Journey to the New World

1852 to 1853

Trust under ev'ry condition, till thou shalt reach thy home;
Trust, till in perfect fruition, that which is real hath come.[1]

THERE IS NO SHORTAGE of immigration stories among first- and second-generation Swedish Americans. Both *Religious Aspects of Swedish Immigration*, by George M. Stephenson, and Lars Ljungmark's *Swedish Exodus* document the impetus for the departure of thousands of Swedes from their homeland. The memoirs of Victor Witting, Gustaf Unonius, and others recount the rigors of transatlantic crossings in the mid-nineteenth century. Alan Swanson notes that Vilhelm Moberg's classic novel, *The Emigrants*, serves as a touchstone for all fictive literature about Swedish emigrations.[2] It also provides an exodus narrative for those whose forbears' stories have been forgotten or lost. The Westergreen family's emigration journey differs from other stories in at least two ways. First, Nels Westergreen left a two-part manuscript autobiography of about five hundred pages, plus over sixty years of daily journals, so there is more detail than other narrators provide. Second, as difficult as most emigration journeys of the period were, the Westergreen family's must rank among the longest and hardest.

1. See Pethrus, "Löftena kunna ej svika" [All that our Savior hath spoken], #254.
2. See Swanson, "Där Ute: Moberg's Predecessors," 279.

The Reverend T. N. Hasselquist, for example, emigrated the same year, 1852, but his circumstances were markedly different from the Westergreen family's. He held a position that meant "prominence, a good social standing, and the comforts of life," to quote one of his biographers.[3] The Westergreens were poor and obscure. When the pastor was recruited by Lars Paul Esbjörn to come to Galesburg, Illinois, and minister to the Swedish Lutherans there, the cost of his passage was paid by other emigrants. The Westergreens had just enough money to pay their fare across the Atlantic, but no idea how they would manage to travel cross-country to the Midwest. As they and one other family were the first from their area to attempt the journey, they were subjected to dire predictions, as well as good wishes. They undoubtedly left Västanå with mixed feelings. Hanna's mother and two youngest sons were buried in Näsum churchyard, and Ola's first wife was buried nearby. Other living members of the extended family would be left behind. They mentioned no resources or friends to sustain them while they got settled in America. And among the five sons, Nels was the only one who had any acquaintance with the English language. His description of leaving the farm could have been written by Moberg:

> Finally the day came when we would leave our home. . . . Although we looked in hope to a better future and freer spaces, yet so many dangers lay between these and us. . . . On the day we traveled our relatives gathered. We packed up our final things. Finally we stood at the door. The hour of departure had come. Our relatives followed us on the way a little distance, where we waved farewell and shed also loving tears at the thought we would never meet again until the other side of the grave. I looked back to our old house, the house garden and hill where part of my youth was spent, and which I perhaps would never see again.[4]

With their loaded wagon, the Westergreens traveled only as far as Vångby the first day, a matter of a few miles. They then headed for Åkarp, and spent several days at the parsonage with Pastor Hasselquist. They heard Hasselquist preach twice on the Sunday, in Åkarp and then Vittsjö, and the following day began their cross-country trip to Halmstad. The somewhat serpentine route may have been a consequence of limited roads, faulty memory, or poor navigation; Halmstad is northwest

3. Ander, *T. N. Hasselquist*, 6.
4. Westergreen, *Lefnads Anteckning*, 105–6.

of Åkarp, but they headed for Markaryd, which is northeast. From Markaryd they went through dry and barren moor heath, which they found long and tiresome, though occasionally they would encounter a tolerably fertile ground surrounding a house or village.

Up to this point in his life, Karlshamn and Kristianstad were the largest towns Nels Westergreen had seen. If he had not emigrated to America, he could have had a career with the local tourism board, writing:

> The city of Halmstad is situated on the Nissa River and has a fine harbor. If the city lacks the size or stately buildings that can be found in Karlshamn or Kristianstad, yet it makes up for it in fineness and coziness. In a word, Halmstad is a beautiful city. It even has a castle on the highest point over the Nissa River, and the most beautiful bridge I have seen in Sweden.[5]

Ola Westergreen booked passage to Göteborg, and they stayed in that city about three weeks. They attended their last worship service in Sweden on Midsummer's Day, and on June 26, 1852, the Westergreens left Göteborg aboard the schooner *Ellen Perkins*.

The *Fall River Monitor* described the *Ellen Perkins* as "a small, ill-looking craft, of only 130 tons burthen, utterly unfit to convey a small, much less a large number of passengers across the Atlantic."[6] Schooners, which are sailing vessels with two or more masts, the foremast being shorter or the same height as the rear mast, were first used by the Dutch in the sixteenth or seventeenth century, but were widely employed in the United States in the nineteenth century. They were used in trades that required speed and windward ability, such as slaving, privateering, and offshore fishing, but were less common as merchant ships. The schooner's captain, Joseph B. Bligh, was less experienced than many of his crew.

On the seventh day after the *Ellen Perkins* passed Norway's south coast, they encountered stormy weather and had to jettison iron bars stored under the deck. Soon after the storm ended, they passed the northern islands of Scotland, rocky and deserted-looking. Nevertheless, some of the passengers would gladly have gone on land if permitted, but the schooner continued. For a few days they had land in sight, but never sailed close enough to see if there were houses or other evidences of human habitation. Once they left the coast of Scotland, they did not see

---

5. Westergreen, *Lefnads Anteckning*, 112.
6. "Arrival of Swedish Immigrants," 2.

land again for ten weeks, when they spotted the shores of Nova Scotia on
September 11, 1852.

Something was obviously wrong aboard the *Ellen Perkins*. The first
voyage of Christopher Columbus to the New World in 1492 took thirty-
three days. The Pilgrims' voyage on the Mayflower in 1620 lasted sixty-
six days, and two persons died during the Atlantic crossing (nine people
aboard the *Ellen Perkins* died).[7] Eric Jansson, leader of the Bishop Hill
Colony, sailed from Liverpool to New York, reaching there late March
or early April 1846. The voyage took six weeks.[8] And T. N. Hasselquist,
who had befriended the Westergreens before their emigration, left Sweden nearly two months after the Westergreens, but nevertheless arrived
in New York only one day later than they.[9] Nels Westergreen noted that
the *Ellen Perkins*' captain was "not skilled in sea voyages," and another
man on board eventually took over leadership, "or else I don't know how
we ever would have reached land." He speculated that perhaps they were
caught in the Gulf Stream and had to double back in order to continue
toward their destination.[10]

The prolonged voyage had a more serious consequence than bore-
dom; the passengers ran out of food and drinking water. The captain
or crew would flag down passing ships to buy or beg some provisions,
and this is turn was shared with the passengers regardless of ability to
pay. Westergreen recalled one occasion when the captain obtained some
cornmeal. For some reason, Nels had no opportunity to get a share during the day, so during the night he made his way to the chest and grabbed
a handful of meal with a scrap of meat mixed in with it. The people on the
Ellen Perkins subsisted mainly on porridge until the ship came closer to
Newfoundland's banks and encountered some fishing boats. The captain
was able to buy fish to be cooked on board, and all received a share.

After sailing along the banks of Nova Scotia, they did not see land
again until they reached the outer side of Cape Cod. On September 21 they
were allowed to disembark for the first time since leaving Göteborg, and
spent the day ashore on an island somewhere between Martha's Vineyard
and New Bedford. The next day they anchored at Newport, then progressed

---

7. Westergreen, *Lefnads Anteckning*, 122. Westergreen noted that for burial at sea,
they simply fastened a weight to the clothed body and threw it overboard. A layman
named Palmblad read some prayers at each committal.

8. Elmen, *Wheat Flour Messiah*, 100.

9. Ander, *T. N. Hasselquist*, 11.

10. Westergreen, *Lefnads Anteckning*, 130.

up Narragansett Bay, into Mount Hope Bay, and finally arrived at Fall River, about forty-five miles south of Boston, on September 27, 1852.[11]

No explanation was given for landing here. In 1852 Boston was a recognized port of entry into the United States, but Fall River had never received arrivals from overseas. It had a town hall, but was not incorporated as a city until 1854. Its harbor was far inferior to Boston's, but it did have a railroad station and an expanding economy, thanks to stonecutting from nearby granite quarries.

The Westergreen family set foot in the New World without provisions or money. A few of them walked into the city and entered a workshop, where they found a Norwegian smith. They told him of their need, and he gave them a dollar to buy food. Along with many others, they camped out in the railroad depot because they had nowhere else to stay. Nels concluded that the citizens of Fall River had not had shiploads of foreigners arrive before.[12] People came down to look at them, bringing them an abundance of food and sometimes offering money. They appeared to the immigrants "like rich lords and ladies."[13] Someone (probably the postmaster, since the first telegraphs were installed in post offices) had the wisdom to send a telegram to a Swede named P. F. Williston in Boston. He most likely worked for the Swedish consulate there, given his response to the immigrants' plight. Williston arrived in Fall River a few days later, and became an advocate for the immigrants, arranging employment and travel for many. For the Westergreens, this proved to be a mixed blessing. Williston arranged that Nels, age eighteen, would get a place working for a doctor named Rice. His fifteen-year-old brother, Erik, would go to another family, and thirteen-year-old Sven would go to a captain named Bowers. Erik was unwilling to leave his family, but ran and hid before being persuaded to be parted from the others. On

11. This is the date Westergreen gives, but the *Fall River Monitor* for September 25, 1852, identifies the *Ellen Perkins*'s arrival as occurring "the previous Monday," which would have been September 20. I believe an error was made in the date given for the newspaper article, since there are other demonstrable errors in the article. For example, it reports the ship left Sweden on June 20. That was a Sunday—and Westergreen gives a description of the Midsummer Day worship service he attended a few days *before* the *Ellen Perkins* sailed from Göteborg.

12. Westergreen was surely correct. In 2012, the director of the Fall River Historical Society was astonished to learn a boatload of immigrants had arrived there in 1852, and the fact that the arrival of the *Ellen Perkins* made the local newspaper underscores that this was unprecedented.

13. Westergreen, *Lefnads Anteckning*, 150.

October 12, Williston told them there had been a change of plans; he had arranged for the family to go by train to Boston and from there on to Chicago, their ultimate destination.[14] In later years, Westergreen's journal mentioned an aged uncle living in Rockford; if the uncle's emigration from Sweden preceded theirs, it was a logical reason for heading west. There was no time to get word of their travel plans to Erik, who by then was working in Somerset, about five miles from Fall River. Nels and Sven agreed to stay behind, get Erik, and bring him with them on a later train. Hanna and Ola took everything except what Nels and Sven were wearing, and promised to stay in Boston with the two youngest sons, Anders and Johan, until the family was reunited and could make its way to Chicago. Williston went with them.

The three teenagers were now on their own, without even a change of clothes. Nels and Sven spent the night on board the ship. The next day they found Erik and returned to the railroad station, where a conductor took pity on them and allowed them to travel free. When they reached Boston, the rest of the family was nowhere to be found. Nels was able to make himself sufficiently understood by a passerby, who led them to another Swedish immigrant named Nyborg. He, in turn, gave them lunch and then took them to Williston's, where they were dismayed to learn the rest of the family had been persuaded to travel to Chicago without them. A misunderstanding led Ola to believe the elder boys were settled in their new places of employment, and would not be meeting them. Even if this were true, it does not explain why the parents did not leave their sons' clothing behind for them. The boys stood alone and directionless, to use Nels's own words. They could not count on another generous train conductor, and at any rate were not sure they still had employment offers near Fall River. Nyborg offered them free meals, and Williston let them use his spare room for about two weeks. The Swedish Consul in Boston promised them train fare to Chicago, but they misunderstood what was offered, and believed it would be impossible to find their family if they traveled before getting a letter telling them of their new address.[15] The

---

14. An unpublished essay written by Henry Westergreen (Sven's son) in 1959 claims that the family needed immigration or clearance papers, and these were not available in Fall River. The essay was given to me in 1987 by Henry's nephew, Arthur Westergreen. There are several discrepancies between this essay and Nels Westergreen's own contemporaneous account.

15. Williston's address served as the contact point for the parents and the sons until they were reunited.

brothers decided to wait to hear from their parents, and in the meantime they would try to find work and save up the money for train fare.

Williston arranged employment for them a second time. Sven and Erik went together to the town of Truro, about fifty-eight miles from Boston by boat, to work for a fisherman. Nels was to be sent to a farm in Minot, Maine. Once again, the brothers experienced the pain of separation from family:

> We were assured by Mr. Williston that we would find pleasant places, and decided to take them. We were together all of Sunday, but on Monday we parted from one another with deep feelings. ... By noon the same day I left Boston I arrived in Portland, over one hundred miles from Boston, where we [presumably he and Williston] stayed a little while before continuing to Lewiston, where I got off and continued my journey on foot to Minot.[16]

It took him two days to reach Minot. The first evening he stayed with a friendly family named Dinsmore, and arrived at the farm of James E. Washburn (1810–1900) by midday the following day. The Washburns were longtime residents of the Minot area. James Washburn's grandfather, Eliab Washburn, came to Minot in 1789 from Bridgewater, Massachusetts, and bought one hundred acres of rolling meadow and forest. His son, Joseph (1770–1858), was a skilled carpenter who built a spacious, two-story yellow home in 1807. It was one of the largest and finest houses in the area. There were two sizeable gardens, several outbuildings, and an orchard. No one there spoke Swedish, and without even a brother for company, it was a lonely and difficult time for Nels. James Washburn had five daughters but no sons, so he was glad to have another young man to help with the farm labor. The first task he was given was churning butter, and when he was finished, he was sent to the orchard to assist another man in picking apples. He enjoyed that, since he was allowed to eat as much as he wanted. As time passed, he also did logging, looked after the livestock, and did general agricultural work. The Washburns were kind to him. Two of the younger daughters, Elizabeth (1849–1937) and Delia (1851–1925), were usually around as he worked the land, and from them he picked up more of the English language. The family included him in their celebrations and encouraged him to attend the local school to learn English; this was probably the Old Pottle Hill School in

16. Westergreen, *Lefnads Anteckning*, 160–61.

Minot, established around 1801.[17] It was a small, poor schoolhouse but had a fairly good teacher. Westergreen was put in the lowest class, and had some difficulty with arithmetic in particular. To his surprise, other students helped him with math and with correct English spelling. His attendance was sporadic. He later wrote he thought he went to school for a total of about ten weeks.

The Washburns were devout Christians who had family morning and evening prayers together. They were also active members of Minot Center Congregational Church. The congregation was established around 1793 and a church erected in 1805, but it was replaced by a newer building on the same site in 1846. A typical New England building of white clapboard, it had a bell tower and single center entrance. The minister at the time was the Reverend Elijah Jones, who lived in a manse across the road, and was the incumbent for about fifty years. Westergreen was initially reluctant to attend church because his Swedish clothes were both different and well-worn. Washburn remedied that by giving him one of his own old suits, and later bought him new clothes. As his language skills improved, Westergreen began to visit the local singing schools, and became better acquainted with other young people in the area. When he was alone, however, he would sing Swedish hymns and songs to assuage his loneliness and encourage himself, and noted that he often felt the drawing of God's Spirit on him. There was no hint of a religious vocation at that time, however.

It was not until March 1853 that Nels heard from his parents; a letter had been sent to Williston, who eventually forwarded it to him. They began writing to each other directly. Springtime came, and he continued to work on the farm, but began to find it tiresome. Then Ola wrote to him later in the spring of 1853, complaining about his circumstances in Chicago and stating that he was ill. This made Nels anxious to reunite with his brothers, and he wanted to set off for the Midwest as soon as possible. Washburn was busy with planting and did not want him to leave. He offered Nels twenty dollars if he would stay there a month longer, or fifty dollars and a winter's schooling if he would stay until the following year. But Nels was determined to go. In his autobiography he admitted his reason was not simply anxiety over his parents; he did not enjoy farming, and wanted to be his own boss.[18]

17. Hodson and Hemond, *Minot Homesteads*, 114.

18. Westergreen, *Lefnads Anteckning*, 176.

Nevertheless, it was with some tears that he parted with the Washburn family. They gave him twelve dollars, and James Washburn walked with him some distance toward the train station. Nels took a train to Portland, and then a steamship to Boston. He immediately went to Mr. Williston's office to inquire about Sven and Erik, only to learn they were out on a fishing expedition with their employer, a man named Giraud Cordis. His sailing vessel fished off the shore of Nova Scotia during the summer and in the winter they went to Florida and gathered oysters. Until they returned, Nels believed he should not leave for Chicago. For the next six months, he drifted from one job to another, mainly in Massachusetts. He went to Medford and stayed briefly with Washburn's brother. He heard that Lowell was a large manufacturing town where he might find work, so he took a train there, arriving at midnight. To save money he decided to walk the streets all night rather than staying at a hotel, but a policeman stopped him and put him in a jail cell overnight. He found work briefly in Pelham, New Hampshire, but left when he heard a fellow Swede from his home village lived in Methuen. His countryman did not know of any job openings. Nels then worked briefly for a machinist in Lawrence, at a flour mill in Methuen, a forge in Boston, a smith shop in East Boston, a flour mill in Boston, and machine shops in Boston and Cambridge. He stayed in boarding houses and visited a variety of churches. In reading his account of this period, his depression and lack of direction become evident. He longed for Christian fellowship and support, but formed no lasting friendships. It seemed his life was on hold.

Finally his parents sent Nels twenty dollars and told him to go to Truro, get his brothers, and come to Chicago. This time he found Cordis, but neither of his brothers. What was worse, on the packet-boat back to Boston, he was robbed of all his money. Once again Nels was without money and separated from his family. His father sent him an additional ten dollars and told him to come without his brothers, if necessary. It was now November 6, 1853, more than a year since the family had been together, and eighteen months since they left their farm in Sweden.

With a new acquaintance named Gaslander, Nels took a train from Boston to Albany, then traveled to Buffalo and took a steamboat from Buffalo to Detroit. His cash supply was twenty-five cents when he left Buffalo, so he subsisted on bread and some pieces of sausage. He remembered he had read in a paper of an old Swedish-Finn named Bloom who lived in Detroit. Amazingly, as the boat came into harbor he could see a warehouse with the name Bloom on it. Once he disembarked, he inquired at a boarding house after Bloom. The proprietor told him it was too late to go to Bloom's that night, but offered to put them up for the night at no charge. The next day they found Bloom and his family. They stayed as their guests several days and attended the Baptist church with them. The Blooms must also have helped them financially, because Nels had ten cents in his pocket when he boarded the train to Chicago.

The train depot in Chicago was not far from Lake Michigan on the south side of the city: possibly the Fort Wayne & Chicago Railroad Depot, located south of Twelfth Street and next to the south branch of the Chicago River. Nels wrote that everything looked so desolate that he could scarcely believe he and Gaslander were in Chicago. They began walking north into the city, uncertain where to go. Even though he had a mailing address for his parents, Nels did not know his way around the city, and Chicago's population at that time was 60,662. On the Clark Street Bridge they encountered a man wearing a white neck-cloth: a sign that he was a minister. Nels asked the clergyman in English if he knew where any Swedes were. The minister gave an affirmative answer, and asked whom he sought. When Nels gave his father's name, the stranger said he knew Ola and Hanna, and would take Nels to them immediately. It turned out the clergyman was Sven B. Newman, a pioneer leader in Swedish Methodism.[19] Ola and Hanna Westergreen had become charter members of the first Swedish Methodist church in Chicago. Newman watched the tearful and joyous reunion between parents and son, and then led them in prayer.

In the meantime, Erik and Sven were still based in Massachusetts. An account remembered by Sven's son, a century later, suggests that Sven was in Boston, not in Truro with Erik. The account differs in some points from his uncle's autobiography. Henry Westergreen recounted that Sven got a letter from Nels three years after the family arrived in Fall River, suggesting that they meet at the Bethel Ship John Wesley in New York City. This recycled brig, moored in the North River, served as a chapel, traveler's aid society, hospital, post office, and currency exchange for Scandinavian immigrants.[20] Sven left his job in Truro, allegedly receiving only $1.50 from Mrs. Cordis in pay for what he claimed was three years' work, and took a train from Boston to New York. He stayed at a cabin

19. Like so many immigrants to America, Nyman soon anglicized his name. He is known as Newman in published works. I have chosen to use the names Nels Westergreen employed in his writing at the time of the event being described, changing the spelling or names concurrently with his own changes.

20. Whyman, *The Hedstroms and the Bethel Ship Saga*, 94.

with some card-playing drunks until morning, then walked to the navy
shipyard instead of the North River. With his still-limited language skills,
he mistook "Bethel Ship" for "battleship." Obviously, he found neither
his brother Nels nor the Bethel Ship, so he took the train back to Boston.
He nearly froze on the train, and could barely walk on his frostbitten
feet. As he stumbled down a street near the station he was relieved to
encounter Nels, who had tickets for both of them to get to Chicago and
their parents.[21]

Nels's account says nothing about a proposed rendezvous in New
York City. By 1856 he was a lay preacher, studying for ordination in the
Methodist Church. His autobiography states that he went from Chicago
to Boston, arriving February 15, and preached at various churches for
almost three weeks. He met Sven in Boston on March 4, and they went
to New York the following day. Nels claimed it was at that point that they
met Pastor Nyman/Newman and O.G. Hedstrom, the minister in charge
of the Bethel Ship John Wesley. The brothers' journey to Chicago took
nine days, mainly because snow that piled up on the tracks and difficult
people along the way. For example, he related that in Cleveland someone
tried to throw them off the train platform.[22]

On February 27, before he met Sven, Nels traveled to Truro to meet
his brother Erik. He was hurt and disappointed when "he seemed almost
indifferent to meeting me, much less to travel with me."[23] The brothers
attended a prayer meeting together that evening. The following day, he
tried again to persuade Erik to go home (i.e., Chicago) with him, but in
vain. Erik accompanied him until they reached Wellfleet, a few miles to
the south, and they parted with many tears. Nels and Erik did not see
one another again for more than ten years. No reason is given for Erik's
unwillingness to go west with his brothers. He earned a pittance working
for Cordis on the fishing boat, and had no other marketable skill except
as a farm laborer. He was now eighteen years old, and had been separated
from most of his family for three years. One can speculate that he was

---

21. Henry Westergreen, unpublished essay, 3–4. It is hard to know what to believe
about these conflicting accounts. Given that Sven's narrative was written as his son
remembered him telling it, over one hundred years after the events occurred, I am
inclined to believe that the amount of detail in this narrative is the result of conflation
of several different events during the period between Sven's arrival in the United States
and his reunion with his parents.

22. Westergreen, *Uppteckningar*, 32.

23. Westergreen, *Uppteckningar*, 30.

still angry at his parents, though not at Nels. Erik was the first son to be sent off to labor after they arrived in America, and when he and his brothers tried to join their parents in Boston, they found they had been abandoned. Eventually Erik became a police officer in Hingham, Massachusetts, and lived there for much of the remainder of his life.

Sven was reunited with his parents and younger brothers three and a half years after they parted in Fall River. When his parents relocated from Chicago to the Galesburg area, Sven and the two youngest brothers, Anders and Johan, went with them. Later Sven became a farmer in Knox County, Illinois, remained active in the Methodist Church, and served as a lay preacher. Unlike Erik (or Johan, the youngest), Sven maintained close ties to his parents, Nels, and Anders his entire life. The Westergreens' journey, then, resulted in two breakups of the family. The first occurred when they left their relatives in Sweden. The second and unexpected rupture happened after they arrived in America. The seven of them were never all together under the same roof again.

3

Call and Discernment

1854 to 1862

O, send us shepherds for your flock, and feed them with your Word;
Against all dangers that assail, equip and arm them, Lord.[1]

WHEN WESTERGREEN WAS REUNITED with his parents and two youngest brothers in November 1853, his role in the family had changed. It had been over a year since they had seen one another, and for the first six months of that period, there had been no correspondence between the parents and their eldest son. Though dutiful and obedient as a young single person in a *läsare* family was expected to be, there was also a role reversal occurring over time. Not only had Nels, as a matter of necessity, learned to fend for himself without parental supervision; he also advocated for his father against an employer when Ola was cheated on some of his wages, and helped build a log house for his parents in Copley Township, Knox County.[2] It was Nels and not his father who made a trip back to the East Coast to find his brothers Sven and Erik. There is never a hint in the manuscript autobiography of a rebellion against parental expectations or authority in the years between his conversion experience in December 1853 until his ordination as a Methodist deacon and first ministerial

1. See Svedberg, "Av dig förordnand, store Gud" [By thee, ordained, great God], 316.

2. Westergreen, *Journal for 1858*, June 22 and July 23 entries.

appointment in 1859. However, during this period, Westergreen formed his first permanent relationships outside the family circle. In addition, he tried his hand at several jobs, pursued more education than either parent had, and had formative religious experiences independent of parental supervision. Westergreen himself later referred to this stage of his life and ministry as "the preparation period."[3]

A few days after his arrival in Chicago, Nels and his traveling companion, Gaslander, went with Ola Westergreen to S. B. Newman's. Newman had prayer with them, and both young men claimed to have been converted.[4] They began attending worship with the Swedish Methodist congregation that O.G. Hedstrom had founded at the Seaman's Bethel Chapel in Chicago in December 1852, and which was now led by Newman.[5] Hanna and Ola, arriving in Chicago in early October of 1852, initially had joined St. Ansgarius Episcopal Church, founded by the Reverend Gustaf Unonius three years earlier.[6] The church's parish register for that period lists every member of the family, although there is no indication the three elder sons ever set foot there. The register also notes that the Westergreens withdrew in January 1853.[7] It is possible the elder Westergreens left for Hedstrom's newly organized Methodist congregation because of its affinity for their own *läsare* orientation. Another possibility is that tensions between the Swedish and Norwegian immigrants within the congregation put them off, particularly since the majority of members were Norwegians.[8] It should be remembered that from 1814 until 1905 Norway was under Swedish rule, and as *Swedish History in Brief* notes, the period was "colored by repeated and progressively sharper conflicts."[9] Those who emigrated did not automatically

3. Westergreen, *Minnen af Min Werksamhet som Predikant* [Memories of my work as a preacher], 1.

4. Westergreen, *Lefnads Anteckning*, 215.

5. Whyman, *The Hedstroms and the Bethel Ship Saga*, 99.

6. This was the first Swedish-language congregation in Chicago, located first at Illinois and Franklin Streets, later moving to Sedgwick near North Avenue. Although raised in the (Lutheran) State Church, Unonius claimed the Episcopal Church was the true equivalent of the Church of Sweden in America.

7. The parents' names are listed as Olof and Hanna Nilson, demonstrating the absence of a fixed spelling of forenames or surnames. The date shown in the register is probably a reflection of when they arrived in America, rather than when they began attending. *St. Ansgarius Parish Register*, 110.

8. See Olsson, "St. Ansgarius and the Immigrant Community," 40.

9. Andersson and Weibull, *Swedish History in Brief*, 43.

relinquish their loyalties and grudges upon setting foot on American soil.
The St. Ansgarius congregation eventually split along these ethnic lines.
The two newly arrived men entered their names on probation in Newman's church, which was located near St. Ansgarius Church in what was
known as Swede Town on Chicago's near north side.

Westergreen and Gaslander found work almost immediately with
the Illinois Central Railroad, but neither stayed long. Gaslander, possibly
captivated by Newman's descriptions of his own time in the American
South, decided to head for New Orleans, and Westergreen lost contact
with him. Westergreen had the opportunity to become the foreman of a
railroad crew, with good pay and opportunity for travel, but he was torn
between worldly temptations on the job and his longing for the depth
of religious experience he witnessed among the Methodists. It appears
that he was going through a period of vocational rootlessness similar
to the interval between leaving his employment with the Washburns in
Minot, Maine, and traveling to Chicago six months later. In both places
he was faithful in church attendance and diligent in prayer, but was not
drawn to any particular vocation. The difference between Westergreen
in New England and Westergreen in Chicago was that in New England,
he continually had a goal in mind: being reunited with his family. He did
not have such clarity regarding a career. After leaving the Illinois Central
Railroad, he tried working for less money at Cyrus McCormick's reaper
factory, established in Chicago only a few years earlier.[10] For McCormick,
work was an all-consuming passion, and he was also reputed to abstain
from smoking, drinking, and cursing, so it is likely Westergreen thought
working conditions would be more in line with the values expressed at
Methodist class meetings.

The trajectory of Westergreen's spiritual growth is easier to track
than his employment. In December 1853, he first attended a Methodist
class meeting with his mother. He had never experienced one before, but
she explained it was a type of meeting where people spoke of their religious experiences.[11] He was uneasy about going, because, as he admitted,

10. According to Northern Illinois University archives, in 1849 the Chicago factory
was housed in a brick building, three stories high and 40 feet by 190 feet in size. The
factory had planing machines, saws, lathes, boring machines, and blacksmith furnaces.
Much of the machinery was driven by a thirty-horsepower engine, one of the first in
Chicago. By 1850 the factory employed about 120 men. A year later, the Chicago newspapers claimed that McCormick's factory was the largest of its kind in the world.

11. It is debatable whether this was truly a novelty for Westergreen, given that
his parents had been *läsare* in Sweden and probably participated in or even hosted

he had no such experience to speak about, but decided to attend because
he thought it might do him some good. Soon after, he attended a second
meeting with his father, held by Brother Newman at the Bethel Church.[12]
He was impressed by the participants' simple and artless speech, along
with the songs and prayers led by Newman, and acknowledged it gave
him "a solemn feeling."[13] When Newman approached him and questioned him on the state of his own soul, he admitted he could not testify
as others at the meeting could. Newman then spoke words of admoni-
tion and encouragement, and the entire group knelt down and prayed for
him. Westergreen later claimed it was at this point he seriously began to
seek entire sanctification. On Christmas Eve of that year, he prayed out
loud for the first time in the presence of other people at a prayer meeting
in his parents' home. Nevertheless, because he did not believe he had the
depth of religious experience as the other Methodists, it was a long time
before he dared to speak in a general prayer meeting.

Newman was clearly a significant and formative influence at this
stage in Westergreen's life. He was one of four Swedish immigrants in
the mid-nineteenth century who, to varying degrees, shaped the trajectory of Westergreen's faith and ministry. The other three were O. G. and
Jonas Hedstrom, both Methodist ministers, and, indirectly, Eric Jansson.
A more detailed history of these men and their ministries offers further
insight into Westergreen himself.

Sven Bernhard Nyman/Newman (1812–1902), was a native of Hö-
ganäs in western Skåne. His autobiography identifies him as the oldest
Swedish Methodist preacher, though in fact O. G. Hedstrom was nine
years his senior. He was confirmed at age sixteen, and said he had a comparatively good religious education, but lacked true peace with God.[14]
He worked as a schoolmaster, wholesale clerk, and briefly for the Russian Consulate in Stockholm before his elder brother persuaded him to
join him in Mobile, Alabama. For the next two years he ran a clothing

---

conventicle meetings in Blekinge and/or Skåne before emigrating in 1852. However,
according to Evangelical Covenant historian Karl Olsson, conventicle meetings were
generally more oriented toward Bible reading and worship *per se* than testimony. See
Olsson, *By One Spirit*, 32–33.

12. Throughout the journals, Westergreen referred to fellow clergy by the title
"Brother____," and their wives as "Sister ___."

13. Westergreen, *Lefnads Anteckning*, 217. This phrase recurs throughout Westergreen's journals as an expression of high praise for a religious assembly. It was a favorite descriptor of many late eighteenth- and nineteenth-century Methodist preachers.

14. Newman, *S. B. Newmans Sjelfbiografi*, 5.

and provisions store with fairly good success. Newman's brother and sister-in-law had joined the Methodist Episcopal Church, and Sven soon became a participant. At a protracted meeting in 1844 he experienced a spiritual awakening, subsequently began studying for the ministry, and was received on probation in the Alabama Conference in 1845. For about six years, Newman served English-speaking congregations in northern Florida. In 1851 he was appointed to assist O. G. Hedstrom on the Bethel Ship in New York, and in this appointment he obtained a strong foundation in ministering to the particular needs of recent immigrants. With the growing Scandinavian population in the Midwest, especially in Chicago and western Illinois, there was a need for Swedish-speaking pastors there. As noted earlier, Hedstrom organized the congregation in Chicago, but Newman remained to serve as its pastor. This is how Newman fortuitously happened to be on Clark Street bridge in Chicago when Westergreen and Gaslander walked into the city from the railroad depot in November 1853.[15] The three coauthors of *Svenska Metodismen I Amerika*, published in 1895, referred to him as "Father Newman," and a great pioneer of Swedish Methodism.[16] Newman was a groundbreaker for new Swedish Methodist classes—which eventually became churches—across the Chicago area and Indiana. He was also an expert at raising funds to erect the first building used by Swedish Methodists in Chicago, and later for putting the new theological school on better financial footing. His work with Hedstrom had made him particularly sensitive to the temporal needs of newly arrived immigrants, many of whom were nearly as impoverished as Ola and Hanna's family. The earliest Swedish arrivals in Chicago lived in overcrowded, rickety frame cottages in an industrial area east of the North Branch of the Chicago River, where cholera and typhoid struck frequently. The Emigrant Aid Society had not yet been established to assist with shelter, food, and employment. Newman's mentoring of Westergreen extended beyond the young man's vocational discernment and ministerial education; he was also the presiding elder of the Chicago District for five years, and subsequently was pastor of many of the Illinois churches later served by Westergreen. These included Rockford, Wataga, Geneva and Batavia, Evanston, Humboldt Park, Moreland, and Austin. There was no one in a better position to advise Westergreen through much of his ministry. Unlike the other

15. In contrast to the years that followed, Clark Street had the *only* bridge crossing the Chicago River at the time.

16. Liljegren et al., *Svenska Metodismen i Amerika*, 188.

religious influences during Westergreen's period of discernment, New-man became a personal friend.

The Hedstrom brothers also shaped Westergreen at this stage of his life, though Jonas (1813–1859) had more direct contact with him than Olof Gustaf (1803–1877), commonly known by his initials. The elder Hedstrom was a tailor by trade, who left Sweden in 1825 and joined the Methodist Church in New York after his conversion in 1829. That same year he married an American woman, Caroline Pinckney. Hedstrom made a visit to Sweden in 1833, returning with his younger brother Jo-nas. In 1835 he was received on probation in the New York Annual Con-ference. George Scott, a Methodist missionary to Sweden in the 1830s, tried to persuade both O. G. Hedstrom and the Missionary Society of the Methodist Episcopal Church to have Hedstrom follow him back to Swe-den in 1842 to strengthen the Methodist movement there, and there ap-peared to be provisional agreement to the proposition. But when Scott's ministry in Stockholm was abruptly terminated, so also were Hedstrom's plans to sail back to his native country. He continued serving in the Catskill and Burham Circuits. In 1843 he was a pastor in Prattsville when Peter Bergner (1797–1866), a Swedish American carpenter and Method-ist lay preacher, wrote to him about the possibility of leading a ministry to Swedish sailors and immigrants coming into New York Harbor. The Wes-leyan Methodist Church, which had stronger leanings toward the "holi-ness" movement than the Methodist Episcopal Church, had purchased a condemned brig and renovated it into a floating bethel church for sea-men. Bergner was holding worship services there in Swedish: the only regular Swedish language services in America at the time.[17] In 1844 the Wesleyans sold the brig to the Asbury Society, a local New York church extension organization of the Methodist Episcopal Church. The work expanded beyond what Bergner could handle alone, and he approached the Missionary Society of the Methodist Episcopal Church to see about professional, full-time leadership for the Bethel Ship. After some initial reluctance, O. G. Hedstrom said he would go the ship if the bishop ap-pointed him. He conducted his first service on the ship—also known as the North River Mission—on May 25, 1845. In addition to conducting Sunday worship in Swedish, there was a 5:00 p.m. service in German and

17. Whyman, *Hedstroms*, 72. Gloria Dei "Old Swedes" Episcopal Church in Phila-delphia may have been a partial exception, if they held occasional Swedish-language services. The other older Swedish church, Holy Trinity in Wilmington, Delaware, dis-continued the use of Swedish in the eighteenth century.

evening service in English. Social services of various kinds were offered, tracts were distributed, and a Sunday School for children and a temperance society for adults were organized. Hedstrom conducted baptisms, marriages, and funerals, and was instrumental in finding temporary and sometimes permanent housing for them. Financial assistance and travel guidance were made available. The Bethel Ship really provided the services of a Swedish consulate or Traveler's Aid Society for seamen and immigrants. A contemporary of Hedstrom's, Joseph Hartwell, described his preaching style this way:

> His mind, though not trained in the culture of the schools, was active, vigorous and clear . . . not inclined to metaphysics but his descriptive powers were wonderful. With a text that suggested an army or a ship, a shepherd or husbandman, he could draw such vivid word pictures as moved even the coolest hearts.[18]

Meanwhile, O. G. Hedstrom's younger brother, Jonas, moved to eastern Pennsylvania and became a blacksmith, which was a trade he had learned in his homeland.[19] He fell in love with a young woman named Diantha Sornberger, whose father was a war veteran. As Whyman explains it, after the War of 1812, the administration of the Illinois Territory designated the area between the Illinois and Mississippi Rivers as a military tract for the benefit of soldiers.[20] The Sornberger family took advantage of this opportunity and moved to Victoria in Knox County, Illinois, in 1837. Jonas Hedstrom followed them, and married Diantha on August 17, 1839. The Sornbergers and the young couple remained active in the Methodist church, and Jonas became bi-vocational, working both as a blacksmith and a local preacher. He organized a Methodist congregation of five persons in Victoria, and preached his first Swedish sermon in December 1846. A gifted speaker and shrewd entrepreneur, he prospered in his business and also dealt in real estate. This wholehearted embrace of private enterprise was one of several points of conflict with Eric Jansson. In 1848 Jonas Hedstrom became a probationary member of the Rock River Conference of the Methodist Episcopal Church, and in 1850 was ordained an elder in full connection.[21]

18. Hartwell, "Chapters from Memory," 60–61.

19. Witting, *Minnen Från Mitt Lif*, 168–70.

20. Whyman, *Hedstroms*, 118.

21. Liljegren et al., *Svenska Metodismen i Amerika*, 172.

Since the Westergreens landed at Fall River, Massachusetts, rather than arriving at New York City, they did not encounter either Hedstrom at that time. Westergreen met with O. G. Hedstrom and worshiped on the Bethel Ship when he returned to the East Coast to search for his two brothers in 1856. In the photograph taken at the first organizational meeting of Swedish Methodist preachers in 1866, O. G. is front row center, holding a large book in one hand: clearly the presiding elder. Westergreen and S. B. Newman are seated next to each other at Hedstrom's right: an evocative arrangement. It was Jonas Hedstrom who signed Westergreen's first license to preach and who supervised his early ministry. And between them, the Hedstrom brothers helped foster the influx of Swedish immigrants to northern Illinois, including the notorious Eric Jansson and his followers. The relationship between the Janssonists and those who joined with Jonas Hedstrom's congregation shaped Westergreen and that entire generation of Swedish Methodist preachers.

Eric Jansson (1808–1850) was raised in a conventional Lutheran home in Hälsingland, Sweden, but at age twenty-two had a vision in a barn while suffering an acute attack of rheumatism. The vision, which biographer Paul Elmen likened to Paul's vision on the Damascus Road or Wesley's Aldersgate experience, led him to believe he had been deceived by Lutheran clergy and teachers; physical and spiritual healing could only come through faith in the power of Christ, as revealed in the Bible.[22] Jansson became active in local conventicles and read the works of Luther and Arndt. He believed he had been commissioned to preach this truth to people, and proclaimed the necessity and attainability of entire sanctification, the experience of sanctification and justification as a single event, and the superiority of his *own* experiences and insights. The State Church was already hostile toward lay preachers, and when Jansson began organizing book burnings—starting with the works of Luther and Arndt—and led other acts of civil disobedience, he did nothing to endear himself to the religious establishment.

Jansson gathered hundreds of followers, and wrote a catechism and songbook for their use. The catechism presented sanctification as attainable, sinless perfection, and consequently, equality with Christ. Though all his followers ostensibly could reach this perfection, it was most particularly manifested in Jansson himself. An excerpt from the catechism demonstrates this:

22. Elmen, *Wheat Flour Messiah*, 3–4.

> Q: Do you believe thus, that the coming of Christ did not occur
> until Eric Jansson came with the true light, just as God in the
> moment of creation called forth light out of darkness?
>
> A: . . . As the splendor of the second temple at Jerusalem far
> exceeded the splendor of the first, so also the glory of the
> work which is to be accomplished by Eric Jansson, standing
> in Christ's stead, will surpass that which Jesus and his apostles
> carried out.[23]

Unlike Wesleyan perfectionist theology, which speaks of the Holy Spirit
perfecting one in love for God and neighbor, Jansson's understanding of
perfection was colored by his delusional mindset and strong anti-intel-
lectual streak. Jansson probably never read Wesley; he would have been
more likely to burn *Wesley's Works*. But he did move in Pietistic circles
where focus on the inner life and spiritual progress were of great importance. Gunnar Westin states that the terms *läsare* and Methodist were
practically interchangeable in Sweden by 1840.[24] What is more, Jansson
was such a persuasive speaker that the pastor of Alfta parish in Hälsingland lamented that 10 percent of his parishioners had become Janssonists
and stopped attending the parish church.[25] Clairvoyance and miracles
were attributed to him, and, as Elmen wrote, the farmers and laborers who
followed him were "an unlikely combination of piety and revolution, of
moral pretension and criminality, of Bible study, prayer, and insolence."[26]
What may have started as a convictional religious experience developed
into an insurrection against the Church and its authorities by laity whose
cultic leader claimed divine sanction. Jansson was arrested for causing
civil unrest and holding conventicle meetings, among other things, but
escaped on his way to prison in Gävle. Through the intercession of his
attorney, Lars Vilhelm Henschen, he obtained permission to leave the
country and emigrate to America.

One of Jansson's deputies, Olof Olsson, had already traveled to New
York in December 1845 aboard the brig *Neptune*. He had been sent by
Jansson to explore a suitable location with available land upon which the
Janssonists could establish a religious community. Olsson was unable to
speak English and had no idea where to turn for help. Someone led him

23. Jansson, *Cateches*, 79. Translated by Paul Elmen.
24. Whyman, *Hedstroms*, 46.
25. Elmen, *Wheat Flour Messiah*, 49.
26. Elmen, *Wheat Flour Messiah*, 76.

and his family to Hedstrom's Bethel Ship. They were given living quarters on the ship for several weeks, spoken to in their own language, and education for Olsson's two children was provided. Olsson became friends with O. G. Hedstrom, who told him about the fertile land available in Illinois, and made arrangements for his brother Jonas to meet and welcome the Olsson family. Olsson was already predisposed to regard the Methodists as friends, given his earlier contact and work with George Scott in Sweden, and decided to join the Methodist Church. Olsson wrote to his fellow Janssonists in Sweden, praising Methodist preaching and worship and expressing thankfulness for Hedstrom's kindness. Eric Jansson was not pleased; before he and another group of followers left for America in April 1846, he exhorted his disciples to pray "that those bewildered followers who have been led astray by the seductions of Pastor Hedstrom should be brought back to the [Janssonist] fold."[27]

When Jansson and his family arrived in spring 1846, Hedstrom invited him to share the Bethel Ship pulpit, but Jansson declined. Instead he preached in private homes and won some additional followers before the long journey to western Illinois. One of these, Anna-Sophia Pollock, had been a staunch Methodist but left the church after hearing "the Prophet." Now she served as translator for the small party as they made their way west. Contrary to Jansson's promise, the new immigrants were not miraculously able to speak the English language as soon as they set foot on American soil. A total of about twelve hundred Janssonists emigrated from Sweden between 1846 and 1854. Many, however, defected as soon as they reached the New World, and others stayed in Chicago. When the first party reached Victoria, they stayed with Olof Olsson and his family in a log cabin owned by Jonas Hedstrom. Jansson's son, Eric Johnson, recalled the violent theological debates and name-calling between his father and Jonas Hedstrom, and his father's anger toward Olof Olsson for defecting to the Methodist Church. Jansson's megalomania, peculiar sanctification theology, and insistence on no interpretation of the Bible but his own were certainly at odds with Wesleyan theology. Anna-Sophia Pollock, who married Jansson three weeks after his first wife died, wrote that Hedstrom was trying to have her husband deported, and furthermore had threatened the colony with arson and Pollock herself with deportation if she did not stop teaching English to

27. Elmen, *Wheat Flour Messiah*, 99. Jansson also prayed that Sweden would suffer worse than Sodom and Gomorrah, and that anyone who doubted this would come to pass would either be cut in two or else drop dead like Ananias and Sapphira.

the Swedish immigrants—assertions that seem as far-fetched as some of her husband's statements.[28] Elmen, writing more than forty years prior to discovery of the Pollock manuscript, lent a measure of credence to the idea that things were getting personal. He wrote that the animosity was not purely theological; there was also rivalry for the support of newly arrived immigrants. Both the Methodist and Janssonist groups grew, and in August 1846 the Janssonists purchased an eighty-acre farm near Red Oak, Illinois. They named the colony Bishop Hill, after Jansson's birthplace, Biskopskulla.

This was a period in American history when utopian communities were common. The Janssonists communicated with the Amana colony in Iowa, the Oneida perfectionist colony, and the Shakers. In addition to Bishop Hill, there were three other utopian colonies in Henry County, at Morristown, Wetherfield, and Geneseo.[29] Farming was the chief occupation at Bishop Hill, but they supplemented their income with the production of linen cloth and corn brooms.

Worship in the Colony Church was similar in structure to nondenominational worship elsewhere. They sang hymns and songs, mainly composed by Jansson, prayed extemporaneously, celebrated the Lord's Supper, and usually Jansson preached. His theology evolved with the various challenges of life in the New World; while in Sweden, sinless perfection was regarded as something any believer could and should attain. By his logic, if a believer had Christ dwelling within him/her, and Christ was without sin, then sin could no longer exist in the believer. This tenet was reflected in the absence of any prayers of confession during worship. The conviction of one's own righteousness before God gave the Janssonists courage to stand against civil and ecclesiastical authority in Sweden. But in America, there was no Conventicle Edict prohibiting their gatherings, and no need for a primitive liberation theology to empower or grant status to the immigrants.[30] What seemed more necessary was a strong, wise leader whom they could trust to keep them alive. Not surprisingly,

28. Butler-Wall, "Anna Sophia," 157. The memoir, written in Swedish, was discovered in the Bishop Hill Heritage Association Archives in 2010. It was written between April 8 and May 11, 1850, i.e., it was completed two days prior to Jansson's murder.

29. Jansson would also have been aware of the former Mormon colony in Nauvoo, Hancock County, Illinois, which broke apart within two years of Joseph Smith's murder by a mob in 1844.

30. The relationship between sanctification/holiness theology and liberation theology is presented in Norén, "Study of Wesley's Doctrine," 388.

the circle of those who had reached perfection grew ever smaller, finally becoming the sole property of Jansson, who routinely likened himself to Jesus Christ. Jansson's teaching also had an impact on the lifestyle and governance of the colony; for the first year or two, marriages were not allowed at Bishop Hill. The reason was practical more than religious; with limited resources, they needed to keep population growth at a minimum. Colonists were expected to seclude themselves from possible contamination or persecution by the outside world. All property was held in common, in accordance with Jansson's reading of the New Testament. If a person wished to leave the colony, there were two penalties: public denunciation by Jansson, and leaving behind all money and labor the person had invested in the colony.[31] Jansson claimed power over physical disease, and illness among his followers was taken as a sign of unbelief. This teaching was sorely challenged in 1849, when a cholera epidemic swept away two hundred colony members, including Jansson's first wife, Maja Stina. Jansson blamed her death on the unbelief of others. Unwise business transactions, defections to the Methodists and Lutherans in the area, the financial impact of the cholera epidemic, and interpersonal conflict led to multiple lawsuits. Jansson was shot and killed by the estranged husband of a colonist at the Henry County Courthouse in Cambridge on May 13, 1850. It is testimony to the colonists' belief in their leader that Jansson's body lay in state for three days in the Colony Church; they apparently hoped he would return to them, rising from the dead.[32]

Jonas Olsson and seven trustees took over leadership of the colony, and the Illinois legislature granted it a charter in January of 1853. As Elmen explains, Bishop Hill prospered financially until the economic crisis of 1857, but divisions rose in the village, and in 1862 the communal idea was abandoned, and each member of the colony received a fair share of the whole.[33] Most of the colonists eventually joined the Methodist church, which was formally organized in 1864. Nels Westergreen was its first pastor.

These men and the historical developments of that period had a lasting impact not only on Westergreen and his ministry, but on the trajectory of Swedish Methodism as a whole. During this period of vocational discernment, however, Westergreen's closest contact was with S. B.

---

31. Elmen, *Wheat Flour Messiah* 128.

32. Isaksson and Hallgren, *Bishop Hill*, 128.

33. Elmen, *Wheat Flour Messiah*, 169.

Newman. An importance difference between Newman and the other men who influenced Westergreen is that Newman was more distant from sanctification and holiness theology, except what he absorbed from Wesley's own writings. He had been converted and ordained in Alabama, and was in ministry there and in Florida until 1851. The Holiness Movement did not make inroads in the American South until the last two decades of the nineteenth century.[34] Nevertheless, Newman's theology and pastoral orientation were typical of evangelical Protestantism in that era.

Because of his distress about his spiritual state, Westergreen sought counsel from Newman on several occasions, as well as sharing his anxiety with others in the church. He recognized that his *läsare* background contributed to his tendency toward scrupulosity, recalling that it was considered common among the *läsare* back in Sweden to go through great struggle and deep sorrow over one's sins before experiencing true blessedness and peace with God through Christ. He also acknowledged that during this period of his life he was over-dependent on the love and sympathy of other participants in the class meeting.[35] But there is reason to hypothesize that Newman was not the sole guiding force. The residual influence of and Wesleyan reaction to the perfectionist teaching of Eric Jansson among Swedish immigrants must be taken into account. Two of Westergreen's closest friends during his discernment period and early ministry were Victor Witting (1825–1906) and Peter Challman (1822–1900). Both men had been part of the Janssonist sect at Bishop Hill before becoming Methodist preachers. They were slightly older than Westergreen, licensed before him, and were therefore in a position to mentor him. Challman joined the Janssonists in 1844, while still in Sweden, and came to America with the sect two years later.[36] He left the Bishop Hill colony after a year, as did Victor Witting, who had joined the Janssonists shortly after Challman left.[37] Like Westergreen, Witting grew up in a strongly Pietist part of Sweden, and also placed high value on personal religious experience.

Another factor affecting Westergreen's spiritual and vocational struggle was his own psychosocial development. A century later, developmental psychologists wrote extensively about the transition from

34. Kostlevy, *Holy Jumpers*, 14.
35. Westergreen, *Lefnads Anteckning*, 3.
36. Liljegren et al., *Svenska Metodismen I Amerika*, 178.
37. Liljegren et al., *Svenska Metodismen I Amerika*, 185.

childhood to adulthood: a period when personal identity and ideology—religious, political, and vocational—must be forged for oneself. The stage is marked by experimentation, self-definition, and self-discovery.[38] One manifestation of this experimentation in Westergreen was the various names he used as his signature during this period: Nils Olsson, N. Olavson, Niles Olson, Nelson Westergreen, and finally Nels O. Westergreen. Another sign of his gradual self-definition may be his vacillation between independence and dependence upon family for religious and personal identity. While he absorbed his parents' Pietist worldview, it was a religious orientation that placed a premium on personal, first-hand religious experience; simply conforming to the community's worship pattern or social mores was not enough. *Leading* his parents and other role models in their religious exercises was one step in the process. Formal education for ministry and ordination was another.

The Westergreen family seemed to have difficulty settling in a community in Illinois. Early in 1854 they moved from Chicago to St. Charles, a community west of Chicago on the Fox River. The only Swedish worship service they found there was Lutheran, and it was not to their taste. A Methodist minister named Cederstrom came and preached in St. Charles, but shortly thereafter he left the Methodist Church to join the Lutherans. It was another sixteen years until a Swedish Methodist congregation was established a few miles down the river in Geneva, Illinois.[39] The Westergreens soon moved north to Rockford, a city with a significant Scandinavian population.[40] There is no record of what sort of employment Ola or Nels had during this period, though Ola's opportunities may have been limited by the earlier injury to one arm. Many of the early Swedish settlers became farmers, but others started small businesses or worked in the city's many factories, so an immigrant would not have had difficulty finding an employer who spoke the same language. In 1853 a cholera epidemic reached Rockford, and during the summer of 1854 a number of Westergreen's friends succumbed. He wrote in his autobiography that he was afraid of dying, and afraid to meet God, but "had no power to resist sin or seek his soul's salvation with seriousness."[41]

38. Erikson, *Childhood and Society*, 261.

39. Liljegren et al., *Svenska Metodismen i Amerika*, 273.

40. "Rockford Illinois History," https://www.gorockford.com/about/history/. Rockford's population in 1850 was 2,563. The first Swedish settlers arrived in 1852, and soon became the largest ethnic group in the city.

41. Westergreen, *Uppteckningar*, 18.

He felt spiritually adrift. It was not until autumn that Pastor Newman came to Rockford and took him under his wing again. Under Newman's leadership, a religious movement broke out among the immigrants. He organized a Methodist class and made Ola Westergreen its leader.[42] He also took Nels with him to Pecatonica and other small farming communities, where he made pastoral calls and preached. He urged Westergreen to try his hand at preaching, and late in the year, during a meeting in his parents' house, Westergreen took Revelation 3 as his text and, with knees quaking, gave his first sermon.[43] Having taken that initial step, Westergreen began to hold class meetings on his own, and preached to his fellow immigrants after Newman returned to Chicago. In the absence of his mentor, Westergreen's lack of self-confidence became more pronounced. He wrote, "I soon found how little equipped I was to speak God's Word. On one occasion, a preacher from the Lutheran Church came in, and fear overcame me. Others could preach about a verse and find more to say than I could about an entire chapter. Both words and ideas escaped me. Yet the Lord blessed this weak effort by movement both on the people and myself, and we often parted with tears."[44]

In the spring of 1855 Westergreen left his family again and moved back to Chicago to look for work. He boarded with a man named Peterson, who was an assistant to Newman, and the two young men became good friends. Newman, seeing Westergreen struggle to find a job, found a place for him at Garrett Biblical Institute, where he arrived on May 4 and stayed several weeks, sitting in on classes and using the library. Westergreen reveled in the resources available in the school library, and incorporated what he learned into his sermons. He participated in prayer meetings and class meetings, but reproached himself for frequently "yielding to the temptation to frivolity and thoughtlessness."[45] On weekends, he would travel into the city to worship at the Swedish Methodist Church, and heard various Scandinavian preachers. In particular, he was impressed by the sermons of Eric Shogren, whom Wallenius and Olson describe as "eloquent, with a pleasing voice and a high degree of skill as

42. *Official Church Record: Historical Record of Permanent Data for Bethany United Methodist Church, Rockford Illinois, 1920*, 4.

43. There are six different sermons on portions of Revelation 3 in the Northern Illinois Conference Archives, but as these are not dated, it is impossible to know whether one of them is Westergreen's first work.

44. Westergreen, *Uppteckningar*, 22.

45. Westergreen, *Lefnads Anteckning*, 241.

a public speaker."[46] After Westergreen left Evanston at the end of June, he and Shogren traveled together and preached in Wataga, Galesburg, Knoxville, and other communities in western Illinois. The preaching tour culminated with an American campmeeting in Victoria followed by a Swedish campmeeting in Andover.

Campmeetings, urban tent-meetings, and protracted meetings (the indoor equivalent) came to be a vital part of Westergreen's ministry as well as his own religious identity and experience, and thus they merit further explication. Open-air preaching had been part of the Methodist movement since its earliest days. In 1739 John Wesley "submitted to be more vile" and preached outdoors near Bristol, England. Even before Wesley's death in 1791, Methodist preacher Daniel Asbury organized a Methodist society near Terrell, North Carolina, and led worship on the banks of the Catawba River.[47] Charles A. Johnson has noted that outdoor services that included celebration of the sacraments took place on the America frontier as early as 1769.[48] Unlike the Cane Ridge Camp Meeting of 1801, the earliest American Methodist outdoor services were a matter of necessity, not choice; circuit riders were eager to establish new congregations on the frontier, and while preaching services were held in private homes, schoolhouses, and public buildings, meeting in the open air allowed them to accommodate larger groups. It also offered the possibility of reaching the unchurched/unbelieving, who might come to scoff but stay to be converted.

The outdoor preaching service offered both freedom of movement for worshipers and an abundance of metaphors for conveying the gospel. Russell E. Richey describes Methodist movement's sacralization of American woodlands in this way:

> . . . as cathedral, as confessional, as challenge—as shady grove (nature's cathedral), as garden (a Gethsemane, where temptations might be fought and spiritual solace sought), and as wilderness (a challenge through and into which the Methodist "gospel" must be taken).[49]

The romantic language of shady grove, garden, and wilderness should not be construed as new physical territory being discovered or explored.

46. Wallenius and Olson, *Short History*, 28.

47. Brown, "Finding America's Oldest Camp Meeting," 253.

48. Johnson, *Frontier Camp Meeting*, 25.

49 Richey, "Shady Grove, Garden, and Wilderness," 258.

From almost the beginning, itinerant preachers had to seek permission from a land owner to hold campmeetings on the property. Sites were chosen on the basis of proximity to a water source, pasturage, shade trees, and accessibility to roads, wagon trails, and/or rivers. It should also be noted that after the Civil War, but particularly following the advent of the first Chautauqua in 1874, permanent campmeeting settings tended to chosen on the basis of proximity to recreational opportunities and amenities such as public transportation.

The type of songs sung by the Swedish Methodists at the campmeetings differed to some degree from those sung at English language campmeetings. In contrast to the sacralization of the American woodlands, noted by Richey, and Charles Lippy's observations in "The Camp Meeting in Transition: The Character and Legacy of the Late Nineteenth Century," nature imagery did not enjoy a prominent place in the Swedish songs. This is somewhat surprising, given the prevalence of such imagery in the larger body of Swedish hymn lyrics, both past and present. Instead, the early Swedish campmeetings would have drawn primarily from three sources: *Den Svenska Psalmboken*, *Femtio Andeliga Sånger*, and whatever American hymns, gospel songs, and choruses the preachers translated into Swedish.[50] The *ordo salutis* was the dominant theological theme in the lyrics. In *Glory, Hallelujah! The Story of the Campmeeting Spiritual*, Ellen Jane Lorenz identifies musical and rhetorical structure of the music used in American campmeetings: simple choruses, many of which were never written down; the "spiritual song" created by a preacher or local leader, often with imperfect rhymes and strained meter; extension refrains (repeating a key phrase from the stanza as a refrain); interrupting refrains, in which the refrain is often unrelated to what comes before and after; "mother hymns," in which a much older hymn text had a refrain added to it (such as "We're Marching to Zion"); and independent choruses, which are very simple, brief songs repeated with variations from six to thirty times.[51] Lorenz also notes that although the Methodists never officially sanctioned a single revival songbook, dozens of songbooks,

50. *Den Svenska Psalmboken* was the Church of Sweden hymnbook published in 1819. O. G. Hedström used this hymnbook on the Bethel Ship, along with whatever Wesley hymns had been translated into Scandinavian languages. If immigrants brought any books with them, the most likely selections were the Bible and *Den Svenska Psalmboken*. *Femtio Andeliga Sånger* was a collection published by T. M. Hasselquist in 1852; it included popular works by Oscar Ahnfelt, Lina Sandell, and Carl Olof Rosenius.

51. Lorenz, *Glory, Hallelujah!*, 41–54.

usually without music, were published throughout the nineteenth century.[52] It appears that few of these had the word "Methodist" in the title. The publication of such songbooks in Swedish did not gain momentum until the 1870s and 1880s; examples and analyses of these works appear in the chapter covering that period in Westergreen's life.

In Illinois, the first known Methodist campmeeting was conducted by the Reverend Jesse Walker in April, 1807, south of Edwardsville, near St. Louis, Missouri. According to historian J. Gordon Melton, Walker was assisted by Charles R. Matheny and Hosea Riggs.[53] In *The Methodist Movement in Northern Illinois*, Almer M. Pennewell traces the history of a number of "permanent" Methodist campgrounds and institutes in the state, in or near Des Plaines, Franklin Grove, Gibson, Lena, New Lenox, Dolton, and Lake Geneva (Wisconsin). Of these, only Des Plaines Campground and Conference Point Camp in Lake Geneva still exist.[54] However, Pennewell and Melton include little information on the locations, history, and distinctive aspects of Swedish Methodist campmeetings.

Westergreen was present at the first independent Swedish Methodist campmeeting, held in Andover Township, Henry County, Illinois, in August 1855. Meetings were held the following two years, but not in a fixed location. During the 1860s and early 1870s, campmeetings were conducted in several locations in Knox and Henry Counties in western Illinois: Red Oak Grove in Weller Township, Lynn Grove in Lynn Township, Victoria, Brush Creek, Altona, Kewanee, Oak Hill, and two different places called Hickory Grove: one near Opheim and one in Galva Township. He wrote about preparing for a campmeeting at Red Oak Grove held September 4–7, 1865:

> We got four men from Andover to help fix up the campground. Found when we got to the place we couldn't get the ground we

52. Lorenz, *Glory, Hallelujah!*, 73.

53. Melton, *Log Cabins to Steeples*, 115.

54. Pennewell, *Methodist Movement*, 273–303. At New Lenox, a large United Methodist church has replaced the cottages, dining hall, and tabernacle. In Lena, there is also a United Methodist church, but Butternut Woods, the site of the former campmeetings, is now a housing development with no religious connection. At Des Plaines Campground, the former Swedish tabernacle is used for worship during the summer months, but the program there has evolved into a variety of recreational, educational, and devotional opportunities. At Lake Geneva, Conference Point has become an independent Christian conference and camping center. The United Methodist Church runs a camping program at nearby Wesley Woods. Neither Conference Point nor Wesley Woods hosts any event that resembles a traditional nineteenth-century campmeeting.

looked out last Friday. Got a new ground, cleared it and hauled logs and boards for seats, and put up a frame for the pulpit. We set up six tents. On the 7th, it was so rainy we had to have our meetings in tents.[55]

Only the latter Hickory Grove was purchased and developed by the Galesburg District Campmeeting Association, Central Swedish Conference. A dining hall, tabernacle, house for ministers, and some cottages were erected.[56] In the years that followed, Swedish Methodist campmeetings were held in New Sweden and Swede Bend, Iowa, Scandia Grove, Minnesota, Sheffield, Indiana, the West Pullman, Ravenswood, and Edgewater neighborhoods of Chicago, Glen Ellyn and Maywood (two Chicago suburbs), New Lenox and Des Plaines, Cambridge, Wisconsin, and other parts of the United States with a significant Scandinavian population.[57] The 1855 campmeetings were significant experiences in Westergreen's spiritual and vocational development. In the years that followed, his journal recorded statistics, speakers, and events at campmeetings in far greater detail than it did church dedications or ordinary Sunday services. His autobiography acknowledged that he had long desired to attend a campmeeting, but he was initially disappointed in this first one. The songs, sermons and prayers did not seem to affect him as he had hoped, though he waited in expectation. He met up with another man, Anders Shogren, who found himself in a similar situation. On the last evening, he suggested that they both go down to the mourners' bench for others to pray over them, and reasoned that even if nothing came from it, it would nevertheless be a blow to their pride. They went forward, and he later wrote, "I never before felt myself as happy as I did in that moment. I thought I could rest in Jesus better than I ever could before. And the following day, I spent some time with Brother Witting, who also attended the campmeeting, and I felt an inner drive to praise God."[58] After such a transforming experience, the Swedish campmeeting that followed was a letdown. Westergreen saw others awakened to conviction, followed by conversion, but he himself wept, prayed, and waited in vain to be filled with peace and joy. In hindsight, he reflected that it was because he was

55. Westergreen, *Journals*, September 4, 1865.

56. See Stoneberg, "Swedish Campmeetings," 160.

57. It should be noted that some of these place-names have changed over the years.

58. Westergreen, *Uppteckningar*, 26.

trying to build on the previous experience with his faith rather than relying on the working cause: Jesus Christ.

After the campmeeting the Methodists held a Quarterly Conference
examination, as was common practice at the time, and Westergreen received his license to preach.[59] One of the questions asked was whether
he knew he had the forgiveness of his sins, and the testimony of it. He
responded, "No," but his license was nevertheless approved and signed
by Jonas Hedstrom, the president, and Otto Lubeck, the secretary. For
the rest of that year he was a colporteur in Chicago and towns to the
west, including Geneva, St. Charles, and Leland. He and Eric Shogren
both preached at a Watch Night service in Chicago on New Year's Eve
of that year. This service was originally adapted from the Moravians by
John Wesley, and was an extended service of hymn-singing, testimony
and prayer that occurred on the Friday night nearest the full moon. Over
time, it transferred to New Year's Eve, and the theological focus shifted
to renewing one's covenant with God and/or welcoming another year of
the Lord.[60]

For the first half of 1856, Westergreen was not under appointment
or earning a steady income, but as a licensed preacher he gave sermons
fairly regularly in Batavia, Victoria, Galesburg, Andover, Rock Island,
and Moline, doing colporteur work, and traveling. Newman gradually
involved Westergreen in worship and outreach ministries of the church:
making as many as twenty pastoral calls per day, occasionally preaching,
and going door to door selling copies of Wesley's "Christian Perfection"
for $.25, though occasionally he also sold *Porter's Compendium*, Nelson's
Counsel, and a few other booklets.[61] Westergreen enjoyed preaching, but
admitted he was often half-hearted in peddling; he would go from house
to house in and around Chicago, knock on the door, and if a servant
girl opened the door he merely asked if the homeowners wanted to buy
any books. This usually received a negative answer, but in his reports he
nevertheless included these as households visited, even though he hadn't
been inside the home or talked with the inhabitants.[62] In February and
March he traveled back to New York and Massachusetts to search for
his brothers Sven and Erik. He preached several times in Boston, and

59. Westergreen, *Uppteckningar*, 28.

60. Tucker, *American Methodist Worship*, 74.

61. Westergreen, *Journals*, February 8 and May 21, 1856.

62. Westergreen, memoranda at end of 1856 *Journal*.

attended worship with Erik at the First Congregational Parish of Truro, on Cape Cod.[63] Nels and Sven met up with Newman and O. G. Hedstrom briefly, and attended a class meeting while in New York City before returning to Chicago in mid-March. Sven moved in with his parents, but Nels continued west to Galesburg and preached several times in the Lutheran Church in Galesburg.

Up to this point, he had preached only in Swedish and to fellow immigrants. Westergreen's first attempt to give a sermon in English occurred July 27, 1856, at a campmeeting at Forest Glen, a wooded settlement about ten miles northwest of Chicago's city center. His text was Heb 2:3, and A. J. Anderson exhorted after him in Swedish.[64] Despite ongoing missionary efforts, it was more than thirty years before a Swedish Methodist congregation was established and a building erected there.

Westergreen's first recorded romance occurred during this period. His journal and autobiography are inconsistent in describing his relationship with Lisa, a young Norwegian woman whose surname may have been Swenson. The 1856 journal scarcely acknowledges the attraction between them. It notes that he had "trifling conversation" with her in two instances. The memoranda at the end of the journal is vague regarding how the relationship developed, though it states they first became acquainted when he lived in Rockford in 1855, and asserts that their intimate company and conversation were grounded in the fear of God. She attended his prayer meetings and was deeply pious. But in the autobiography, composed years later, he relates that he and Lisa used to go for walks together. They corresponded during his study time in Evanston, and their mutual regard was renewed when he returned from preaching in Victoria. He was deeply attracted to her, but his parents disapproved of the relationship because it provided fuel for gossip, and because he admitted to them that he didn't really want to marry her.[65] Then the young woman fell ill with consumption, and finally died in February or March of the following year. Westergreen himself fell ill with what proved not to be consumption, and he also experienced a spiritual low point. He came to regard his infatuation as foolish and sinful, and vowed never to become ensnared that way again. As for Lisa, the autobiography notes

63. Founded in 1709, it is one of the oldest churches on Cape Cod. Erik's employer, Giraud Cordis, was a member, which is probably why Erik also worshiped there. The graves of Cordis and his wife are in the adjoining churchyard.

64. Witting, *Minnen från mitt Liv*, 360.

65. Westergreen, *Uppteckningar*, 35.

that he believed she "realized her error and entered into the blessed rest of the Lord" before she died, but this account was written more than ten years after the fact. His 1857 journal recounts it with more immediacy and tenderness:

> I preached at Brother Witting's at the request of Sister Lisa, who lay sick there. My text was 1 Peter 5: 6–8. I do not know but I believe it was the final sermon Sister Lisa heard in time. After a long illness of consumption (of nine months, I believe) she entered gladly in the Lord, leaving behind her in death the clear testimony that her soul was saved. The final hours were full of joy and gladness. . . . [The following day,] with tears I took my farewell for the last time of Sister Lisa and went to Galesburg with thoughts of continuing my studies again.[66]

The last sentence is significant. There is a silence or opaqueness in the journals about many aspects of Westergreen's life aside from his religious experiences and some familial relationships. He had so compartmentalized his world that he could leave his sweetheart's deathbed and neither attend her funeral nor mention her again in his writings. The reticence was not limited to affairs of the heart; in the early years of ministry, he seldom noted how he traveled from one preaching appointment to another, whether and how much he was paid for his work, what they sang during worship, or how he interpreted a text for preaching.[67] He never gave the names of his professors or classmates. In his later years, the journals became more introspective, but during this early period, reflection on his experiences was minimal.

In the autumn of 1856, rather than returning to Garrett Biblical Institute, Westergreen enrolled at Knox College in Galesburg, Illinois, taking courses in Greek, English grammar, and German. He heard Senator Stephen Douglas speak at a Democratic meeting in Galesburg, but was not present for the Lincoln-Douglas debates in 1858. After becoming an American citizen, Westergreen nearly always voted Republican if there was not a Prohibition Party candidate listed on the ballot.

On January 1, 1857, a Swedish Methodist Church was dedicated in Galesburg. Prior to this, the Swedes had met in the (American) Methodist Episcopal Church or in private homes. Westergreen had already

66. Westergreen, *Journals*, February 14 and 16, 1857.

67. In many of the journals, however, one can draw conclusions about Westergreen's financial circumstances from the accounts kept at the back of the book. One must infer his method of biblical interpretation from the sermons themselves.

been preaching in the area every Sunday and sometimes during the week:
a total of 109 times in 1856, and 154 times in 1857. Once the Swedish
Methodists had their own building, Westergreen participated in nightly
protracted meetings that lasted two weeks at the beginning of the year,
with Jonas Hedstrom, Peter Challman, Victor Witting, and Eric Shogren
also taking turns preaching and exhorting. Later in January, Westergreen
and Witting held protracted meetings in Berlin (Swedona) for two weeks.
His account of the end of the meetings was typical of his recollections
from this period:

> I preached the final sermon of our protracted meetings in Ber-
> lin. My text was John 1:22. We have the greatest reason to praise
> the Lord. We arrived in Berlin with dim prospects and no great,
> unusual gifts, but we know our dependency upon God, and he
> opened the way for unworthy us more than we had expected.
> Seldom have I encountered greater friendship from both the
> Americans and Swedes than here, and seldom were any ser-
> mons given without any movement follow. At least if we can
> judge by what we saw with our eyes, when we asked if there was
> any troubled soul who wanted to come forward to the altar, or
> any who knew they stood in grace who wanted to pray for them.
> Almost every night someone came. About fifteen people joined
> themselves with the congregation. O, may the Lord help them to
> be received in grace and become steadfast to the end.[68]

This reflection is quite similar to Joseph Pilmore's assessment of a
campmeeting near Philadelphia, written eighty-five years earlier, and it is
typical of the rhetoric used by Methodist preachers of the time:

> I found a vast concourse of people assembled in the grove where
> I preached before. I began immediately and was greatly assisted
> from above while I explained the parable of the fruitless fig tree.
> It was one of the most solemn seasons I ever know in preaching
> abroad, and had great reason to believe the Word of the Lord
> was made the Savior of life to many of the people.[69]

Even as a novice, Westergreen was noted for expository preaching
across the entire Bible; the 1857 record shows he used seventeen different
Old Testament books, fifteen New Testament books, and all four Gospels.
All this pastoral work must have taken a toll on his academic work; he

68. Westergreen, *Journals*, February 13, 1857.
69. Maser and Maag, *Journal of Joseph Pilmore*, 91, 142.

mentioned his studies in his journal only a few times before taking exams in Latin and other subjects in June.

Although there was competition for the immigrants' denomination-al loyalty at the time, the exigencies of frontier life nevertheless resulted in more cooperative and ecumenical activity than we might suppose.[70] In western Illinois, cordial relations between the Augustana Lutheran Church and other immigrant denominations were encouraged by the example of T. N. Hasselquist, who became pastor of the Swedish Lutheran congregation in Galesburg in 1852 and attended some of the protracted meetings held by the Methodists. Hasselquist was known to have worn a white frock coat to lead Sunday morning worship, rather than traditional vestments, and he used Ahnfelt's revival songs in his services.[71] It is therefore not surprising that when Westergreen began preaching in the late 1850s, Lutherans attended his preaching services, he was invited to preach in a Lutheran church (probably at Mission Point in Illinois), and he exhorted after the Reverend Andreas Andreen, a Lutheran pastor, preached near Lafayette, Indiana.[72] Andreen had arrived in America a year after Westergreen, and for over a year he associated with O. G. Hedstrom and the Methodists before being called to serve as an assistant to (Lutheran) Erland Carlsson in Chicago. Westergreen praised Andreen's ministry, and expressed his desire for more ecumenical ventures:

> How good it was [to work together]! I had not thought about the different Protestant denominations coming closer to one another in love, sometimes preaching together and harmoniously seeking to forward God's work.[73]

The friendship with Andreen was strained the following year, when the Lutheran preacher "laid great obstacles in our way" during a protracted meeting in Berlin/Swedona, and then visited Andover and presented what he thought were the differences between their traditions to a general congregation. Westergreen thought he did not do justice to the Wesleyan

---

70. Conversation with the Reverend Dr. Daniel Swinson, conference historian for the Northern Illinois Conference, United Methodist Church, August 18, 2012. According to Swinson, it was not uncommon during this period for pastors of different denominations to hold impassioned public debates about various theological points, yet still do pulpit exchanges and maintain friendly relations.

71. Tredway, "Two Anniversaries and Five Historians," 65.

72. Andreas Andreen was the father of Gustav Albert Andreen, born 1864, who later became president of Augustana College in Rock Island, Illinois.

73. Westergreen, *Uppteckningar*, 52.

point of view. Nevertheless, Westergreen continued to attend Lutheran services when he could. Perhaps because Westergreen's first exposure to distinctively Methodist teaching was Wesley's "Christian Perfection," and because his studies at Knox College put him in close proximity to the Bishop Hill colony, he gained some awareness of differences between Janssonism and Methodism. He preached against "the fallacy of antinomianism," and noted in another instance that Peter Challman gave a clear and powerful talk about "the difference between justification and holiness" at a preachers' meeting.[74] It is unfortunate that no manuscript for this presentation is known to exist, since Challman's first exposure to teaching about sanctification/holiness was from Eric Jansson, not the Methodists.

Though not yet ordained, Westergreen was connected to the church in Galesburg for most of the year. After the Methodist Conference in Abingdon, Illinois, in September, he was assigned to the Victoria circuit, but not appointed as minister of the charge. It is probable that he had an informal arrangement with these congregations; such arrangements were not uncommon when presiding elders had the freedom to exercise such authority, and usually did so when they wanted to keep a gifted preacher in their district. This would also be in keeping with John Wesley's perspective that itinerant preachers and evangelists did not require ordination as sacramental administration did. Westergreen baptized a sick child in its home early in 1858, but licensed preachers were permitted to baptize in emergency situations when an ordained minister was unavailable.

During the early part of the new year, a revival broke out in Victoria, mainly among the Americans but also to some extent among the Swedes. Westergreen preached several times a week both in English and Swedish. He was taken aback by the raucous shouting and cries of thanksgiving during prayer by the Americans, but he trusted their sincerity. Westergreen's parents and at least one sibling were now living in Galesburg, and his brother Sven (who Americanized his name to Swan) attended for a week and returned to Galesburg claiming a fresh religious experience. It was common practice during protracted meetings to hold "after-meetings," either to continue praise and worship or to pray over those who had come forward at the invitation. When the latter occurred, the hope was that the seeker would experience the Holy Spirit's power and testify to it for the edification of others and the building up of the church. A danger inherent to the situation was evaluating the authenticity of the preacher

74. Westergreen, *Journals*, August 7 and May 28, 1857.

and presence of the Holy Spirit by the degree of experience manifested. Westergreen's journal and autobiography demonstrate the pitfall:

> On August 13 I traveled to a campmeeting in Iowa. Never can I remember I was so sluggish at a campmeeting as I was at the beginning of this one. . . . Never do I remember to have been so cold and careless. I preached in the morning from Matthew 10:7 but had no power. There was no great revival [here], but praise be to God for what we saw. There was a general seeking after sanctification among the friends.[75]

Perceived failure to yield the desired revival caused self-doubt and introspection among the preachers conducting protracted meetings. On more than one occasion, Westergreen and his fellow revivalists met privately after a disappointing service and confessed to one another their most secret sins, followed by prayer for one another.[76]

During this period Westergreen studied on his own a great deal, reading the sermons of Henric Schartau, Charles Haddon Spurgeon, and Christmas Evans, along with Benson's commentary, a history of the French Revolution, Blake's *History of Slavery and the Slave Trade*, Spener's work on the spiritual priesthood, and Watson's *Theological Institutes*. He preached across northern Illinois, riding on horseback or more often walking from one appointment to another, and he gave sermons in Swedish, English, and Norwegian, depending on the primary language of his listeners. There were very few Swedish Methodist congregations with their own buildings, so he preached in railroad depots, schoolhouses, courthouses, peoples' homes, American Methodist churches, some Lutheran churches: anywhere he could gather listeners. He preached a total of 285 times in 1859, and noted that he "enjoyed good liberty" or made other positive remarks about his experiences in the pulpit about 25 percent of the time. He also felt free to comment when the evangelistic work was not going well. At Princeton, Illinois, he commented, "Prejudice keeps people from coming to our meetings," and described the English congregation in Leland as "hard." When preaching at Mission Point, on the Fox River, he wrote, "The enemy is at work to hinder people to come out and hear."[77]

75. Westergreen, *Journals*, August 14, 1858, and *Uppteckningar*, 62.

76. Westergreen, *Uppteckningar*, 61, 63.

77. Westergreen, *Journals*, April 12, January 2, December 21, 1859.

Preaching at the Otter Creek Settlement in LaSalle County, he had one of several powerful religious experiences that punctuated his life. He broke down while preaching, but recorded the following in his journal:

> Was never so happy in my life as I was last night. Never before could I say my sins were forgiven with full assurance—but could now in looking up to Christ through faith, it seemed as I did not fear death. No wonder I felt happy—I was almost afraid of going to sleep for fear I should lose—never, whatever changes I may have to pass through, shall I forget the time. I believe I was not deceived, for though I this day have not felt the overflowing happiness, peace and joy that I felt last night, yet, bless the Lord, I can rest in my Savior. Yet I will have a brighter evidence, and will not stay short of it, believed that the Lord will give it, and also save me from all self-deception, which would be very dangerous.[78]

The parallels between this account and Wesley's famous "Aldersgate" experience on May 24, 1738, are unmistakable:

> In the evening I went very unwillingly to a society in Aldersgate Street, where one was reading Luther's preface to the Epistle to the Romans. About a quarter before nine, while he was describing the change which God works in the heart through faith in Christ, I felt my heart strangely warmed. I felt I did trust in Christ, Christ alone for salvation: And an assurance was given me, that he had taken away *my* sins, even *mine*, and saved *me* from the law of sin and death.[79]

One cannot say whether Westergreen was consciously echoing Wesley's language. Aside from the disparity in their ages, a theological difference between the two accounts is that Wesley, reflecting on the Aldersgate experience, placed greater emphasis on the peace he received, but acknowledged he did not have the "transports of joy that usually attend the beginning of [salvation]."[80] Westergreen, on the other hand, wrote primarily about the joy and happiness he felt. However, both men's journals mentioned being assailed by various temptations in the days that followed their religious experiences, though Wesley was far more specific in his writing about the nature of those temptations.

---

78. Westergreen, *Journals*, May 15, 1859.

79. Wesley, *Works of John Wesley*, May 24, 1738.

80. Wesley, *Works of John Wesley*, May 24, 1738.

In September 1859 Westergreen was ordained a deacon (probationary minister) in Kewanee, Illinois. Other than noting he preached that day on Rev 2:17, he wrote little about the event. In the memoranda at the end of the year he wrote:

> At Conference I made the solemn promise to execute my office with faith and received deacon's ordination. May the Lord help me that I not become a promise breaker, but with decency live out my calling, that I may eventually know the joy of giving a good account of my work.[81]

The second volume of his manuscript autobiography is not much more informative:

> Sunday, September 4, 1859, I was ordained deacon by Bishop Janes of the American Methodist Church in Kewanee. May God's blessing stream down upon me that I may be able to exercise my call faithfully and diligently, and also oversee the flock profitably.[82]

Westergreen was appointed to the church in Victoria, Illinois. It was the oldest Swedish Methodist church in the country, founded by Jonas Hedstrom in 1846. Westergreen would have had reason to feel Elijah's mantle had fallen on him; not only had the founder died just four months earlier, but Hedstrom had reproved him sharply for a sermon on the parable of the wise and foolish maidens Matt 25:13 that Westergreen preached the previous year. This left Westergreen despondent for days.[83] Whyman described Jonas Hedstrom as a person of strong faith and commitment, but also doctrinally polemic and an able debater and administrator.[84] His forensic skills were much in evidence in his clashes with Eric Jansson, and later with Lars P. Esbjörn, the Lutheran pastor who began work among the Swedish immigrants in 1849. In addition, Westergreen's immediate predecessor at Victoria was his friend Victor Witting, himself a former Janssonist. All these elements combined to foster a Methodist culture with the following characteristics: (1) sanctification was regarded as an essential part of the *ordo salutis*; (2) Wesleyan doctrine as opposed

---

81. Westergreen, *Journals*, 1859, memoranda.
82. Westergreen, *Uppteckningar*, 72.
83. Westergreen, *Journals*, March 6, 1858.
84. Whyman, *Hedstroms*, 125.

to Janssonist was taught; (3) a free church orientation challenged the assumption that every Swedish immigrant was Lutheran.

A month after ordination, Westergreen officiated at his first funeral, and also helped administer the sacrament for the first time, with his friend Peter Challman. These events were significant enough to him that he noted the occasion in his journal, but did not engage in any reflection on their meaning. Throughout his ministry, he kept a record of baptisms, funerals, weddings and services of Holy Communion at which he presided, but as liturgical acts they never appeared to be central to his identity as a Christian minister. In *American Methodist Worship*, Karen B. Westerfield Tucker notes that in the middle of the nineteenth century, the funeral sermon "functioned as the core of the religious observances surrounding death, with the Scripture readings and prayers from the rites providing authoritative theological support for the sermon content."[85] For Westergreen, preaching of the Word was the core of his vocational identity, and it was an identity forged before a bishop laid hands on him. That core, along with his Pietist orientation and the perfectionist milieu in which he discerned his vocation, meant that his journal gives scant detail about what was sung or worn in worship, but focused instead on what texts were preached, who exhorted afterward, and how many came forward at the end. He did occasionally preach or lecture *about* the Lord's Supper, but in recounting worship services at which it was celebrated, his focus was chiefly on Word and not Table.

Westergreen's family continued to figure prominently in his journals, chiefly in terms of their spiritual state. Andrew and Swan were still living with their parents; Swan "seemed to rest securely in faith in his Savior," but he categorized Andrew as a seeker, even though his father wrote him in January and said Andrew was converted, because "he could not believe with certainty in the forgiveness of his sins, although he had once dared believe it and even was joyful." His brother Erik, who was then twenty-two years old, wrote from Massachusetts, telling the family he had gotten married. John, the youngest brother, had been living with their parents, but in 1858 hired out to a Mr. Goldsmith in Ontario Township. He did not last long in the job, and took off for parts unknown, losing contact with his family. In July 1861 Westergreen received a letter from his parents, informing him that they heard a rumor that John was dead. He was so distraught he was barely able to walk the two miles from

85. Tucker, *American Methodist Worship*, 209.

the post office to his home. Anxiety over his brother's "immortal soul" caused him to preach through his tears the following day. He tried to bargain with God, promising that John's soul was spared, he would serve more faithfully than before.[86] In August the elder Westergreens finally received a letter from John, written three months earlier. There was much rejoicing in the family, and even more when Nels unexpectedly met him at a train station in December. However, John continued a pattern of disappearing or getting into trouble, being assisted by his eldest brother, and promising to amend his ways. Over a century after his death, Westergreen family descendants still refer to John as the black sheep of the family.[87]

At the Annual Conference of 1860, Westergreen was appointed to the Leland Circuit, covering Leland and Norway, whose congregations had church buildings, but also Mission Point, Indian Creek, Freedom, Otter Creek, Rutland, and Newark. These smaller settlements were located in what eventually became the Elgin and DeKalb districts of the Northern Illinois Conference. Though Leland and Norway, in LaSalle County, were less than twenty miles apart, the entire circuit was 150 miles around. In addition to the aforementioned communities, some of which had church buildings, he preached and led prayer meetings in homes, churches erected by other denominations, and any other available space in the vicinity of his circuit. This meant Westergreen was moving from one preaching appointment to the next and visiting families most of the time. What is more, he traveled the entire circuit on foot. In a typical week in January of that year, he preached seven times in four different settlements, visited five families, and spent one day writing letters and sermon outlines. Brothers Anderson and Witting helped him lead a Norwegian campmeeting in Leland in June, followed by a meeting in Norway with Witting only. Thirteen people united themselves on trial with the congregation.

During this period, Westergreen's scrupulosity and scholarly exactness expressed themselves in his ministry and personal life. His journal is punctuated by laments: "I do not feel that peace that passeth understanding. O, for more Religion, I need it"; "I gave way to temptation to anger at a [church] sister"; "How cold in heart and powerless in prayer I am. Lord, help me"; "Another week has passed away. How many more shall I pass through the Lord only knows. Death's solemn hour is fast approaching."[88]

86. Westergreen, *Uppteckningar*, 110.

87. Interview with Robert Beekman, great-grandson of Swan Westergreen, June 6, 2017.

88. Westergreen, *Journals*, April 10, January 12, January 19, and May 12, 1860.

He preached his first sermon on the topic of sanctification in May. Based on 2 Cor 7:1, it lasted two hours and twenty minutes, and he reported, "The Lord granted me his gracious support . . . tears ran down many cheeks and I hope that the sermon was, with God's help, not entirely in vain."[89] In September he and Brother Petterson entered a covenant to seek sanctification. They set aside three days for fasting, but it did not seem to show any results or give them increased power in prayer. At the Swedish campmeeting in Andover, he was among those who preached, and he was pleased to see that on the last night of the meetings, the altar was full of people praying and seeking sanctification. But they also preached in defense of Methodist doctrine against Lutheranism, and he sometimes had occasion to converse seriously with people who had become Mormons.[90] The latter is not surprising, given the varied immigration patterns of Mormons of that time from Nauvoo to Iowa City.

At Conference in Macomb in September, Westergreen was sent to the Indiana Mission: Yorktown, Beaver, and Attica, but also Buena Vista and Bunkum.[91] He preached his farewell sermon in Leland September 30, and wrote in his journal that it was not hard to leave. The memorandum says, "I was well satisfied to leave for it has seemed with few exceptions I couldn't be of much use among the Norwegians there."[92] As demonstrated by circumference of the Leland Circuit, Methodist preachers of this period were expected to be evangelists and entrepreneurs, not managers or shepherds of one or two settled flocks. As such, a congregation or class did not anticipate the preacher would be present to lead worship at 11:00 every Sunday morning, nor even that a service would occur at that time. Westergreen was away from his charge often, and sometimes for prolonged periods. He went north to the Chicago area at least three times in 1861; from January 31 to February 4, he preached a missions sermon there and assisted at a protracted meeting. He returned to the city March 20–27 for the Swedish preachers' meeting, at which he presented his lengthy sermon on sanctification; it was so long that he was able to give only half of it. August brought another trip westward to Victoria for the Swedish campmeeting, which he characterized as "tolerably good," and a brief reunion with his family. In December he preached for the Swedish

89. Westergreen, *Uppteckningar*, 85.

90. Westergreen, *Journals*, May 20 and August 23, 1860.

91. Bunkum has since been renamed Iroquois. The postal address for Beaver was Donavan, Illinois, i.e., the circuit straddled Illinois and Indiana.

92. Westergreen, *Journals*, 1860 memoranda.

soldiers at the newly opened Camp Douglas, on the south side of Chicago. Westergreen also preached for the Swedes in Calumet, Baileytown, Hobart Station, and Lake Station in northern Indiana, and was in Effingham and then Norway/Leland, Illinois, from April 5 to June 19.

Westergreen was ordained elder by Bishop Ames in Lacon, in Marshall County, Illinois, at Conference in 1861. His autobiography has more reflection on the event than was the case for his deacon's ordination:

> Sunday the 1st September 1861 I was ordained, along with Brother Anderson and several Americans to the order of Elder. Strangely enough, when I was confirmed I was the first to stand before the altar. Then I was ordained deacon I was also called forward first, and likewise when I was ordained Elder. . . . O, that I may yet be clothed with the Spirit and power from on high, that I may fulfill my office with faithfulness, and my call with sincerity and diligence, that my own soul may be saved and may joyfully win others for the Kingdom of God. My prayer is that the Lord will give me greater success in my work during the coming year than during the previous one.[93]

The bishop reappointed him to the Indiana Mission, and Westergreen preached a total of 303 times that year.

Why did he label this "The Preparation Period?" His education did not conclude after this; he continued taking courses at Garrett and at Knox College, and began studying German on his own in 1865. Ordination did not seem to be the milestone it is in many ministers' lives. One possibility is that these years marked the formation of his theological orientation. Raised in a Pietist household, he classified himself as a seeker when he arrived in Chicago. His formative spiritual experiences occurred in Methodist class meetings and worship services, and the first Wesleyan literature he read was "Christian Perfection." He quickly learned to distinguish the differences between the Wesleyan and Janssonist doctrines of sanctification, and soon after had to defend Methodist teaching against challenges from Swedish Lutheran pastors. The frontier/missionary culture in which he began preaching fostered an orientation toward Word rather than sacramental worship. Though his writing makes explicit his desire for "a deeper work of grace" within himself, there is also an implicit desire for ongoing education in order to become more effective in ministry.

93. Westergreen, *Uppteckningar*, 114.

4

The Civil War Years

1861 to 1865

I believe in God, and know he has measured my destiny.
I fear God and nothing else: no, not even death.[1]

At first glance, Nels Westergreen did not seem the type to become deeply invested in the War between the States. In all his writings, he came across as someone with firm convictions and a tender conscience, but never a combative personality. His obituary described him as "a model pastor who would rejoice with the joyful and weep with the sorrowful."[2] Almost thirty years after Westergreen's death, one scholar, analyzing *Sändebudet* (The messenger) and the apparent biases of various editors, noted that Westergreen was not as interested in politics as his predecessors were.[3] Unlike many young Swedish men who emigrated, Westergreen had not undergone any compulsory military training in his native land. Prior to the events culminating in the Civil War, he wrote no political commentary in his autobiography or journals. This raises questions as to why he became as involved as he did at this juncture of American history,

---

1. See Wallin, "Jag tror på Gud och vet, att han" [I believe in God, and know], 380.

2. Wallenius, "Dr. N. O. Westergreen Ingången I Vilan" [Dr. N. O. Westergreen Enters into Rest], 2.

3. Andersen, "*Sändebudet* and American Public Affairs 1862–1872," 5.

how he understood the events unfolding around him, and how it affected his ministry.

One possible influence on Westergreen and other Swedes of that era was *Den Svenska Psalmboken* (The Swedish hymnal), published in 1819 and edited by Johan Olaf Wallin, theologian and Archbishop of Uppsala. The hymnal was used for the next hundred years in Sweden, and was also used on Hedstrom's Bethel Ship in New York. Unlike subsequent hymn and song books produced in Sweden and by Swedish Americans, *Den Svenska Psalmboken* contained a section titled "war hymns." It included this one, written by J. M. Altenburg and revised by Wallin:

> Be not dismayed, thou little flock,
> Although the foe's fierce battle shock
> Loud on all sides assail thee.
> Thou o'er thy fall they laugh secure,
> Their triumph cannot long endure,
> Let not thy courage fail thee.
>
> Thy cause is God's—go at His call,
> And to His hand commit thine all;
> Fear thou no ill impending;
> His Gideon shall arise for thee,
> God's Word and people manfully
> In God's own time defending.
>
> Our hope is sure in Jesus' might;
> Against themselves the godless fight
> Themselves, not us, distressing;
> Shame and contempt their lot shall be;
> God is with us, with Him are we;
> To us belongs His blessing.[4]

One can imagine Swedish immigrants, already predisposed by geographical location to sympathize with the Union cause, recalling this hymn and being convinced of the rightness of taking up arms against the Confederacy. Another war hymn of Wallin's would have fostered resignation if not confidence in the face of battle:

---

4. See Altenberg and Wallin, "Förfäras ej, du lilla hop" [Be not dismayed, thou little flock], 378.

> I believe in God, and know that he has measured my destiny/fate.
> I fear God and nothing else: no, not even death.
> For freedom, right and homeland,
> I bear my weapon secure. . . .
>
> . . . The Lord, who gave us life
> Has inscribed how long life shall be.
> With joyful hope in the Lord's Word
> We embrace danger.[5]

Wallin's concept of what was morally right was based not on an act itself but on "the disposition of the person acting, and where norms of behavior are derived both from biblically grounded general rules and from what promotes the greater good of one's neighbor and the welfare of society."[6] From the Union perspective, the greater good of one's neighbor was the elimination of slavery and, admittedly, preachers on both sides of the Mason-Dixon Line used Scripture to defend their viewpoints. As a Pietist raised by *läsare* parents, Westergreen would have been receptive to antislavery rhetoric bolstered by biblical citations. And as a preacher leading "meetings" (his preferred term) that consisted primarily of singing, preaching and prayer, it is inevitable that he would have known and used Wallin's hymns as well as *Femtio Andeliga Sånger* (Fifty spiritual songs).

A second and nonliturgical influence upon Westergreen was his independent reading. He was in his mid-twenties, had studied at Knox College, and was serving churches when he read part or all of Harriet Beecher Stowe's *Uncle Tom's Cabin* in July of 1858.[7] He had a low opinion of the book, commenting that "it was poor reading for a minister," but it appeared to influence him as it did thousands of other readers.[8] He had also read William O. Blake's *The History of Slavery and the Slave Trade*, and wrote in his journal, "Is it possible that such things as the cruelties of slavery and the abusive traffic [of] the slave trade can be carried on in a Christian land? Yet I believe it is true."[9]

---

5. See Wallin, "Jag tror på Gud och vet, att han" [I believe in God, and know], 380.

6. Fyrlund, *Tro och Helgelse*, abstract.

7. *Uncle Tom's Cabin* was first published in 1852, and became the best-selling novel of the nineteenth century. In the year after publication, three hundred thousand copies sold in the United States and over one million in Great Britain.

8. Westergreen, *Journals*, July 17, 1858.

9. Westergreen, *Journals*, October 21, 1858.

At the time he read the novel, he was preaching in the Galesburg Circuit of Illinois. The setting of his ministry was a third strand of influence. Galesburg, the county seat of Knox County, had been the principal depot of the Underground Railroad in western Illinois, although the first recorded instance of assisting fugitive slaves occurred not in Galesburg but nearby Knoxville in 1843.[10] The town of Galesburg and the first anti-slavery society in Illinois were both incorporated in 1837. The first black people, Mr. and Mrs. Henry Van Allen, moved there in 1840.[11] Galesburg became known as a fiercely abolitionist town, where a runaway slave was considered as free from capture when within its limits as if in Canada.[12] Although Westergreen's appointment was changed from Galesburg to the Norwegian settlement in LaSalle County, Illinois, in October of 1858, the rest of his family remained by choice in the Galesburg area, and he regularly returned to Knox County to visit them and to preach over the next few years. As was previously noted, Westergreen spent a few years appointed to the Indiana Mission: a demanding circuit. For example, from Beaver, Illinois, to Attica, Indiana, was between fifty and sixty miles on horseback. From Attica to Yorktown was between thirty and forty miles. There was a train connection, but the journey was shorter on horseback. From Attica to Buena Vista was 120 miles by train. Between Beaver and Attica were high river crossings. Westergreen's normal pattern was to spend four weeks in Indiana followed by three weeks in the Beaver area. In 1862 the bishop sent him back Leland and Norway for a year, and then to western Illinois, to the Galesburg and Bishop Hill Circuit.

Westergreen was not alone in being influenced against the Confederacy. American geography played a role in fostering sympathy for the Union cause among most immigrants from Scandinavia. The census for the decade between 1850 and 1860 showed an increase of almost fifty-five thousand Americans born in Scandinavia, but only about a thousand of these lived in states that joined the Confederacy. Among the Southern forces only nineteen men claimed Scandinavian descent, but twenty thousand Scandinavians served in the Union Army, about 1 percent of the total forces.[13] It is estimated that 25 percent of the Union Army was foreign born, with the largest non-native representations from

10. Chapman et al., *History of Knox County*, 203.

11. Perry, *History of Knox County Illinois*, 762.

12. Chapman, *History*, 209.

13. "Scandinavian-Americans in the American Civil War," n.p.

Germany and Ireland. Some immigrant soldiers formed their own regiments; Company C of the 43rd Illinois Regiment and Company D of the 57th Illinois Regiment were mainly Swedish.[14] Even taking into account the anglicizing of some surnames, it is estimated there were at least fifteen hundred Swedes scattered throughout Illinois regiments. The 15th Wisconsin Regiment was also Scandinavian, although Norwegians were fewer in number because the Norwegian Synod split on the question of slavery. The great majority of the Swedish soldiers enlisted for three years. It can be argued that the Swedes, like some other European immigrants, adapted more readily to military discipline because many had already undergone a course of compulsory military instruction in their native land.[15] The Swedish company of the 43rd Illinois Regiment joined General Grant's expedition against Fort Henry and Fort Donelson, the Battle of Corinth and eventually mustered out of service at Little Rock in 1865.

Two Swedish Americans who distinguished themselves by their service to the Union forces were John Ericsson, inventor of the screw propeller and designer of the ironclad ship the *Monitor*, and Admiral John Adolph Dahlgren, inventor of the Dahlgren Gun and commander of the Washington Navy Yard at the beginning of the war. Westergreen is likely to have read in the newspaper of their contributions to the war effort.

His ministry in Indiana had yielded mixed results, and Westergreen was relieved when he was moved. He was happiest at Beaver, in part because when he was there he stayed with the Grant family. They seem to have welcomed him as one of their own. He tutored two of the sons in their arithmetic lessons, and the elder Grants took care of him when he fell ill with fever and chills. Westergreen had the leisure to continue his theological reading when staying in Beaver, and the Methodist congregation there was the largest and most stable one in the circuit. Since the Methodist church was the only one in the community that held services in Swedish, there was no competition for the immigrants' loyalty. In Attica, on the other hand, there was rivalry between the Methodists and Lutherans, due mainly to the efforts of the same Rev. Andreen who had been so cordial a few years earlier. The memoranda from Westergreen's 1862 journal stated:

> I spent about half my time [in Attica] and laid out considerable labor but it seemed to a great extent to have been in vain. . . .

14. Olson, *History of the Swedes of Illinois*, 627.
15. Olson, *History of the Swedes in Illinois*, 630.

Hardly ever saw the Lutherans more prejudiced against us and
at the same time appear more smooth and kind than they were
there. I tried almost every way to draw them out to our meetings
but failed. . . . I went across the river into Warren County where
a good many of them were settled and tried to hold meetings
in the home, but could not draw them out to hear. It seemed
especially since Rev. A. Andreen came and became their pastor
that they had either agreed to not go to our meetings or that they
were afraid of each other. So I had to give up in disappointment.[16]

In the Lutherans' own history of their missionary efforts in Attica,
they validate Westergreen's perception of prejudice. The congregation's
anniversary celebration booklet reads as follows:

In 1855 there were already about five hundred Swedes in this
locality. . . . If they were not all Christians they were at least
churchly, yet they were as sheep without a shepherd. A Methodist pastor, "Father" Newman of Chicago, was the first minister
who found his way to this colony. He did not succeed in interesting them in Methodism, however. . . . [In 1858] Rev. A. Andreen
again took up the work at Attica and it became the principal
station from then on. Services were held in the schoolhouse or
in the Swedish Methodist Church.[17]

A handwritten commentary on the Lutheran church's beginning is even
more critical of Methodism:

In the beginning there were some Methodists in the town would
sought to secure proselytes. They even had a little church, which
for many years was used as a prayer house. . . . Dr. Norelius wrote
about Attica, saying that our countrymen had a great hunger for
God's Word, and were drawn in through the sectarians' tireless
working on them, to draw them away from our church . . . however, they did not succeed in winning many for Methodism, and
after a time they gave up completely.[18]

Westergreen himself thought at the time that the Methodist
Church's prospects in Attica were poor, but he did enjoy the kind and
devoted Christian friends that he made there. He was more critical of
Buena Vista, noting that "there were very few if any Christians in town.

16. Westergreen, *Journals*, 1862 memoranda.
17. *History of First Lutheran Church of Attica, Indiana*, 5–6.
18. Author unknown, handwritten commentary on the history of the First Lutheran Church of Attica, Indiana, 2–3.

Most of them were inclined to drinking, and when I heard about their drinking I was sorry and discouraged. I don't know if any soul was at all converted under my labor there. The Lord have mercy on them."[19]

After attending Conference in Galesburg in September, Westergreen returned to Leland and Norway, in the Fox River Valley southwest of Chicago. While he never claimed to be satisfied with the fruits of his ministry at Leland, the location made it easier for him to continue his studies in Hebrew and Greek at Garrett Biblical Institute, placed him in closer proximity to his family in Knox County, and allowed him to enter more fully into the affairs of the Conference. During the period of 1858 through 1862, Westergreen preached nearly thirteen hundred times.

In addition to spending years as minister in an area renowned for its advocacy for runaway slaves, Westergreen spent considerable time in and around Chicago, both as a student at Garrett and as a minister regularly attending meetings of the Swedish Methodist preachers. For example, in 1861, though serving the Indiana Mission, Westergreen made record of at least six trips to Chicago. President Lincoln said about the city, "After Boston, Chicago has been the chief instrument in bringing this war on the country. . . . You called for war until we had it. You called for emancipation and I have given it to you."[20] Senator Stephen A. Douglas supported the North in the Civil War, and his 1861 "Save the Flag" speech to the Illinois General Assembly pleased Union sympathizers.[21] However, it should not be supposed that Chicago was as hospitable as Galesburg to the black migration that began in the 1840s. In 1860 there were about a thousand black inhabitants in a city with a total population of 109,000; they faced discrimination and segregation in nearly every aspect of life. Westergreen did not comment on racial injustices he may have seen there; it was not until he served as a Union Army chaplain that he mentioned any contact with or observations about black people.

The Civil War began April 12, 1861, while Westergreen was serving the Indiana Mission. He had seen troops being trained at Morris, Illinois, and elsewhere, but did not write much about the war until the following year. He encountered wounded soldiers when he took the train to Chicago, attended meetings for the relief of Union troops, read accounts of the

19. Westergreen, *Journals*, 1862 memoranda.

20. Levy, *To Die in Chicago*, 5.

21. See Johannsen, *Letters of Stephen A. Douglas*, 437.

Battles of Fort Donelson, Shiloh, and Corinth. There were regular visits to preach at Camp Douglas as well as Camp Reynolds, near Indianapolis.

After the firing on Fort Sumter, the federal government was not initially organized for recruiting, training, and equipping volunteer regiments for the Union Army. It was left to states and municipalities to gather and organize the troops until late in 1861. In Chicago, volunteers gathered in makeshift camps on the prairie just south of the city: land that was owned by Stephen Douglas and Henry Graves, a local farmer. Judge Allen C. Fuller selected this site for a permanent army camp because it was just four miles south of the city, and had easy access to Lake Michigan. In addition, the Illinois Central Railroad, running between the camp and the lake, meant that public transportation was already in place. A total of eighty acres, it ran from 31st Street to 33rd Place, from Cottage Grove Avenue to what is now Martin Luther King Drive, with the main entrance on Cottage Grove. It was, however, a poor location in that it was low-lying, swampy land with only one water hydrant and no sewage system. The camp officially opened on September 30, 1861, and the first cheaply built barracks were completed on November 1 of the same year. Each building was 105 feet long and 24 feet wide, intended to house 180 men. They were built of a single thickness of pine boards, without plastering or ceiling, and the roofs were covered with tar paper.[22] Each barrack had a kitchen with a long table and benches for the men. Although the barracks were considered clean and comfortable for the time, the construction was inadequate protection from harsh Chicago winters, and the lack of sanitation made it a breeding ground for disease. Westergreen made his first visit to Camp Douglas in November 1861, and returned to preach the following month.

There was a post chaplain, the Reverend Edmund B. Tuttle, and the YMCA and Christian Commission built a chapel in the camp's Garrison Square in 1861. When Fort Donelson fell on February 16, 1862, between twelve and fifteen thousand Confederate soldiers were taken prisoner, and the government scrambled to find places to them. The responsibility fell to General Henry W. Halleck in St. Louis. Colonel Joseph H. Tucker, who was commandant of Camp Douglas, wired General Halleck and said that Chicago could take eight or nine thousand of the prisoners.[23] The men were transported by steamboat to Cairo, Illinois, and then by

22. See *Official Records of the War of the Rebellion*, 56.
23. Levy, *To Die in Chicago*, 17.

train to Chicago. When approximately forty-five hundred Confederate troops arrived on February 20, there were no prison barracks, so they were housed with the Union troops. In less than a week, the first religious service for prisoners was conducted in the chapel by Dr. Pratt of Trinity Church. A few days later, the Rev. Dwight L. Moody held services, and until the camp closed in 1865, religious services were conducted on a voluntary basis by local and visiting clergy, such as Westergreen, and those serving through the Christian Commission and the Chicago Bible Society. The Catholic Bishop of Chicago also sent priests, who baptized hundreds of Confederate prisoners and brought food to hospital wards. Moody and other clergy helped provide for the needs of prisoners' families, as well as conducting services and distributing religious literature. By 1862, doctors and clergy were the only nonmilitary persons allowed to enter the camp—and they were certainly needed. A total of 26,871 Confederate soldiers and their slaves passed through Camp Douglas. It had the highest mortality rate of all Northern prisons, yet only eighty of the 4,009 deaths were due to battle wounds, other injuries, and unspecified diseases. By contrast, fourteen hundred died of smallpox and malaria, and nearly thirteen hundred of pneumonia and pleurisy.[24]

Although Westergreen did not become a United States citizen until September 1864, his personal interest in and allegiance to his adopted country increased as the war went on.[25] His ministry was primarily among Scandinavian immigrants, though he did preach occasionally in English, especially when he was the visiting preacher in a church of another denomination. An example of his sense of American identity can be found in his 1861 journal, while he was serving the Indiana Mission. A rumor had reached Westergreen that his youngest brother, John, was dead. A month later he learned the rumor was false, but during the time of uncertainty, in his words, "I even made the promise that if the Lord saved my brother's soul then I would be ready to go wherever he wanted

---

24. Levy, *To Die in Chicago*, 272.

25. Westergreen's delay in obtaining citizenship is a mystery. The Naturalization Act of 1790 allowed any free white immigrant (usually a male property owner) to apply for citizenship after two years in the United States with one year in the state where application was being made. By 1850, this had been amended; a free white immigrant was required to go to court and file his/her intent to become a citizen after two years in the country, but had to wait an additional three years to seek naturalization papers that completed the process. It may be that Westergreen delayed in applying because as an itinerant minister, he did not own property and/or he lived in three different states during his first decade in America.

to send me to proclaim God's word, *even if it meant going back to my ancestral land*."[26] Sweden was now the "ancestral land," while America was home.

It is uncertain when Westergreen first learned about the United States Christian Commission, which was created in 1861 in response to the suffering after the First Battle of Bull Run. The YMCA (only ten years old at the time) plus Protestant ministers formed the Commission, and about five thousand volunteer delegates served during the war and afterward. The aim of the Commission was advancing the spiritual and temporal welfare of soldiers in the army and sailors in the navy, in co-operation with the chaplains. The Commission's national office was in Philadelphia, but numerous other cities, including Chicago, served as regional clearinghouses. The Commission appointed clergy "delegates" who served on a volunteer basis for terms averaging six weeks.[27]

Westergreen closely followed the progress of the war. In April 1861 he watched recruits drilling for the war between Newark and Mission Point, Illinois, and recruits attended his worship services in Morris, Illinois. As mentioned earlier, he first visited Camp Douglas in November 1861, and from then until the war's end he visited the Camp nearly every time he was in Chicago. There were a little over four thousand troops stationed there. He found the soldiers very attentive to his preaching, and prayed that the Word would bear fruit in their hearts.[28] He knew, after the capture of Fort Donelson, that the first Confederate prisoners were transported there. Westergreen was still serving the Indiana Mission when he wrote in his autobiography:

> [On] Monday the 17th February [1862] I received the news of the capture of Fort Donelson by our troops. For awhile my feelings soared with a general stream of joy for the victory won. But soon my thoughts took another turn. When I thought about how dearly bought it was, how many lives it cost, how much sorrow this will spread in the land and how many souls who perhaps have hurried unprepared into eternity: when I remember this I felt driven to pray for our land and our soldiers and that peace will soon be restored—so much that when I preached that

26. Westergreen, *Uppteckningar*, 110, emphasis added.

27. Although clergy had served as chaplains to military personnel since the Revolutionary War, it was not until World War I that chaplains were actually members of the military.

28. Westergreen, *1861 Journal*, memoranda.

evening in the city of Peru, Indiana, and after the sermon several
came forward for prayer, I could scarcely turn my thoughts from
the war's battlefields to unite my prayer with theirs.[29]

In 1862 Westergreen was writing regularly on the progress of the
war and his reaction to it. On April 9 he walked to Attica and "heard the
mournful news of the last great battle of Pittsburg. I felt a great deal. O
Lord, how long before the sword now already drunk with blood shall be
put in the scabbard?"[30] He wrote about the war four times that month,
acknowledging his mind was very much occupied by it. During the summer he spoke briefly at a war meeting in Stockwell, Indiana. He noted
that the war and drafting engaged the minds of the people, challenging
the progress of evangelizing and starting new churches. He prayed that
God would make an end to the war, and wept when two of his immigrant
friends left to join the army.

In addition to following news of the war through the newspaper
and visiting Camp Douglas, Westergreen took time off to visit the troops
while serving in the Indiana Mission. In January and again in September
and December 1863 he traveled to the military hospitals in Cairo and
Mound City, Illinois, particularly to visit the Scandinavians there and
give them spiritual counsel.[31] He rejoiced when he heard the news that
Vicksburg was taken in July, and mourned when he preached the funeral
sermon of an acquaintance who died in the army.

At Conference in 1863 Westergreen was appointed to the church in
Galesburg, and took the train to the city every week for classes at Garrett
Biblical Institute, but admitted did not feel a great interest in them. He
nevertheless passed his examinations in Greek, Hebrew, and homiletics. In his journal he noted that he had never had a comparatively more
easy and pleasant field of labor than Galesburg. In 1864 he became the
first minister of the Bishop Hill congregation. Though he remarked it
was not as pleasant or convenient an appointment as Galesburg, this
appointment was an interesting and ultimately fruitful time in Westergreen's ministry. He had occasion to compare his Wesleyan theology and
homiletical method with both Lutheranism and Janssonism. Of course,
Westergreen did not come to America until two years after Eric Jansson's

---

29. Westergreen, *Uppteckningar*, 121.

30. Westergreen, *Journals*, April 9, 1862. The Battle of Pittsburg is better known as
the Battle of Shiloh. It was a Union victory, but the bloodiest battle of the war up to that
point. Westergreen's lament paraphrased Isa 34:5.

31. Westergreen, *Uppteckningar*, 133, 139.

murder, but he had access to Jansson's catechism and songbook, which were first published in 1846. In late February he listened to Jonas Olsson, former deputy of Eric Jansson, preach in Bishop Hill's Old Colony Church. Westergreen wrote:

> He did not give us much exposition of the scripture but a very good exhortation. But how greatly they must have changed in their preaching since a few years ago. The old man preached, as far as I could judge, just about like the Lutheran preachers except a little better.[32]

Despite this mixed review, he seemed to get along well with members of the former colony, which had dissolved as an economic entity in 1862.[33] It was Jonas Olsson who heard A. J. Anderson preach in Andover in 1860, and invited him to preach at Bishop Hill. The Methodists were allowed to hold their own meetings/worship in a room in the northeast corner of the Colony Church.[34] This arrangement ceased when, according to a history of the Bishop Hill Methodist Church, Anderson wore out his welcome.[35] Various Methodist circuit riders then held meetings in the village schoolhouse or in private homes. This continued until April of 1865, when Westergreen bought rooms over the blacksmith shop to fix up for a meeting house. His journal notes, "Thank God we have at least a place now in Bishop Hill that we can call our own."[36] The blacksmith shop was not to be the congregation's permanent home. In July, Westergreen did a preaching tour of the Keokuk area, preaching in several different churches in both Swedish and English, raising money for a free-standing building for which only the congregation held keys: a project not completed until 1869, when Alfred Anderson was pastor.

The heated theological debates between Eric Jansson and Jonas Hedstrom were never repeated between Westergreen and the Janssonists who remained at Bishop Hill. There are a couple of likely factors that account for a more irenic relationship. First, the colony leaders after Jansson's death did not have his bellicose and megalomaniacal personality.

32. Westergreen, *Journals*, February 19, 1865.

33. Elmen, *Wheat Flour Messiah*, 169.

34. The Seventh Day Adventists also held some meetings in the Colony Church in the late 1860s. A few colonists joined, but the majority affiliated with the Methodist Church.

35. *Church Messenger: History of Bishop Hill Methodist Church*, 18.

36. Westergreen, *Journals*, April 24, 1865.

Second, the Olsson brothers and other Janssonists experienced earlier contact with Methodist teaching through George Scott before emigrating from Sweden, and had adopted much of the same vocabulary for describing sanctification. What is more, they benefited from the hospitality and guidance of the Hedstroms upon arriving in the United States. It appears that during this period Challman, Witting, Brown, and other former Janssonists who became Methodists found the transition to a Wesleyan understanding of Christian Perfection a fairly easy and natural one. Jansson biographer Paul Elmen even commented, "The Janssonists were corrupted Methodists."[37]

Westergreen's relationship with the Lutheran Church during this period was more complicated and varied. As noted earlier, he and his father became acquainted with the Reverend T. N. Hasselquist in Åkarp prior to their emigration from Sweden, and Hasselquist served the Lutheran church in Galesburg from 1852–1863. Westergreen occasionally heard him and other Lutheran pastors preach in Galesburg, and the clergy did pulpit supply in one another's churches. In August 1864 both Methodists and Lutherans preached at the Red Oak campmeeting in western Illinois. Westergreen was so well-known and respected across denominational lines that in May 1865 he was invited to become the pastor of the Lutheran Church in Swede Bend, Iowa: an offer he declined.[38] At the same time, there was theological tension between the groups. In February 1865 an Augustana Synod Lutheran preacher in Galesburg, A. W. Dahlsten, allegedly attacked Methodism from the pulpit, using Wesley's sermon, "On Sin in Believers," as a weapon.[39] Two weeks later, A. J. Anderson preached a rebuttal sermon "exposing the errors of the Lutherans." The back and forth homiletical debate continued for about a month, and the Methodist gatherings drew standing-room only crowds. Westergreen's final comment about it was at the end of March, when he wrote, "I went to the Lutheran church in the evening, expecting to hear Andreen preach,

37. Elmen, letter to Norén, November 1980.

38. Westergreen, *Journals*, May 18, 1865.

39. Wesley, "On Sin in Believers," in *Sermons on Several Occasions, First Series*, 144–55. As E. H. Sugden comments in the 1921 edition of *Wesley's Standard Sermons*, "This [1763] sermon is most valuable as a corrective to the conclusion which might fairly be drawn from some of the earlier sermons, that after conversion, the believer is entirely free from sin; and that the existence of sinful desires in him is proof that he has not exercised saving faith in Christ."

but he had not come, so Dahlsten preached a long, dragging message."[40] The following month he went to Wataga to hear a Mr. Larson preach, and when the man did not show up, Westergreen was asked to give a message instead; evidence suggesting the quarrel had blown over, though not his misgivings about the Lutherans' homiletical method. We do not know whether Dahlsten was naturally combative or was simply trying to defend his church on two perceived fronts simultaneously. As Karl Olson describes the situation, in the 1860s a substantial group of dissidents in Dahlsten's church favored the more democratic and evangelistic orientation of the (American) Synod of Northern Illinois, and eventually left to form the Second Lutheran Church of Galesburg. Dahlsten, who distrusted the Rosenians and opposed greater lay representation in synod deliberations, lost a substantial percentage of his congregation: Christians who claimed they were loyal to "the pure and unaltered Scriptures" rather than Lutheran faith and usages.[41] Small wonder that Dahlsten would look askance at the Swedish Methodists, whose *modus operandi* was more compatible with Rosenius, and who might also siphon off congregants.

Westergreen's ambivalence toward Lutheranism seems to have persisted throughout his ministry, though it does not appear he relished the conflict. On another occasion he wrote:

> I heard Mr. Andreen preach in the evening a sermon about part of the passion of Christ. His text was in the Canticles, and made a somewhat wonderful twisting to apply it to his subject. Some may think this is smart, but I think it rather weak and deficient in sound sense and judgment.[42]

The following February he traveled to Milwaukee to attend meetings between Methodist and Lutheran clergy in the basement of an American Methodist church. A heated debate arose when the Methodists declared the true church to be visible and the Lutherans asserted the true church was invisible. Other topics discussed were the call to ministry, baptism, and Christian perfection. Regarding the latter, Westergreen noted:

> The debates were close and warm but we had evidently the advantage. But in the evening, when the sacrament of the Lord's Supper came up, the Lutherans seemed determined to storm the

---

40. Westergreen, *Journals*, March 28, 1865.

41. Olson, *By One Spirit*, 228–29.

42. Westergreen, *Journals*, April 6, 1865.

ground, and they succeeded, at least, to spread confusion. Broke
up the meeting in the midst of confusion. Felt very sorry.[43]

He attended the Lutheran conference in Chicago several months
later—not as a debater or guest preacher, but merely an observer. His
only comment on the meetings was, "Heard Dahlsten preach in the evening. Rather dull."[44]

Thirty years after the dust-up in Galesburg, and twenty years after
the Galesburg Rule adopted by the Lutherans' General Council stated,
"Lutheran pulpits are for Lutheran ministers only," Westergreen was
still regularly invited to preach in Swedish and Norwegian Lutheran
churches. But in *Svenska Metodismen i Amerika* (Swedish Methodism in
America), published in 1895, Westergreen devoted a chapter to outlin-
ing Methodist beliefs and contrasting them with Lutheran teaching, with
special sections devoted to holiness and Christian perfection as well as
the sacraments.[45] This was another assertion of differentiation from the
American offspring of the state church in which he was raised.

The thirty-year-old Westergreen did not spend all his time riding
from one preaching appointment to the next; he was also in search of
a mate. His loneliness manifested itself in regular journal entries about
dissatisfaction over his present spiritual state and a desire for "a melting
time" in communion with God, along with periodic confession that he
had "yielded to temptation" while alone. In one entry he lamented, "I
live as near as possible the life of a monk at present, finding there is not
a little truth in that passage, It is not good for man to be alone."[46] His
mood was always more cheerful when he spent time in the company of
others, particularly the safe and structured intimacy of campmeetings
and protracted meetings. Many of his closest colleagues in ministry were
married by this time. He knew that Jonas Hedstrom's wooing of Diantha
Sornberger led to the establishment of Swedish Methodism in western
Illinois. Peter Challman married and had at least six sons. Victor Witting,
who was then living in Chicago, had not found singleness necessary for
itinerant ministry. Nor did Westergreen's own family hold up celibacy as
a higher calling than marriage; his father sired a total of nine children in
his two marriages, and all Nels Westergreen's surviving brothers married.

43. Westergreen, *Journals*, February 15, 1866.

44. Westergreen, *Journals*, October 8, 1866.

45. Liljegren et al., *Svenska Metodismen i Amerika*, ch. 5.

46. Westergreen, *Journals*, July 17, 1866.

Unfortunately, Westergreen's ambivalent relationship with Lisa in 1856 seemed to set a pattern for thwarted or abandoned romances throughout his life. Any expression of interest, any levity or "frivolous conversation" with a woman was followed by self-recrimination and determination to walk more closely with God in the future.

In April of 1864 he appeared to be attracted to an unnamed woman in Bishop Hill. He wrote in his journal, "Have had somewhat of a pleasant time at Bishop Hill during this visit for some reasons. I am very glad I had Brother Challman in company with me this time . . . as in any other way I might have acted somewhat unwisely."[47] A few days later, he talked with his parents about his situation, and they counseled him to "try to get married." His journal entry adds, "If it is the Lord's will may he point out the suitable person is my wish."[48] In October, after moving to Chicago, he wrote about two possible mates. The first one, Miss Borg, was active in the Methodist Church and met with Westergreen several times. After a lengthy conversation with her in the office of *Sändebudet*, he described her as highly accomplished and possibly devoting her whole life to the service of God, adding, "The more I become acquainted with her the more I admire her, uniting great talents and accomplishments with the most simple and un-artificial manner."[49] It is strange, then, that he never mentioned her again. The following week he received a letter from a friend in Geneseo, Illinois, informing him that Miss Hannah Siberg—possibly the young woman from Bishop Hill—was dead. He wrote:

> She left a bright testimony of her soul's salvation behind her. I had on her perhaps more than on any other woman fixed my attention for [my] future life. These hopes are now cut off but thanks be unto God, who does all things well. However, I cannot help but feel somewhat downcast in my mind.[50]

True to form, he never wrote about Hannah Siberg or his grief after this entry. To be fair to Westergreen, his journals rarely mentioned his feelings about *anyone* outside his immediate family, so it is not remarkable that there is scant acknowledgment of the women to whom he was attracted. It should not be surmised that he didn't really like women and/or was attracted to men. He appeared to have close relationships with his brother

47. Westergreen, *Journals*, April 24, 1865.
48 Westergreen, *Journals*, April 29, 1865.
49. Westergreen, *Journals*, October 22, 1865.
50. Westergreen, *Journals*, October 30, 1865.

Andrew's wife, Selma, and his brother Swan's daughter Nellie. Following his father's death, his mother lived with him almost a quarter century. A few years later Selma, now a widow, became his paid, live-in housekeeper. He also seemed to have happy and respectful relationships with women in the church; his assessment of women preachers and speakers he heard occasionally had no patronizing or misogynist slant. He attended "sister meetings" of the various churches he served with the same regularity as meetings of clergy brethren. It could be that Westergreen was consciously or unconsciously emulating John Wesley's nonsexual relationships with devout women in the early Methodist movement, or perhaps modeling himself after Francis Asbury's celibate lifestyle and Asbury's praise for itinerant preachers who refrained from marrying. We cannot know, given the scanty information given by Westergreen. C. G. Wallenius, writing in *Sändebudet* in 1937, claimed that Westergreen had been betrothed three times, but in each case the bride-to-be died during the engagement period, and this led Westergreen to conclude he was called to a life of singleness.[51] Given that Hannah Siberg died before Wallenius was even born, it seems more likely that in old age, Westergreen told his colleague about Hannah and/or other fleeting attractions as a young man, and Wallenius reimagined it into a whole story.

In September 1864, while serving the Bishop Hill charge, two critical events occurred in Westergreen's life: he became a United States citizen and, while attending the Methodist Annual Conference in Rock Island, Illinois, he visited Union soldiers and Confederate prisoners at what is now Arsenal Island. He wrote:

> The Southern prisoners were held under guard. Although they probably have it better than many of our prisoners in the South, it is not surprising that many die. We visited their graves, and if I am not mistaken, there were over 1700 already buried there. They are buried in pits long enough for a body and wide enough for several bodies. They are set out side by side until the grave is full; then there is a funeral and a new grave is dug.[52]

Visiting the soldiers and prisoners strengthened his resolve to involve himself more deeply in his adopted country's fortunes. During the Annual Conference, Westergreen and his old friend Peter Challman, the

51. Wallenius, "Några uppgifter om tidnings utgivare, redaktion och sätteri" [Some statements about the paper's publishing, editing and composing room], 15.

52. Westergreen, *Uppteckningar*, 155–56.

former Eric Janssonist, decided to volunteer for the Christian Commission during the coming year. He exercised his new right to vote in November, casting a ballot for Lincoln, and a month later traveled to Peoria with Challman to be recommended for service with the Christian Commission. During their absence, the presiding elder of the district would arrange for other preachers, both ordained and lay, to full their pulpits.

Just before setting off for chaplaincy service, Westergreen fulfilled a previously made promise to preach several times in Keokuk, Iowa. The brief detour is worth mentioning because his oldest surviving sermon manuscript on sanctification was from this preaching tour. His theme was "Every Christian ought to be like Christ," and the text was Phil 2:5, "Let the same mind be in you that was in Christ Jesus."[53] The phrase "having the mind of Christ" functioned as synonym for holiness/sanctification. The structure of the sermon is similar in some ways to John Wesley's sermon, "Christian Perfection," in that there is a brief introduction followed by an enumeration of the ways in which we can *not* be like Christ, and then a list of way in which we *can*. The Westergreen sermon has an "application" section at the end; this generally signaled that an exhorter would not follow the preacher in bringing the message to bear upon listeners. Wesley's sermon does not have a conclusion marked as "application," but the final point functions as one; the pronouns shift to exhort/address the listeners as "you." (It should also be remembered that Wesley endlessly revised his writings for publication.) Another similarity is the interweaving of multiple supporting texts into the sermon. For Westergreen, virtually all the texts were from the New Testament; the single Old Testament passage cited, Isa 53:7, is used to illustrate the patience of the Savior. Another aspect of the sermon worth noting comes after the fourth main point of the sermon, which raises the question of how to receive the mind of Christ. It is followed by six imperative statements, of which the first three are almost a verbatim quote from Wesley's "The Scripture Way of Salvation":

1. We must accept the possibility of receiving this.

2. We must perceive the necessity of being in possession of it.

3. We can only receive it through a childlike faith in Christ.[54]

53. Other sanctification sermons he preached during his visit to Keokuk were based on 1 Thess 3:12–13 and 1 Thess 5:23. They may have been part of a five-sermon series on sanctification preached earlier in the year in Galesburg.

54. Westergreen, "Hwarje Kristen Bör Likna Kristus," III.5, quoting Wesley, "The

Five of the six statements contain the word "must." The resulting tenor of the sermon maximizes human responsibility and says much less about the activity of the Holy Spirit in attaining the mind of Christ. Only the last point of the application mitigates this, when the sermon speaks of possessing the mind of Christ as the privilege as well as the duty of every Christian. The emphasis on human responsibility may to some degree account for Westergreen's endless striving for a religious experience that seemed to elude him, and his repeated attempts to "consecrate himself wholly" at campmeetings.

On December 15 Westergreen and Challman arrived in St. Louis, visited Benton Barracks, and spoke with some of the soldiers in English. From there they went to Memphis and visited Swedes from the 8th Illinois Regiment, and visited encampments and hospitals for two days. They took the steamboat *Fanny Ogden* down the Mississippi to the junction with the White River, and went up the White River to Duvall's Bluff, which Westergreen described as "a dirty little place, but still has several regiments of our soldiers encamped there, and they have also thrown up some earthwork fortifications."[55] The next leg of their journey was by train to Little Rock, where they encountered Swedes from the 43rd Illinois Regiment. Some were from the Galesburg area, and he knew them from home. Westergreen considered it an excellent situation for ministry, though he noted that Challman's opportunities for preaching would be hindered by his limited English. He attended a Catholic mass for the first time in his life the morning of Christmas Day, and then Challman preached for the Swedish soldiers after lunch and Westergreen preached in English for the 29th Iowa Regiment. The following evening he preached in English in the Methodist Church in Little Rock. Westergreen wrote that it felt strange to fill the pulpit once occupied by "the notorious" John Newland Maffitt (1795–1850), a brilliant preacher and journalist whose later career was marred by divorce and accusations of sexual impropriety.[56] Maffit's son and namesake was a privateer and Confederate Captain.

For the first week or so in Little Rock, Westergreen and Challman appeared to work together, preaching and distributing newspaper, booklets, tracts, and New Testaments among the soldiers of the 9th and

---

Scripture Way of Salvation," 14–16.

55. Westergreen, *Uppteckningar*, 162.

56. Westergreen, *Uppteckningar*, 165.

28th Wisconsin Regiments, Company C of the 43rd Illinois Regiment, 50th Indiana Regiment, 1st Missouri Regiment, 29th and 40th Iowa Regiments.[57] On New Year's Eve, they held a Watch Night service with the 43rd Illinois Regiment. Westergreen preached in Swedish and Challman exhorted, and Westergreen reported, "We had a moving time at the turn of the year."[58] They had fairly comfortable and pleasant circumstances in Little Rock, but there were four chaplains from the Christian Commission there at the same time, and Westergreen may have felt redundant. He thought there would be a wider scope for his ministry elsewhere. After obtaining a clergy pass from the general's headquarters, he set off for Duvall's Bluff, Arkansas, on January 6, 1865. He stopped at Bayou Metoe for one night, and preached to a Norwegian company of the 27th Wisconsin Regiment. Once he arrived in Duvall's Bluff, the local agent for the Christian Commission, a man named Sacket, told him there were no accommodations for him, but Westergreen stayed with him a few nights before being offered the "narrow accommodations and even more narrow shared bed" of a Swedish Lieutenant by the name of Olson. At Duvall's Bluff, Westergreen preached and distributed literature to 3rd Minnesota and 12th Michigan Regiments. With another Christian Commission volunteer, he preached and led worship for the 57th Negro Regiment.[59] He noted that it was easy to speak to the black soldiers, because they were generally more simple than the whites and received the Word willingly. Their worship services were lively and even noisy, with acclamations during prayer, and sometimes singing religious songs in their barracks until late at night.[60]

From Duvall's Bluff, Westergreen made brief trips to Little Rock and Brownsville, located northwest of Duvall's Bluff near Des Arc. They had a chapel at Brownsville, and when he preached in English to the

57. Westergreen's journal for January 3, 1865, reveals that in addition to preaching, on a single day he distributed fifty-six Testaments, five hundred "soldier books," four hundred papers, and thirteen hundred pages of tracts. This was typical of his chaplaincy work.

58. Westergreen, *Uppteckningar*, 167.

59. This was 4th Regiment Infantry (African Descent), organized at Duvall's Bluff on December 2, 1863. It was attached to the District of Eastern Arkansas, 7th Corps, until March 1864. Its designation changed to the 57th US Colored Troops on March 11, 1864.

60. Westergreen, *Uppteckningar*, 177. It should be noted that Westergreen's use of the term "simple" should not be construed as condescending. Throughout his writings, the term connotes childlike receptivity to the gospel and/or purity of faith.

3rd Michigan Cavalry Regiment, the building was full to overflowing. He wrote, "The Lord gave me grace to speak with liberty. May the Word also have fallen on good ground."[61] Once he returned to Duvall's Bluff on January 14, he learned that Sacket had now arranged lodging and food for him. He shared a bed with a captain of the 57th Negro Regiment, and the following morning attended the funeral of a soldier in that regiment before preaching outdoors to the 35th Wisconsin Regiment. In the evening he preached to the 3rd Minnesota Regiment and then "visited the negroes' meeting, which lasted long into the night."[62] He remained in Duvall's Bluff another five days, visiting the hospital, preaching for the Swedes in the 3rd Minnesota Regiment and in English for cavalry. He was pleased with the opportunities for ministry.

On January 19 he received a letter with disturbing news; his brother John had gone AWOL and been arrested as a deserter in Springfield, Illinois. Westergreen's surprise was even greater since he had not known John was in the Union army, serving in the 29th Michigan Infantry Regiment.[63] He was advised by Mr. Ensign, who seems to have been the director of the Christian Commission in Little Rock, to return north and seek whether his brother could be helped. Westergreen met up with Peter Challman again. They knelt on the riverbank and prayed for the wayward brother, and then boarded the steamboat *Tycoon*. Two other ministers, Evans and Hall, were also on board, along with many soldiers. They conducted worship services morning and afternoon, and arrived in Memphis on January 24, 1865. Westergreen sought the counsel of a man named Burnell, who oversaw the Christian Commission's work in Memphis. Later in the evening Westergreen and Challman took passage on *The City of Cairo* up the Mississippi River to Cairo. They then took trains first to St. Louis and then to Springfield, where they checked into the St. Charles Hotel. Westergreen described himself as weighed down with sorrow the following morning as he prayed and then made his way to Camp Butler, a few miles northeast of Springfield. He asked for Captain Henry Snow, from whom he had received the letter with news of his brother's arrest. Snow was friendly and good-natured, and explained to him that although John had been arrested and charged, he was not in custody but had been sent to the front along with the 51st Illinois Infantry.

---

61. Westergreen, *Uppteckningar*, 178.

62. Westergreen, *Uppteckningar*, 180.

63. Ancestry.com, *Westergreen Name in History*, 24.

Westergreen's spirits lifted and he praised God; though he was sorry not to have encountered John, and knew that his brother had been sent to a place where the danger was great, he was thankful that John's fate was not worse. Having heard that Peter Cartwright was scheduled to preach in Williamsville on the following day, he traveled there and heard the congregation's pastor, Mr. Smith, preach a good sermon. In his autobiography Westergreen muses, "O, how solemn I thought it was to come in again to a regular congregation in the North. It felt to me like coming home after being away."[64] When Cartwright did not arrive the next day, Westergreen was asked to fill the pulpit. He then continued his journey back to Galesburg, arriving January 31, 1865. He wrote:

> O, how glad and thankful I felt to be happy and well, among old and trusted friends again. And after the Lord's particular help in anxious times and answers to prayer I now felt like Samuel, who could raise up a stone of remembrance and say, "The Lord has helped me up to now." I still felt rather tired after my assiduous work and I needed some rest."[65]

Westergreen wrote out a report of his work for Mr. Reynolds, the Peoria coordinator for the Christian Commission, and sent him eight dollars that he owed. Reynolds wanted him to recruit others in western Illinois to serve as chaplains.

Back at home, Westergreen resumed his studies at Knox College in March, but it was hard for him to concentrate on his Greek and Latin studies. His chaplaincy work had given him a taste for life outside the classroom and chapel; he wrote that he liked to be out visiting, praying and talking with people. He assisted with protracted meetings in Galesburg and resumed his routine of preaching, studying, and making pastoral calls. On April 3 he heard that Richmond was taken, and the following day learned that a large part of the city was in flames. Strangely enough, his journal did not note the surrender of Lee on April 9, 1865. The same month he received a letter from his brother John, who was then in Bulls Gap in eastern Tennessee. There had been a Confederate victory after a small battle there in November of 1864. On the day before Easter, the sorrowful news of Lincoln's and Seward's assassinations reached them.[66]

64. Westergreen, *Uppteckningar*, 193.

65. Westergreen, *Uppteckningar*, 195.

66. Westergreen, *Uppteckningar*, 203. Of course, the initial news was not entirely accurate. Secretary of State Seward was wounded but not killed.

Funeral bunting hung in the doorways to houses, as well as the flags being at half-staff. Westergreen's autobiography noted:

> The sad news spread a strange gloom and melancholy feeling
> among the people. The flags were hung at half-mast as a sign of
> mourning, along with funeral bunting hung in the doorways to
> houses. Lightheartedness and jesting are heard no more, and it
> seems as though sorrow marks every face and gravity is stamped
> upon it. . . . It seems as though one and all, without regard to
> political affiliation or viewpoint, felt together the country's great
> loss. . . . It was for several days almost as one will feel when one
> loses a close acquaintance, dear friend, or relative.[67]

Churches held special services on April 19, the day of Lincoln's funeral.
Westergreen chose 2 Sam 3:33–34 as his text.

Westergreen's journal mentions the capture of Jefferson Davis in
May, but the rest of the year is devoid of any political comment or involvement, even though he moved to Chicago in September and must
have been aware of the search for over four thousand dead Confederate
prisoners and the unfolding investigation of Camp Douglas.[68] When the
war ended, Westergreen's interest shifted to the growth of Scandinavian
churches in the city and the plight of impoverished recent immigrants.
For the remainder of his life, he devoted energy to social issues such as
temperance and, to a lesser extent, workers' rights and safety. His journal
made note of other current events, both national and international, but
he did not otherwise involve himself deeply in political matters.

---

67. Westergreen, *Uppteckningar*, 204–5.
68. Levy, *To Die in Chicago*, 290.

5

The "Golden Age"

1865 to 1875

Give me a new, a perfect heart, from doubt and fear and sorrow free;
The mind which was in Christ impart, and let my spirit cleave to Thee.[1]

THE YEARS IMMEDIATELY AFTER the Civil War brought Westergreen to positions of greater prominence and leadership. At the beginning 1865, Westergreen was pastor *in absentia* of the Bishop Hill church; he was actually serving with the Christian Commission as a Union Army chaplain, mainly around Little Rock, Arkansas. Although appointed in September 1864 to a triweekly circuit of Bishop Hill, Wataga, and Kewanee, he had preached there many times before; in 1863 he had been appointed to the Galesburg and Bishop Hill circuits, but lived in Galesburg because he was continuing his studies at Knox College.[2] His journals for 1864 and 1865 show that he preached extensively in northwestern Illinois, particularly Knox, Henry, Stark, Henderson, Rock Island, and Warren Counties. He also made preaching trips farther afield to Iowa and the Chicago area, and when Conference met in late September he was appointed to Chicago.

Westergreen went to the city on September 13, 1865, where he met with Victor Witting, Peter Challman, and A. J. Anderson, who was then

1. See Wesley, "God of All Power, and Truth, and Grace," 562.

2. The first *resident* pastor in Bishop Hill, A. J. Anderson, came in 1866. *Church Messenger*, 20.

83

pastor of the one Scandinavian Methodist congregation in the city with a church building. Anderson preached on the west side in the evening, and Westergreen exhorted after him. The Illinois Street church, sometimes called First Swedish Methodist, was founded by O. G. Hedstrom in December 1852 but led initially by S. B. Newman. The congregation erected its own wooden building, located just north of the city center, in 1854. Like St. Ansgarius Church, the Scandinavian Episcopal congregation established by Gustav Unonius in 1849, the congregation had as many Norwegians as Swedes. During the pastorate of Nels Peterson, Westergreen's successor, the Norwegians left to establish their own congregation on the west side. Some of the Swedes continued to worship at the Illinois Street church until it was destroyed in the Chicago Fire.

The Chicago appointment opened a new range of opportunities for him. Unlike Bishop Hill, which remained a small farming community and was often an end point for the immigrants who chose to go there, Chicago was growing rapidly; it served as the gateway for Scandinavians settling anywhere but along the eastern seaboard. By the 1850s, over thirty railroad lines entered the city, and it was the terminus for trains from the east. As the city's population expanded, the numbers in Westergreen's congregation were increasing.[3] In late September he recorded:

> I found that there is a great deal to do for a preacher in Chicago. Felt somewhat cast down in my mind today, yet, I was much encouraged in the evening at the prayer meeting which I led. There was a good attendance. The Sabbath school room was entirely filled and some warm and earnest prayers were offered.[4]

Saying "there is a great deal to do" was an understatement. His predecessor at the Illinois Street Church had revived a moribund congregation in a ramshackle building, rebuilding the frame structure and increasing the congregation by 160. Then Eric Shogren took charge for a year, and added another hundred members. Thus Westergreen was attempting to make pastoral calls on around three hundred members in a city with only a rudimentary local public transportation system.[5] The church building on Illinois Street was too small for the number attending, so Westergreen

3. For example, between 1860 and 1870, the city's population grew from 112,172 to just under 300,000.

4. Westergreen, *Journals*, September 28, 1865.

5. A single-track, horse-drawn streetcar ran down State Street beginning in 1859, but it was not until the 1880s that several other lines were established. Chicago's elevated train system was built in 1892.

and his colleagues were establishing another church at Market (now Orleans) and Oak Streets. In addition, Westergreen was helping Victor Witting, who was editor of *Sändebudet*, translating articles into Swedish for publication, and he consoled the Wittings when their youngest child died. Witting, in turn, assisted Westergreen in his new appointment, while also raising funds for the Swedish Methodist theological seminary that finally started in 1870. Like other Methodist preachers of the time, Westergreen was also preaching outside his own church, both to established immigrant congregations and to smaller groups of Scandinavian immigrants who were forming classes and meeting in homes, schools, and other borrowed premises in rural areas. He participated in camp-meetings in Rockford, Leland, and Des Plaines in Illinois, plus Scandic Grove, Minnesota, and Clinton, Iowa. He made time to visit his family in western Illinois only twice, in conjunction with attending Annual Conference and preaching in the area. Nevertheless, they continued to play a significant role in his life. He fretted about his wayward brother John, and remonstrated with his brother Andrew when he learned he "had yielded to temptation while at Galva and attended a ball."[6]

Westergreen's pastoral care responsibilities extended beyond church members and prospects. He was frequently called to the bedsides of the sick, and conducted many funerals during the cholera epidemic of 1866–67. Before the flow of the Chicago River was reversed in 1890, sewage and other contaminants ended up in the drinking water drawn from Lake Michigan, resulting in regular outbreaks of typhoid and cholera. In 1854, for example, 5.5 percent of the population succumbed to cholera. Westergreen noted there were nine coffins on a train he and O. G. Hedstrom traveled on in October 1866.

Near the end of the year, Westergreen started a protracted meeting on the west side, with O. P. Peterson, A. Haagensen (both Norwegians), and a Brother Carlson also preaching and exhorting at the nightly services. On December 22, a religious revival broke out. It is described this way in Westergreen's journal:

> Brother Carlson preached in the evening and I exhorted. Led prayer around the altar and had a blessed time. Though I believe I sometimes have felt a greater joy, yet I believe I never could trust more firmly on the Savior's merits for salvation than tonight. My soul is happy. Bless the Lord. Praise God. Hallelujah—yet, O for more of Christ's love. . . . I trust it may be the

6. Westergreen, *Journals*, October 12, 1865.

means in hands of God in shaping my course of usefulness here,
as I hope by the help of God to be more able to present Christ as
a present Savior to the people. Thus I have much to thank God
for at the close of this year, and yet my soul longs for a greater
baptism from on high.[7]

This was clearly a spiritual high point for Westergreen, and the experience was shared by many in the congregation, so that the protracted
meeting continued several weeks. When he preached two days later, on
Christmas Eve, he had to interrupt his sermon several times, because
someone in the pews "came to peace with God."[8] In the memoranda at
the end of his 1866 journal, he reflected:

> The protracted meeting at the beginning of this year was, I think,
> a real success. I witnessed then what I may say was the first more
> extensive revival that I ever have had on any charge since I en-
> tered the ministry, if not the most extensive I have witnessed
> under the labors of any of our Swede brethren. It is true I had
> revivals on my charges before, and also witnessed and partaken
> in revivals on the charges of other brethren, but I think none so
> extensive as this. Brother Witting and myself have worked in
> peace and harmony, and thank God he has graciously crowned
> our labors with success.[9]

In addition to the success of the protracted meeting, several significant developments took place beyond Westergreen's immediate congregation that contributed to the growth and organization of the Scandinavian
Methodists. First, at one of his prayer meetings he and others became
convinced of a calling to help newly arrived immigrants, and believed
they would be most effective if various denominations worked together.
They and a committee formed the Scandinavian Emigrant Aid Society.[10]
Westergreen had made several trips to the Union Station on Kinzie Street,
and encountered Swedish and Norwegian immigrants as destitute and
lost as he and his family had been years earlier, when they arrived in Fall
River. Westergreen and a Lutheran minister, Erland Carlson, visited the
Galena and Chicago Railroad Company and received the promise of six

7. Westergreen, *Journals*, December 22, 1865, and memoranda from end of year.
8. Westergreen, *Uppteckningar*, 225.
9. Westergreen, *Journals*, memoranda from end of 1866.
10. Liljegren et al., *Svenska Metodism I Amerika*, 265.

hundred dollars, plus four hundred dollars from another company.[11] This philanthropic work, which included a shelter for newcomers from Scandinavia, predated the organization of Vasa, Svithiod, and other mutual aid societies. A second endeavor to which he and other clergy devoted their energies was the temperance movement. Westergreen was not part of the Independent Order of Good Templars, organized in New York in 1851; this organization was censured for being a secret society.[12] However, 1866 was the year he and Witting began holding regular temperance meetings at the church, including one on Easter Sunday evening. Westergreen recorded the numbers who "signed the pledge" as diligently as he kept track of those who joined the church on probation or in full membership.

The most far-reaching event in 1866 for Westergreen and the larger church was the October convention of all Scandinavian Methodist preachers in the United States. It took place at the First Swedish Methodist Church in Chicago. The photograph taken on that occasion shows twenty-six preachers, with O. G. Hedstrom sitting in the middle of the front row.[13] At least three concerns were catalysts for this meeting. In 1856, at the conference session in Peoria, Illinois, all Swedish Methodist congregations were made part of one district that covered Illinois, Indiana, and Iowa, with Jonas Hedstrom as its superintendent. By the mid-1860s, Kansas had been added to the district. It was far too large an area for one superintendent to supervise and visit regularly. At the 1866 convention, the ministers drafted a petition to General Conference to form a semiautonomous Scandinavian conference to carry out missionary work and establish churches among their people in America. They also passed a resolution to send one or two missionaries to Sweden to organize the Methodist movement there. Victor Witting applied for a leave of absence and obtained funding from a private individual to pursue this goal. And finally, they resolved to establish a Scandinavian school for ministerial candidates, possibly in conjunction with Garrett Biblical Institute in Evanston.[14]

11. Westergreen, *Uppteckningar*, 232.

12. Westergreen, *Uppteckningar*, 218.

13. Peter Challman does not appear in this photo, though he was a minister in good standing at the time, and served as presiding elder of the Swedish district from 1857–1865. At the time of the convention in 1866 he was visiting Sweden. After he returned, he left the Methodist Episcopal Church and joined with the Free Methodists for several years.

14 Liljegren et al., *Svenska Metodismen I Amerika*, 215.

According to Victor Witting's autobiography, the idea of a Scandinavian professor and/or seminary first came up at the annual conference
in Kewanee, Illinois, in 1859. Four years later he published an editorial
in *Sändebudet*, raising the question once again and noting that such a
school could be in conjunction with Methodist institutions of higher
learning in Bloomington or Evanston, Illinois.[15] At the outset, it would
be limited to ministerial candidates, but the eventual goal would be to
expand to general education. Albert Ericson was chosen to be a teacher
in the proposed seminary, and, since his education up to that point had
not included theology, he went to Sweden for six months to prepare for
the work. Upon his return, the school was not ready to start, so instead he
became editor of *Sändebudet* until the 1871 Chicago Fire destroyed the
newspaper's office and printing press. He then served the large church in
Worcester, Massachusetts. It was not until 1883, thirteen years after the
seminary was established, that Ericson became principal and a teacher.

Westergreen remained in Chicago, appointed to First Swedish
Methodist Church, until the Annual Conference of 1868, but he did not
limit himself to the care of a single congregation. His daily journal shows
he preached in over twenty-five other churches across the Midwest, as
well as four different campmeetings during the summer months and
protracted meetings in Victoria and Chicago, both his own congregation
and a German Methodist church on Clybourn Avenue, where he noted
he "enjoyed good liberty." Critical of manuscript preaching, he spoke
from outlines or extemporaneously, perhaps in part because he was con-
stantly invoking the Spirit's power to fill and guide him as well as working
within the hearts of his listeners. His work with the Emigrant Aid Society
continued on a regular basis. Peter Challman returned from his trip to
Sweden in July of 1867 with a large number of immigrants, and Victor
Witting, after reporting on his own recent visit to Sweden, obtained a
leave of absence to establish the Methodist church in the land of his birth,
and departed at the end of September. Westergreen continued to assist
in translating materials for *Sändebudet*, though only Ericson's name appeared on the masthead.

He never complained of overwork in his journals from these years;
on the contrary, he seemed to thrive on the busyness and variety that
his Chicago pastorate offered. He was usually preaching between 150

15. Witting, *Minnen Från Mitt Lif,* 505.

and 200 times per year during this period.[16] Nevertheless, there are occasional notes of frustration or discouragement over situations he encountered in his ministry. For example, in August of 1867 he went by
train to Rockford to preach to the congregation where his parents had
been charter members, and for whom he preached his first sermon.[17] The
Swedish Methodist congregation experienced its ups and downs over
the years, but in 1863 was able to purchase a small building that was
previously owned by Presbyterians. They then purchased a lot in a better
location, and planned to move their building. When Westergreen arrived
to preach, he found the work was not finished, and recorded that he was
tempted to leave without conducting worship. He stayed, however, and
preached in both English and Swedish before returning to Chicago. During the same month he tried to reconcile a difficulty between two women
in his congregation, and wrote that they parted in tears. There was also
stress within his family. His brother John fell into what was described as
loose company, and gambled away his money, so that Nels had to rescue
him financially several times. The older brother's exhortations to seek
his soul's salvation seemed to fall upon deaf ears. In December 1867 he
received a telegram that his mother was critically ill and not expected to
last the night. He rushed to western Illinois and stayed at her bedside a
few days, and eventually she recovered. His degree of anxiety over her
health suggests the emotional bond with her was stronger and more complicated than with his father, who died in 1874, although all indications
are that his relationship with his father was good.

Westergreen continued to preach mainly in Swedish, but occasionally in English, Norwegian, or German as the situation required. In 1868
he traveled as far west as Omaha, and preached at campmeetings in Swede
Bend, the Andover area, and Des Plaines. Besides his ongoing work with
the Emigrant Aid Society, the temperance movement, and helping with
Sändebudet, he now undertook translation of "The Lord Our Righteousness" and other works by John Wesley into Swedish. These would be
published in the newspaper, which featured "A Page from Methodist History" as well as contemporary church news in every issue. Westergreen

16. It was not until he was appointed editor of *Sändebudet* in 1872 that he admitted
he felt overwhelmed. He was also preaching far less as editor, so it may be that preaching and face-to-face ministry energized him, but sitting alone at a desk depleted him.

17. Ola Westergreen was in charge of the class that started in 1854. The usual practice was for Methodists to form a "class," and if/when it reached sufficient size and
strength, it organized formally as a congregation.

was not the first or only one to put Wesley into Swedish, of course; a translation of "Christian Perfection" had been circulating for a number of years. Westergreen distributed it as a tract a decade earlier, when he was working as a colporteur among immigrants in Chicago. Victor Witting had translated some of Charles Wesley's hymns into Swedish. It is likely Westergreen took on this new project because he had more theological education than any of his peers in ministry at that point. He also wrote the formal petition for the General Conference regarding the establishment of a Scandinavian Methodist seminary. He and his colleagues held meetings to discuss the particulars of this venture, but the stars did not align for its debut.

When the Annual Conference met in Washington, Illinois, in late September, Westergreen was discouraged when the cabinet appointed him to Galesburg. The reason for his disappointment is not disclosed, but from the memoranda at the end of his journal, it appears that his work and his own religious experience while in Chicago had flourished, so that he was reluctant to leave it behind. He reflected:

> While I tonight cast a retrospect over the past year I can truly say that goodness and mercy have followed me through the same. If it has not been the best yet it has been one of the most prosperous in my whole ministry. The Lord at the beginning of the year was pleased to bless my soul with a sweet happiness and peace in believing. During the latter part of the year [presumably after moving to Galesburg] I have even been much down-pressed in my spirit, especially as I have felt greatly concerned for the salvation of my brethren who are yet unsaved and I hope the Lord will answer our prayer. . . . On the 26th day of February while at prayer my soul was blessed in the same manner as I received in the blessing on the 22nd of December 1865. I was happy in faith in my Savior. While I was riding to Leland the following day I avoided all conversation and held an unbroken communion with my Savior and the day following while I was riding in the cars to Chicago I was so happy occasionally that I could hardly keep from praising God aloud. My joy at this time was perhaps greater than it was the first time in Chicago but then it appeared to me greater as it was so new and of course that time will be looked upon by me as of greater importance as it to a great extent changed my course of labor and enabled me from thence to preach a more free, full, and personal salvation than I had done before. . . . This year has not been so successful

in my ministry as the two previous years and yet we have met with some success.[18]

There were other factors that could have contributed to his lack of enthusiasm over leaving Chicago. He had been appointed to the Galesburg and Bishop Hill circuits a few years earlier, while studying at Knox College, so this may have felt like a step backward in his vocation. When Westergreen returned to Knox County that autumn, he moved back into the family home with his parents. His brother Andrew, who was now working as a store clerk, was also under the same roof. Since Westergreen had been living on his own for over a decade, he may have felt some awkwardness at the situation. It is evident his presence was advantageous for the rest of the family; he helped bring in the hay, picked cherries to be preserved, emptied the cellar when heavy rains flooded much of the town, and bought out his brother Andrew's share in the property. One amusing and atypical incident occurred in connection with his manual labor during this period. When mowing the hay in July, he became so tired and thirsty he accepted the offer of some cherry wine one of the neighbors was making. He drank three or four glasses quickly and admitted, "I could feel the effect of it in my head a little."[19] Given his support for any Prohibition Party candidate for public office, it is surprising he acknowledged the episode ever happened.

Despite his misgivings about the move, he acknowledged that the congregation in Galesburg received him very kindly, and he knew many of the people. The Swedish Methodists had been organized by Jonas Hedstrom in 1849 or 1851, making it one of the oldest churches in the connection, and it was also one of the largest.[20] The congregation's genesis was not without difficulties. The town of Galesburg and Knox College, established in 1837, had been founded by Congregationalists and Presbyterians. To this day, the Congregational Church (now United Church of Christ) is the largest and grandest religious edifice in the town. Jonathan Blanchard, then president of Knox College, opposed the advent of rival churches, and persuaded many who had been drawn to the Methodist church to withdraw their pledges to their building fund. During one

18. Westergreen, *Journals*, 1868 memoranda.

19. Westergreen, *Journals*, July 22, 1869.

20. Wallenius and Olson claim the earlier date, while *Svenska Metodismen I Amerika* gives the date as 1851. Only Victoria (1846) was definitely older, but Galesburg had more members.

bitter debate with Jonas Hedstrom, the latter is alleged to have declared, "Do you see the sun in the heavens? You might as well try to stop him in his course as to attempt to shut the Methodists out of Galesburg. We have come here to stay."[21] Competition came from other quarters, too. Six months after Hedstrom had organized a Methodist society, a Swedish Lutheran church was established in Galesburg. Its first pastor, T. N. Hasselquist, was on cordial terms with Westergreen, having met him before both men left Sweden, but when Hasselquist left Galesburg in 1863 to become president of Augustana College, his successors were not as friendly toward the Swedish Methodists. In 1852 a Baptist movement swept through Galesburg, to the detriment of the fledgling Methodist congregation. Many of the members were rebaptized, and even one of the Methodist preachers of the time left to affiliate with the Baptist church.[22]

Unfortunately, there was also some tension with the American Methodists. In 1851 the Swedish and American congregations decided to construct a shared building that would seat around two hundred. They would take turns using it for worship. After a few years, the Americans wanted the building for themselves, and at a meeting of the trustees—the majority of whom were Americans—the Swedes were voted out. Hedstrom and his flock did not give up and disperse, but managed to erect a small building of their own, which was dedicated on New Year's Day, 1857. At Conference that year, A. J. Anderson was appointed the first full-time pastor of the church, and stayed for two years. He was followed by Peter Newberg and Lot Lindquist, then Westergreen, a second stint by Anderson, and S. B. Newman. When Westergreen returned in 1868, the Galesburg congregation was in many ways the flagship church for Swedish Methodists in the area. It was, however, in transition and possibly decline at the beginning of Westergreen's second stint there. In the mid-1860s an independent church organized in Wataga, northeast of town, and decreased the Galesburg congregation by fifty members.

An additional complication for Westergreen during his first year in Galesburg was some conflict among the Swedish Methodist clergy. His friend Peter Challman, who had returned from Sweden and was living in Knox County, had left the Methodist Church. This was partly due to an article Albert Ericson published in *Sändebudet* the previous year, which angered Challman. *Svenska Metodismen I Amerika* does not acknowledge

21. Wallenius and Olson, *Short Story of the Swedish Methodism*, 35.

22. Liljegren et al., *Svenska Metodismen I Amerika*, 204.

Challman's departure, but in his journal Westergreen indicates there was
also an interpersonal conflict with Eric Shogren over Challman's attempt
to organize a Free Methodist Church in Victoria: an effort that ultimately
failed. It escalated to the point of letters from each being read aloud during Conference. Westergreen wrote in October:

> Brother Challman preached yesterday with such feeling and
> influence that the whole congregation was in tears. It is to me
> strange how a man who cherishes such feelings as Brother
> Challman against most of his former brethren in the ministry
> can preach with such influence and feeling.[23]

The friendship between Challman and Westergreen survived this un-
pleasantness. Challman covered his preaching appointments when
Westergreen was sick in January 1869. While the conflict later in the year
made Westergreen somewhat anxious, he continued to meet with Challman and enjoy his company. In 1884 Challman moved to northwestern
Iowa, and according to Wallenius and Olson, he regretted having left the
"old Methodist church" and rejoined it in 1900.[24]

Westergreen was anything but idle during his first full year back in
Galesburg. He preached more than twice a week to his own congregation,
and eighty-six times at other churches and protracted meetings from
Burlington, Iowa, to Hingham, Massachusetts. He attended temperance
lectures at Caledonia Hall, the new opera house and auditorium in Galesburg, and sat in on the Lutherans' conference in April. In August and
September he spoke at campmeetings at Lynn Grove (near Woodhull),
Gibson, and Bardolph, Illinois. His energy and zeal were reflected in his
most-preached sermon text for the year, 1 Tim 6:12: "Fight the good
fight of the faith; take hold of the eternal life to which you were called
when you made the good confession in the presence of many witnesses."
When the Conference met in Canton, Illinois, in September, Westergreen
asked for and was granted a few weeks' leave of absence. He used the
opportunity to make a trip east, where he visited his younger brother
Erik/Alex (Westergreen's journal that year refers to him by both names)
in Massachusetts. His brother had not enjoyed the same education and
opportunities in the Boston area. Now married, he was frustrated in
seeking better employment, and planned to go back to sea. Erik was
described as a seeker in the journal, despite his regular attendance at a

23. Westergreen, *Journals*, October 25, 1869.

24. Wallenius and Olson, *Short Story of the Swedish Methodism*, 26.

local church and the fact that the two brothers prayed together earnestly. When they parted, Westergreen headed to New York City and met with O. G. Hedstrom . He preached on the Bethel Ship and in Brooklyn at the Swedish Methodist Church organized in 1845. Perhaps the most significant event of this trip, however, was that Hedstrom took Westergreen to one of Phoebe Palmer's Tuesday Meetings for the Promotion of Holiness, held in her home. Westergreen wrote, "It was a good meeting, and my own soul was touched especially under the prayer of Mrs. Palmer."[25] This may have been the first meeting between Westergreen and Palmer, although she spoke at the Des Plaines campmeeting in 1865.[26] Palmer was a lifelong Methodist who experienced entire sanctification in 1837. Westergreen had probably read *The Way of Holiness*, published in 1843, and O. G. Hedstrom's implicit endorsement of her teaching helped shape Westergreen's theology of Christian perfection still further.

Two related events in November 1869 had both an immediate and long-lasting impact on Westergreen. First, his brother Andrew was granted his exhorter's license: a step toward ordained ministry. However, Andrew had no advanced education as his brother did. He would need further training, preferably in the seminary that had been planned at the 1866 organizational meeting of Swedish Methodist preachers. Second, Albert Ericson, who had been editor of *Sändebudet* since returning from his study leave in Sweden, tendered his resignation as head of the nascent theological school. The men at the preachers' meeting that ran from October 29 through November 1 tried in vain to persuade him to accept the position. Westergreen wrote, "We were no nearer the end at noon with our business than when we commenced, and after much speeching [*sic*] and refusing I consented to take the school for the present."[27] Instead of Evanston or Bloomington, the school would have to begin in western Illinois.

After his trip to the East Coast, Westergreen returned to Galesburg to continue serving his congregation while simultaneously starting classes for the seminary's first three students: Alfred Anderson, August Wigren, and Andrew Westergreen. Wigren (1849–1874) had taken some courses at Hedding College in Abingdon, south of Galesburg, and was serving the congregation at Swedona, a settlement north of Galesburg in

25. Westergreen, *Journals*, December 21, 1869.
26. Saliers, *Des Plaines Campground*, 2. The National Holiness Camp Meeting Association had one of its annual meetings at the campground in 1870, reflecting the growing holiness movement within the denomination since before the Civil War.
27. Westergreen, *Journals*, November 1, 1869.

Mercer County. Alfred Anderson (1851–1921) had less prior education than Wigren. He emigrated from Sweden at age fifteen and was converted under the preaching S. B. Newman in Beaver at the end of 1868. He studied under Westergreen for about a year before being ordained in the Central Illinois Conference and being appointed to New Sweden, Iowa. While serving that congregation he continued his studies at Mt. Pleasant College. Andrew Westergreen (1842–1903), as noted earlier, was a novice to higher education, though given his upbringing, he was familiar with the Bible and Christian faith.

Few records remain from the earliest years of the Swedish Methodist seminary, aside from minutes taken at the 1866 preachers' meeting, which are included in *Svenska Metodismen I Amerika*, and Westergreen's journals. S. B. Newman's autobiography shows that his involvement with the seminary was limited to fundraising, an endeavor at which he excelled. Witting's autobiography acknowledged he could not describe the history and development of the seminary from 1867 to 1877, because he was in Sweden those years, organizing the Methodist church there. The dearth of records may also be attributed in part to the history of ministerial training/theological education in the denomination. As Frederick Norwood explains in *The Story of Methodism*, most of the early leaders in American Methodism did not have much formal training, but rather an apprenticeship:

> Theological education in its first form was completely personal; one man learned from another more experienced. . . . The presiding elders were key figures in this early form of theological education. They took the younger men under their wing and showed them how.[28]

What Westergreen undertook in Galesburg seemed to be akin to the ministerial course of study developed in 1816 and standardized throughout the Methodist Episcopal Church in 1848. It aimed to give candidates a more substantial understanding of Christianity and its history, Wesleyan theology, and equipment for the practical tasks of ministry, such as preaching, administration, and pastoral care. The Swedish Methodist seminary did not, at the outset, try to replicate the three-year curriculum of Garrett Biblical Institute, founded in 1853. The latter institution's history states that its curriculum was meant to *supplement* the denomination's prescribed course of study, with a particular focus on biblical

28. Norwood, *Story of American Methodism*, 220.

learning, including Greek and Hebrew.[29] Garrett's educational model was patterned more after the scholastic focus of Andover Theological Seminary, founded in 1805, and Princeton Theological Seminary, established in 1809. These two institutions' three-year curriculum focused on three areas of study: Bible, church history, and theology, with a specialized faculty and sizeable library.[30] It was not until years later, when Westergreen's fledgling school moved to Evanston and coordinated curriculum with Garrett, that the program of study more closely resembled the American Methodist pattern. Even then, the Swedes developed a more general education program as well as training for Methodist ministry.

Westergreen arranged for his students in Galesburg to preach and lead worship regularly—sometimes with supervision—as well as studying under him. The schedule for tutorials appeared to be arranged around preaching appointments. The first subject the men studied was Swedish grammar. This may seem surprising, but Wigren left Sweden when he was only three years old. Andrew Westergreen was ten. Like O. G. Hedstrom, they had to relearn their mother tongue in order to minister to the growing immigrant community.[31] The initial journal entry about instructing the men was written the second week of February 1870, though Alfred Anderson did not begin his studies until March. Westergreen sometimes taught them as a group, and other times in individual tutorials. He examined the students regularly, though it is not clear whether these were written or oral exams. In April he received a box of books for the school, presumably from Hedstrom. One text Westergreen used that first year was Ralston's *Elements of Theology*, which they read in the Danish because they had no theology textbooks in Swedish. A new student, Andrew J. Wicklund, began studies in June and was recommended for a license to preach in late July, but apparently did not go on to ordination; his name is not listed in *Svenska Metodismen I Amerika*. The following year Henry W. Eklund and John A. Gabrielson became Westergreen's students.[32]

It is testimony to his stamina and dedication that Westergreen was able to get a seminary up and running while simultaneously serving the largest Swedish Methodist Church in western Illinois. One of the few

29. Garrett-Evangelical Theological Seminary, http://www.garrett.edu/history.

30. Shelley, "Seminaries' Identity Crisis," 43.

31. Whyman, *Hedstroms*, 74.

32. Westergreen's *Journal* adds the names of John Lind and August Elming, with Bro. Palmlund from Brooklyn intending to come a few weeks later. However, Palmlund and Elming are not listed in *Svenska Metodismen I Amerika*.

sermon manuscripts with a date on the first page was preached on Pentecost 1870 in Galesburg, and again in 1880, when he was living in Chicago. The sermon theme was taken from the first line of his text, 1 Thess 3:23: "May the God of peace sanctify you wholly." He did use this text when preaching a series of sermons on sanctification in Keokuk in December 1864, and perhaps he developed this message from the earlier one. However, the 1870 sermon mentions Phoebe Palmer by name, acknowledging that her religious pilgrimage was exceptional. He did not meet Palmer until 1869, so it unlikely he would have mentioned her before she even spoke at Des Plaines Campground. The sermon provides a theological contrast to the sanctification sermon on Phil 2:5. Where the earlier sermon focused on human responsibility in attaining "the mind of Christ," the emphasis in this message is the work of the Holy Spirit as sanctifier. This is immediately apparent from the five points of the introduction:

1. The Holy Spirit as a person

2. In his office and work

3. The promise of him

4. His outpouring

5. His continuing work[33]

The vocabulary in this sermon is also different from the earlier sermon. "Sanctification" and other forms of the word appear thirty-seven times, and "holiness" and related forms are used seven times. Even taking into account the greater length of the manuscript, the rate at which these theological terms are used (as opposed to simpler expressions like "every Christian ought to be like Christ") suggests increasing theological sophistication on the part of his listeners. After all, he mentions Phoebe Palmer without needing to explain who she is. He and the listeners have a shared frame of reference, unlike his stint as guest preacher in Keokuk several years earlier. Sanctification is presented in this message in two ways: first, as a possibility to be realized through the work of the Holy Spirit, as promised in Scripture; second, the experience of sanctification is validated, to a large extent, by the feelings of the sanctified person and the fruits manifested by him/her.

33. Westergreen, "Men Fridens Gud Sjelf Helga Eder Till Hela Eder Warelse" [May the God of peace sanctify you wholly], III.2.

As the sole professor of the fledgling school, Westergreen occasionally had to deal with issues that nowadays would be delegated to a dean of students. A rumor of scandalous behavior between Andrew Wicklund and Inga Peterson resulted in Miss Peterson being expelled from the congregation, much to the chagrin of the young woman's father and sister. They eventually left the church. A month later Westergreen took John Gabrielson to task, telling him he did not believe Gabrielson was Christian at all if he would not leave off using strong drink. Gabrielson became angry and threatened to leave the church, and discussion of his situation caused friction at the quarterly conference held in March 1871. It was eventually resolved, and Gabrielson was ordained a deacon in 1873 in the Central Illinois Conference, and elder by Bishop Peck in 1877. Still another student, August Elming, had such difficulty learning that when Westergreen examined him he could not answer a single question correctly, and burst into tears. Westergreen was sympathetic, and regarded him as an excellent young man in other ways, but Elming did not continue preparing for ordained ministry.

The start of the 1871–1872 academic year was not markedly different from the previous one. Theological tensions between the Methodists and other denominations flared up occasionally, though never instigated by Westergreen. He wrote about visiting the Second Lutheran Church and hearing a discussion about sanctification, commenting that the Lutherans seemed to think justification and sanctification were one and the same thing. He continued to worry about his brothers; in April, he expressed the wish that Swan could find an occupation other than farming, given his health problems.[34] The vocation he had in mind, not surprisingly, was full-time ministry, but Swan continued farming in Copley Township of Knox County for the rest of his life. In June, he fretted about his youngest brother, John, whose whereabouts were unknown. Then in August John wrote to the family and announced he had gotten married—and once again needed money. Westergreen reluctantly sent him fifty dollars.

The board of school directors met in late summer and discussed the possibility of Albert Ericson and Westergreen changing places, i.e., Ericson would lead the school and Westergreen take charge of *Sändebudet* in Chicago. This proposal was suspended when Chicago was devastated by

34. Swan was, in fact, a local preacher in the Methodist Church for forty years, that is, a layperson licensed to preach and conduct worship without being in itinerant ministry.

the fire of October 8, 1871. Though the exact cause was unknown, the fire began in a shed behind 137 Dekoven Street, southwest of the city center. It spread as far north as Belden Avenue to the north and 20th Street to the south, and from Lake Michigan on the east to as far west as Halsted Street at some points, although most of the western boundary was the north and south branches of the Chicago River. Almost one-third of the city's population was left homeless. Westergreen traveled to the city a few days afterward, and wrote about what he saw and experienced:

> Over one hundred thousand persons are reported homeless and how many lives have been lost can probably hardly be fully ascertained. . . . I went to Chicago in the morning, arriving there in the afternoon at half past three. The cars stopped far down on the west side. Then I walked up north until I came to the place where the first had started and the sight that at once burst upon my vision I cannot describe, and hope I may not see such a sight again. . . . Took a walk out on the north side among the ruins. When the evening shades drew about it appeared to me as I was walking in an awful dreamland. Brother Ericson and myself went out on the north side as far as some way up Lincoln Park before we could see the end of the desolation, then walked south until we could see the end of destruction there. We were then tired, having walked I think six or seven miles, all through ruins on every side. Not a house in the way except Mr. Ogden's, which has been saved as by a miracle. Though we saw the tract of destruction we could hardly realize that it was the city of Chicago we were in, so complete was the destruction, and though it was an awful reality, it seems almost as a dream.[35]

There was now no point in having Westergreen and Ericson change places; the offices of *Sändebudet* had been destroyed, and the biweekly newspaper did not resume publication until a year later. It can be argued that the Swedes were more affected by the great Chicago Fire than any other immigrant group, because in 1871 they were concentrated in the parts of the city that burned, while other immigrant groups, such as the Irish and Germans, were spread out in different areas of the city.[36] Hundreds of Swedish homes and five Scandinavian churches were destroyed, including the Swedish Methodist church. The congregation met temporarily in a Norwegian Methodist church on Indiana Avenue, then

---

35. Westergreen, *Journals*, October 10 and 11, 1871.
36. Liljegren et al., *Svenska Metodismen I Amerika*, 220.

in a German Methodist church until they purchased some empty lots on
May Street for a new building. The basement was completed first, and
the congregation had its dedication service on November 1, 1872. It took
another seven years, during the pastorate of John Wigren, until the main
floor of the church was completed and dedicated. It became known as
Second Swedish Methodist Church, although Westergreen usually referred to it as May Street. The church at Market and Oak retained the
name First Church, but it was also referred to as Market Street Church
and North Side Swedish Methodist Church.

Westergreen returned to Galesburg and two days later wrote a lecture about "the great conflagration and its lesson . . . may it serve as a
warning for us."[37] He then resumed his teaching and preached at least
twice a week. Life seemed to return to its normal routines, except for
a self-appointed committee from the church approaching him in mid-
November and asking him to change the style of his preaching. It was the
first criticism of his homiletical method recorded in his journal since Jonas Hedstrom had taken him to task about his exposition of Matt 25:13,
thirteen years earlier. This time the criticism made him angry as well as
depressed. He wrote:

> [I] have been very much tempted today occasionally from the
> meeting we had yesterday, especially the criticizing of my way
> of preaching. Oh! How much I need patience and so little I have
> of it, but alas, I find a great deal of unsubdued pride within that
> only wants for an opportunity to break out.[38]

His agitated feelings were soothed somewhat by an invitation to return
to Beaver to preach for several days at the end of the year. He enjoyed
spending time with old friends there, and five people joined the congregation on probation. He did, however, report "some extravagances that
disturbed the meeting, especially by Brother Swan, who first came and
fell flat in [sic] the altar and prayed, then thought he had got the power
to cast out the devil."[39] This suggests that while some manifestations of
the Holy Spirit's work were welcome and even sought after during worship, phenomena associated with more radical holiness traditions were
not. Westergreen rejoiced when several came forward seeking salvation,
when someone claimed to have found peace with God, when testimony,

37. Westergreen, *Journals*, October 14, 1871.

38. Westergreen, *Journals*, November 14, 1871.

39. Westergreen, *Journals*, January 2, 1872.

singing and prayer continued long after the meeting had ended, and
when he could describe a particular service as "a melting time." But he
never aspired to speak in tongues. He did not conduct healing services
himself, and did not even mention exorcism in his journals.

When he returned to Galesburg, he continued teaching Swedish
grammar, theology, and Greek to his students. His personal reading
included the entire Bible, the writings of Phoebe Palmer, Johan Arndt's
True Christianity, and Thomas Chalmers's *Lectures on the Epistle to the
Romans*, among other works. He also spent time raising money for a new
church building. There was debate over what house and lot to buy, and
whether to have frame or brick construction. The cornerstone of the new
Swedish Methodist Church was laid in June 1872. Westergreen attended
a campmeeting in Washington, Illinois, which was conducted in German and English, and then preached at campmeetings held near Bishop
Hill and Gibson. His brother Andrew also preached at the former, and
Swan at the latter. Annual Conference was held in Geneseo, and here
Westergreen had a temporary falling out with Eric Shogren (1824–1906).
He had privately been critical of Shogren's preaching, commenting in
his journal that while his colleague spoke in an easy, flowing manner, he
doubted that Shogren had the influence on the masses that he exercised
in earlier years.[40] At Conference, they disagreed over who would be the
next presiding elder of the district. Westergreen became so angry he left
Conference before it ended. He was nevertheless pleased when he heard
his brother Andrew had been appointed to Rockford, and was satisfied
that he was to take over as editor of *Sändebudet*. He had already met with
his class for the last time in August, and reported they prayed and wept
together before they closed.

Shortly after Conference, the fledgling seminary was moved from
Galesburg to Galva, a little over thirty miles to the northeast, and Christopher Wiren, who was pastor there, took charge of the school. It was not
until January 1875 that the Swedish Methodist Seminary moved to Evanston and eventually erected buildings near Garrett Biblical Institute. William Henschen became rector and professor: a post he held until 1883. In
that year Albert Ericson, the original candidate to lead the school, finally
took the reins and served until 1909. The change in location and leadership did not spell the end of Westergreen's involvement, however. Once
he was based back in Chicago, he resumed his involvement, teaching

---

40. Westergreen, *Journals*, May 8, 1872.

1880–1881 and serving as assistant 1896–1897, attending examinations, and often teaching both theological and basic courses.

Prior to his move, Westergreen sought the advice and support of his old friend Victor Witting. They had a pleasant time together, but Witting's health was poor at that point, and he told Westergreen he had heart disease. This placed limitations on his ability to provide assistance, particularly since the Swedish publishing committee assigned him to translate *The Book of Discipline* into Swedish for publication in Sweden, as well as selecting Swedish books to be sold in the Methodist bookstore in Chicago. Despite Witting's encouragement and counsel, Westergreen's return to Chicago was not easy. For example, we may assume that when he lived with his parents in Galesburg, at least some of his meals were prepared by his mother. She maintained the family home and did the laundry. In Chicago, Westergreen had what he called a "boarding place" rather than a home of his own, and the nature of his appointment meant that although he still preached regularly, he could not do pastoral visitation and nurture personal connections as he had before. Another reason this year was hard for Westergreen is that he was charged with reviving *Sändebudet* after a year's hiatus due to the fire. When Witting started the paper in 1862 it was a four-page periodical published twice a month; now readers expected an issue every week. As a newspaper for immigrants, many of whom had not yet learned English, *Sändebudet* covered not only denominational news, but also current events, both national and international. For example, Westergreen translated President Grant's second inaugural address into Swedish for inclusion in the paper. *Sändebudet* also had regular columns on agriculture and farming, news about other denominations and Methodism in other countries, Sunday School lessons, book reviews, instruction on Methodist history, the schedule for quarterly conferences, camp-meetings and protracted meetings, announcement of weddings, funerals, and clergy appointments, an editorial, sometimes a serialized novel translated into Swedish, and advertising. It was a daunting task for any editor, and Westergreen had no one to proofread for him or give other assistance. The office for *Sändebudet* was a small, drafty corner of the Methodist bookstore. On October 9, the first issue under Westergreen's editorship was printed: exactly a year and a day after the great Chicago fire started.

His work did not earn him the appreciation and support of all clergy colleagues. Less than two weeks after *Sändebudet* resumed publication, another minister attacked his work in another periodical. In early

December, he received an angry letter from Albert Ericson, his predecessor, criticizing his language in the newspaper. Westergreen decided not to answer Ericson, but try to do the best he could with the paper, hoping that the Lord would help him with it.[41] Friction in his relationship with Ericson continued into the next year. There is no evidence to suggest they quarreled face to face, but in one instance Westergreen admitted he was tempted to anger with Ericson, and in another instance he wrote, "This has been a day of real anguish to my soul" when Ericson visited the *Sändebudet* office.

Despite a grueling schedule and some interpersonal conflict, Westergreen wrote in his journal that 1873 was mostly uniform and pleasant. His friendship with Alfred Anderson, one of his first three students in Galesburg, deepened when Anderson was appointed to Chicago as an assistant to Eric Shogren. The three colleagues conducted a successful protracted meeting early in the year; Westergreen described one of their meetings as glorious, and noted that Anderson preached with great unction. Westergreen and Anderson were about the same age, came from neighboring counties in Sweden, and were both converted or spiritually influenced by the preaching of S. B. Newman. Westergreen described their friendship this way:

> By conversation on religious topics and experiences, we have learned to know the spiritual condition of each other better than we perhaps did before. In fact our relation to each other while I was associated with him in the work in the congregation has been just what I believe it should be between brethren in Christ and in the Christian ministry.[42]

Westergreen felt the loss of Anderson's company as well as Shogren's when both were sent to new appointments near the end of the year. He had enjoyed long conversations with them on personal religion and holiness, two of his favorite topics. After their departure, Westergreen continued to preach frequently at the church at Market and Oak and elsewhere, but the fact that nearly a third of the sermons were "repeats"—far more than his usual practice—is an indication of how demanding it was to produce *Sändebudet* every week. Sanctification or holiness continued to be a prominent theme in his sermons.[43] That summer he preached at four

41. Westergreen, *Journals*, December 18, 1872.

42. Westergreen, *Journals*, memoranda for 1873.

43. Westergreen tended to use the word sanctification in his sermons, but holiness

campmeetings: Des Plaines, Hickory Grove, the district campmeeting at New Lenox, and the Free Methodists' campmeeting. In his limited free time, he went to see President Grant at the Chicago Chamber of Commerce, and attended the laying of the cornerstone for Mount Vernon Military Academy in Morgan Park, south of the city.

During this period, Ola and Hanna Westergreen could take pride in their three sons living in Illinois; two were in full-time ministry and one was a local preacher and farmer. Their youngest son, living in Pennsylvania, followed a different path. They were shocked by the news that John had been arrested and was in jail, awaiting trial. Westergreen traveled to Philadelphia in November to offer what help he could, but to little avail. John had been charged with larceny and released on $800 bail. The evidence against him was probably not enough to convict him, but he broke bail and fled south before being rearrested, tried, and ultimately sentenced to several months in the penitentiary, leaving his young wife dependent on the support of her brother-in-law and her family of origin. Once again Westergreen had several earnest and prayerful conversations with his youngest brother, hoping for his soul's salvation.

When Westergreen returned to Chicago and his work on the newspaper, more challenges awaited. A smallpox pandemic that had started a few years earlier now swept through Chicago, claiming Eric Anderson, a clergy colleague, in early March. Westergreen went to be vaccinated the same day. August Wigren, Westergreen's former student, contracted the disease while in Sweden and died there. Meanwhile, deaths from diphtheria and whooping cough soared in the 1870s. Swedes, Germans, and Poles living south of 37th Street were devastated by another cholera outbreak. O. G. Hedstrom, the patriarch of Swedish Methodism, contracted typhoid, and anecdotal evidence suggests he never regained his strength. Sorrow struck even closer to home. In April, Westergreen received the news that Eunice, the infant daughter of his brother Swan and wife, Betsy, had died. He visited them and his parents the following month, in conjunction with a preachers' meeting in Galesburg, and found his mother and father well. They had a long, earnest conversation about sanctification and how to seek it wholeheartedly. On the first of July he received a telegram suggesting he come home immediately if he wanted to see his father alive. He arrived to find Ola in great pain. Two doctors administered chloroform and operated twice, but the man

when discussing a person's religious experience or aspiration.

died a few days later, at the age of seventy-five. The symptoms described in Westergreen's journal suggest the cause may have sepsis following a ruptured appendix.[44] Local ministers led the funeral, rather than Nels or Andrew, and Ola was buried at Hope Cemetery in Galesburg. Before the month ended, Andrew brought Hanna to Chicago to live with her eldest son. She remained with Nels until her death, twenty-four years later. Needless to say, he scrambled to find more suitable housing. Alfred Anderson helped him find temporary accommodations in a house on May Street. They later moved to a house on Granger Street in what is now the Old Town neighborhood on the near north side of the city.

The next year, 1875, brought slightly fewer family emergencies and an easing of the demands on Westergreen's energy. He continued to edit *Sändebudet* and preach at North Side, and participated in protracted meetings that ran for nearly two months. In addition, his schedule allowed him to attend more lectures and local ministerial meetings than seemed to be the case in the previous few years. It may be that having his mother, who was then in her late sixties, living with him allowed him to shift some domestic responsibilities to her. In March he went to Galesburg, where he and brothers Andrew and Swan visited their father's grave and prayed together. He traveled to Rockford to preach at Easter, and to the East Coast after the annual campmeeting at Des Plaines. In Philadelphia he met with his brother John, who was now released from prison. Westergreen believed he was a changed man. His journey continued to the Boston area, where he spent time with brother Alex/Erik and his family, and then to New York. He visited O. G. Hedstrom on Staten Island, but stayed with Daniel Sörlin, a Methodist minister who had recently emigrated from Sweden.

At Annual Conference in Moline in September, Westergreen was appointed to the north side of Chicago, and William Henschen was to take over as editor of *Sändebudet*. When he returned home to Chicago the following week, there was a letter from Alex/Erik with the news that he had lost everything he had. Westergreen's journal does not explain the cause of this calamity, but one result was that Alex temporarily left his wife and daughter in Hingham, outside of Boston, and came to Chicago in December to look for work. Westergreen located a man in Galva who offered to give him a job. In the meantime, brother John left his wife

44. Unfortunately, birth and death records for Knox County during this period were destroyed in a fire, and none of Ola's present-day descendants know his cause of death.

in Philadelphia and came to Chicago in search of employment, though he would occasionally disappear for a day or two without explanation. Westergreen tried to put the best possible face on it, remarking that being with his brothers for Christmas in 1875 reminded him of olden times when they were happy children together around their parents' table. The description, along with his account of the entire year, is consistent with psychologist Kevin Leman's presentation of characteristic behavior of the firstborn in a family: reliable, conscientious, perfectionistic, and serious.[45] With Ola's death, Westergreen took on the role of head of the family, and seemingly felt responsible for everyone else's welfare.

The end of 1875 marked the conclusion of what Westergreen himself referred to as "the Golden Age" or "the Magnificent Period" when, as an old man, he divided his life into several periods. Other than the four-year "Renaissance Period" that began about a decade later, he clearly thought of these years as the acme of his ministerial career. What would lead to this self-assessment? I believe at least two factors come into play. The first and predictable element is that Westergreen was hitting his vocational stride. No longer a beginner in ministry, psychologically if not administratively under the mentorship of those with longer tenure, he was now in a position to exercise greater autonomy in decision-making with individual congregations, in establishing the seminary, and in editing *Sändebudet*. Within Methodism's connectional system, he was no longer trying to live up to the legacy of Jonas Hedstrom or looking to S. B. Newman for guidance. His intellectual and pastoral gifts were also being recognized by the larger church; this is evidenced in his being appointed to two of the largest Swedish Methodist congregations, being entrusted with the training of other immigrants for ministry, and being given the task of restarting and editing the newspaper.

The second factor, I believe, was one of which Westergreen himself may not have been entirely aware. During this period a major focus in his ministry was the newly arrived Scandinavian immigrant: organizing other clergy and congregations to address their immediate temporal needs, acclimatizing them to an unfamiliar culture through the newspaper, and preparing young men to minister to those who had not yet learned English. In the course of his work he was also articulating the theological differences between Wesleyan and Lutheran theology. This, naturally, was of greater interest to those who had left a state church behind in the

45. Leman, *Birth Order Book*, 14–15.

old country than it would have been to English-speaking Methodists in America. In the decades that followed Westergreen's "Golden Age," social service agencies and local governments gradually took on some of the physical needs of the poor, and fraternal organizations and newspapers, as well as secular entertainment, competed for the attention and loyalty of immigrants. In the "Golden Age," the Swedish Methodist seminary would not have existed without Westergreen; in subsequent years, he sat on the school board, attended examinations and graduation, and sometimes taught courses, but others took the reins of primary leadership. In the decade that followed, Westergreen was not less active or effective in ministry, but the challenges for his vocation and his family were different.

6

The Elder Brother

1876 to 1886

In sorrow and in joy, I would in thee, my Lord, abide;
Obey your statutes with a heart now wholly sanctified.[1]

DURING HIS LATER YEARS, Westergreen sketched an outline of his life divided into chapters to which he assigned titles but not dates. His "golden age" or "magnificent period" was distinguished by his vocational maturation, the groundbreaking work in establishing the Swedish Methodist Seminary, the cultivation of his literary and managerial skills in editing *Sändebudet* and working on other Swedish-language publications. It was also a period of growing involvement in social issues of the day, particularly the temperance movement and the Emigrant Aid Society.

Westergreen labeled the decade following this "the mixed period." In reconstructing his life map, it seems most likely that this period ran from approximately 1875 or 1876 to the Annual Conference in 1886. He gave no reason for this designation. He never referred to it as such in his daily journals, and his two-volume manuscript autobiography covered only the years from his birth until October 1866, so no clues can be found there. Nevertheless, in reviewing his ministry during the period, along with considering events in his personal and family life, several themes emerge that set it apart from the years that preceded and followed. First,

1. See Kingo, "Nu skall ej synden mera" [No longer shall sin hold me], 209.

Westergreen served as presiding elder over the Galesburg District and then the Chicago District.[2] It was a position of some authority that involved considerable travel; the schedule for second quarterly conferences printed in a January 1883 issue of *Sändebudet* shows the Chicago District extended west to Moline, Illinois, and east to Jamestown, New York. Instead of focusing pastoral care and administration on one or two congregations, he had to be conversant with the strengths and difficulties of many churches. He functioned as a superintendent or overseer among his peers, and occasionally had to exercise discipline on one or another of them. In his journals, Westergreen nearly always referred to clergy colleagues by the title "brother"; when he became presiding elder, that did not change, but Westergreen became "the elder brother."

He was elder brother in the more literal sense in his family of origin. For at least fifteen years Nels had regularly come to the rescue of his youngest brother, John, and the pattern continued during this period. In addition, however, his brother Andrew was disabled by depression for several months, and Alex/Erik now came to him for help when he was out of work and unable to support his family. Only Swan, still farming and serving as a lay preacher in western Illinois, did not come to him for aid in the midst of a crisis.

Another leitmotif characterizing this period was the further development and articulation of his sanctification theology. During the periods that he or Victor Witting edited *Sändebudet*, there were articles on various aspects of holiness on a regular basis, such as "Sker helgelsen ögonblickligen eller småningom?" (Does sanctification happen instantly or gradually?)[3] and "Huru wet du att du är helgad?" (How do you know that you are sanctified?) In 1876, when William Henschen was editor, he published at least three articles on Christian perfection. Two of these were by Westergreen, but stylistic evidence suggests the third, "Är du ett

2. The boundaries and names of Swedish Mission Districts were fluid in the early years of Swedish Methodism; in 1874, for example, the Illinois Central Conference included congregations located in Kansas, Iowa, Illinois, and Indiana. At the General Conference of 1876, a petition was approved for the Swedes to organize the Swedish Northwest Conference, and they divided into three new districts: Chicago (which included Galesburg and other western Illinois congregations), Kansas and Nebraska, and St. Paul. By 1893, there were five districts: Chicago, Burlington, Kansas, Nebraska, and Superior. At that time they divided the Swedish Northwest Conference into three annual conferences: Central, Western, and Northern.

3. Janes, "Sker helgelsen ögonblickligen eller småningom?" [Does sanctification happen instantly or gradually?], 2.

helgon?" (Are you a saint?) was by the editor.[4] In 1878 Westergreen attended the Holiness Convention in Moline. Seven years and several holiness meetings later, he wrote *Skillnaden På Sann Helighet och Religiös Svärmeri* (The difference between true holiness and religious fanaticism). It further sharpened his focus on what constituted an orthodox Wesleyan understanding of sanctification. In addition, the friendship that developed between Westergreen and E. A. Skogsbergh of the Mission Friends led to Westergreen contrasting Wesleyan theology with Waldenström's: a subdued and far less contentious echo of his debates with the Lutherans in Galesburg the previous decade.

The first few years of Westergreen's "mixed period" would be considered unsettling for almost any pastor. His change of appointments was more frequent than any previous period of his ministry. At the beginning of 1876 he was the editor of *Sändebudet* and preaching regularly, most often at the First/Market Street Church in Chicago, but also to the fledgling Fifth Avenue congregation on the south side. At Conference that year Henschen took over as editor and Westergreen was appointed to Geneva and Batavia, so he and his mother moved from what is now the Old Town neighborhood of Chicago to the Fox River valley, about forty-five miles to the west. In 1877, he was made the presiding elder of the Galesburg District, and given pastoral responsibility for Moline, Rock Island, and Geneseo. This made it necessary for him to move to Moline. Just one year later, in 1878, he was appointed to Fifth Avenue Church in Chicago, and moved again.[5]

A mitigating factor in the midst of these changes was Westergreen's degree of familiarity with the congregations and locales in question. His family had lived in St. Charles briefly in the 1850s, before moving to Rockford; he therefore knew the terrain around neighboring Geneva and Batavia, and the challenges Methodism had faced in establishing a congregation. Galesburg was also familiar ground; he had studied at Knox College, served the church, and owned property in the area. His brother Swan and his family still farmed in Knox County, and for a time brother Andrew served the church in Galva. He knew the Fifth Avenue Church

4. Henschen, "Är du ett helgon?" [Are you a saint?], 1.

5. The name of the church was not finalized until 1880, when it was designated Third Swedish ME Church of Chicago. Westergreen usually referred to it as Fifth Avenue, but in *Svenska Metodismen I Amerika*, it is called Sydsidan [South Side]. Adding to the confusion was the existence of several other Swedish Methodist churches on the south side of the city. These also went by more than one name.

because prior to its formal organization in 1875, when the congregation
was still meeting in a rented hall, he shared leadership of worship services
with Eric Shogren and Alfred Anderson.[6] And Westergreen had preached
in Moline as early as 1857. Like other Swedish Methodist clergy of the
time, he generally took itinerant ministry in stride, though he did express
disappointment about being sent to Moline at Conference in 1877.[7] Although he never states it directly, Westergreen's journals suggest that he
considered Chicago his home. He traveled extensively during this decade,
but did not express a desire to work or eventually retire somewhere else.

His pastoral schedule followed a predictable pattern. The first Monday in January began the Week of Prayer, with services every evening and
sermons on texts suggested by the Evangelical Alliance. Methodist clergy
met together on Mondays, usually at the Clark Street Church, now known
as the Chicago Temple or First United Methodist Church of Chicago.
From Westergreen's account, it appears that these were not primarily business meetings. Ministers took turns presenting papers or had discussion
on theological and pastoral subjects; for example, in 1879 Bishop Merrill
presented a paper on the atonement. At an 1886 meeting the bishop read
a paper against universalism and the liberalism of the times. The Swedish
Methodist clergy had monthly meetings. In addition to this, there were
district meetings of the Swedish clergy and various Conference-appointed
committees. Protracted meetings were often held early in the year, after
the Week of Prayer but before Lent began. For Westergreen, this period
often meant guest-preaching at former pastoral appointments or traveling
further afield. In 1876 he observed the Week of Prayer, and then traveled to Donovan and Beaver, where he preached three times and attended
quarterly conference. Of interest at this quarterly conference was that the
Beaver congregation voted unanimously in favor of a separate Swedish
Annual Conference. Westergreen then attended several meetings of the
building committee to consider erecting a structure for the Fifth Avenue
congregation. After brief trips to preach in Galesburg and Norway, Illinois, and two slightly longer trips to Moline, Westergreen limited himself
to the Chicago and Rockford areas until late June.

He was just as busy at home in Chicago. In addition to his own ministerial duties, he visited the sewing society and "sister meetings" on the
south side. During one week in April 1886 he went to the Union Park

6. Wallenius, *Historik över Fifth Avenue Svenska Metodist Församling i Chicago
1875–1917*, 3.

7. Westergreen, *Journals*, September 26, 1877.

Congregational Church on the near west side and heard Joseph Cook give a lecture on "the certainties in religion," and then to another lecture hall to hear Henry Ward Beecher give a lecture on the reign of the common people. In addition, went many times to witness the preaching of D. L. Moody and music of P. P. Bliss at Farwell Hall. The auditorium, located on Madison between Clark and LaSalle Streets, was named for John V. Farwell, treasurer of the YMCA. The main floor and gallery allegedly could accommodate three thousand people in theater seats rather than pews. On Pentecost, when attendance was small at Westergreen's nearby Methodist church, he wrote that he supposed many were at Moody's church, but it appears he was not competitive with the evangelist. Both men had been part of the Christian Commission and done chaplaincy work at Camp Douglas during the Civil War, though it is unclear whether they were personally acquainted. Now, more than ten years after the war ended, Westergreen wrote, "Heard Moody lecture at Farwell Hall in the evening. His subject was Daniel. It was a good lecture but not extraordinary in any way except for the earnestness that Mr. Moody seemed to have in the delivery of his lecture."[8] Moody had a previous connection with Swedes in Chicago; he allowed the Lutheran Mission Friends to use his building for some meetings in the 1860s.[9] He had also gained renown in Sweden, after news of his 1873 and 1875 preaching missions in London and other parts of the UK reached evangelicals in the Scandinavian Peninsula. His sermons were translated into Swedish and published in tracts and newspapers. Just as the Wesleyan revival in the eighteenth century was due in part to the hymns of Charles Wesley, so also Moody, teaming up with two gifted musicians, P. P. Bliss and Ira Sankey, added to his ability to draw and engage crowds.

A few days after attending Moody's services for the third time, Westergreen took the Michigan Central Grand Trunk and then the New York Central Railroads to Buffalo and on to New York City. He stayed with Daniel Salomon Sörlin and his wife. Sörlin (1830–1888) had become a Methodist in Sweden under the influence of Albert Ericson in 1868. He was working for a steamship company in Kalmar and serving as a lay preacher part-time when Victor Witting advised him to enter full-time ministry. Sörlin was ordained before emigrating to New York in order to work with O. G. Hedstrom on the Bethel Ship. Later in 1876 he

8. Westergreen, *Journals*, June 6, 1876.

9. Olsson, *By One Spirit*, 200. The fledgling denomination eventually became the Evangelical Covenant Church in America.

was reassigned to the May Street Church in Chicago, also known as Second Swedish Methodist Church. In addition to being a gifted preacher, Sörlin composed hymn texts and tunes, and at least two songbooks were published by him in the 1880s. A selection from his 1881 songbook, in which both text and tune were by Sörlin, is typical of his work:

There Is Yet Room

The Father's doorway is open
And you may enter therein.
So turn to home, for there is room,
Our Lord calls from within:

Refrain:
There is yet room! Yes, there is room
Why will you longer delay?
The greatest gift here awaits you;
Make haste! And enter today.

A heavenly choir is watching;
Why do you tarry, dear soul?
Leave all behind, the Savior, kind
Will heal and make you whole.

So turn toward home now, beloved.
In sin no longer remain.
Leave shame and guilt all behind you;
A great inheritance gain.

Now is the time, now the moment
To claim his peace and his grace.
Assured that one day in glory
To see his wonderful face.[10]

When Westergreen visited in late June of 1876, Sörlin arranged for him to preach on the Bethel Ship, at the Swedish Methodist Church in Brooklyn, and in English at the 27th Street Methodist Episcopal Church. In addition they visited a traveling preacher's Gospel tent somewhere in the city, and went to Madison Square, where "a great number of Swedes had

10. See Sörlin, "Ännu Rum" [There is yet room], 10.

gathered to serenade the Prince of Sweden."[11] From New York he and
Sörlin traveled to Philadelphia, where they met Victor Witting and attended a July Fourth celebration of one hundred years since the Declaration of Independence was signed. Westergreen stayed with his brother
John and his family, but returned to Chicago two days later without them,
although they had previously planned to move there.

Back in Chicago for most of the summer, Westergreen attended a
campmeeting in Lake Bluff, participated in the three-day Holiness Convocation on Wabash Avenue, and preached seven times in both English
and Swedish at the Des Plaines Campground during its summer meetings from August 21 to 30. At least two of his seven sermon texts had
to do with the work of the Holy Spirit and/or holiness. The manuscript
of one sermon has survived. Its text is John 7:37–39. Drawing on the
text's metaphor of living water, Westergreen asserts that through faith,
the Christian can be filled and satisfied just as thirst can be satisfied:

> We must not only believe in God's institution, or the work of
> grace, but in Christ personally. We must believe in Christ and
> what God has done for us in him. We must believe in Christ as
> the Scriptures bear witness to him. . . . Such belief brings about
> perfect satisfaction and rest in Christ. We have the witness that
> we are children of God, according to Romans 8:15–16, and the
> indwelling and filling to holiness.[12]

One clue that it is indeed the sermon preached at the campmeeting
is the abrupt ending after the word *tillämpning* (application); in sermons
preached at protracted meetings and campmeetings, an exhorter immediately followed the preacher's sermon and made application of the main
points and an invitation. The Swedish Methodists did not yet have a tabernacle on the grounds, but held their worship services in a large tent. At
the close of the campmeeting everyone marched around the grounds and
shook hands: a custom observed by the National Campmeeting Association for the Promotion of Holiness. Westergreen wrote in his journal:

> Broke up the campmeeting and went home in the forenoon.
> This has been one of the best campmeetings I have been on for

---

11. Westergreen, *Journals*, June 27, 1876. Presumably this was the future Gustav V,
who would have been eighteen years old in 1876.

12. Westergreen, sermon on John 7:37–39, August 1876.

a long time. When I came home, I felt my own soul blessed by believing in Jesus Christ. Blessed be his holy name.[13]

Both Sörlin and William Henschen, who was then editor of *Sändebudet*, participated in the campmeeting with Westergreen. He did not make note of his fellow preachers' sermon texts or topics, but Henschen's sympathy with the holiness movement is demonstrated by both his presence there and his articles in *Sändebudet* mentioned earlier. For example, in "Är Du Ett Helgon?" (Are you a saint?) he wrote:

> Reader! If you are not becoming a saint in this life, and weighed as such by God in the hour of death, you are by no means fit for the kingdom of heaven. What is a sanctified person, if not a saint? The Bible says: "Without holiness shall no one see the Lord." Hebrews 12:1.... Being sanctified means being not of the world, and having God's Spirit dwelling in your heart.... God's Spirit shall perform the work in you and with you.[14]

There are at least two similarities between Henschen's articulation of holiness theology and Westergreen's during this period. First, there is a balance between divine and human activity. Being "not of the world" is possible because of the prior sanctifying activity of the Holy Spirit. Second, his supporting texts in the essay are from New Testament epistles; Westergreen also drew heavily though not exclusively from the epistles when preaching on sanctification. Unlike Westergreen, Henschen was not consistent in using the same Swedish Bible translations in his quotations, suggesting he may have been doing his own translation.

In September 1876, Andrew Westergreen married Selma Hanson (1854–1930) in Keokuk, Iowa. His elder brother was present for the ceremony, but Bro. A. J. Anderson officiated, assisted by someone named Wheeler. A few days later, when Annual Conference met in Pekin, Illinois, there was a nearly unanimous vote to establish a separate Swedish Conference. Westergreen was not enthusiastic about the idea, just as he had expressed reservations when the congregation in Beaver had voted for it earlier in the year. He nevertheless expressed the hope that the Lord would work it out for the best. He recorded no reasons for his misgivings. After this Conference, Nels was appointed to Geneva and Batavia, and Andrew to Swedona.

---

13. Westergreen, *Journals*, August 30, 1876.
14. Henschen, "Är Du Ett Helgon?" [Are you a saint?], 1.

The rest of the year seems to have unfolded without incident in his ministry, but he did make note of the terrible railroad accident in Ashtabula, Ohio, at the end of December. A trestle bridge collapsed and nearly one hundred people died as a result of the fall and resulting fire. Among the casualties were Moody's songwriter, P. P. Bliss, and his wife.

Though he had now moved west of Chicago, Westergreen continued his ecumenical interests along with his activities in the temperance and holiness movements. The following spring he had his first recorded connection with the "Mission Friends." This name originated in Sweden as a Pietistic renewal movement led by Paul Peter Waldenström (1838–1917) and others within the state church. In the United States, it was initially known as the Swedish Evangelical Lutheran Mission Synod. Westergreen had almost certainly encountered them before; they had organized as a society as early as 1868 in Swede Bend, Iowa, and soon established a society in Chicago. Their first church building, on the near north side, was dedicated in 1869, and before long there were societies of Mission Friends in the same immigrant neighborhoods and towns that had Swedish Methodist congregations. It was in March 1877 that Westergreen noted he had met Erik August Skogsbergh on a train when he was traveling to Galva. Skogsbergh (1850–1939), who was born in Värmland and converted at age nineteen, began preaching throughout Småland and Västergötland provinces while he was still a student at a Bible institute. His zeal, oratorical skills, and musical gifts drew enormous crowds in that part of Sweden.[15] In 1876 the Swedish Evangelical Lutheran Mission Association in Chicago persuaded the lay preacher to emigrate to Chicago and minister to immigrants at their church on Franklin Street, not far from the Swedish Methodists' church at Market and Oak. Skogsbergh came with considerable reluctance, but soon established himself as a charismatic preacher among his fellow Swedes. His congregation was larger than the building could accommodate, so he approached D. L. Moody and asked if he could use the evangelist's church when Moody was not holding his own services. He soon earned the nickname "the Swedish Moody." In 1877, the board of the Swedish Evangelical Lutheran Mission Synod received a request for Skogsbergh's ordination from the Franklin Street congregation. He passed an examination before a committee and was ordained on January 22, 1877, in Princeton, Illinois.[16]

15. Olsson, *By One Spirit*, 158.

16. Dahlhielm, *Burning Heart*, 83.

That same year he purchased three city lots at 30th and LaSalle Street, and construction began on what became Tabernacle Church. Skogsbergh was in ministry in Chicago until 1883, when he moved to Minneapolis.

The relationship that developed between Westergreen and the Mission Friends was an interesting one. Skogsbergh was not mentioned by name again in the 1877 journal, but in the years that followed, it is clear Westergreen and Skogsbergh worked together in ministry on the south side of Chicago. The nearby Swedish Methodist congregation, organized in 1875 but meeting in rented rooms for several years, was located at what would now be 33rd and Wells Street, just a few blocks from the Tabernacle.[17] Westergreen wrote of union services held by the Methodists and Mission Friends as early as 1878. He was conversant with Waldenström's atonement theology and mentioned enjoying discussions of it with various people in 1877 and 1883, but noted in July 1879 that he had explained to someone "the reasons we cannot accept it."[18] After moving back to Chicago following Annual Conference in 1878, Westergreen's involvement with Skogsbergh and the Mission Friends was deeper and more sustained than it ever seemed to be with the Swedish Lutherans. He preached at the Tabernacle as often as eleven times per year. Sometimes Skogsbergh would preach and Westergreen exhort afterward, and other times it was the reverse order. Westergreen was a guest at Skogsbergh's wedding at the end of May 1879, as well as the ordination of ministers at the Tabernacle the following month. The two ministers met with each other apart from worship, and discussed how their respective missionary efforts among Scandinavian immigrants were going. Their only point of disagreement on theological matters was recorded in April of 1881, when Westergreen wrote, "I was at the meeting in the Mission Tabernacle in the afternoon and evening. Spoke some in the afternoon. Could not agree with them in regard to the first resurrection. Can agree with them more in their views about the millennium."[19] The lack of accord on this doctrine did not prove to be an impediment to the friendship, since Westergreen continued to be invited to preach for Skogsbergh. A somewhat surprising critique by Westergreen's brother John provides a fleeting glimpse of a Saturday evening service at the Tabernacle:

17. Westergreen and his colleagues referred to this as the Fifth Avenue Church that was the street name at the time. It was changed from Fifth to Wells in 1916. Construction of the Dan Ryan Expressway in 1961–62 replaced the intersection altogether.

18. Westergreen, *Journals*, July 4, 1879.

19. Westergreen, *Journals*, April 16, 1881.

> Brother John and I went over to the Mission Tabernacle. Mr.
> Franson spoke first, after which they had the sacrament. I par-
> took with them. Brother John did not like their meeting as well
> as ours. He did not like especially their reciting scripture texts.
> He thought it broke too much the solemn silence which ought
> to prevail on such an occasion.[20]

Did Westergreen's younger brother really make such a remark, or were
the words merely attributed to him? Only a few days earlier, the elder
brother had written, "[I] felt very solemn in regard to my brother John.
O, that he may soon be saved": a sentiment that seems incongruent with
a desire for more silent reverence in worship.

Westergreen's association with the Mission Friends extended beyond Skogsbergh. He, Skogsbergh, and C. A. Björk participated in and
spoke at Swedish Union meetings at Moody's church in 1881. He attended the organizational meetings of what became the Swedish Evangelical
Mission Covenant in February, 1885 at the Tabernacle, and noted that he
heard two preachers: Brother Carlson from Kansas and Brother Peterson
from Oakland, Nebraska. His one critical comment was "They spoke
well enough, but there is very little system in their preaching."[21] Two
days later he was at Farwell Hall, where the Mission Friends held a large
union meeting. Here Westergreen heard David Nyvall, S. W. Sundberg,
and Skogsbergh, and his report was more favorable. The cordial relationship between Westergreen and the Mission Friends was uninterrupted
in the ensuing decades; he continued to preach at the Tabernacle and
other Mission Friends' churches. When Paul Peter Waldenström gave a
lecture to a packed auditorium at North Park College in September 1905,
Westergreen was invited to sit on the platform near the speaker.[22]

Although he was closer to the Mission Friends than to other non-
Methodist groups, Westergreen's interest in Christian unity and participating in others denominations' worship was ongoing. Between 1877 and
1879 he preached at Baptist and Lutheran churches in Moline and other
towns, a Presbyterian church, at Norwegian Methodist churches, and at
numerous denominational and nondenominational campmeetings in
the city and rural areas. In addition, he attended the Holiness Convention
in Moline, healing services at Quinn Chapel,[23] the German Methodist

20. Westergreen, *Journals*, January 22, 1881.

21. Westergreen, *Journals*, February 20, 1885.

22. Westergreen, *Journals*, September 2, 1905.

23. Quinn Chapel African Methodist Episcopal Church, organized in 1844, is the

Conference, the Augustana Lutheran Synod meeting, and various nondenominational "Gospel tents" in the city. He wrote an essay on Christian
unity in October 1879, which was presented in Minneapolis. Unfortunately, this document was not preserved among his papers.

As noted earlier, Westergreen's brother John stayed with him and
attended church for an interval in 1881. His moments of serious purpose and stability were the exception rather than the rule during these
years. He seemed incapable of settling down in any place or vocation.
After being released from the penitentiary in Philadelphia in 1874, John
did not find regular work to support himself and his wife, Annie Black
Westergreen. He spent some time in Chicago, and at the beginning of
1876 left for Philadelphia so that he and Annie could pack up their belongings and settle permanently in Chicago or western Illinois. This is
where Nels or Swan hoped to line up employment for him. Instead, John
wrote from Pennsylvania and asked for money for train fare. John and
Annie still did not come, even after receiving the funds and having a
visit from Nels in July. There was no word from them until the following
May. John appeared in Chicago briefly and without his wife in June of
1877, but then took off for North Dakota, returning to Chicago in time
to move to Moline with his elder brother and mother. After a few weeks
working there, he quit his job and went to Houston, Texas. Meanwhile,
Annie was relying on financial support from her family of origin and her
brother-in-law. John was out of touch for a year, and finally wrote to his
family from Cheyenne, Wyoming. It seems his wife joined him there at
some point, for the correspondence in 1880 appears to have been with
both John and Annie.

John's erratic and often irresponsible *modus operandi* continued
unabated during this decade. By 1881 Annie was back in Philadelphia
while John, after a brief stay in Chicago, went to Galesburg and then dis-
appeared for five weeks. Westergreen next mentioned him early in 1882,
when John had returned to his wife. By 1883 he had a job working on a
railroad, and Annie wrote Nels and said she had not heard from John
for three months. The following year he wrote to his family from Ogden,
Utah, explaining that he had left Pueblo, Colorado, and was contemplat-
ing a trip home in the fall after he visited the World's Fair in New Orleans.
The journals do not mention if he ever made it to either place, but John
next wrote to his family from San Francisco early in 1885. He asked for

---

oldest black congregation in the city of Chicago.

money, and his elder brother helped him once again. There was a second bailout request in May, when he claimed he had pawned all his belongings. He visited his mother and elder brother three times in 1886, always requesting money so his wife in Philadelphia could come to Chicago.

The other Westergreen brothers did not leave correspondence or daily journals, so we cannot describe their relationship with the youngest brother. Based on the journals left by Nels, along with stories that have been passed along to succeeding generations of the Westergreen family, it seems that Nels was the only brother to whom John turned for regular assistance. He was the eldest and had been working the longest. Nels was also the one who took responsibility for Hanna, their mother, after Ola's death in 1874. The other brothers were married and all except John had children, while Nels remained single. With no other dependents to feed and house, Nels must have seemed the logical choice to assume his mother's care and come to the financial rescue of the wayward sibling.

Andrew, the next-to-youngest brother, was serving the church in Galva at the beginning of this period, though he preached on a circuit that included Wataga, Altona, Peoria, and Kewanee. At Annual Conference in 1879 he was appointed to Bishop Hill, which seems to have been one of the happiest periods in his ministry. Like his elder brother, he was a gifted preacher, and also a shrewd fundraiser and organizer. During his time at Bishop Hill, he raised more than $1,600 to build a new parsonage, sold the old parsonage, and had it moved across the village.[24] Though shorter and somewhat stockier than Nels, he had an attractive face and darker, wavy hair. Judging from the multitude of extant photographs of him from the 1860s and 1870s, each sporting a slightly different hairstyle and beard, one may speculate that he was preoccupied with his appearance. He and Selma had two sons, Edmund Theodore ("Teddie") and Wesley. After being moved to Swedona for one year, he was appointed to Rockford at the Conference held in Minneapolis in 1883. This was the congregation to which his family had belonged nearly thirty years earlier. It was at this point that crises began to unfold and his elder brother had to step in and help.

In mid-January 1884, Selma became ill. The family attributed it to a difficult pregnancy and was not unduly worried. About a week later she gave birth to a stillborn child. Nels and Andrew conducted the graveside service at the Swedish cemetery in Rockford. In October of the following

24. *The Messenger: Bishop Hill Community Methodist Church*, 25.

year, Andrew wrote to his brother and said that Teddie was sick with diphtheria. That he contracted a highly contagious disease was not surprising; without most modern vaccines or knowledge of how diseases were spread, people living in urban areas were particularly vulnerable. In addition to Rockford's cholera epidemic in 1853, there was a scarlet fever epidemic in 1881. The city's first sewer lines were not laid until 1886. The city leaders began to quarantine people for smallpox and scarlet fever in 1882, but did nothing to halt the spread of diphtheria.[25] Records do not show how many children contracted the illness in 1885, but Teddie became ill on October 16, and a few days later symptoms appeared in his younger brother, Wesley. The extended family waited for word of the prognosis, and received a telegram on October 25 that Teddie had died at 1:00 that afternoon, a few weeks short of his eighth birthday. Westergreen and his mother traveled to Rockford, where they met Selma's sister at the depot before going to the house. The funeral was the following day, with burial at the Swedish Cemetery. Westergreen wrote:

> At 3:00 in the afternoon Theodore's funeral was appointed. I tried to preach his funeral sermon from Revelation 22:5 but I was too much excited to succeed well. Bro. Lindskog spoke some afterward. I performed the last rite at the graveyard over little Teddie. The other boy, Wesley, was also sick but he is better.[26]

Westergreen was more deeply attached at this point to brother Andrew's sons than to Swan's offspring in Knox County. The next day he wrote:

> O, how we all miss Teddie. What an intelligent and pleasant child he was. . . . I spent part of the forenoon with Andrew and Selma, then went to Chicago. Wesley was better today, thank God. But O, how empty the house seems without Teddie. We feel the loss of him; we miss his happy face, his cheerful smile, his kind and clear look. How much more shall the parents feel it! No wonder they are sad and often weeping. May God comfort them.[27]

A few weeks later Andrew sent him a photograph of Teddie, surrounded by the flowers that were on his coffin. The other boy, Wesley, eventually made a complete recovery, but Andrew's difficulties and grief did not subside. He and possibly Selma sank into a depression that made continuing in ministry problematic. Four months after the funeral, Nels

25. Empereur, *Development of Public Health*, 4.

26. Westergreen, *Journals*, October 26, 1885.

27. Westergreen, *Journals*, October 27, 1885.

traveled to Rockford to conduct a series of services at Andrew's church. His brother and sister-in-law did not attend them all, and Andrew was described as "unwell." A month later Selma wrote to Nels, begging him to come immediately, because Andrew was "in critical condition." He went, and was told his brother had not slept for nine or ten nights. Nels took him back to Chicago, where Andrew stayed with his elder brother and mother, completely bedridden. A doctor visited him and prescribed some medicine to quiet his nerves and help him sleep. A week later the doctor said his condition had deteriorated, and brought in another physician for a second opinion. They feared that "his mind would give way entirely." There was no psychotherapy available at the time; by coincidence, Andrew's first breakdown occurred in the same year Sigmund Freud began therapeutic practice and research in Vienna. Andrew remained under his brother's roof for over two months. Selma and young Wesley came and visited for several days in May, and brother John also visited for a short time. The overcrowding and caregiving proved to be too much for Hanna, who was now in her late seventies and also prone to depression. Nels took her to stay with friends for awhile, leaving him to take care of his brother and provide hospitality for the expanded household, all while serving as presiding elder of the Chicago District and leading the Fifth Avenue congregation. Andrew was finally well enough to return to Rockford later in May, though it is doubtful he resumed ministry; the 1886 conference journal lists him as a member, but with supernumerary status. In 1888, when he and Selma had another baby that lived only a few weeks, he appeared more resilient. His next major breakdown happened about sixteen years later, though he periodically suffered from bouts of depression. Once again, his elder brother took care of him and Selma.

Alex/Erik, the brother closest in age to Nels, was of necessity as self-sufficient as his older brother in many ways, but he, too, turned to Nels in crisis. Alex had remained on the East Coast after Nels and Swan made their way to the Midwest to rejoin the rest of the family in the 1850s. He had married in 1860 and had one child. As noted in the previous chapter, in 1875 Alex somehow lost all that he had. Unable to find other work, he left his wife, Eunice, and daughter, Annie, behind and came to Chicago to enlist his elder brother's help, arriving the day before Christmas and staying with Nels and Hanna. Between Christmas and New Year's Eve, the two men went out looking without success for some new employment. Nothing suitable seemed to be available in Chicago, but Nels and Andrew heard of someone in Galva who was looking for workers. Alex went there and worked in Galva a short time before moving to Galesburg, finding employment as a police officer. He then brought Eunice and Annie to make a new home there. When Nels went to Galesburg twice in July 1878, he was surprised to learn that his brother's family had gone on a month-long journey, possibly back to Massachusetts to visit Eunice's family. The fact that he had told no one in his family about the trip suggests the relationship was not as close as the one between Nels and Andrew. Though not as flighty as his youngest brother, Alex, too, seemed to have difficulty settling into a vocation. For a time he worked for a company called Brown's. In 1881 Alex wrote to Nels and said he couldn't stand the job any longer, and was returning to police work. Early in 1882 he decided to move back to the Boston area. After packing and shipping their belongings, he and his family stayed with Nels and Hanna until their departure. It was an emotional parting:

> This has been a solemn day. When mother in the forenoon parted with my brother Alex and his family perhaps for the last time on earth, no wonder they were quite overcome by their feelings. Alex and his family [left] . . . a little after midnight. May God give them a safe journey to their destination.[28]

Once back in familiar territory, Alex was hired by the Hingham Police Department and both he and his financial situation became more stable. He was active in the church and became president of the local temperance reform club.[29]

Three of the brothers, then, depended on Nels to varying degrees during his "mixed period." John's reliance on his elder brother was nothing new, and Alex's vocational crisis was eventually resolved. It was Andrew, the brother in ministry as well as by blood, whose needs placed the greatest emotional as well as physical demand on Nels. An unexpected result of Andrew's crises was the development of a closer relationship between his wife, Selma, and Nels. Prior to this, Westergreen's journals acknowledged her presence at family gatherings, but there was no particular affinity mentioned. The deepening of their friendship proved to be mutually beneficial in later years.

28. Westergreen, *Journals*, March 13, 1882.

29. Westergreen never specifies whether his brother united with a Methodist church, Swedish or otherwise. Alex and Swan had attended the Congregational Church of Truro after they were separated from the rest of the family in 1852. The Swedish Methodist church closest to Hingham was in Quincy, but it was not established until 1886.

Aside from the demands of family life, in the early 1880s Westergreen continued to be invested in the temperance movement and relief
for the poor, particularly immigrants. The temperance banner was flying
in Methodist societies long before Westergreen's birth; J. Gordon Melton
notes that John Wesley told the early Methodists that wine or beer in
moderation was allowed, rather than insisting on total abstinence,
though he did oppose the use of distilled spirits. The temperance movement evolved in the years after Wesley's death, both in Illinois and the
rest of the United States.[30] The General Conference of 1836 prohibited
ministers from making or selling spirituous liquors. The consumption of
alcohol sufficient to compromise a minister's effectiveness was a major
cause of dismissal; nevertheless, there was not a general ban on *all* drinking, particularly for laity. The denomination's observance of Temperance
Sunday on the last Sunday in June dates from 1868. In 1871 Westergreen
had scolded John Gabrielson, one of his seminary students, for his use of
strong drink, but the matter was eventually resolved and Gabrielson went
on to be ordained. In the 1880s, concurrent with the rise of the Women's
Christian Temperance Union, the mood shifted from temperance to total
abstinence. Under the leadership of Frances Willard, a Methodist living
in Evanston who became national president of the WCTU, the cause also
became political as well as ecclesiastical and personal. More than once,
Westergreen demonstrated his commitment at the ballot box:

> I went early and deposited my ticket, and in so doing, I voted the
> straight Republican ticket, as I have done the last twenty years.
> If there had been any show for a prohibition ticket I would have
> gone for that for the sake of the principle.[31]

Individual Methodist congregations had their own temperance societies, though these do not appear to have been linked to the WCTU.
Westergreen wrote a temperance hymn in 1884, which was probably sung
when he preached a temperance sermon in Geneva at the end of March.
The local Lutheran minister also spoke. The hymn contains allusions to
Prov 23:31–32, and was included in the *Swedish Methodist Hymnbook*,
published in 1884 and 1887:

---

30. Melton, *Log Cabins to Steeples*, 304.
31. Westergreen, *Journals*, November 4, 1884.

Where are misery and groaning?
Where are hearts oppressed with pain?
Where do souls in needless anguish
Shed remorse's tears again?

There, in much inebriation,
There, where wine and spirits flow;
After brief exhilaration
Freedom, reason, sense all go.

Do not look on wine, I pray you,
As it shimmers in the glass,
As it beckons to the eye and
Sweetly o'er the tongue doth pass.

But it quickly turns upon you
Like a deadly serpent stings;
And, as Scripture warns the drinker
Everlasting peril brings.

Therefore, make the resolution
Walk in pure sobriety.
Seek and save the lost around you,
From temptation help them flee.

For alone we do not struggle
God's own power is on our side;
He will give us holy victory
That his name be glorified.[32]

Andrew Westergreen also preached and participated in temperance meetings. Once Westergreen became presiding elder of the Chicago District, and much of his preaching was tied to conducting quarterly conferences, he wrote less about the issue, but his commitment to it did not waver. Melton speculates that the late nineteenth-century temperance movement was linked to anti-Catholic sentiment.[33] There is minimal evidence of this in Westergreen's writing, though in his declining years he was prone to attribute civic disturbances or crime to Italian

---

32. See Westergreen, "Hvar är klagan, hvar är jemmer" [Where are misery and groaning], #579.

33. Melton, *Log Cabins to Steeples*, 306.

or Irish immigrants, both of which would have been overwhelmingly Roman Catholic.[34]

Westergreen's concern for the poor and the immigrant followed a trajectory similar to his commitment to temperance in this period, that is, while his interest in their needs did not diminish, his involvement while serving as presiding elder was perhaps less hands-on and more institutional. During a preaching tour of Marinette, Menomonie, and Menekaunee, Wisconsin, in May of 1880, he observed many Swedish immigrants waiting at the Marinette depot. He believed some were heading to the mines in Michigan but more were headed for Minnesota. In Chicago, in addition to being active in the Emigrant Aid Society, he would make trips to the depot in Chicago to ask if any immigrants had arrived, needing assistance. Depending on their needs, he would take the indigent to a county agent to try to arrange for lodging, draw upon the Relief Fund, and even occasionally provide temporary shelter on church property.

His commentary on and involvement in social issues extended beyond temperance and aid to immigrants. In 1884, he and the Reverend Bernard Swanson discussed starting a monthly Christian Workers' Society on the south side, similar to the one already in existence on the north side.[35] Westergreen preached regularly at the Rock Island car shops and in the mission house by the McCormick Harvesting Machine Company, and ministered to the temporal needs of those who worked in both places. This is not to suggest that Westergreen had socialist leanings similar to those of Samuel Fielden, a British-born American Methodist lay preacher in Chicago at the time. On May 4, 1886, there was a nonviolent demonstration of workers at Haymarket Square. They were striking in support of an eight-hour work day. The previous day, police had killed one worker during a demonstration at the McCormick factory. Mayor Carter Harrison attended part of the Haymarket demonstration and called it peaceful. Samuel Fielden had just finished addressing the crowd when someone—the identity of the person was never proven—threw a bomb that killed seven police officers and at least four demonstrators, and injured many others. Westergreen did not mention Fielden by name, but his journal entry reflects the common bias reflected in the local press:

34. In June of 1894, he attributed the disturbance outside a Methodist tent-meeting in the city to "foreign-born Catholics, who did not understand our language."

35. This is not to be confused with the World Movement of Christian Workers, which is a Roman Catholic organization.

Last night there was a terrible riot on the west side between the
anarchists and the police. Several were killed and wounded on
both sides. There is a great deal of excitement in the city today.
Bro. Wigren came in the afternoon and we went in the evening
to the casino rink to hear Moody, but found it had been closed
by order of the mayor on account of the late troubles.[36]

Along with seven others, Fielden was tried, convicted of murder, and
sentenced to death on the grounds they conspired to work with the unknown bomber. Only four were actually executed, and one committed
suicide in prison. The sentence of Fielden and the others was appealed
and later commuted to life in prison by Illinois's governor, Richard James
Oglesby. Westergreen reflected on the executions in November of 1887:

I heard that Ling, one of the anarchists, had committed suicide
in the jail by placing a cartridge in his mouth and igniting it.
What a miserable end. . . . When I read today in the papers of the
defiant hardness of the five men who were executed in Chicago
yesterday to the very last, yes, in the very moment of death—I
have felt very strange the whole day. It is certainly a mystery, for
generally in view of death stubbornness either gives way to de-
spair or melts into repentance, but here it seemed to be neither.[37]

Based on his concern for immigrants, his desire to organize workers
into Christian societies, and his zeal for abstinence from alcohol, one might
conjecture that for Westergreen, growing in the Christian faith went hand
in hand with improvement of one's general lot in life. This would be congruent with his colporteur work after he arrived in Chicago, his agreeing to
start a Swedish seminary for the preparation of men for ministry, and his
writing and publishing. Both education and edification were components
of a better life and stronger faith, as well the path to upward mobility.

Westergreen served on the board of the Swedish Theological School
(as it was initially named): an assignment that was not without its head-
aches. One significant problem was that the school was "homeless" for
its first eleven years, holding classes in the community where its professor was already appointed to a church. From 1870 to 1872, that meant
"*den gamla stugan*" (the old cottage) in Galesburg, described in a history of the seminary as low and small enough that it could accommodate

36. Westergreen, *Journals*, May 5, 1886.
37. Westergreen, *Journals*, November 10 and 12, 1887.

only the professor; students had to find lodging independently.[38] Then classes moved several times to various locations, depending on where the minister who would be teaching was otherwise appointed. At the Annual Conference held in Bishop Hill in 1881, the clergy were united in wanting the seminary to have a permanent location and its own building, but not in agreement as to where it should be. It was finally put to a vote, with thirteen in favor of Galva and twenty-one for Evanston. The selection of Evanston was providential, as it was already home to a Methodist university with a substantial library, and the city abuts the transportation hub and cultural offerings of Chicago. Galva, on the other hand, had three railroad lines running through it, but its population was just over 2,000 in 1880, and the closest academic library was in Galesburg, some twenty-six miles away. C. G. Nelson was appointed the agent for raising funds for a building. The trustees of Northwestern University agreed to a ninety-nine-year lease at nominal cost on a large piece of land near the northern edge of campus: now the location of the university's Technological Institute at 2145 Sheridan Road. The building was not completed until October 1883.[39] The syllabus from 1905 describes the seminary's location and mission in grandiloquent terms:

> This "department" of Northwestern is hid away in a quiet little nook "twixt the Lake and the Rubicon"—otherwise called the Valley of Hinnon—away from the clamor and din of commercial life, away from the glare and scrutiny of publicity, away from the gaze of all but the peaceful, beauty-loving lakeside strollers of the upper campus. It is the Valhalla of a small band of theological descendants of the daring Vikings, who labor early and late to equip themselves as their ancestors did, for conquest. . . . Soon they will go forth, not in the strength of grim Odin—whose name they still hold in kindly remembrance—but by the might of Jehovah of Hosts to spread consternation, to be sure, but among the works of wickedness and ignorance only. Their van will be composed of a triumvirate of doughty warriors, who though diminutive in stature yet are magnificent in bearing and ability. Following them will be a company of stalwart sons of Svea, led by him who found his name in a field of rye. Then will come an indomitable band of Smalandings with their leader of exidental [sic] origin. The minors with their superabundance of zeal and inexperience, together with their acknowledged

38. Alfred Anderson, *Historiskt föredrag*, 9–10.
39. Liljegren et al., *Historik öfver Svenska Metodismen*, 110.

leader, who dreams of the "pale moonlight of Melrose," will be suppressed at the rear. Now and then one will be stricken, but in the quiet of Valhalla, planted sweetly twixt the Rubicon and the Lake, others will be preparing to take their places and the conquest will go on adding to the domains of the Kingdom.[40]

Before construction of the building, classes were held in borrowed rooms: probably in the Swedish Methodist church in Evanston, given that examinations and graduations often took place there. The close of the academic year was a multiday event. In 1888, it began with a Sunday baccalaureate sermon by the rector. On Tuesday and Wednesday there were public examinations in elocution and general subjects, and on Wednesday evening they had orations by the graduates, songs, prayers, and presentation of diplomas. The actual graduation service was not always at the Evanston church but moved several times to various locations: Fisk Hall, Memorial Hall, and even First Swedish Methodist of Chicago, until 1907. At that time, a larger seminary building was erected at Lincoln Street and Orrington Avenue, a few blocks from the original address. All the closing exercises were in Swedish until the early years of the twentieth century, when they had a morning worship service in English and an evening one in Swedish.

Since he was living in Chicago again, the school directors decided Westergreen ought to resume teaching the second level students, meeting with them on Wednesday and Friday mornings.[41] This presented some additional difficulties. First, he was living on the south side, and had to rely on public transportation to get to Evanston and his classes. This added significantly to the time commitment involved. Second, the students in the ministerial course of study were also serving local churches part-time. The Evanston congregation known today as Emmanuel United Methodist Church was led by students for the first years of its existence, but as was the case when the seminary was at Galesburg, some students were serving further afield. This occasionally made convening them for class a challenge. On one occasion Westergreen noted that only two of the four enrolled in the course were present. *Svenska Metodismen I Amerika* states that Westergreen taught "various subjects," which most likely means all subjects. A bibliography for the ministerial course of study appeared in *Sändebudet* in the 1880s. Prior to being received on trial as preachers,

40. *Syllabus Brochure, 1905*, n.p.
41. Westergreen, *Journals*, May 20 and September 16, 1880.

candidates were expected to have studied George Rawlinson's *Ancient History*, William Smith's *Old Testament History* and *New Testament History*, Marcius Wilson's *History of the United States*, Abel Stevens's *American Methodism*, C. Heaven's *Rhetoric*, Samuel Wakefield's *Christian Theology*, and the *Discipline of the Methodist Episcopal Church*. The textbooks for the second level, which Westergreen taught, included the following:

- F. G. Hibbard, *On Baptism*
- Francis Wayland, *The Elements of Moral Science*
- D. D. Whebon, *The Freedom of the Will*
- Bishop Emory, *Defense of Our Fathers*
- Samuel Porter, *Compendium of Methodism*
- L. L. Gandsen, *The Bible: The Divine Origin and Inspiration*
- George Rawlinson, *The Historical Evidences of the Truth of the Scripture Recorded*
- William G. Shedd, *Homiletics and Pastoral Theology*[42]

Even more telling is the list of readings for the first level of study:

- Watson's *Theological Institutes*
- John Wesley, *Christian Perfection*
- George Babbington, *History of the Church*
- Oliver S. Munsell, *Psychology; or, The Science of the Mind*
- *Wesley's Sermons*
- Abel Stevens, *History of Methodism*
- L. T. Townsend, *The Sword and Garment*[43]

The bibliography, particularly for the first year of study, is emphatically Methodist/Wesleyan rather than giving a broader perspective of Protestant theology. Norwood identifies Watson's *Institutes* as emphasizing the Wesleyan concept of sanctification.[44] Singling out one particular writing of Wesley's, *Christian Perfection*, signals the importance of the doctrine for Swedish Methodists in America. In the prerequisite

---

42. *Sändebudet*, January 25, 1886, 4.

43. *Sändebudet*, January 25, 1886, 4.

44. Norwood, *Story of American Methodism*, 293.

readings, one jumps from New Testament history to American history, with nothing in between. From a twenty-first-century perspective, it is easy to identify what is left out, but it is more instructive to consider the nature of ministerial formation that *is* suggested by the bibliography. For example, the centrality of preaching is reflected by textbooks on rhetoric, homiletics, and Wesley's sermons. Knowledge of the *Book of Discipline*, plus a period of supervised ministry in local churches and some lectures during the third year of study, were considered sufficient preparation for church administration.

The list of textbooks is reflected in the curriculum itself. A circular used for fundraising in the late 1880s includes the courses offered in each of the three years.

Junior Year:

- Theology—introduction to systematic theology
- Biblical Introduction
- History—ancient and modern
- Geography—physical and political
- Swedish Language—grammar, reading, dictation, translation from English
- English Language

Middle Year:

- Systematic Theology
- Church History
- Swedish Language—grammar completed and reviewed, rhetoric, and essay once a month
- Elocution
- Sacred History
- Biblical Archaeology
- English Language

Senior Year:

- Swedish Language—literature, rhetoric, and essay every third week
- Dogmatics—completed and reviewed

- Church Polity—ME discipline and lectures
- Pastoral Theology
- Homiletics—the preparation and construction of sermons
- Hermeneutics
- Church History—completed and reviewed
- Elocution
- Sacred History
- English language[45]

As can be seen from the bibliography and course list, prospective students were required to be proficient in reading English, but were also required to take courses in English and Swedish during all three years of study. When Westergreen started the seminary in 1870, his three students had to study the Swedish language because they had lost fluency in their native tongue after years in America. The fact that nearly twenty years later the seminary had courses in Swedish *and* English suggests that their ministry post-seminary would be primarily to newly arrived immigrants with minimal competency in English. One could also infer that two classes in elocution reflects the hope that graduates would be able to hold their own among American Methodist clergy peers, as well as the centrality of preaching among Swedish Methodists.

Westergreen continued to write and lecture while he was teaching, serving as presiding elder of the Chicago District, and ministering to the congregation at the Fifth Avenue Church. He was on the hymnbook committee for the Swedish Methodist Conference, which met regularly from 1880 through 1884, when they finished working on proofs for the new hymnal. His friends Victor Witting and Daniel Sörlin were also on the committee. Witting had already independently published at least two volumes of songs for worship. *Andeliga Sånger för Böne, Klass, och Förlängda Möten* (Spiritual songs for prayer, class, and protracted meetings), which was published in 1870, included translations into Swedish of hymns such as "Rock of Ages," "Sweet Hour of Prayer," and "Nearer, My God, to Thee." During this era, denominations and individuals were publishing songbooks all the time. The independently printed ones rarely identified the composer, lyricist, or translator. For example, P. P. Bliss published the Gospel song "Whosoever Will," based on Rev 22:17, in

45. Brochure from 1889, Swedish Theological Seminary, Evanston, Illinois.

1870. In 1880, a songbook titled *Barnvännens Lyra* (utan noter) *Andliga Sånger för Hemmet, Kyrkan och Skolan* (The children's lyre [without music]: Spiritual songs for the home, church, and school) was collected and self-published in Chicago by someone identified only as A. Hult. Song #35 is "Hvar och en som vill," i.e., the P. P. Bliss song translated into Swedish, without attribution. Before, during, and after Westergreen's years as editor of *Sändebudet*, the paper carried advertisements for an impressive list of songbooks published by Hitchcock & Walden, including English and Swedish titles such as *The Tribute of Praise, Hallowed Hymns (utan noter)* [without music], and *Hymn and Tune Book for Methodist Episcopal Church.* Witting and Westergreen were certainly not opposed to the use of small, inexpensive and portable songbooks, but they were intended for less formal and more social settings than the Sunday morning worship service.[46] However, they were concerned that Wesley's own hymns, rich in biblical allusion and doctrinally sound, were given good translations and put into the pews of immigrant churches.

Westergreen's writing and lecturing went beyond the work of the hymnal committee, important as that was. In 1880 he was asked to write a history of Scandinavian Methodism in Chicago, past and present. It was presented at the regular preachers' meeting in November of that year, and it is safe to assume that portions of it were incorporated into *Svenska Metodismen i Amerika*, since Westergreen was a coauthor of the book. He met with Dr. Walden of Walden & Hitchcock, the church's publishers, to see about publishing a Sunday School paper in the Swedish language. It was possibly also in 1880 that he began writing the first part of his autobiography, *Levnads Anteckning Från Min Barndom* (Life notation from my childhood). The 241-page manuscript, never published, covers the period from his birth to the beginning of his studies in Chicago. In 1882 he presented a ninety-minute lecture on the unity of the Christian Church in Moline and continued writing articles for *Sändebudet*. He presented the lecture again in Racine in June 1884, and at Pullman in May of 1885.

In 1884 and 1885, while continuing to work on the hymnal, his commitment to sanctification theology came to the forefront. He was not an anomaly in his pursuit of holiness; Bishop Matthew Simpson (1811–1884), who became president of Garrett Biblical Institute in 1859, was sympathetic to the Holiness Movement, and was the first bishop to participate in the National Campmeeting for the Promotion of Holiness.

46. See Armstrong, "Wrestling Jacob," 175.

Simpson was elected to the episcopacy in 1852 and presided over annual conferences all over the United States.[47] Westergreen was acquainted
with Simpson, of course, but his renewed zeal for holiness may have been
triggered in part by a religious experience that took place in March 1884,
between preaching appointments. His journal records the following:

> While on the train between Winnetka and Highland Park [Il-
> linois], I felt such a spirit of prayer poured out upon me, that I
> have not felt for a long time. My soul went out in the most ear-
> nest desire after a more heartfelt religion, a sweeter communion
> with Jesus. And soon my soul was blessed, and I felt more joy in
> believing than I have done for a long time.[48]

Although Westergreen did not explicitly label this as having attained perfect holiness, it led him to preach on the new birth at a district ministers'
meeting in Beaver several days later. His text was 1 John 3:9: "Those who
have been born of God do not sin, because God's seed abides in them;
they cannot sin, because they have been born of God." The next day he
preached on sanctification, taking for his text 2 Cor 7:1: "Since we have
these promises, beloved, let us cleanse ourselves from every defilement of
body and of spirit, making holiness perfect in the fear of God." Unfortunately, neither sermon manuscript remains. A sermon from this period
that has survived is "Not as Though I Had Already Attained," based on
Phil 3:12. Westergreen preached it during Lent at the Lakeview/Elim
Church, within two weeks of his experience on the train. The absence of
the term "sanctification" and low incidence of "perfection" and "holiness"
in the manuscript may be a subtle reinforcement of the sermon theme:
the idea of going on to something not yet attained. Listeners are invited
to identify with two aspects of Paul's behavior: humility in the knowledge
of one's own imperfection and in increased desire to attain perfection:

> Christ saw what evil Paul had already done. He had compelled
> some to blaspheme. . . . But Christ saw what good Paul could do
> in the future, if he was grasped—he was a chosen instrument.
> No one made a greater contribution to the rapid spreading of the
> Gospel. No one gave to Christianity so much of its evangelistic
> direction as Paul. . . . How Christ apprehended Paul is an example
> of how he still apprehends sinners in order to save them.[49]

---

47. "Matthew Simpson," https://en.wikipedia.org/wiki/Matthew_Simpson.

48. Westergreen, *Journals*, March 15, 1884.

49. Westergreen, "Icke Att Jag Allredan Hafver Det Fattat" [Not as though I had

From the issues addressed, the choice of biblical citations, and the use first-person plural pronouns as he addressed the congregation, it is clear Westergreen assumed he was speaking to people who were biblically literate, already Christian, and striving after holiness. The dearth of behavioral directives, especially in the "application" section, is somewhat surprising, given Paul's own language in the text of "pressing on and straining forward." Instead, the longer-than-usual application addresses questions of how Christ may apprehend us, how we can apprehend him still more, how our feelings in connection with Christ's teachings are perishable, and how "the world" loses its attractiveness to Christians. In other words, the behavioral and social implications of holiness (which, given Westergreen's own lifestyle, we may assume include everything from diligent Bible reading to helping the poor to refraining from worldly amusements) come as the *result* of Christ apprehending us and our faithful response of seeking him still more.

Unlike many in the sectarian movements in Methodism that sprang up in the second half the nineteenth century, Westergreen did not align himself with those who believed the single solution to all social ills was the conversion of individuals. In this sense his views were congruent with those of Bishop Simpson, who had worked for social reform, particularly abolition, as well as participating in the holiness movement. In October 1884 Westergreen went and heard some Scottish preachers he described as belonging "to this class of come-outers that are giving against all churches more or less. Sorry that they have had some influence upon some of our people."[50] Early in 1885 he witnessed that influence firsthand in his ministry when a married couple who had been part of the Methodist Church abruptly stopped attending. He wrote in his journal:

> Had a talk with Brother Bostrom and his wife. Both profess to have received a special blessing, and at the same time they have left off entirely to come to church and have meetings in their own home. I believe they are very religious, though some of their notions, I think, are rather queer and somewhat overdrawn.[51]

Melvin E. Dieter describes the widening gap between the sectarian perfectionists and the more traditional Methodists this way:

already attained], 2–3.

50. Westergreen, *Journals*, October 19, 1884.

51. Westergreen, *Journals*, March 26, 1885.

"The independent movements of the 1880s constituted an un-
bearable embarrassment to the leaders of the moderate holiness
center who were pursuing their own holiness reform almost
exclusively in terms of their Methodist loyalist context."[52]

Westergreen's fidelity to the Methodist Church and simultaneous
longing for entire sanctification are demonstrated in his participation
in the Holiness Convention at Park Avenue Methodist Church in May
1885.[53] He attended, but did so in company with four other Swedish
Methodist ministers: Eric Shogren, Karl H. Elmström, Henry V. Eklund,
and his own brother Andrew. He noted:

> It was a very good meeting and the power of God was manifest.
> It was somewhat noisy, perhaps a little more than I should have
> wished, yet I leave that with the Lord. I went forward for prayer
> both in the afternoon and evening. I tried to consecrate myself
> to the Lord the best I could, but I have no special feeling yet.
> May God help me.[54]

Ironically, he wrote that he was blessed while sitting on the street
car *on his way* to the holiness meeting, rather than while he was there.
He spent part of six days at the Holiness Convention, longing for the
witness of an inward work and "resting [my] faith in Jesus"; this speaks to
his enthusiasm for the pursuit of holiness. However, on those same days
he gave a lecture at the Pullman church, celebrated Pentecost at the Fifth
Avenue Church (preaching on holiness both morning and evening), conducted a quarterly conference on the south side, and visited a healing service at Quinn Chapel with his brother. In other words, Westergreen was
not so focused on attaining this "second blessing" that he neglected his
ministerial responsibilities or left the Methodist church behind. A month
after the Holiness Convention, Westergreen and his brother attended the
Free Methodist campmeeting near Wayne Station, and said there was a
good spirit prevailing. In August, the annual campmeeting in Des Plaines
included a holiness meeting. Westergreen reconsecrated himself wholly
to God while alone in the grove. At the conclusion of the campmeeting,
he wondered how many had been converted or sanctified. This suggests
that at least two distinct religious experiences might be expected as result

52. Dieter, *Holiness Revival of the Nineteenth Century*, 230.

53. Park Avenue Methodist Episcopal Church was located at Park Avenue and
Robey Street (the latter is now Damen Avenue).

54. Westergreen, *Journals*, May 21, 1885.

of the preaching, testimonies, and prayer, but also that such experiences might happen either within the context of corporate worship or when one was alone and at prayer.

On Maundy Thursday of 1885, about a week after his conversation with Mr. and Mrs. Bostrom, Westergreen felt moved to begin writing an essay about "true holiness." He finished the first draft a little more than a week later: a remarkable feat, given that Easter Sunday, a quarterly conference in Geneva, and a visit to Asbury Chapel to hear the evangelist D. W. Potter occurred during the same period. The paper was presented at the district clergy conference in Racine, Wisconsin, in May, and according to *Sändebudet*, his colleagues persuaded him to have it published.[55] It seems likely that the finished product was an expansion of the initial essay, since the resulting book, *Skillnaden På Sann Helighet och Religiöst Svärmeri* (The difference between true holiness and religious fanaticism) is about fifty pages long, and sold for thirty cents. Even that did not exhaust the topic; a month later an essay by him titled "Allmänna Helighets Principer" (General principles regarding holiness) was published in *Sändebudet*.[56] *Skillnaden På Sann Helighet och Religiöst Svärmeri* is an interesting variation on a theme Westergreen had played before. Years earlier, in Galesburg, he had defended the Wesleyan concept of Christian perfection against criticism from the local Lutheran minister. In the late 1870s and in a much milder fashion he had spoken about the differences between Waldenström's atonement theology and what he believed was orthodox Wesleyan doctrine. The 1885 book is not so much devotional reading as it is a comparative analysis of two stances. It is a diagnostic rather than prescriptive work.

The structure of the book is reminiscent of Wesley's sermon "Christian Perfection," first published in 1741. Both abound in biblical references. "Christian Perfection" takes as its primary text Phil 3:12, while Westergreen does not identify a particular text as the foundation for his thesis: perhaps because it is an essay and not a sermon. "Christian Perfection" has a brief introduction and then has two main sections: (a) in what sense Christians are not perfect and (b) in what sense they are perfect. The sermon has nine numbered paragraphs under the first section, including imperfect in knowledge and not free from ignorance, mistake, or infirmities. There are thirty numbered "senses" in

55. Elmström et al., "En Värdeful Bok" [A valuable book], 4.

56. Westergreen, "Allmänna Helighets Principer" [General principles regarding holiness], 4.

the second section. The attainable aspects of perfection include ceasing from outward, willful, or habitual sin, being freed from the necessity of sin, evil thoughts, and evil tempers.

Westergreen's introductory paragraphs have the most pastoral tone of the whole treatise. Using his own translations of Heb 13:8 and other passages, he explains that while Jesus Christ is unchangeably the same forever, the variable spirit of the times confuses human discernment, so that realities are sometimes taken for illusions, and silhouettes are thought to be realities. It is as though he wishes to give those he considers in error the benefit of the doubt, that their intentions may be good. Like Wesley, he also uses two categories to present his arguments, but his contrast is between true holiness and religious fanaticism: ways in which they are superficially similar, and then ways in which they are markedly different. Among the similarities he identifies are (a) both involve a separation, (b) both occupy a person's mind and striving, and (c) both can sometimes lead to self-denial and sacrifice.[57] The force of Westergreen's argument regarding the difference relies on logic as well as the authority of Scripture. He reasons that one may speak of "true holiness" just as Johan Arndt was able to write about "true Christianity." The adjective "true" would not be required if there were not something being received as valid Christianity in his time that he found not to be so. Likewise, "true holiness" implies the presence or possibility of a counterfeit, which he names as religious fanaticism.

Without reiterating the entire book, some of the contrasts he identifies are particularly interesting when considering the temporal and cultural context in which he was writing. For example, Westergreen claims that holiness is always the same, wherever one finds it, but this is not the case with fanaticism. The latter may take on a political-religious direction, as it did during the Crusades, a superstitious direction, as it did during witchcraft trials, an antinomian direction, or a sensual direction, degenerating sooner or later into carnality.[58] This observation could be a reaction against both the separatism of the Come-Outers and the growing politicization of the temperance movement. He also delineates a comparison between the sanctified person's reading of the Bible and a fanatic's. About the former he states:

---

57. Westergreen, *Skillnaden På Sann Helighet*, 17.
58. Westergreen, *Skillnaden På Sann Helighet*, 29.

The liberating, life-giving and directing truths, which speak of
Christ, of salvation, of the mind of Christ and other words about
holiness: these never become worn-out or too old for him. They
not only retain their former light, but also become more precious over the years.[59]

By contrast, he notes that while a fanatic may focus on interpreting the
prophets, he will ignore biblical history as much as possible, pull passages out of context, devote undue attention to minutiae, and/or insist on
a method of interpretation frowned upon by the church. *Skillnaden På
Sann Helighet och Religiöst Svärmeri* was published during the "Golden
Age of Free Thought," which ran from approximately 1875 until 1914. It
was also a period when historical criticism of the Bible threatened some
Christians' understanding of Scripture's authority and immutability.
Without identifying him by name in the book, it may be that Westergreen
had in mind Robert G. Ingersoll (1833–1899), the agnostic orator and
writer, as a threat to orthodox faith. In his journal, he refers to Ingersoll
as "the great blasphemer."[60] A third difference between true holiness and
religious fanaticism is in human relations. Westergreen asserts that holiness is patient and mild, broad-minded and tolerant, hoping the best
of fellow Christians. Fanatics, on the other hand, are full of suspicion
toward others, including Christians, think highly of themselves, and do
not associate with the lowly.[61]

It is worth noting that Westergreen used a broader range of terms
for discussing sanctification/holiness in *Skillnaden På Sann Helighet och
Religiöst Svärmeri* than he had used in his sermons during the previous
decade, though the term *fullkomlighet* (perfection) is not prominent. It
is also hard to find a simple definition of the experience of sanctifica-
tion/holiness. For the most part, the book stays on the safer ground of
describing *people* with the experience than describing the experience
itself. Westergreen's writing attempts to defend entire sanctification with
Scripture and logic as something apprehended not just cognitively but
experientially: an experience which, to his mortification, he did not seem
to believe he had. That said, his understanding of sanctification could be
summarized as a work of the Holy Spirit that occurs after justification,
evident in the Christian community not merely by testimony (though it

---

59. Westergreen, *Skillnaden På Sann Helighet*, 40.

60. Westergreen, *Journals*, July 21, 1899.

61. Westergreen, *Skillnaden På Sann Helighet*, 50.

may include testimony), but by changes in the recipient. It is received by faith, and nothing less than a total consecration of oneself to Christ enables one to appropriate this gracious gift. Such consecration is evaluated in terms of (a) feelings of total consecration and subsequent sanctification: an elusive test, at best; (b) demonstrating the ethical behavior supposedly possible only after sanctification has taken place. Holiness, in this work, is presented as opposed to fanaticism, rather than being described as an entity in itself. When the term appears in concrete form, it is used in connection with volitional human acts and speech after sanctification has occurred. Perfection is understood in the Greek sense, as in Phil 3:12 τετελείωμαι, suggesting a completion or culmination of sanctification.

The article Westergreen wrote for *Sändebudet*, "General Principles of Holiness," appeared in the July 20, 1885, edition. It is a recapitulation and translation of a paper presented at the Holiness Convention two months earlier, though the vocabulary and some of the concerns addressed suggest that Westergreen gave prominence to what was of greatest congruence with his own theological perspective. The essay begins with thanksgiving to God for the spread of the holiness movement across the United States and Canada. It then outlines twelve plain principles concerning holiness:

1. Justification by faith come first, and includes forgiveness of sin, the new birth, and adoption as God's child.

2. Perfect holiness is a work subsequent to justification, and is carried out by the Holy Spirit in those who trust in the unending power of Christ's cleansing blood, and who make a solemn and perfect sacrifice/consecration of body, soul, spirit and all earthly things to God.

3. It is the duty of the sanctified person to witness to the experience to the glory of God.

4. It produces holy character.

5. It results in the fruits of the Spirit.

6. It leads to further growth in grace.

7. It seeks out holy relationships in life and shuns anything/anyone who would hinder growth.

8. It is nurtured in the fellowship of a congregation, rather than separating one from other Christians.

9. It is non-sectarian. Rather than being the property of a particular church, it is available to all.

10. It results in generosity in sharing one's resources. Sanctified people have no need of bazaars, suppers, or dramatic societies to raise funds for the church.

11. It supports protracted meetings as a means of reaching other with evangelical simplicity.

12. It leads a person to read holy literature that will promote deeper knowledge of Jesus Christ.[62]

Given that this article was published within weeks of his book on holiness, it is worth observing the similar and different emphases. Both devote much more space to describing characteristics of the sanctified person than to explicating the work of the Holy Spirit. Neither addresses the dilemma Westergreen confronted at a personal level, i.e., how to account for the absence of or ambiguity about this stage of the *Ordo Salutis* when the believer has consecrated him/herself repeatedly? The two works differ in that the *Sändebudet* article gives more attention to demonstrable outcomes of sanctification in the believer, e.g., good stewardship, ecumenical activity, participation in protracted meetings and reading spiritually edifying literature.

Victor Witting, who was the editor of *Sändebudet* during this period, published more than theological discussions in the weekly paper. During the Civil War years, for instance, he included detailed updates of battles, particularly Union Army victories. Arlow Andersen claims that under Witting's years as editor, the paper was generally Republican in sympathy, but the editorial pages were generally silent on matters pertaining to American foreign relations.[63] The same was true under Westergreen's leadership. In addition, other than during the Civil War, Westergreen did not frequently mention local, national, or world news in his personal daily journal, which makes his selection of current events he *did* write about during this period all the more significant. As already noted, he reflected the local secular newspapers' bias in writing about the Haymarket Riot in May 1886. Death and disaster seemed to be most noteworthy for him. He recorded in detail the shooting and subsequent death of President Garfield in 1881, the 1883 Diamond Coal Mine disaster in

62. Westergreen, "Allmänna helighets-principer," 4.
63. Andersen, "Sändebudet and American Public Affairs," 7.

Braidwood, Illinois, a convent fire in Belleville, Illinois, in 1884, in which twenty or thirty girls perished, and race riots in Cleveland the same year. He took grim satisfaction when fire destroyed part of the baseball ground at 39th and Wabash, saying, "I should have had no objection if the whole concern had burned down, as it is only held open for the desecration of the Sabbath."[64] During 1885, he made mention of the Kankakee Insane Asylum fire in January, in which seventeen people died, the opening of Niagara Falls National Park, and General Grant's death in July. A personal journal does not serve the same function as an immigrant newspaper, of course, but it would seem that during the years 1876 to 1886, Westergreen's interest in the world outside the church diminished. Family struggles, various aspects of his ministry, and the pursuit of Christian perfection occupied his attention.

His vocation plus family concerns were certainly demanding enough to prevent him for focusing on current events. He had been made presiding elder of the Chicago District at Annual Conference in the autumn of 1881. His schedule, printed in an 1882 issue of *Sändebudet*, shows he was conducted an average of seven quarterly conferences per month, each generally being a two-day commitment with him preaching at one or more worship services. This required him to travel from western Illinois to Jamestown, New York, several times per year. His journals during his time as presiding elder were atypical in that there was little mention of his reading for his own enjoyment or ongoing education. Possible romantic interests were also cast aside. In one humorous journal entry written while visiting Galesburg in 1883, he said:

> That strange woman Luisa Hill was in today. What she wanted
> I don't know, for I did not speak to her, and I was glad that Bro.
> Swan and Sister Betsy were in so that we did not need to open a
> conversation with her. The woman must be much over fifty and
> yet the poor woman is lovesick after me.[65]

Westergreen, who turned forty-nine that year, was clearly not interested. He never mentioned her again. Supervising the students who were preaching at the Rock Island car shops, Pullman, and other fledgling congregations plus his own preaching schedule, which averaged over two hundred times per year, hindered the pursuit of outside interests. It should also be remembered that given Westergreen's social conservatism,

64. Westergreen, *Journals*, December 12, 1884.
65. Westergreen, *Journals*, March 12, 1883.

leisure enjoyments were limited to church-related picnics, birthday parties, and other gatherings with fellow Christians.

Annual Conference was held in Dayton, Iowa, in 1885 with Bishop Bowman presiding. Westergreen expected his term as presiding elder would end, but was dismayed when he met with the cabinet and learned they were planning to send him to Rockford and his brother Andrew to Moline. He managed to get it changed so that Andrew was reappointed to Rockford while he remained at Fifth Avenue for one more year. His longtime colleague Eric Shogren was made presiding elder; he and Westergreen met a week after Conference ended to draw up a plan for Shogren's first quarter on the Chicago district. Westergreen's final year of ministry at the Fifth Avenue church was without major incident, which was just as well, given what a tumultuous and demanding period it was with his family. When Conference met in Galesburg the following September, Westergreen was appointed to Evanston, and N. M. Liljegren became his successor at Fifth Avenue. Westergreen wrote that both he and his mother were satisfied with his appointment. He preached his farewell sermon at Fifth Avenue on September 19, 1886, taking Acts 20:27 as his text: "I did not shrink from declaring to you the whole purpose of God." The congregation held a surprise party for them at the church on the night before they moved.

Evanston would be a new chapter in Westergreen's life, signaled, perhaps, by his preaching to the Sunday School in English his first Sunday there. He called the four years that followed his "Renaissance Period," succeeded by years of personal loss. It is to that era of his ministry we now turn.

Hanna and Ola Westergreen

Gammalstorp Church, where Nels Westergreen
was baptized, in Bjäraryd, Sweden

Medieval bridge in Västanå, Sweden, the village where Westergreen was raised

The Washburn Farm in Minot, Maine

Minot Center Church, which Westergreen attended with the Washburn family

Westergreen as a young man

Erik/Alex Olsson and Swan Westergreen

Andrew and Selma Westergreen

Victoria Swedish Methodist Church, the oldest Swedish Methodist building

1866 meeting of Scandinavian Methodist preachers in Chicago. Row
1: Nels O. Westergreen, S. B. Newman, N. Peterson, O. G. Hedstrom,
O. P. Peterson, P. Nyberg, A. J. Anderson, Victor Witting. Row 2: J. H.
Ekstrand, A. Haagensen, Albert Ericson, L. Lindqvist, J. Ölund. Row 3:
Ole Petersen, C. J. Anderson. O. Gunerson, O. C. Simpson, A. Vigdal,
J. H. Johnson, Karl Schou, Andrew Westergreen, N. Christofferson, John
Wigren, P. Jensen, R. Peterson, C. G. Hofflund, Gustaf Wetterlund

First Swedish Methodist of Chicago (also known as Market Street Church)

Nels Westergreen in middle age

Westergreen's house in
Humboldt Park, Chicago

Betsy, Arthur, and Nellie Westergreen

Westergreen at Desplaines campground for "Old Peoples'
Day" (front row, fourth from the right)

The Swedish Methodist Theological Seminary in Evanston, Illinois

Westergreen's funeral at the Swedish Methodist Church in Galesburg, Illinois

Westergreen's grave at Hope Cemetery, Galesburg

7

Renaissance and Requiem

1886 to 1898

Be not dismayed or troubled, my friend,
soon in the homeland all grief shall end.
There free from sorrow, sin, and distress,
we through the Savior find perfect rest.[1]

AT ANNUAL CONFERENCE IN 1886, Westergreen was appointed to serve
the immigrant Methodist congregation in Evanston, Illinois. He and his
mother moved into the furnished, two-story parsonage near the corner
of Sherman and Grove less than two weeks later. Though he was pleased
with the appointment, Westergreen's early days there were not without
setbacks and frustrations. When the congregation was formally organized
in 1874, it had a documented membership of seventy-five. In the decade
following that, record-keeping became haphazard. Westergreen found
no record of addresses of families in the congregation and no record of
pastoral visits, making it much more difficult to assess pastoral care needs
and call upon members. In addition, prior to Annual Conference he had
already committed himself to preaching engagements in Jamestown,
New York, and Galesburg, Victoria, and Galva, Illinois. He also attended

---

1. See Ottander, "Trust in the Savior, O Precious Soul" [Håll dig vid klippan], 402.

the Rock River Conference and the Swedish Baptist Conference. These all took time that might have been spent settling into a new pastorate.

There is no mention of the congregation complaining about his absences. In the twelve years since their organization, they had changed leadership at least six times, making it likely they had come to rely on the continuity of lay rather than clergy leadership. They could trace their roots back to a devout layman named Otto Larson, who came to Evanston from Sweden in 1868, with his wife coming a year later. Another early leader was Karl Shou, a Danish immigrant, who had been converted in Indiana and was then studying for the ministry at Garrett Biblical Institute. Shou organized the congregation in 1872; it was part of the Norwegian-Danish district of the Methodist Episcopal Church. Initially they met in a schoolhouse at Benson Avenue and Clark Street.[2] Otto Larson was part of this congregation for two years, until he and other newly arrived Swedes withdrew and formed their own congregation, which affiliated with the Swedish Mission District of the Central Illinois Conference.[3] This happened at roughly the same time the Swedish Methodist Theological School relocated to the campus of Northwestern University, with the fortuitous result of having faculty and student pastors available to serve the new congregation. The first leader, J. B. Anderson, was a theology student who earned a stipend of three hundred dollars per year. In 1875, another student named O. J. Stead took charge of the congregation. Its membership rose to seventy-five, and in 1876 they built a thirty-two-by-fifty-foot building in what is now downtown Evanston. *Svenska Metodismen i Amerika* includes a photograph of the structure; it has four lancet windows on each side and a rose window above the center entrance. The building could reflect nearly any Protestant tradition (or one-room schoolhouse, aside from the shape of the windows) of that period. The style is less recognizably Scandinavian than Union Avenue Swedish Methodist in Chicago, built in 1895, for example, or Malden, Massachusetts, Swedish Methodist, built in 1894.

2. Norwegian-Danish Methodism in America began in 1843 with a class meeting at what was known as the "Norwegian Settlement" at Fox River Valley, La Salle County, Illinois. The first congregation was established at Cambridge, Wisconsin, by the Reverend Christian Willerup, a Dane. Its building, dedicated in 1852, was the first Norwegian-Danish Methodist Episcopal Church ever built.

3. Conference relations are sometimes confusing. It was not until 1876 that the Swedish Methodists had their own Annual Conference and published their own journals, entirely separate from the Central Illinois Conference journal. And although Westergreen was ordained in the Central Illinois Conference, he normally attended the Rock River Conference along with the Swedish Methodist Conference.

These churches have a square tower with belfry in one corner topped by a pitched roof of distinctive design: possibly reminiscent of the *klockstaplar* (detached bell towers) in Sweden. The main entrance is at the base of the tower, sometimes on the diagonal rather than flush with one side of the tower. A local example of the diagonal style was the Cheltenham / South Shore Church at 79th and Burnham, built in 1906. The interior would follow a modified Akron plan, with central pulpit, altar table below, and pews arranged in a half-moon pattern radiating from the pulpit. Sliding doors on one side of the room could be opened to accommodate overflow crowds or to conduct classes. Often the main floor and sanctuary were a half floor above street level. The reason for this elevation was the congregation would build and use the lower level until funds could be raised to complete the rest of the building.

There were other Scandinavians in Evanston who chose not to affiliate with the Swedish Methodist Church, or who left the church to join other congregations. A group of Lutheran women began holding house-meetings the same year that Westergreen was appointed to the Methodist Church. By 1888, about sixty people gathered in Union Hall to organize a church. They were soon able to buy a German Lutheran church building, and used it for ten years until they erected their own building on Lake Street. A few in Westergreen's congregation transferred their membership: Lars Erik Larson and the August Johnson family were among them.[4]

The Evanston church was accustomed to learned clergy as well as brief pastorates by the time Westergreen arrived in 1886. His immediate predecessor was Albert Ericson, who was rector of the Swedish Methodist Theological Seminary, and prior to Ericson, the church enjoyed the ministry of William Henschen (1842–1925). Henschen's father, Lars Wilhelm, was the attorney who had served as Eric Jansson's defense counsel in Sweden, as well as being a member of the Swedish Parliament. Henschen himself was probably the most educated minister in the Swedish Methodist Church at the time, having studied philosophy, natural history, and medicine at Uppsala University with further studies in Berlin. Henschen taught high school in Sweden, emigrated to the United States in 1870, was a citrus grower in Florida and newspaper editor in New York City before coming to Chicago. He became editor of *Sändebudet* and part-time instructor at the Swedish Methodist Seminary. The ministers

4. *Original parish register of Immanuel Lutheran Church*, Evanston, Illinois.

who followed Westergreen, Richard Cederberg and Oscar F. Linstrum, were good men, but had far less education and ministerial experience than Ericson, Henschen, and Westergreen.

Once he returned from his travels at the end of 1886, Westergreen stayed close to home the following year. He preached almost exclusively at the church in Evanston, mainly in Swedish, but more often in English when addressing the Sunday School or conducting funerals. In this respect, Westergreen adopted what many Swedish American clergy of the time were doing. In *Swedish Chicago: The Shaping of an Immigrant Community 1880–1920*, Anita Olson Gustafson notes that Sunday School and young people's groups were recording their minutes in English in the 1890s, although Swedish was still the primarily language for sermons and worship services.[5] The second generation did not have the same competency in Swedish that their immigrant parents commonly had.

Victor Witting and his wife were now living in North Evanston, and Westergreen was glad to have old friends nearby. He and his mother participated in a Midsummer outdoor supper at the Wittings's home. Other clergy colleagues were having their troubles. The Reverend John Melcher Öjerholm, the man who replaced Andrew Westergreen at Rockford, was brought up on charges (not specified in the *Conference Journal*) and Westergreen was called on to serve as defense counsel at his trial. Öjerholm was not suspended, but told to settle the matter before Conference. When that was not accomplished, he was expelled, to Westergreen's disappointment. Öjerholm eventually transferred to the Texas Conference. Westergreen's former mentor, S. B. Newman, was facing a trial of a different sort. His wife had died of cholera in July 1885, and he seemed to have developed a problem with substance abuse. He was now seventy-three years old, and may have suffered from a variety of ailments, but he was also very lonely, and the word among his colleagues was that he was "taking too much medicine." Westergreen called upon him with another minister, Eric Shogren, but they did not find Newman at home. Westergreen wrote him a long letter the next day. If Newman *was* over-medicating, it may have been unintentional. The United States Food and Drug Administration was not established until 1906, along with the passage of the Pure Food and Drugs Act. Prior to that, patent medicines with dubious ingredients were readily available. Even *Sändebudet* occasionally ran

5. Gustafson, *Swedish Chicago*, 170. Another transitional pattern among the Swedes and Norwegians was having morning worship in language, and evening worship in the other.

a half-page advertisement for "Maltos-Cannabis," a breakfast drink that allegedly would cure catarrh, anemia, weak stomach, scrofula, nervous temperament, insomnia, and lung sickness.[6] Westergreen himself took patent medicines; on one occasion he wrote to Swan's daughter Nellie:

> I have been very weak and nervous, and very much troubled with cough and slime that come upon me in spells . . . and one time I was also troubled with cold night sweats which were not only uncomfortable, but weakened me. I went to the doctor twice, and took a lot of medicine, but it did not seem to help much. I have now begun to take a patent medicine that is highly recommended; it is called Cannabis Sativa Remedy. It is made in this country in Rochester, New York. . . . I have taken this medicine now for nearly three weeks, and I think is has helped me some, for I have got better appetite, more nights' rest, and I think it has strengthened me some, though it has not done so much yet to rid me of my troublesome cough.[7]

Westergreen did not make note of Newman's reaction to his letter, nor whether the alleged over-medication was addressed. It did not cause a break in the friendship; Westergreen's journals note that Newman preached along with Westergreen at Des Plaines Campground in 1887 and 1889. They saw each other regularly at the monthly meetings of Swedish Methodist preachers, and otherwise socialized together. Newman did continue to be a cause for concern among his ministerial brethren, particularly when he remarried in 1894.

Andrew Westergreen, recovering from the breakdown after his son's death, had supernumerary status until the Annual Conference of 1887, and there were lingering signs that all was not well. In early April, Nels wrote that he and his mother had not heard from Andrew in a long time, and that made them anxious. He went to Rockford the first week of May for a district meeting, and while he was there he visited Andrew and Selma. Andrew returned to Evanston with him, and stayed for about two weeks. On at least one occasion the two brothers went out to do some pastoral calling, but Andrew stayed outside most of the time, while Nels did the actual visiting. Adding to the stress in Andrew's life was being appointed to Lakeview/Elim in 1887, but unable to move the family's belongings from Rockford into the parsonage for awhile. Then Selma became pregnant again. She had a baby boy in early March, and came

6. Advertisement for "Maltos Cannabis," 18.
7. Westergreen, letter to Nellie Westergreen, October 15, 1914.

down with childbed (puerperal) fever. For more than ten days it was unclear whether she would recover, and part of the time her mind appeared to be affected. Westergreen's journal brimmed with anxiety over his sister-in-law, writing things such as, "I am not very much fit for study at present. I am filled too much with anxiety for the life and welfare of Selma, my brother's wife. We are earnestly praying to God that she may be spared."[8] Selma *was* spared, but her infant son, Ernst, died unexpectedly in April, possibly from sudden infant death syndrome. Westergreen lamented that the child had not been baptized. He preached the funeral sermon at Graceland Cemetery in Chicago. No marker was purchased for the baby's grave.

The youngest brother, John, continued to struggle in his marriage and employment. He and his wife separated in 1885, but eventually reunited. In May 1888 he wrote from Omaha, saying he was sick of his job and wished he could find other work. Five months later he sent another letter, telling the family he had fallen and broken a leg, and had thus been laid up and unable to work for several weeks. Nels sent him money to cover his expenses. But family life was not all trouble and sorrow during the first two years in Evanston. Swan's daughter Nellie wrote of her conversion in March 1887, and the following year she came and spent about a month with her uncle and grandmother. The three of them attended class-meetings, went to Lincoln Park Zoo, and to "the panorama of the crucifixion" presented by a man named Dahlgren from Bishop Hill.

His mother was in fairly good health, considering she was eighty years old. This allowed Westergreen time to pursue some of his interests beyond ministry to the Evanston congregation. Perhaps this was why he referred to this as his renaissance period. He served on the publication committee of the Swedish Methodist Book Concern, which had produced the first official Swedish Methodist hymnbook a few years earlier. He continued writing articles for *Sändebudet*, of which Witting was editor, *Väktaren* (The watchman), a Methodist paper that began publishing in the late 1880s, and wrote a history of the Swedish Methodist Seminary. To facilitate his continued intellectual growth, he sat in on the final examinations at the seminary, and took a Hebrew course at Garrett Biblical Institute. He gave numerous temperance lectures at various churches between 1886 and 1890. His involvement in the Swedish Emigrant Aid Society seems to have waned during the appointment to Evanston, but his

---

8. Westergreen, *Journals*, March 10, 1887.

care for "the orphans and widows in their distress" did not. Thanksgiving Day services were an opportunity to take up a special offering for the poor. In January of 1890 he was part of a committee that worked toward securing a home for orphans and the homeless: a project spurred on by the promise of up to five thousand dollars in matching funds.[9] On Easter Day of that year, he and Alfred Anderson were able to raise over a thousand dollars toward the cause. The Swedish Methodist clergy adopted a constitution and elected trustees for a home that would be for the sick or elderly. They rented a house in Evanston for that purpose, but a few years later were able to buy land and dedicate the institution that became known as The Bethany Home, located in Ravenswood near the Swedish Methodist Church. He and his fellow ministers also discussed "the labor question" at a weekly clergy meeting.

The ministers' meetings during this period usually featured theological presentations, such as the state of revival meetings, the witness of the Spirit, and how to retain sanctification. They also discussed the pension fund, and whether women should be delegates to General Conference. Occasionally the topics simply reflected the biases of the time. On one occasion Westergreen wrote:

> I went to the Monday preachers' meeting. Mr. White, a Cumberland Presbyterian minister, read before the meeting extracts from the Catholic confessional which were very filthy, and made remarks over them. Of course there was no boys or women allowed to be in. What a church that is, which not only allows, but enjoins such filthy talk in the confession box upon its members: especially the female members.[10]

Prior to the Civil War, it was unusual for Westergreen to mention current events in his journal, but starting with the Great Chicago Fire of 1871, he commented on them more often. This was certainly the case during his ministry in Evanston. In 1887 he wrote about the death of Henry Ward Beecher, the famous Congregational minister, abolitionist, and champion of women's suffrage: "one of the great men of this country" is how Westergreen described him. He described the Chatsworth (Illinois) train wreck in August of the same year. It was one of the worst railroad accidents of the nineteenth century; over eighty people were killed, and about 150 seriously injured. Westergreen witnessed the parade in

9. Westergreen, *Journals*, January 1, 1890.
10. Westergreen, *Journals*, December 8, 1890.

Chicago when President Cleveland laid the cornerstone of the Auditorium Theater. In 1888 he attended the Republican National Convention
held at the Auditorium. Another significant development he wrote about,
in which he and other Protestant clergy were involved, was plans for the
Columbian Exposition of 1893. They appointed a committee to meeting with those who were planning the World's Fair, and drafted a petition to be presented to President Harrison, asking that the exposition
not be opened on a Sunday. Westergreen's journal commented on the
Thingwalla and *Geyser* disaster: two ships that collided off the coast of
Nova Scotia, in which over a hundred drowned. The Johnstown Flood of
1889 was acknowledged, with speculation that thousands of lives were
lost. The typhoid epidemic that began in January of 1889 in Chicago was
mentioned repeatedly by Westergreen, as friends and church members
succumbed to the disease. He was seemingly more prone to make note of
death and disaster than celebratory events, perhaps because the latter did
not offer opportunity to reflect solemnly on the brevity of life and need
to put one's trust in God.

Pastoral duties took up most of his time. In addition to conducting
services in Evanston, he made a trip to the East Coast in January of 1889,
preaching in Manhattan and Brooklyn plus Boston and other cities in
Massachusetts. Later in the year he preached in Galesburg and western
Illinois, campmeetings in Hickory Grove and Des Plaines, including the
National Holiness Campmeeting at Des Plaines. The following summer he went further west to Nebraska, preaching in Omaha, Saronville,
and Stromsberg as well as at a campmeeting in Shappard's Grove. He
attended the Swedish Methodist Annual Conference, but also the Free
Methodist General Conference, Central Illinois Methodist Conference,
and Norwegian-Danish Methodist Conference. No reason was given for
attending these conferences; he was not a guest preacher, or asked to rep-
resent Swedish Methodism to these bodies. The fact that he frequently
commented on the quality of preaching at these meetings suggests that
spiritual hunger and/or a desire to sharpen his own homiletical skills
were the impetus for his attendance. As a connoisseur of sermons, he
could be critical but was never mean-spirited. For example, he became
acquainted with C. G. Wallenius (1865–1947) in 1889, a year after Wallenius emigrated from Sweden. The first time he preached in the Evanston
church, Westergreen's comment was, "[it was] a plain, good sermon, but
he spoke a little too much in a low monotonous voice." The next evening
Westergreen preached and Wallenius exhorted afterward. Westergreen

complained that he spoke too long and so they did not have much time for prayer.[11] However, a year later he wrote, "Wallenius preached for me in the evening a very good sermon. He has certainly improved greatly in preaching since he came among us."[12] Westergreen could be critical of peers who were veterans in the ministry, too. When Albert Ericson (1840–1910) served as head of the Swedes' seminary and gave the baccalaureate sermon in 1890, Westergreen's evaluation was that "it was a long and strong sermon, but as it was written and read throughout, I think it lost some of its force."[13] He gave a more favorable review to William Henschen's pulpit skills at Annual Conference a few years later, writing, "In the evening Dr. Henschen preached the annual missionary sermon in our church. It was a splendid sermon for conciseness and clearness."[14]

A major event in his personal life was the purchase of a house in Humboldt Park in 1890. Up to this point in his ministry, he had lived in rented rooms or, as was the case in Evanston, in a parsonage. He was satisfied with his change of appointment to the Humboldt Park church at Annual Conference that year, and after looking for a place near the church, rented an apartment from a man named Seaberg. It had less room than the Evanston parsonage, but the greater problem was a noisy Irish family living upstairs. This took a toll on Hanna's nerves as well as his own. Fortunately, brother Andrew repaid him a substantial loan in November, and this allowed him to make a down payment on his own house at 1722 N. Richmond. It was a two story, narrow frame building, and when Westergreen converted it into two apartments, he was better able to pay property taxes, utilities, and other expenses. His mother was glad to be settled in their own place: something she had not enjoyed since her husband's death, almost twenty years earlier. The house was conveniently close to the church and public transportation. This meant that when Westergreen's appointment changed at Conference in 1892, he could get to his new charge without much difficulty, and without having to move again.

Andrew Westergreen was serving the Lakeview/Elim Church at this time. In some respects it was similar in design to the Evanston building: a simple structure with a raised, center entrance, but without the lancet

11. Westergreen, *Journals*, March 14 and 15, 1889.

12. Westergreen, *Journals*, April 23, 1890.

13. Westergreen, *Journals*, June 8, 1890.

14. Westergreen, *Journals*, September 17, 1893.

and rose windows suggesting its ecclesiastical identity. A more significant difference was the 1883 building in Lakeview was not in good repair
when Andrew became its pastor in 1887. Under his leadership, the congregation grew to over two hundred, with more than that in the Sunday
School. It is likely that the parsonage next door served as overflow space
for all the activities taking place there. A larger, more substantial building was needed, and Andrew had proven to be an effective fundraiser
when he served Bishop Hill 1879–1882. Given the scope of the building
project, the new, immense brick church building was not completed and
dedicated until September 1898.

The adjective "renaissance" that Westergreen used to characterize
this period seems to have continued, to some extent, to his two years serving the Humboldt Park Swedish Methodist Church. He was enthusiastic
about his work and interested in current affairs around him, and despite
his tendency toward hypochondria, his health was good. His journals
reflect less spiritual self-laceration than in some earlier and later years,
and at least two positive religious experiences. The first occurred in July
of 1891, when he wrote, "While walking on the street I had almost inces-
sant communion with God in prayer. I have not felt that way for a long
time."[15] No noteworthy events seem to have precipitated this experience;
he had preached "with good liberty" twice the day before, and preached
again that evening. The second experience was more predictable, as it
happened at the close of the campmeetings at Des Plaines. Westergreen
had preached at least twice during the campmeeting, and attended holiness meetings led by others when he wrote the following:

> Blessed be God for the good time we have had. I cannot say
> that I feel very happy, at least I have not felt any ecstasy of joy as
> some have during the meeting. But I think if I understand my-
> self aright that I am more given up to Christ and can better trust
> in Him than I could before the campmeeting. Blessed be God.[16]

Westergreen did not travel much in 1891; the farthest journey from
home was to Burlington, Iowa, for the start of protracted meetings. On the
way he stopped in Galesburg to attend a quarterly conference and meet
with his brother Swan. In March he participated in the opening of the
Bethany Home in Evanston. Brothers Newman, Henschen, and Bernard
Swanson made short speeches, after which they all had lunch in the home.

15. Westergreen, *Journals*, July 30, 1891.
16. Westergreen, *Journals*, August 17, 1892.

At the weekly clergy meetings, they now addressed social issues more often, along with presenting theological papers for discussion. Among the topics they dealt with were "the Negro question and the present status of evangelical work among colored people, especially in Chicago," mission work among the Cree Indians, "religious sentiment in connection with the Columbian Exposition," and "the labor question."[17] In addition, Westergreen wrote about the drought in Kansas, in which over thirty thousand farmers were bankrupted, the lynching of eleven Italian prisoners in New Orleans, the death of Charles Haddon Spurgeon, and still more outbreaks of typhoid. He continued to write or translate articles and sermons for *Sändebudet*, the *Northwestern Christian Advocate*, and his colleague Witting's series, *Stilla Stunder* (Quiet moments). His involvement with the Swedish Seminary was less during this period; aside from noting that he went to hear senior class recitations about sanctification theology, he did little beyond attending examinations and commencement.

Concerns about immediate and extended family continued to figure regularly in Westergreen's journals. His mother began a slow decline often marked by depression, which made her weepy and peevish by turns. His niece Nellie wrote that her father, Swan, was sick. The anxiety continued when brother Alex wrote that his wife, Eunice, was ill. His two youngest brothers and their families continued to depend on him for emotional and financial support. Andrew borrowed a large sum of money from him. Andrew's surviving son, Wesley, developed pneumonia, and Selma broke an arm that took several months to heal. John and Annie separated again for awhile, and John seemed to be working as a courier, taking trains all over the country. Despite these challenges, Westergreen was satisfied with his two years at Humboldt Park. If he did not find the congregation as vital as his previous appointment in Evanston, it was nevertheless growing. It was close enough to other Swedish Methodist churches to offer opportunities for pulpit exchanges and involvement in ecumenical ventures, outreach to the unchurched, and investment in temperance and other social concerns.

When Conference met in Moline during September 1892, Westergreen was appointed to Melrose Park and Moreland. The former was at 601 N. 14th Avenue, and the latter was located just east of Cicero Avenue on Ontario Street, in what is now the West Garfield Park neighborhood.

---

17. Westergreen, *Journals*, February 16 and October 5, 1891, February 15 and May 16, 1892.

In addition, he preached regularly in Oak Park, though the Swedish Methodists never had their own building there.

If Evanston and Humboldt Park represented a renaissance for Westergreen, the sense of rebirth diminished in the years that followed, culminating with a requiem in 1898. It was an unsettled and often unhappy time for him. He had briefer appointments than in the previous decade; one year at Melrose Park and Moreland, one year at Ravenswood, one year with supernumerary status, a second year at Moreland, one year as a teacher at the seminary, one year at Englewood, and finally, one year at Forest Glen. Even by Methodist standards of the day, that was a lot of moving around. He and his mother remained in their house in Humboldt Park, and he commuted to his different churches, often finding a place to board overnight; for example, he stayed at the Bethany Home when activities at the Ravenswood church required him to be there late in the evening.

In some ways, he took the changes of appointment with equanimity. In 1893 he preached 173 times, with thirty-one times at Melrose Park, thirty-four times at Moreland, twenty-seven times at Ravenswood, and ten times at Oak Park. The remaining seventy sermons were presented at other Swedish Methodist churches, campmeetings, and funerals, but none at churches of other denominations. This is somewhat surprising, given his friendships with the Swedish Baptists and Mission Friends. There were protracted meetings at Moreland in early January, followed by Oak Park later in the month and Melrose Park in April. The only problems related to his appointment that he reported were occasional low attendance and the congregations being delinquent in paying him. At a quarterly conference meeting in June 1893 he noted that the church owed him about one hundred dollars in salary. He finally received it in September. The same problem arose the following year when he was at Ravenswood; at the quarterly conference in February 1894 he was still owed half his salary for the quarter.

If day-to-day life in the local church was routine for Westergreen in 1893, his activities beyond his appointment were stimulating and evolving, and current events in Chicago beyond the life of the church were exciting. He was made vice president of the Church Extension Society, and listened with interest to Lucy Rider Meyer (1849–1922) speak about deaconess work and the Chicago Training School, which she and her husband founded. He and his clergy colleagues hosted speakers from the Freedman's Aid Society, which promoted education for former slaves and their descendants in the American south. The ministers also discussed what could be done for the poor and unemployed in the Chicago area: a pressing concern during the Panic of 1893. Westergreen participated in both the stockholders' meeting of the Swedish Methodist Book Concern and the annual business meeting of the Des Plaines Campground. He and his brother Andrew visited the penitentiary in Joliet after district meetings at Richards Street Methodist in Joliet. And, as usual, he enjoyed preaching and participating in the annual Methodist campmeeting in Des Plaines and the National Holiness campmeeting that followed it.

As mentioned earlier, 1893 was one of the most momentous years in Chicago's history, and Westergreen's journal provides commentary on many of the events that happened, starting with President Cleveland's visit to the city on Saturday, April 29. The president had come to open the Columbian Exposition on May 1. Westergreen wrote that the streets were crowded with people, and he seemed amused that on the Monday, the muddy streets had been swept for the president's visit. His brothers Andrew and John visited the fair during the first few days of July, but their oldest brother went alone a few days later. He wrote that the caravels arrived in the afternoon, and were received with great excitement. He marveled at how much there was to see. Three days later there was a fire in the smokestack of cold storage plant on the fair ground, resulting in the deaths of sixteen people, including thirteen firefighters who were crushed or burned when the smokestack collapsed. The tragedy was witnessed by about twenty-five thousand fair attendees. Westergreen was not present when it happened, but acknowledged the terrible sorrow it spread. July 20 was "Swedish Day" at the fair, but Westergreen did not visit again until August, when he took his brother Swan and nephew Henry to see the Exposition. In October he accompanied Swan's daughters Nellie and Emma to the fair, and made two additional visits on his own before the fair ended. It is interesting that Westergreen, who ordinarily shunned anything he considered a worldly amusement, was drawn to the Columbian Exposition so many times. It may be that he was caught up in what Anita Olson Gustafson suggests, "The celebration of Sweden's Day at the Columbian Exposition [served to] display the Swedish community's strength and to publicize Swedish cultural and national achievements."[18] Other than noting its size, how much there was to see, and how hungry and tired he was by the end of each visit, Westergreen did not describe what he saw and did while there.

18. Gustafson, *Swedish Chicago*, 122.

Soon after the Columbian Exposition opened, there was a national economic crisis. The collapse of the Philadelphia and Reading Railroad and the National Cordage Company started a panic in the stock market. When Westergreen was on his way home from a preachers' meeting on June 5, he witnessed a crowd in the street outside the church, and learned they were trying to make a run on the Dane Savings Bank.[19] In the weeks and months that followed, five thousand banks closed and fifteen thousand businesses failed. The unemployment rate reached 25 percent in Pennsylvania, 35 percent in New York, and 43 percent in Michigan. President Cleveland was blamed for the panic.[20]

Three other significant events occurred in or near Chicago during the Columbian Exposition, which ran from May 1 to October 30, 1893. First, in early July a devastating tornado struck the town of Pomeroy, Iowa, a town of one thousand people. It destroyed 80 percent of the homes and other buildings, including the Methodist Church. Over seventy people were killed and two hundred injured. Westergreen's brother John, who had been traveling, brought the family a photograph of the destruction when he visited on July 18. A second major event occurred in September, when the Parliament of the World's Religions met in what is now the Art Institute of Chicago. It was the largest congress held in conjunction with the Columbian Exposition, and the first organized interfaith gathering, designed to create a global dialog of faiths. Christianity was represented by G. Bonet-Maury, a French Protestant historian. Westergreen never mentioned this important meeting, perhaps because he was in Galesburg attending Annual Conference at the time. Given his intellectual curiosity and ecumenical inclinations, one might expect him to comment on the significance of the parliament. His overall conservatism might have prompted him to censure a meeting with different religions on equal footing. We cannot know the reason for his silence. The third momentous event occurred just before the Columbian Exposition ended. On October 28, 1893, Chicago's five-time mayor, Carter Harrison Sr., was assassinated in his home. Westergreen wrote of long lines of people waiting to see the remains of Harrison, which were lying in state in the city hall. The funeral was November 1. The planned closing celebration for the Columbian Exposition instead became a large public memorial assembly in the fair's Festival Hall.

19. Westergreen, *Journals*, June 5, 1893.
20. "Panic of 1893," https://en.wikipedia.org/wiki/Panic_of_1893#.

Of more immediate concern to Westergreen were ongoing difficulties within his family and home. After disappearing for a few days in early February, John began working for the Illinois Central Railroad, attended church, reunited with his wife and mother-in-law, and they settled into their own place: all positive developments. However, entries in Westergreen's journal strongly suggest that John, like other family members, suffered from depression. On one occasion Westergreen wrote, "Brother John felt sad this morning, and in making his morning prayer wept and asked the Lord to give him something to do that he should not need to go out on the train on Sunday . . . he was crying bitterly."[21] John's claim for a pension was refused in Washington.[22] In October he quit working for the railroad and announced he would seek other work. He was not successful in that endeavor, and went back to working as some sort of courier for the railroad. His marriage was never stable or placid. John, like his eldest brother, was a Republican, and it dismayed the entire family when it was revealed that Annie and her mother were staunch Democrats. Hanna Westergreen thought her daughter-in-law was lazy and a burden to John, and did not hide these sentiments from Annie. Even John remarked on more than one occasion that he wished he could send his wife and mother-in-law back to Philadelphia. The faltering national economy and labor strikes affected John more than any other family member, and he frequently called on Nels to lament and weep. Meanwhile, brother Andrew fell off a streetcar in Chicago, injuring one hand. He also fell into debt, and went to Nels for assistance. Hanna's depression worsened, and she seemed to be in the early stages of dementia. In June and July of 1893 the journal notes:

> In the morning Mother opened the faucet to the bathtub and forgot to shut it so the water overflowed. Then afterwards Brother Wiström's good canary bird singer got out of his cage and was lost. . . . Mother is crying because the Wiströms downstairs were doing a lot of cooking, and the heat from their stove made our kitchen too warm for comfort. . . . Mother was not well today on account of the heat last night and as she is nervous she has been weeping a good deal today.[23]

---

21. Westergreen, *Journals*, February 19, 1893.

22. This was presumably a military pension for his service in the Union Army.

23. Westergreen, *Journals*, June 20 and 30, July 25, 1893.

In her despondency, she "prayed in a feeble voice that the Lord might soon take her home."[24] Home was not a happy, restful place for Westergreen.

Then there was the matter of the house itself. The frame building Westergreen purchased lacked adequate insulation, resulting in frozen pipes and consequently no water a number of times during the winter. Finally, at the most intimate level, in his journal Westergreen acknowledged at least four times during the year that he was struggling against "carnal lusts." He prayed for deliverance from them, but wrote that it seemed to give him only momentary relief. He did not mention being attracted to any woman that year, so it is impossible to say whether these sexual temptations were something new, or simply something he had not admitted to himself before.

The following year was a low point in Westergreen's life, with elements so ambiguous and sinister he did not commit them fully to paper. He did write about some aspects of his life causing stress: his brother Andrew's discouragement over poor attendance at protracted meetings; a neighbor on the next block shooting and killing himself because of poverty and the inability to find work; his mother's ongoing melancholy. There were two other unexpected developments that caused Westergreen and his closest friends anguish and soul-searching: an unanticipated pastoral move and a wedding.

The appointment process is the one that retains an element of mystery more than a century later. At Annual Conference in 1893, Westergreen had been appointed to the Ravenswood church, located at Ashland and Winnemac Avenues. The small church building was quite close to the new Bethany Home for the aged. Westergreen wrote that he was satisfied with the appointment since it would not require him to move. When services or meetings ran late into the evening, he would spend the night at the Bethany Home or with ministerial colleagues in the area. His only critical comment about the appointment was regarding the quarterly meeting in February; he noted the winter weather had interfered with the stewards' work, so that he had received less than half his quarterly salary. This left him so short of funds that he had to withdraw all the money he had in the bank to pay his various debts.

When he went to Evanston just prior to Annual Conference in August 1894, he learned that of all the fourth year students, only one, Carl A. Albrektson, was joining their conference. All the rest of the class

24. Westergreen, *Journals*, April 4, 1894.

planned to join other conferences. That being the case, it was no doubt a surprise when Alfred Anderson told Westergreen he could not stay at the Ravenswood church for another year. The only appointment offered him was Emmanuel Methodist on the southwest side. The small congregation was an offshoot of the May Street church; some of the members had moved such a distance from May Street that they wished to start a new congregation, and did so in 1892. Under S. B. Newman's leadership, they bought a piece of land, built at least the basement level of a church, and were meeting there at the time Westergreen was offered the appointment. He did not want it. The only reason he stated clearly in his journal was that it was deeply in debt, but it is just as likely that he considered the inconvenience of trying to maintain his residence in Humboldt Park while serving a congregation on the other side of the city. He requested supernumerary status instead, which dismayed the presiding elders. They offered him Waukegan and Lake Forest. He held his ground and took supernumerary status for a year, but decided to supply Waukegan as though he had been appointed. It was an awkward situation for everyone, and caused a rift between Westergreen and Alfred Anderson. He was not the only one displeased with the presiding elders; Andrew was moved to Geneva and Batavia, and he and Selma were both unhappy and angry about the secret manner in which the appointments were made.[25] Arvid Sörlin, son of Westergreen's friend the late Daniel Sörlin, was appointed to Ravenswood in Westergreen's place. Westergreen bore him no ill will for the change; at least three times in 1894 he made favorable comments about the younger minister's preaching. A possible reason for bishop's cabinet forcing Westergreen to make way for Sörlin was that the latter was a student at the seminary, and likely requested a place not far from Evanston to fulfill supervised ministry requirements.

Westergreen remained perturbed about the cabinet's decision for some time. At the end of October he went to the preachers' meeting but wrote, "My present position is somewhat strange, and I also feel somewhat strange in connection with the brethren in the regular work."[26] He had a long letter from his brother Andrew, which repeated a remark allegedly made by Alfred Anderson in the cabinet, and another attributed to Bishop Vincent. He took the letter and it to his old friend John Wigren and they discussed it at length, concluding that they believed they still had many

---

25. Westergreen, *Journals*, August 30 and September 5, 1894.
26. Westergreen, *Journals*, October 29, 1894.

brethren in ministry who were good and true to them. One can only speculate what remarks engendered such a response. A week later, he received
an invitation from Alfred Anderson and his wife to come to their house
in Ravenswood for the monthly Swedish preachers' meeting, which would
also be a celebration of the Andersons' twentieth wedding anniversary.
Westergreen wrote, "I wrote back and thanked [him] for the invitation but
declined to come for reasons I did not want to state just now."[27]

Because he was supernumerary rather than having a pastoral appointment, he generally went to Waukegan and Lake Forest only on Sundays, and not every Sunday at that. The Waukegan people did not have a
church building until 1896, but met in the WCTU Hall on Washington
Street. The Lake Forest congregation met on Sunday afternoon in the
chapel of a Presbyterian church, and never grew to sufficient size to have
its own building. This meant Westergreen had no place to use as a base
for ministry in either town. For the first time in his life, time weighed
heavily on his hands. He busied himself with household chores, calling
on fellow clergy, going to the park, and writing letters and articles. In his
journal he lamented, "It seems so strange that I have not any meeting
in the week as I have been used to have. It seems to me that I have not
enough to do, and yet how much worse it would have been if I had not
any place at all to preach in even on Sundays."[28]

In the meantime, his mother was melancholy and weeping a great
deal, without any apparent provocation. It was a difficult period. Other
than listing his sermon texts for each time he preached in Waukegan or
Lake Forest, he gave little detail about his ministry there, though it must
have been fruitful, since the Waukegan congregation grew and raised sufficient funds to erect their own building twenty-four months after he left.
Their appreciation for him was expressed on his final Sunday there, when
they presented him with a silver water pitcher with a plate and goblet. The
church's thirty-fifth anniversary program referred to Westergreen as "one
of our leading ministers."[29]

During the year of supernumerary status, he did find enjoyment in
his usual pursuits: preaching at Des Plaines and local tent-meetings as
well as at a Holiness Conventions in February and December, working
on his reminisces of his first five years in the United States as well as

27. Westergreen, *Journals*, November 8, 1894.

28. Westergreen, *Journals*, September 20, 1894.

29. *Thirty-Fifth Anniversary 1892–1927*, 2.

a general history of Swedish Methodism, and writing and lecturing on sanctification and the Second Coming.

The famous Pullman Strike occurred between May 11 and August 2, 1894. Westergreen did not comment about it by name, though it affected his brother John directly and himself perhaps indirectly. In late June, John came home downcast because he was having difficulty making a living, much less paying his debts. It was a common complaint among those who worked for the railroad, particularly those living in Pullman neighborhood, because Pullman owned both the houses and utilities for his workers. In the recession, he cut wages, denied workers the opportunity to buy their houses, and he raised utility rates. John escaped at least that aspect of economic hardship. In July he telegraphed his brother from Bloomington, Illinois, saying he could not get back to Chicago because of the strike. Westergreen and his colleagues participated in tent-meetings in Pullman that summer, yet he did not write about the demonstrations he surely encountered, other than noting that some railroad cars were burned on July 6.

The other unexpected development in 1894 was a romance between S. B. Newman, who was then eighty-two years old, and Miss Anna C. Ohman, who was twenty. Westergreen and Wigren were aghast at the prospect of them marrying. Westergreen wrote a long letter to Newman in which he "tried to show him the unfitness of it on account of the great difference in age between them.[30] He received no written response, but Newman and Anna Ohman visited him at home. Westergreen admitted that she seemed to be a sensible girl. The couple then went to Wigren's to try to win his approval. They had a "long and plain talk," and Wigren agreed to perform the ceremony at his house—but first Wigren wrote out a will for Newman to sign, making his bride the sole beneficiary of his estate. Newman's friends reasoned, "We think it is no more than right that a young woman who throws away her chances by marrying such an old man should also have undisputed rights to his property after him."[31] Westergreen and the bride's parents were the only witnesses to the ceremony. About a week later, Westergreen called on the newlyweds and found them well-pleased with their life together. However, Newman reportedly felt bad over the position most of his colleagues in ministry took against him on account of the marriage. The union lasted eight

---

30. Westergreen, *Journals*, September 7, 1894.
31. Westergreen, *Journals*, September 13, 1894.

years, until Newman's death in 1902. May and December romances cause raised eyebrows even today, so it is not surprising there was gossip about Newman's unlikely match. One could speculate about the reasons for Westergreen and Wigren voicing their misgivings so freely. At the time, Westergreen was sixty and Wigren was sixty-eight: not as old as Newman, but old enough that either of them could have been Anna Ohman's father or, in Wigren's case, perhaps even her grandfather. There may have been an element of envy.

At Annual Conference in September 1895 Westergreen's appointment was changed once again. He was sent to Moreland, though he claimed he had been promised Forest Glen. Instead, Claus Olaf Sherman was appointed there. Sherman was four years younger than Westergreen, but had been in ordained ministry just over a year, compared with Westergreen's decades of experience. It was an awkward and discouraging situation; when Westergreen went to Moreland to preach his first midweek service, he learned that the congregation had wanted to keep his predecessor—none other than Sherman—and people were not pleased with the change. In addition, he had considerable difficulty finding a boarding place near the church. He went to S. B. Newman's home in Austin, not far from Moreland, and discussed the matter with him. Eventually the difficult beginning seems to have smoothed out; the Moreland congregation had a surprise party for him in November, and presented him with a gift of nearly twenty dollars.

Two high points in the life of the larger church that year were the jubilee Sunday of Swedish Methodism on May 26, marking fifty years since O. G. Hedstrom preached his first Swedish sermon on the Bethel Ship in New York, and the jubilee celebration of the church in Victoria, Illinois. One jubilee-connected event was the presentation of an original cantata about the history of Swedish Methodism, composed by Adolf Edgren and performed at the Central Music Hall in Chicago on May 30, 1895. The second piece in the cantata, for solo, quartet and choir, describes Eric Jansson's rivalry with Jonas Hedstrom:

> Now, Eric Jansson, from the North
> Found friends in Hälsingland;
> They wished, like him, to try their luck
> Upon a foreign strand.

Pursued in Sweden, Jansson fled
To western Illinois,
He staked his claim at Bishop Hill
New freedom to enjoy.

His fellow pilgrims gathered 'round
And other strangers, too;
The Prophet Jansson wanted all
To follow teachings new.

But Jansson was compelled to yield
In preaching and debate
To Jonas Hedstrom, Methodist,
Whose pulpit skill was great.

To Hedstrom, then, the people turned,
And he gave God the praise;
Preached hope, salvation, holiness,
To guide them all their days.[32]

The cantata alternates between recounting Methodist history and praising God for divine guidance. One section, apparently to be read rather than sung, comprises poetry about various leaders in the early days of Swedish Methodism. The poem about Peter Challman, who had died six years before this celebration, further emphasized the rivalry between the Janssonists and Methodists:

Though eloquent he might not be,
Our Challman knew theology.
With sermons bold he fished for men,
A thoroughgoing Wesleyan.
He left behind the Janssonists,
Joined forces with the Methodists.
Presiding elder, pastor, friend
He served his Lord until the end.[33]

A. J. Anderson and Westergreen were grouped together in a two-part poem, in which this was written about Westergreen:

---

32. Edgren, *Kantat vid Jubelfesten*, pt. 1, p. 2.
33. Edgren, *Kantat vid Jubelfesten*, pt. 2.

And Westergreen, hero of old,
Has heavenly treasures more than gold.
A noble warrior, strong and brave
Who wields the Gospel sword to save.
From early days has fought the fight
To build the church and shine the light.
A servant of the Word and prayer
For victory in Christ to share.
His labor has not been in vain;
A precious harvest he will gain.
To Westergreen and Anderson
The Lamb of God will say, "well done."
And with the patriarchs of yore
They'll dwell with Christ forever more.[34]

The Chicago-area clergy held simultaneous jubilee meetings in three of their largest churches. C. G. Wallenius and Oscar Linstrum led the celebration at the Fifth Avenue Church, William Henschen and Alfred Anderson presided at the May Street Church, and Westergreen and A. J. Anderson were at Market Street. Westergreen and A. J. Anderson were the two main speakers at the celebration in Victoria the following month. A week before they took the train to western Illinois, Anderson had asked to borrow the manuscript of Westergreen's already completed jubilee speech, presumably to avoid duplication. When he had finished studying it, Anderson gave it to his daughter Emma to return it to Westergreen, and somehow she lost it en route. Emma and her mother came to the Westergreen home to apologize for the mishap, and he had to spend the next few days reconstructing it from memory. Nevertheless, he had a good time back in Knox County in mid-June. He visited his brother Swan and family, saw the newly built Maxey's Chapel Methodist Church, not far from the family farm, and described the celebration in Victoria as a great day. On the Sunday morning he preached from Ps 89:15–17. The church was crowded and there were as many outside as inside. Anderson preached in the afternoon, and in the evening they both spoke in English. There were about three hundred at the noonday dinner, and two hundred at supper.

Westergreen preached mainly at Swedish Methodist churches this year, the majority at Waukegan, Lake Forest, and Moreland, but also to at least ten other congregations. He also preached for the Mission Friends, at tent-meetings, and at Des Plaines Campground. He finished writing

34. Edgren, *Kantat vid Jubelfesten*, pt. 2.

his history of Swedish Methodism, and compiled statistics on the Swedish Methodist seminary for a memorial meeting in May. By his reckoning, more than a hundred men had studied there since its genesis twenty-five years earlier. Of these, five had died, four left the denomination, two resigned due to health reasons, and the rest were in ministry in the United States and Sweden.[35]

He would have given himself mixed reviews in terms of his own spiritual life. Although he continued to struggle with sexual temptation, regarding it as a "defilement of the flesh" against which he invoked divine assistance, he also enjoyed moments of religious consolation. In late June, after his ailing mother felt somewhat better, he wrote, "While I was out walking, I began to think and study about salvation by faith until my heart got warmed and I felt a sweeter rest than I have for some time, bless the Lord." A few days later, riding on a streetcar, he mused, "I was thinking about Christ and salvation until I came into a very happy frame of mind and felt a joy that I have not felt I think for nearly two years."[36]

Such moments of sweet communion and calm were becoming fewer and farther between because of concern about family members, particularly his mother and his youngest brother. His mother's eyesight was failing and, combined with her depression and progressive dementia, she required a full-time caregiver. John's wife, Annie, helped care for her until her own mother became ill. Westergreen hired a widow who lived nearby, Mrs. Malmström, to do the housekeeping and care for Hanna. Several times Hanna fainted, had long crying spells, and appeared to have minor strokes. When she was awake and alert she was nevertheless confused and querulous. On one occasion she accused her son of having a surreptitious romance with Mrs. Malmström, which provoked him into losing his temper and speaking harshly to her; it also caused Mrs. Malmström to depart for a period. Another time he wrote in his journal:

> Towards evening Mother was again making some remarks that were so entirely different from the facts, when we bought our house in Galesburg, which I thought I ought to correct. But I was foolish in that, for she fell into one of her hysterical states of weeping. I see now that we have to treat Mother nearly as a child. God give me patience and help me to do what is right to her. . . . Mother has been weeping nearly the whole day and I have not been able to engage in any conversation with her. May

35. Westergreen, *Journals*, May 16, 1895.
36. Westergreen, *Journals*, June 27 and July 1, 1895.

God help both her and us for if this shall continue, I do not
know where it may end.[37]

His brother John became ill in January, and they suspected consumption. Nels accompanied him to a pension agent and signed an af-
fidavit that John had indeed served in the Union army under another
name; they hoped that a pension would assist John and Annie in their
financial straits. John recovered sufficiently to resume working for the
railroad, but suffered a stroke while in St. Louis. He made it back to Chicago, but was unable to walk and could not speak clearly. It was the first
of several strokes. He appeared to recover from the first one, and was
well enough to accompany Nels to a preachers' meeting in early March of
1896. Within a few weeks, however, he was admitted to Wesley Hospital
in Chicago. He showed little improvement, and after a week his physi-
cians said he might as well go home. Had the medical staff known of
his stressful domestic situation, perhaps they would have reconsidered.
Shortly after his return home, creditors threatened to repossess the family's furniture to cover their debts. John continued to decline, and Annie, her mother, and Nels took turns keeping vigil at his bedside. The
journal notes, "The doctor was here and tapped him of water, and he
had no encouragement to give about him. I said to my brother, now try
to think on your Savior; you have nothing else to do now, to which he
nodded assent."[38] John died around 4:00 a.m. on June 5, 1896. They had
the funeral from the house, since they did not expect many would attend.
Andrew and Selma came from Geneva, as well as some Americans, and
Hanna was able to be up and witness the service. John Wigren spoke in
English, and Brothers Alfvin and Iverson in Swedish. The burial was at
Rose Hill Cemetery, and Nels paid all the funeral expenses.

Soon after John's first stroke in 1895, Annie, who suffered from epilepsy, fell while having a seizure downtown, and had to be helped home.
The seizures became more frequent, and a physician they consulted suggested she should undergo an operation for her ailments. A few weeks after John's death, the family received word that brother Alex's wife, Eunice,
had died in Hingham, Massachusetts. Westergreen displayed pastoral
empathy in his condolence letter to Alex and daughter, commenting that
"she died happy in her Savior, so all is well, though it must be lonely in

---

37. Westergreen, *Journals*, April 26–27, 1895.
38. Westergreen, *Journals*, June 4, 1896.

the house after her."[39] He also remarked after John's death that the house seemed empty. Nevertheless, he was not bowed down with grief as he had been after other deaths in the family. His journal in the weeks following the funeral mentioned John and Annie only in connection with settling financial matters: helping Annie and her mother move across the street, following up on the pension claim, and going with Annie and his brother Andrew to Northwestern Loan and Mortgage to pay up the rest of the chattel mortgage on their furniture. His emotional investment in his brother was manifested through prayers for healing and salvation in journal entries during John's illness, but after his death there was no introspection about the state of his brother's soul, their relationship with one another, etc. His kindness toward his brother's widow was evident; after all, he paid the first month's rent on her apartment, and continued to subsidize her periodically, but there was not the same degree of friendship he had with his brother Andrew's wife, Selma.

The journal entry for December 24, 1896, was rather lugubrious. Annie and her mother, Mrs. Black, spent the evening with Westergreen and his mother. He noted that he received a letter from his brother Alex, answered it immediately, and went on to write, "[I] gave some Christmas presents. Had a pleasant Christmas Eve at home. Who shall be living another Christmas Eve, God only knows. Last Christmas Eve brother John was living but now he is gone. Who shall go next of us God only knows."[40]

Hanna Westergreen's health continued to deteriorate, so that she needed constant care and supervision. Westergreen's ministry frequently required him to be gone overnight. This made Mrs. Malmström an essential part of the household. As noted earlier, she had left for awhile the previous year in protest of Hanna's accusations about a romance with Nels, but returned to her post in the Westergreen household. She left a second time in November 1896, albeit only for a few days, when Hanna took a sudden dislike to her. Westergreen reflected, "I hope she may come back again. She has taken such good care both of mother and the house so we cannot spare her. Sister Annie has been in and stayed with mother, but she has her own home and cannot do what Mrs. Malmström has done."[41]

It was in one sense fortunate that Hanna had limited mobility and almost no vision, because like many dementia patients, she had the urge to

---

39. Westergreen, *Journals*, June 22, 1896.

40. Westergreen, *Journals*, December 24, 1896.

41. Westergreen, *Journals*, November 5, 1896.

wander. On occasion she would angrily announce she was going out, stand on the porch for awhile, and eventually come back inside with no recollection of her decision to leave. The words Westergreen most often used to describe his mother's condition were weak, weepy, and above all, nervous.

Under such circumstances it is understandable that he suffered periods of discouragement and depression himself, and that he immersed himself in his work. He had long admired Ole Peter Petersen (1822–1901), the founder of Methodism in Norway, and went to hear him preach, admiring Petersen's "new and original thoughts." Now he also became friends with Henry Danielsen (1846–1920), the minister at the Norwegian-Danish Methodist Church in Moreland, and the two held union meetings for the annual week of prayer in January. Westergreen was subsequently invited to preach to Danielsen's congregation several times, as well as to other Norwegian Methodist congregations in the city. As in the previous years, he spoke at temperance rallies and holiness meetings. In July he enjoyed the annual campmeeting at Des Plaines, preaching three times and participating in meetings; these included testimony meetings, prayer meetings, after-meetings, and preaching services. In addition to Westergreen himself, other leaders included C. O. Karlson, Oscar Linstum, William Swenson, M. L. Wickman, Claus Sherman, A. J. Anderson, Peter Magnus Alfvin, Knut Hanson, Eric Adolf Davidson, John Bendix, Karl Herman Elmström, Isaac Anderson, C. J. Nelson, J. B. Anderson, and Westergreen's brother Andrew. For the first time in his ministry Westergreen wrote of participating in anointing of the sick with three other ministers, one of whom was a Mission Friends pastor. Though he had never written anything in opposition to this liturgical act, adopting it late in his ministry—without comment or explanation—was unexpected.

Westergreen continued to be invested in ministerial education and furthering his own intellectual development. His leisure reading included Tertullian, Hippolytus, Cyprian, apocryphal works of the Ante-Nicean period, and *The Apostolic Canons* and *Constitutions*, along with a prodigious amount of Bible reading. His ministerial and educational leadership was recognized in June of 1896, when John Wigren came and told him he had received the title of Doctor of Divinity from Hedding College in Abingdon, a town about twelve miles south of Galesburg. Westergreen sounded ambivalent when describing the honor:

> When I came home I found my Doctor of Divinity diploma had come. It is all in Latin, printed on parchment. So I have got at last the honor or the title—whatever it implies—but feel just the

same as I did before. It will sound awkward when persons are calling me doctor. . . . I wrote a letter to Dr. Evans and accepted the doctorate they had conferred upon me. I also sent twenty dollars for the same. What is the honor or the doctor's title, after all, against a full assurance of a good standing with the Lord? No higher title can be given than to be called a child of God.[42]

It was just as well that Westergreen's reputation as a scholar was recognized in this way, because when Annual Conference was held in Jamestown, New York, at the end of August, he was appointed as an assistant teacher at the seminary in Evanston. He described the appointment as "being left without a charge," but wrote that he hoped he could be as happy and useful as he was when he was editing *Sändebudet* (and without pastoral responsibility) years earlier. Despite not being the shepherd of a congregation, he preached nearly a hundred times in at least thirteen different churches and two campmeetings in 1897.

He found the school had changed significantly since his previous stint there in the 1880s. In addition to the ministerial curriculum with which he was familiar, it now offered general education courses. He was expected to teach arithmetic, geography, physiology, general history, English, and the history of the United States. The first three had not been among the course offerings when he last taught, and he found arithmetic particularly demanding, and wryly commented that "some of them [his students] are not very brilliant scholars." When the fall term began on September 29, they had about fifteen students. The following June, the seminary trustees concluded that because they anticipated a small enrollment for the following academic year, they could manage with just one professor: Albert Ericson. Westergreen was not upset about the decision, but commented that he hoped he would get some pastoral work to do, because he felt better in that and it agreed with him more. One might say he enjoyed being a scholarly pastor rather than a full-time professor. An account of a religious high point supports this conclusion:

> While riding in the cars today to Evanston it appeared to me that the plan of salvation was very simple and for awhile I was really rejoicing in it. How is it that it cannot appear in the same way always, as there cannot be any deception in it. Lord, help me. When shall I get out in *the clear light not only of theology, but of spiritual enjoyment?*[43]

42. Westergreen, *Journals*, July 10 and 13, 1896.

43. Westergreen, *Journals*, March 3, 1897, emphasis mine.

During the year at the seminary, he both lectured at local churches and went to hear other speakers, both homiletical and scholarly. In June 1897 he gave a lecture on Luther at a church in Grand Crossing, and gave a temperance talk in North Cape Building on North Avenue. Westergreen continued to preach at Des Plaines, at tent-meetings, at holiness meetings, and, for the first time noted in his journal, at open-air street meetings. One such meeting was held at the corner of Erie and Elizabeth Streets, and another at the corner of North Avenue and Fairfield, close to the Humboldt Park Church. He heard D. L. Moody speak about being endowed with the Holy Spirit to do Christian work, and he regularly visited Lutheran and Norwegian-Danish Methodist churches. At one preachers' meeting, a professor gave a talk about Christian communism with Christ's Sermon on the Mount as the foundation. Westergreen noted some remarks were made afterward, but no strong criticism. He was still occasionally critical of the preaching style or worship practice at other churches. For example, when he went to Wicker Park Methodist Episcopal Church, he heard Dr. Holmes preach and was invited to help administer the sacrament. He noted, "There were a number of children that partook. I did not like it, for while we administered it I saw two little boys giggle right there at the altar railing, showing evidently not enough respect for that ordinance."[44] Of A. J. Anderson, he wrote, "[He] preached an excellent sermon on the gifts of the Holy Spirit. He advanced some new ideas but I think he stood on scriptural ground, and made his views clearer than when I have heard him on that subject before."[45]

At Annual Conference, which was held in Galva the first week of September 1897, Westergreen was appointed to Englewood, while his brother Andrew was sent to do a second term at Bishop Hill. Westergreen's predecessor at Englewood, C. G. Wallenius, was slow in moving out of the parsonage, leaving him with nowhere to stay overnight his first weeks on the new charge. He continued to use the Humboldt Park house as his home base, in large part because Hanna could not be moved. The Englewood congregation threw him a welcome party after a Thursday evening service, and gave him over ten dollars.

As was the case in other years, Westergreen mentioned current events and life in the city around him. He rejoiced when William McKinley was inaugurated as president because McKinley was "a professing

44. Westergreen, *Journals*, February 2, 1897.
45. Westergreen, *Journals*, March 26, 1897.

Christian man and a member of the Methodist Church." The war between Greece and Turkey was noted. He wrote about large fires at the Union Stockyards and on Madison Street between Clark and Dearborn. One amusing narrative consistent with his general disapproval of sports was written after visiting the park; "there was a large crowd gathered and they played what some said was football, but I thought it was the most foolish play I have ever seen, and not at all like the original football game."[46] The comment is made more entertaining by the fact that prior to this entry, Westergreen never mentioned having *seen* a football game, much less having played in one.

In the Englewood appointment, Westergreen encountered some of the same difficulties he had in previous churches. Attendance was irregular, and he wondered whether it was a waste of time to hold Thursday evening services, when so few people attended. He was perplexed by how few came out on major feast days, such as Pentecost. He was not paid in a timely fashion; in his last monthly meeting of the conference year, he noted that they still owed him twenty-eight dollars of his salary, adding that he expected it would never be paid. Both the congregation and their building were relatively new; the former had been organized in 1883 under Eric Shogren, and the latter was constructed at a new location west of Halsted Street in 1894. It may be that the congregation's debt on the building made paying the minister a secondary priority. The highlights of his ministry at Englewood seemed to be holding protracted meetings in January with John Lundeen, the minister appointed to the Union Avenue Swedish Methodist Church, followed by protracted meetings at Lundeen's church. Westergreen did not describe unpleasant situations at Englewood; he simply did not have any circumstances that brought him satisfaction or joy. The congregation may have felt the same way about him, since after his last service there before being moved, no parting gift or social occasion was mentioned.

His ministry required him to stay on the south side often, making quick trips back to Humboldt Park to check on his mother and see how Mrs. Malmström was coping with an increasingly demanding situation. In late January Westergreen arranged to have the prayer group (probably from the Market Street congregation) meet at his house because his mother was no longer able to go out. He managed to get Hanna into the room for only a little while before she said she had to go back to bed.

---

46. Westergreen, *Journals*, October 13, 1897.

When his brother Andrew came from Bishop Hill to visit Hanna in April 1898, she did not know who he was until they told her. The same thing happened when Peter Magnus Alfvin, who was then pastor at Humboldt Park, and A. J. Anderson, the presiding elder, called. A few months later Alfvin's wife came and stayed with them for several hours, taking supper with them. She brought the gloomy news that A. J. Wicklund, who had been a minister in the Swedish Methodist Conference before joining the Free Methodists, and become deranged and died recently in the insane asylum in Elgin. Fortunately, this news did not seem to register with Hanna. John Wigren, whom Hanna saw more often than the others, paid her several visits and prayed with her, which cheered her up.

Although Westergreen tried to stay close to home for his mother's sake, he maintained a busy preaching schedule, giving over 150 sermons to about a dozen Swedish Methodist congregations. In addition, he preached at Skogsbergh's Tabernacle on the south side, a Swedish Baptist church, Des Plaines Campground and in a revival tent set up on Oakley Avenue. In his limited free time he attended Norwegian Methodist and Salvation Army tent-meetings in the city, a pan-Scandinavian temperance meeting, heard a presentation by social worker Jane Addams at a preachers' meeting, and went to hear General William Booth, the founder of the Salvation Army, speak in the Central Music Hall. Westergreen made no comment about Addams, but of Booth he wrote, "He gave us a plain good evangelical talk and they had fine music and singing."[47] He made one journey to Bradley, Illinois, and a brief trip to Knox County to visit family and friends in November. During that visit he noted that his brother Swan looked very thin, and was told by his niece Nellie that he was not strong.

A few weeks prior to Annual Conference, which was held at the Union Avenue Church, A. J. Anderson told Westergreen that he would likely be reappointed to Englewood for the following year. Westergreen went to Conference in fairly good spirits, noting the high point of one of the evening services was the singing of J. A. Hultman (1861–1942), the Swedish-born musician who was one of the founding members of the Evangelical Mission Covenant Church (Mission Friends), whose nickname was "The Sunshine Singer." He described the Conference as pleasant and peaceable, but for the second time in five years, he was given an unexpected appointment: the little charge of Forest Glen, miles

47. Westergreen, *Journals*, March 29, 1898.

northwest of Humboldt Park. Westergreen did not express disappointment or anger at the time, but a few days later he took a walk around Forest Glen and commented, "It is very beautiful in summer time, but I am afraid it will be dreary in winter." On a rainy day, a week after that journal entry, he wrote, "I stayed at home and tried to write some. Have felt a kind of melancholy, probably on account of the weather. How little, O Lord, am I doing anyhow. It seems to me sometimes as [though] my life has been to a great extent a failure. Lord, help me."[48]

Reading between the lines, one could infer the low spirits came not only from the inclement weather, but also anxiety about his mother and less than wholehearted enthusiasm about changing appointments again. There are laments at intervals throughout the sixty-three years of daily journals, but this was the first time he questioned whether his *life* was a failure: an indication of how discouraged he felt.

The news event that preoccupied his writing in 1898 was the Spanish-American War, which lasted from April until August. Westergreen first mentioned the conflict in February, when the US battleship *Maine* was blown up at Havana Harbor. In the first half of April he wrote, "There seems to be dissatisfaction with the President's message to Congress as not definite or warlike enough. And really, President McKinley is a weak man or he is a very consummate statesman; which it is will soon be seen. I hope, however, in spite of the excitement that war may be averted."[49]

Less than ten days later, the United States was fully involved in the conflict, which forced Spain to relinquish claims on Cuba, and to cede sovereignty over Guam, Puerto Rico, and the Philippines to the United States. Westergreen recorded the following in his journal:

> The papers are full of war and it seems that we have fired the first shot. God only knows what the outcome shall be when it begins in real earnest. May God help us. . . . At the preachers' meeting there was some talk about getting up an organization something like the Christian Commission was during our Civil War. . . . Troops are leaving Chicago today for the war.[50]

As spring and summer progressed, he made note of Admiral Dewey's victory over the Spanish at Manila, the bombardment of San Juan, Puerto Rico, and the destruction of Spanish Admiral Cervera's fleet and the

48. Westergreen, *Journals*, September 22, 1898.

49. Westergreen, *Journals*, April 12, 1898.

50. Westergreen, *Journals*, April 23–25, 1898.

surrender of Santiago, Cuba. His choice of words, such as "our fleet" and "may God be with us," are indications of how he considered himself an American, despite the focus of his ministry being to Scandinavian immigrants. He was proud of his adopted country and loyal to it.

Westergreen preached his first sermons as minister to Forest Glen on the last Sunday of September. He attended the Epworth League in the afternoon, and stayed there overnight. His only comment about being in his new charge was that he enjoyed good liberty the entire day. A few weeks later when he went there for the Thursday evening service in the midst of a storm that changed from rain to snow, he and the sexton were the only ones who showed up. They sat there awhile, had prayer together, and then went home. For the last two months of the year, he wrote less about his ministry and was focused primarily on his mother's illness. Even when he traveled to Knox County in November, he visited his father's grave in Galesburg and mused that perhaps it would not be long before his mother would be brought there. The journal entries communicate a sense of mournful inevitability. By the end of November Hanna Westergreen was nearly deaf as well as blind, and hardly able to speak, let alone get out of bed without assistance. His brother John's widow, Annie, was sympathetic but could offer no practical help; in June of 1898 she suffered a stroke and had difficulty walking and talking. Westergreen remarked there was little hope of her ever getting well again. He sent updates on Hanna's condition to his brother Swan every few days, usually by postcard.[51] Hanna's physician, Dr. Hess, visited and said she had "a kind of paralysis of the spinal column, and medicine would not do her much good." Two women from the church visited the same evening, and their presence seemed to make her feel better than she had for several days. But it was a temporary reprieve. She sank into semi-consciousness, moaning occasionally but not speaking again. Mrs. Carlson, a friend who lived on North Avenue, was brought in to assist Mrs. Malmström, so that she and Westergreen could get some respite. Hanna seemed to rest easier, and occasionally smiled. On the fourth Sunday of Advent, Westergreen went to Forest Glen and preached in the morning from 1 Pet 1:1–3, which, after the opening salutation, reads: "Blessed be the God and Father of our Lord Jesus Christ! By his great mercy he has given us a new birth into a living hope through the resurrection of Jesus Christ from the dead." Unfortunately, the manuscript for the sermon has been lost. The text was an

51. Presumably he sent similar messages to Andrew in Bishop Hill and Alex in Massachusetts, but only the messages to Swan were preserved.

odd one for the Sunday before Christmas, but turned out to be a poignant choice. When he came home after morning worship he found his mother sinking, but did not believe her end was near, so he and Mrs. Malmström had dinner and noon prayer as usual. When they finished praying, they found her dying, "so still that it seemed almost like a tired child going to sleep, and so she entered her rest."[52] His postcard to Swan, written later that afternoon, was brief: "Dear Brother, Mother has just died. I can say no more. Your brother, N. O. Westergreen." The cause of death listed on the certificate is illegible.

The following day he wrote Swan and his family a letter; both the pages and the envelope were edged in black:

> Dear Brother Swan and family,
>
> Grace and peace! Our dear mother died yesterday about 1:45 o'clock in the afternoon. She did not regain the power of speech so that we could get a dying testimony from her. But on Saturday she had more rest and seemed to be happy, occasionally folding her hands on her breast as in prayer, and speaking to herself, but we could not catch the words. But I thought I heard her say once, "and they crucified him" so she had no doubt communion with her Savior. She seemed to be happy occasionally and smiled, what vision she saw we do not know, but [the Lord] she trusted has taken her to himself and that she has entered her eternal rest. She died so quiet like a tired child goes to sleep. We intend to bury her in Galesburg next Thursday in the forenoon. We have her funeral services here on Wednesday at the north side church at 2:00 o'clock in the afternoon and start for Galesburg 5:30 in the evening. I will write to Brother Andrew that he goes to Galesburg and order the grave dug and also a hearse and three carriages and bearers. Could you help him some, Brother? I cannot express my feelings of loneliness, but Jesus helps.
>
> Your brother,
> N. O. Westergreen[53]

Hanna's body lay untouched in the Westergreen home for two days, until the undertaker arrived with a casket. She was dressed and placed in it, and remained there another twenty-four hours until P. M. Alfvin performed services in the house: probably some version of a wake service.

---

52. Westergreen, *Journals*, December 18, 1898.

53. Nels Westergreen, postcard and letter to Swan Westergreen, December 18 and 19, 1898.

Then they all went to the Market Street Church where A. J. Anderson, who had known Hanna for over forty-three years, gave a "very touching and also instructive address" as well as writing the obituary that appeared in *Sändebudet* about two weeks later. John Wigren and A. J. Anderson also spoke, and there were about ten ministers present. No mention was made of what hymns were sung or what else occurred during the course of the worship at Market Street Church, but silence on the subject would have been consistent with denominational practice of the time. Following the service, Westergreen had the casket loaded onto a train bound for Galesburg. A second funeral service took place at the Galesburg Church, where Olof Johnson and O. A. Rabe spoke. She was buried next to her husband Ola in Hope Cemetery. Westergreen noted that "her corpse, which was natural and even beautiful for her age, had been well preserved." The funeral expenses may seem minimal compared to modern prices, but they were a financial burden for Westergreen. His total income for 1898 was less than a thousand dollars. He had been cheated of four months' back rent—forty-eight dollars—when the Flacks moved out. The bill from the Chicago undertaker was forty dollars, plus twenty-five dollars in Galesburg, over fourteen dollars in train fare to and from Galesburg, three dollars for flowers, and whatever it cost to open the grave. Fortunately, friends stepped forward to help him. He received a total of sixty-seven dollars from A. J. Anderson, A. G. Johnson, and other friends.

Hanna's death was without question the greatest bereavement Westergreen ever endured. The day after the funeral, he wrote:

> Stayed in Galesburg over this day and took long walks, but O, how lonesome since my dear mother, the best friend on earth, is gone. The world appears so bleak now. None can fill the empty void except Jesus. O, may he come in and take such possession of me that all my sorrow and loss may be swallowed up in him. But I will not complain. God has been good and merciful to take my mother home to rest.[54]

He spent Christmas away from his pastoral appointment that year—only the second time in his ministry to do so—and went to be with Andrew and Selma in Bishop Hill instead. Again, uncharacteristically, he did not attend the service early Christmas morning, but stayed in bed. He did preach the afternoon of Christmas Day, repeating the sermon he had

54. Westergreen, *Journals*, December 23, 1898.

preached the day his mother died. He returned to Chicago on the twenty-seventh, and wrote in his journal,

> When I came home today, O how sad and empty everything looked. There was mother's bedroom and bed now empty. There was her chair, now empty. I moved about the house silently and speaking in a low voice almost as on [*sic*] a funeral. O, for something to fill this empty void. Nothing but Jesus can do it.[55]

The depth of grief he describes was not unusual, but his ownership of it was uncommon for him. He had shared his home with his mother for the twenty-four years since Ola's death; combined with his first eighteen years under the parental roof plus living with them when appointed to Galesburg, it meant Nels and Hanna had lived together at least forty-two of his sixty-four years. Far from being an unhealthy attachment, the journals demonstrate he was more candid about the ups and downs of that relationship than he was about any other friendship or romance. Her death was more than a loss. It was the end of a major chapter in his life. In the months that followed, his journals included periodic laments even as he resumed his ministry at Forest Glen. But Hanna's death ushered in an era of multiple bereavements, the onset of his own physical ailments associated with the ageing process, and official retirement.

55. Westergreen, *Journals*, December 27, 1898.

8

Ten Thousand and More

1899 to 1907

Keep me, dear Savior, bless and sanctify me!
In loving favor, let me thy countenance see![1]

AT THE START OF 1899, Westergreen was preoccupied with the death of his mother. His sense of loss was reflected in his preaching: not just sermon content, but in his choice of texts. Of the 144 times he preached that year, the most frequently used texts were Luke 14:33 (*None of you can become my disciple if you do not give up all your possessions*), and John 16:32 (*The hour is coming, and indeed now is, when you will be scattered, each one to his home, and you will leave me alone*). Both passages, at face value, convey a sense of loss and abandonment. He preached ten times from the "Farewell Discourses" of John, his favorite of the four gospels, but only four times on resurrection narratives from the same gospel. Westergreen's journal entries echoed St. Paul's words in 1 Thess 4:13, in which the apostle reminds his brothers and sisters that they do not grieve as others do who have no hope. He wrote the following in his journal a few weeks after Hanna's death:

> Feel sad and lonely after mother. How empty the world looks to me now. How alone it seems to me I am in the world. Tried to

---

1. See Sandell, "Jesus, in Stillness Longing I Wait" [Herre, mitt hjärta], 327.

write something but I feel little inclined for anything now. O, for a filling up of this void with Jesus himself. He alone can satisfy me now. . . . Weather cold and the wind is brisk. Three weeks ago I had my mother with me. Now she is by the grace of our Lord Jesus Christ at rest and in glory. Bless the Lord in the midst of my loss and sorrow. But O, Jesus, fill the emptiness both around and within with thyself. My soul longs for it. May it soon come.[2]

He was not, however, entirely alone. Mrs. Malmström stayed on as his housekeeper even though she was no longer primary caregiver for Hanna. His sister-in-law Annie and Mrs. Black, Annie's mother, lived nearby, and he saw them frequently; in fact, these two women took care of the house when both Westergreen and Mrs. Malmström were ill in late January. Andrew and Selma were living in Bishop Hill, but Westergreen was in regular contact with Andrew in particular, since they were colleagues in ministry as well as brothers. And Westergreen remained close to his friends John Wigren, who had retired in 1895, and Victor Witting, who had lately returned from Sweden.

Several factors added to the misery of the first months of bereavement. First, there was record-setting cold in Chicago, with the pipes freezing as the mercury dropped to minus twenty-one. Second, Westergreen found himself short of funds after paying for the funeral and suffering the loss of rent, when his tenants left abruptly. His congregation at Forest Glen fell behind in paying him his salary. Things seemed to be looking up when a new tenant moved into his first-floor apartment. Then, almost immediately afterward, he learned that his brother Swan was very sick with "lung fever" and not expected to live. The following day he traveled to Victoria, where he had to spend the night before proceeding to Swan's home. Brother Andrew was also there. Swan was improving but was very weak and could not talk much. The three brothers wept and prayed together. Nels spent the night and then went on to Galva, where his colleague William Henschen was holding protracted meetings. He invited Westergreen to preach for him before returning to Chicago the following day.

Once he returned from western Illinois in mid-March, Westergreen seemed to regain his emotional and spiritual footing. His journal contained periodic laments over Hanna's death, but he wrote mainly about his ministry, including his ecumenical activities. His colleague Witting spent an afternoon talking with him before Westergreen went to hear

2. Westergreen, *Journals*, January 2 and 7, 1899.

him lecture at the Humboldt Park Church about the earliest days of
Swedish Methodism in America and his missionary work in Sweden.
Westergreen attended a Swedish Lutheran church on Good Friday, and
sat in on the diocesan convention of Swedish Episcopal clergy at St. Ansgarius Church. Afterward he went to the parsonage to look at the oldest
church records, and found his parents' names (and their five sons) listed;
Ola and Hanna had briefly affiliated with St. Ansgarius when they arrived
in nearly a half-century earlier.

No longer having the responsibility of caring for his mother allowed
him to be away from home more frequently during the next few years,
though he never commented on the fact. He preached at or attended no
fewer than eight tent-meetings in the city and campmeetings in 1899,
where the previous year he preached only at Des Plaines Campground
and a tent in the Pilsen neighborhood. It is true he had stopped in at
two other tent-meetings in the city, but he visited both the same day,
and preached at neither. Now, however, he preached twice at "a colored
campmeeting" in Forest Glen, at the Free Methodist campground in Glen
Ellyn, Sterling campground in Massachusetts, and at three tents or street
corners in the city, as well as at Des Plaines. His sermon texts for tent-
meetings and campgrounds gravitated toward conversion and the work
and fruits of the Holy Spirit in a believer.

His sister-in-law Annie lived nearby with her mother, and had received financial support from him since John's death in 1896. Now Annie's health took a turn for the worse. In early May 1899, she suffered
another one of her "attacks": probably epilepsy. She was unable to accompany Nels to place small flags on John's grave on Memorial Day. She
suffered another seizure in September, causing her to fall down a flight of
stairs and knock her unconscious for several hours. Thus began another
bedside vigil, seemingly at home rather than a hospital. A doctor came
in early October and said she had spinal meningitis. She died on October
10, 1899, without giving a dying testimony but also without much struggle. Westergreen and Mother Black went to Rosehill Cemetery, but were
unable to obtain two plots adjacent to John's, so they chose Mt. Olive on
the west side of the city, and had John's remains reinterred there.[3] The

---

3. There are three separate markers at Mt. Olive for John, Annie, and Annie's
mother. John's stone has his full name and the years of his birth and death. Annie's
stone, which is in the middle, reads "his wife Annie" with no surname or dates, and
poor Mrs. Black's stone simply reads "mother-in-law." The reason for these designa-
tions can be inferred from Nels Westergreen's will, in which he left $150 for the three

funeral was at Annie's church, and Westergreen spoke after Mr. Wilson, the pastor. Aside from floral tributes from friends, Westergreen covered all the funeral expenses, and Mother Black stayed with him for several days after the funeral. He was more affected by her death than one might expect: only the journal pages describing Hanna's death and Annie's are edged in black, and he wrote that "though poor, she had many friends, and she was lovely in her character."[4]

He did not travel farther than Galesburg in 1900, but in addition to serving his church in Melrose Park, he preached at sixteen different Swedish Methodist congregations, at American Methodist and non-Methodist churches, several campmeetings, and funerals. In contrast to the previous few years, family concerns did not figure largely in his journal or claim a significant amount of his time and energy. Instead, he turned once against to reflecting on current events, writing in service to the church, and renewing his interest in sanctification theology. He also continued to cross denominational lines and encourage his congregation to do the same. Surprisingly, his involvement in ministerial education this year was less than usual; he attended a celebration of the thirtieth anniversary of the founding of the seminary, held at the Lakeview church in March of 1900. His brother Andrew was invited to preach, possibly because he was one of the first three students. Westergreen attended the closing exercises of the seminary in Evanston, but did not otherwise seem to play an active role in the life of the school.

In January of that year he invited Victor and Maria Nordlund, who worked for the Scandinavian Alliance Mission, to speak at his church about the China Inland Mission.[5] He was fascinated by their ministry and in the artifacts from China they exhibited. Perhaps the Nordlunds' presentation accounts for his interest in the Boxer Rebellion, which took place between 1899 and 1901. In July he described an Epworth League Social, noting that some of the money raised would be sent to the suffering in India, but adding, "The rumors of the war in China are dark. What

---

headstones. This instruction would have been carried out by James T. Wigren, a son of John Wigren and also Westergreen's executor. One may conclude that Wigren, a generation younger than Westergreen, did not know Mother Black's correct name, and did not check with the cemetery office to learn it.

4. Westergreen, *Journals*, October 10 and 14, 1899.

5. Their daughter, Esther Nordlund (1896–1948), was martyred in China along with two other missionaries from the Evangelical Covenant (formerly Mission Friends) Church.

shall the end be?"[6] The Second Boer War (1899–1902) was occurring at the same time as the Boxer Rebellion, and Westergreen was not the only Chicago clergyman concerned about it. At a preachers' meeting early in the year, a Presbyterian minister named McKenzie read a paper about the conflict to the gathered clergy. Westergreen described it as excellent, and said it generated an animated debate, noting, "McKenzie cleared himself on every point, although he sided with the English."[7] In May, Westergreen joined with his fellow Chicagoans in observing Dewey Day, marking two years since Admiral Dewey won the Battle of Manila Bay during the Spanish-American War. Mayor Carter Harrison, Jr. hosted a dinner for fifteen hundred at the Chicago Athletic Association, with Dewey as the guest of honor. Westergreen was not at the dinner, but saw the parade in the city and wrote about it. When the Galveston Hurricane struck in September, Westergreen acknowledged the loss of life—as well he might, given that it was the deadliest natural disaster in US history—but surprisingly, he did not engage in his customary rumination about the spiritual readiness of those who perished.

In addition to writing a number of articles for *Sändebudet, Nordstjernan* (The North Star), and *Västra* (Western) *Sändebudet*, early in the year he finished a major writing project for Victor Witting, who was working on *Minnen från mitt lif som Sjöman, Immigrant och Predikant, Samt en historisk afhandling af Metodismens Uppkomst, Utveckling, Utbredning bland Svenskarne I Amerika och I Sverige* (Memories of my life as a sailor, immigrant and preacher, together with a historic treatise on Methodism's beginning, development and spread among Swedes in America and Sweden). More than century after it was published, it is impossible to say exactly how much of the book is Witting's work, and how much is Westergreen's. In October Westergreen mentioned: "I picked up a large registered letter package . . . some of Witting's manuscript for his history of Swedish Methodism, which he wants me to look through. I found only a couple of places where it needed a little correction of dates, which I did."[8]

Of the book's twenty-three chapters, only the first seven are unambiguously autobiographical. The last five chapters detail the history of Methodism in Sweden; this must be Witting's work, since he returned to

6. Westergreen, *Journals*, July 13, 1900.
7. Westergreen, *Journals*, February 19, 1900.
8. Westergreen, *Journals*, October 22 and 23, 1900.

Sweden to establish the church, while Westergreen never made a journey back to his native land. The remaining eleven chapters of the nearly six-hundred-page book give the history of Swedish Methodism in different parts of the United States. Although the book was published in 1902, the history only goes as far as 1877. Since Witting was abroad from 1867 to 1876, it is likely that Westergreen supplied both the statistics and narrative of Methodism's development during that period. Helping his friend Witting was not his only scholarly endeavor; he presented lectures on the life of Martin Luther, and spent four weeks preparing a lecture/paper on baptism, which was presented at the Swedish preachers' district meeting.

Westergreen never abandoned his striving after Christian perfection, but during the years just prior to 1900, the pursuit was somewhat eclipsed by his mother's and Annie's final illnesses and deaths. Now both his circumstances and changes in Chicago's religious climate brought it to the forefront again. At the annual campmeeting at Des Plaines, he preached three times. None of the sermon texts were specifically about sanctification (Ps 116:9–14; John 1:35–39; and Heb 7:25), but an afternoon sermon by Knut Hanson, a Norwegian preacher, moved him to go forward with others to seek sanctification on July 31. He wrote, "I cannot say that I got any special blessing or any evidence of a work wrought within me, but it seems that I can rest more quietly on my faith in Christ."[9] On the final night of the campmeeting, after a Communion service with the American Methodists, the Swedes went to their own tabernacle and continued until after midnight. Others adjourned to a grove, where they sang and prayed the whole night. Westergreen testified that he felt an emptiness and returned to the altar for healing of the Spirit. His fellow clergy prayed with him, and he "sought and found rest to his soul."

In mid-September Westergreen attended Annual Conference in Galesburg, and he was invited to have dinner with Bishop Fitzgerald. Alfred Anderson, who was once again the presiding elder, told Westergreen they had a good appointment for him. When the appointments were read out on the final day, he learned he was being sent to the small charge of Melrose Park, which he gave faint praise as being "better than what I had last year." His journal did note that "it seemed that most of our large and important charges are filled with men of inferior talents."[10] He had a point; from a contemporary perspective, the pattern

9. Westergreen, *Journals*, July 31, 1900.

10. Westergreen, *Journals*, September 18, 1899.

of appointments appears counter-intuitive. For example, from the time of the first meeting of Northwest Swedish Annual Conference in 1877, the two largest congregations were Market Street / First in Chicago, with 278 members, and Galesburg, with 275 members. At that Conference, Westergreen was made supervising elder of the Galesburg District and also served the charges of Moline, Rock Island, and Geneseo, with a total of 170 members. The Forest Glen and Melrose Park congregations did not yet exist. By 1883, Westergreen was presiding elder of the Chicago District. The largest congregations were again Market Street, with 436 members, and Galesburg (which was now part of the Chicago District) with 295 members. In 1897, these two churches were still the largest, with 490 and 300 in full membership, respectively. Logic, along with current denominational practice, would suggest that younger, less experienced ministers be appointed to smaller churches, and veterans in ministry be sent to larger, flagship congregations. In Westergreen's case, the opposite seems to have happened. He had served as an assistant to Erland Carlson in Chicago in 1865; this appointment included the Market Street Church. He served the second largest church, Galesburg, for three years in the 1870s. Now, however, he was sent to Melrose Park, which had only fifty-eight full members, after serving Forest Glen, which had the same number. His younger brother Andrew, whom he had trained for ministry, was appointed to Bishop Hill, which had 150 members. In other words, although Westergreen had served the largest congregations in Illinois, edited *Sändebudet*, started the Swedish Methodist seminary, and twice served as a presiding elder, in the final ten years before his retirement, he was given the smallest, fledgling congregations.

Alfred Anderson's role in this and in the larger church also comes into question. Seventeen years younger than Westergreen, he also was one of the first three students at the seminary in Galesburg. After serving churches in Iowa, he, like Westergreen, served as an assistant at the Market Street / First Church and then was pastor at Galesburg. From 1881–83 he was presiding elder of the Galesburg District, and in 1886 became presiding elder of the Chicago District for fifteen years: a extraordinarily long term. Only O. G. Hedstrom's appointment to the Bethel Ship ministry was longer among the Swedish Methodists, and that was to a single charge, not a Conference administrative position.[11] Anderson was also a delegate to General Conference several times, representing

11. The General Conference did not lift the term limit for pastorates until 1900.

the board of the theological seminary, and served as board member and
fundraiser for the Bethany Home. His relationship to Westergreen appears to have been mixed. At least twice he led Westergreen to believe he
would be appointed one place, only to change course at Annual Conference. He sent Andrew Westergreen to Batavia and Geneva in 1894, when
Andrew had been at the Union Avenue Church only a year and did not
want to move. Furthermore, Andrew and Selma disliked the manner in
which the change was made. This caused a temporary rift between Anderson and the Westergreen brothers. Unfortunately, since only a few of
Anderson's personal and professional papers have been preserved in the
Northern Illinois Conference Archives, there is no way to know if there
was animosity from his side, or if it was administrative clumsiness. To
be fair, it could also have been either a desire to lighten the workload
of a minister nearing retirement, or a strategy on the part of the bishop
and presiding elders to send an experienced and effective minister to
struggling and/or recently organized congregations. If we consider the
matter from the second perspective, Westergreen's latter appointments
make more sense. For example, Market Street Church had its genesis in
1852. The Galesburg church was a little older. But Melrose Park was a
"preaching station" served mainly by theological students until around
1887, when a church building was dedicated. Forest Glen did not have an
organized congregation until 1885. Moreland, which, with Melrose Park,
was Westergreen's appointment beginning with Annual Conference in
1892, had been organized only two years earlier. And Waukegan, where
Westergreen served during his supernumerary year, was also just two
years old, and still met in a hired room. In other words, it is possible that
Westergreen's evangelistic zeal, preaching, and administrative and pastoral skills were recognized and put to use where they were particularly
needed. As one of the pioneer ministers of Swedish Methodism, he was a
groundbreaker. To borrow a metaphor from St. Paul, often Westergreen
sowed and another watered, but only God gave the growth (1 Cor 3:6).
For example, Witting noted that his friend had done evangelism in the
Boston area in 1869, 1873, and 1875, before a congregation was finally
established until 1878.[12]

12. Witting, *Minnen Från Mitt Lif*, 493. It should be acknowledged that Albert Ericson, Eric Shogren, and O. G. Hedstrom also did evangelistic work in Boston before Otto
Anderson was able to organize a Methodist class. *Svenska Metodismen i Amerika* puts the
date at 1880, but perhaps that reflects when the class was organized into a congregation.

In the autumn of 1900 Westergreen had a visit from Anders Gustaf Milton, who was serving a church in Nebraska.[13] Milton spoke of his own experience of the blessing of sanctification, and reported that several ministers in the Kansas and Nebraska district both professed and preached this blessing as a special work of grace. In retrospect, this may have foreshadowed the controversy between the Methodist Episcopal Church and what came to be known as the Metropolitan Church Association in Chicago.

Urban perfectionist missions had spread rapidly in the two decades after the Civil War. There was a degree of theological polarization—some would say ecclesiastical and liturgical snobbism—within the Methodist Episcopal Church during this period. For example, an authorized Methodist hymnal was issued in 1878. Of its 307 authors, only ten were members of the Methodist Episcopal Church, and none represented Methodism's holiness or revivalist wing.[14] At the General Conference of 1894, an episcopal spokesman rebuked the formation of holiness associations in the denomination with these words:

> There has sprung up among us a party with holiness as a watchword; they have holiness associations, holiness meetings, holiness preachers, holiness evangelists, and holiness property. Religious experience is represented as if it consists of only two steps, the first step out of condemnation into peace and the next step into Christian perfection. . . . We do not question the sincerity and zeal of their brethren; we desire the church to profit by their earnest preaching and godly example; but we deplore their teaching and methods in so far as they claim a monopoly of the experience, practice, and advocacy of holiness, and separate themselves from the body of ministers and disciples.[15]

Borden P. Bowne of Boston University was extremely critical of holiness spirituality and "the witness of the Spirit," suggesting that the majority of seekers at campmeetings and other revivals were "aiming at an experience instead of surrendering themselves in faith to Christ."[16] The National Holiness Association, founded in 1867, had been invited to conduct holiness

13. Milton was born in Sweden in 1861, came to America at age eighteen, and worked as a carpenter in various states before being converted in 1885. At the point at which he wrote to Westergreen, he had been in ministry for ten years.

14. Case, "United Methodism," n.p.

15. Sweet, *Methodism in American History*, 343.

16. Kostlevy, *Holy Jumpers*, 24.

campmeetings at Des Plaines in 1870, 1889 and 1897, and the holiness movement spread across denominational lines. Nevertheless, it was most strongly rooted in the Wesleyan tradition.

By the 1890s, fault lines were visible both between Methodism's holiness/revivalist and non-holiness wings as well as within the holiness movement itself. Methodist preachers drawn into the movement prior to 1890 stayed within the Methodist Episcopal Church, for the most part. Younger ministers and laity, some of whom were attracted first by the pursuit of holiness and second to the denomination that hosted the holiness association, were more likely to leave and ally themselves either with newly forming denominations or launch unaffiliated ministries of their own. Subtle differences between Wesley's articulation of sanctification theology and Phoebe Palmer's must also be acknowledged as a factor. Wesley emphasized perfection as a process made possible by the Holy Spirit at work within the Christian, and developed a discipline for attaining perfect love; Palmer spoke of sanctification as a present possibility, emphasizing "a sudden crisis experience accompanied by emotional exuberance."[17] Although Westergreen's first exposure to sanctification theology *per se* was through reading Wesley's "Christian Perfection" translated into Swedish, followed by exposure to the distorted perfectionist theology of the Eric Janssonists, his journal makes it clear that he incorporated some of the "crisis experience" orientation of Palmer and American holiness theology of the last half of the nineteenth century. His critique of "come-outers" and what he believed were erroneous expressions of holiness theology found expression in his 1885 book, *Skillnaden på Sann Helighet och Religiöst Svärmeri*, as well as in sermons and articles for *Sändebudet*. He also presented a paper at a ministers' meeting titled, "What Attitude Should We Assume toward Those Who Spread Error among Us?" In it he identified multiple errors being promulgated: higher criticism taken to the point of questioning the truth and authority of Scripture; a worldly spirit, manifested in "carnal liberty" and the lodge meeting and secret societies encroaching on the prayer meeting; certain religious emotions as a substitute for holiness; imposing forms, ceremonies, and beautiful liturgy as a substitute for the requirement of a true Christian life, experience and profession.[18] Westergreen's upbringing in Shartauan Pietism and loyalty to the church as an institution were

17. Jones, *Perfectionist Persuasion*, 4.
18. Westergreen, "What Attitude Should We Assume," 2–8.

manifested in this critique of some of the non-affiliated ministries that
were flourishing during this period:

> The presentation of the church in the Bible as a divine institu-
> tion; the historical testimony of the church in her spread and
> evangelization of the world, the church as the depository of
> truth, even during the dark ages, and God acknowledging him-
> self to the church, by pouring out his Spirit upon it occasion-
> ally, and blessing its work and giving success to the spread of
> the Christian religion: all that means nothing to this class. The
> church is still something of an evil, a cumbrance, a hindrance
> for God's work that ought to be removed and then how glorious
> it would be.[19]

Westergreen's prescription for addressing error included an explanation of why he attended gatherings of religious groups he thought were
heretical; he stated that it was necessary to have a good understanding
of the foundations of error in order to address it effectively. He acknowledged that there could be difference of opinion on some matters of faith
and practice without one side or the other being in error. One example
given was the different numbering of the Ten Commandments in various Christian traditions, or the emphasis on a partly sacramental view of
salvation, as in the high church camp. Westergreen did not quarrel with
these differences as long as there was agreement on what he regarded
as essentials: the authority of the Bible, the doctrine of the Trinity, the
divinity of Jesus Christ, a general atonement, repentance, faith, justification, regeneration, and "partly even sanctification." The errors that
were pointed out included Second Adventism (Millerites), Mormonism,
Swedenborgianism, Christian Science, and Islam (Eric Janssonism was
referred to obliquely). He counseled his listeners to know enough about
the error to be able to address it intelligently, to speak politely but clearly,
and to waste no time with belligerent fanatics who would not listen in
any case. He also advised his fellow clergy not to be frequent visitors to
groups they believed were in error: first, because they might be seen as
spies or subversives, and second, because if church members happened
to be visitors and saw their pastors there, they might take it as validation
of the fanatics.

The holiness movement in Chicago and elsewhere was never a monolithic organization, but rather found expression through many groups,

---

19. Westergreen, "What Attitude Should We Assume," 9–10.

both clergy- and lay-led. In addition to the National Holiness Association, immigrant and English-language churches sponsored independent holiness meetings within their own congregations. The Metropolitan Methodist Mission, for example, was lay-initiated in a heavily German and Scandinavian neighborhood at the corner of Chicago Avenue and Ada Street. The mission opened its four-story brick building in 1894. It was led by Marmaduke Mendenhall "Duke" Farson (1863–1929), a businessman whose father had been a Methodist minister in Indiana, and Edwin Harvey (1865–1926), who owned several low-priced hotels that catered to business travelers. Farson and Harvey had attended the National Holiness Association campmeeting at Des Plaines in 1897, but were dissatisfied at the lack of what they called the Full Gospel, and so they started their own campmeeting in a vacant lot near the church in 1898.

The Metropolitan Methodist Mission functioned like a settlement house with various classes, including some vocational training, and had a tent revival a block away. The mission had invited Seth C. Rees (1854–1933), a Quaker and president of the International Apostolic Holiness Union, to preach for them in 1897. Rees, as Westergreen observed, favored boisterous demonstrations in his meetings, and was suspicious of denominational loyalty. Harvey, meanwhile, wrote against the formal worship and structure of the Methodist Episcopal Church. The outcome was predictable; the Metropolitan Methodist Mission separated from the denomination in 1899 and became the Metropolitan Church Association, also known as the Burning Bush Movement, so named because its periodical was the *Burning Bush*. In addition to having its own newspaper and having "holy jumping" in its meetings, beginning in 1906 the MCA taught that truly sanctified Christians should live communally without personal possessions, and relocate to Waukesha, Wisconsin, to expect the imminent return of Jesus.

The clash between holiness groups in Chicago was public and sometimes ugly. In March of 1901, the Metropolitan Church Association held a well-publicized holiness convocation at the Clark Street Church. They met at noon in that building, but at various other north side churches for evening meetings. The convocation lasted seventy-five days, and an estimated twenty-two hundred people sought salvation or sanctification. Meanwhile, S. B. Shaw, a Chicagoan, persuaded George Hughes of the National Holiness Association to hold its own holiness convocation. In May of 1901, the General Holiness Assembly began holding meetings at the Clark Street Church—in the sanctuary right across the hall from the

MCA meetings. William Kostlevy, author of *Holy Jumpers: Evangelicals and Radicals in Progressive Era America*, notes that the stated purpose of this assembly was "to pray for revival, encourage cooperation in evangelistic endeavors, and remove prejudice from extreme, erroneous and fanatical positions assumed by some so-called holiness workers."[20] Westergreen sampled both meetings. At the General Holiness Assembly he reported hearing sermons by a Presbyterian evangelist, a woman Baptist preacher, Seth C. Rees, and others. He was critical only of Rees; after one sermon, he said Rees spoke sharply and "there was a good deal of shouting and jumping so that even the stovepipe fell down."[21] Two days later Westergreen said Rees seemed openly to attack the Holiness Association as backsliders from what they once were. The General Holiness Assembly was more staid, had lower attendance, less press coverage, and yielded fewer conversions, while the MCA convocation had screamers, jumpers, general theatrics, and focused on millennialism as much as the Wesleyan concept of perfection.

Westergreen did not mention Rees again in his journal, but continued to visit what he called Farson's Revival periodically. Why he went is not clear, since Farson's preaching style employed regular use of a rhetorical sledgehammer. In July 1903, Westergreen alternated between the Des Plaines campmeeting and Farson's meetings. After one of Farson's meetings he wrote, "Mrs. White preached and Farson exhorted.[22] They were very denunciatory especially against the Methodists," thus manifesting the sort of anti-church error Westergreen had described in his earlier lecture.[23] The following day he noted that they were dancing in the meeting; one can imagine his reaction to seeing this in a worship service, given that on an earlier occasion, when visiting a "colored peoples campmeeting" in Maywood, he witnessed a picnic party near the campground having a dance, "and I am sorry to say that I heard some speak Swedish."[24] Returning to the Des Plaines campmeeting, he heard Billy Sunday denounce the Methodist preachers who skipped hearing Sunday himself to go listen to Farson.[25] Westergreen heard Gipsy Smith at the

20. Kostlevy, *Holy Jumpers*, 60.

21. Westergreen, *Journals*, May 9, 1901.

22. Alma White (1862–1946) founded the Pillar of Fire Church and was the first female bishop in the United States.

23. Westergreen, *Journals*, July 20, 1903.

24. Westergreen, *Journals*, June 20, 1901.

25. William Ashley "Billy" Sunday (1862–1935) was a professional baseball player

same campmeeting, but Smith's style was more irenic, and fit in well with the holiness meetings taking place there.[26]

The Holiness Movement, as seen from the list of speakers at the 1901 General Holiness Assembly, was a phenomenon that crossed denominational lines during this period. Sometimes it developed into sects, such as the Metropolitan Church Association, or further evolved into new denominations, such as the Church of the Nazarene. Westergreen was certainly affected by the movement in conscious and unconscious ways, but it should be remembered that his ecumenical interests and ventures were not limited to churches and speakers who identified with the Holiness Movement. Furthermore, as one can see in examining the trajectory of his ministry and interests, a commitment to cooperative and ecumenical evangelism and social outreach was continuous from the time he began preaching. For example, he visited the Mormon Conference in Salt Lake City more from intellectual curiosity than affinity. He preached at Mission Friends' churches because of a shared commitment to evangelize and minister to the temporal needs of Scandinavian immigrants, and also, it is likely, because of his friendship with August Skogsbergh. He went to hear Billy Sunday many times, probably sympathetic to Sunday's fervent preaching against beverage alcohol. He lectured about Luther not to repudiate Lutheran theology, but drawing on Luther's emphasis on grace, and possibly remembering his own religious roots in the Swedish state church. He visited Moody's church regularly, and in April 1902 wrote about hearing G. Campbell Morgan preach there and at the Fourth Presbyterian Church, noting, "He gave us there a sort of New Testament analysis. He is certainly a remarkable man."[27] What was distinctive about the ease with which Westergreen sampled other preachers and traditions was his ability to admire the effectiveness of others while reflecting

---

who was converted at Pacific Garden Mission in Chicago. He was ordained in the Presbyterian Church and worked with the YMCA and as an assistant to J. Wilbur Chapman before becoming a full-time independent evangelist.

26. Rodney Gipsy Smith (1860–1947) was converted at age sixteen in the Primitive Methodist Church, and worked with the Salvation Army, the British Methodist Church, and the National Free Church Council, as well as doing evangelistic preaching around the world.

27. Westergreen, *Journals*, April 20, 1902. G. Campbell Morgan was born 1863 in Gloucestershire, England. Rejected as a Methodist preacher, he became Congregationalist. When Moody preached in England, he invited Morgan to come to the United States and serve as lecturer in the Northfield Bible Conference. He was an expository preacher, though he lacked formal a theological education.

thoughtfully on the differences between their theology and his understanding of Wesleyan theology. This is how he could do pulpit exchanges
with Mission Friends and Lutherans while holding different views of the
atonement from the former and of sanctification theology from the latter.

Invitations to preach across the country came in 1901 and 1902.
Early in January he received a letter from Brother Falk in Seattle, asking
him to preach there, and in February he left on a journey that was the
longest he had made since he left Sweden almost fifty years earlier. He
first took a train to St. Paul, Minnesota, where he preached at the Second
Swedish Methodist Church. The following day he continued northwest
through North Dakota, Montana, and Idaho, arriving in Spokane two
days later. He preached and lectured in Spokane and Moscow, Idaho,
for several days before continuing on to Seattle. His journal for March
of that year reads like a travelogue; there are admiring comments about
the views of Mount Rainier, the beautiful parks overlooking the bay, the
north branch of the Skagit River, etc., as well as describing his ministry.
He preached at Seattle's Wayside Mission, and lectured on the baptism
of the Spirit and sanctification as well as on biblical chronology in connection with archaeological discoveries.[28] On one occasion he preached
on sanctification from 1 Pet 1:14–16, after which they had a powerful
altar meeting. He wrote that "a young man stayed on his knees after
the meeting was broke up until he came out in the clear and then he
was so excited with joy that he jumped out and shouted, so that it created considerable excitement outside."[29] From Seattle he took the train
to Oakland, California, where he preached and lectured again, staying
about a week before moving on to Salt Lake City. He preached, attended
the Mormon Conference and visited the tabernacle before moving on
to Denver, where he preached twice on Easter Sunday. He arrived back
in Chicago more than two months after his departure. But his travels
for the year were not over. In late September he arranged for Brother
Ossian Johnson to fill his preaching appointments so that he could travel
to the East Coast the following month. He preached in Brooklyn, Bat-
tery Park, and Lexington Avenue ME Church, focusing on sanctification.
One sermon, based on Heb 12:14–15, was "Sanctification as a Particular
Work of Grace." An interesting aspect of this message is that Westergreen
appeared to be articulating the experience of sanctification in contrast to

28. Westergreen, *Journals*, February 26, 1901.
29. Westergreen, *Journals*, March 14, 1901.

what he might have called the religious exhibitionism of the full gospel movement. Unlike some of his sermons on sanctification/holiness, there is a more even balance of Gospel and New Testament texts cited. After differentiating sanctification from justification and the new birth, he laid out how sanctification must be sought and is obtained as an experience:

- We must be awakened to the necessity of it.
- We must not seek it as an abstract experience of the Spirit.
- We must not seek it merely as a supplement to what we already have . . .
- It is received by faith from outside ourselves.
- It is received by faith as we seek Christ, rather than a spiritual work of grace being our aim.
- It is received by faith as we are, and we can receive it now . . .
- We must leave our theological designs so that we become like children to receive it.
- Then we will be satisfied with Christ alone, so that we grow in his likeness and find rest.[30]

The final three pages of the eight-page manuscript outline the ways people can lose sanctification even after experiencing it, the ways to keep it, the things that are a threat to peace and holiness, and the things that can be compromised or contaminated as a result of these threats. The eight points in the "application" section are a series of rhetorical questions for listeners, which recapitulate the main points of the message.

Altogether, he preached at twenty-six churches besides his own appointment and numerous campmeetings. In 1902 he did not make as lengthy a journey, but he did go to Worcester and Quinsigamond, Massachusetts, to preach and visit his brother Alex. He preached at more than eighteen different Swedish Methodist churches, plus campmeetings and guest-preaching for the Mission Friends and Lutherans.

During the first few years of the twentieth century, Westergreen's journals showed an occasional intersection between the news he reported and specific ministries he launched or supported. Queen Victoria's death in January of 1901 evoked nothing more than a platitude about the

---

30. Westergreen, "Helgelsen Såsom ett Särskildt Nådeswerk" [Sanctification as a particular work of grace], 5.

inevitability of death, but when President McKinley was shot in September of the same year, Westergreen followed the medical reports closely. He was attending Annual Conference when word came of McKinley's death. There was a recess in conference business while Bishop Fowler paid tribute to the dead president. On the day of the funeral, all the trains and street cars in Chicago stopped and were silent for five minutes. Westergreen reported that during those minutes they sang "Nearer, My God, to Thee," which was one of the late president's favorite hymns. During the Coal Strike of 1902, Westergreen's sympathies were with the miners. He was critical of President Roosevelt, saying the negotiating conference called by the president didn't seem to have any results. At his Sunday evening service, Westergreen took up a collection for the striking miners: one his most political acts not explicitly linked to tenets of his faith. Another social issue he wrote about during this period was "secret societies." Anita Olson Gustafson notes that between 1880 and 1920 Swedish immigrants founded over 145 social organizations in Chicago; some of these were temperance clubs, but others were imbibing fraternal lodges and/or secret societies.[31] Westergreen went to Moody's church and heard speeches against membership in these secular groups, concurring that "the secret society business is a great hindrance to the church in its work."[32] And, as in the previous decade, he continued to speak at temperance meetings and vote for any Prohibition Party candidates.

Westergreen had always been concerned about the plight of immigrants—particularly Scandinavians—who arrived in the city without money, housing, or employment, and he helped establish the Emigrant Aid Society. In the new century, his interest was renewed in the work of Lucy Rider Meyer (1849–1922) the founder of the Chicago Training School. She spoke at a weekly preachers' meeting in April of 1903, and the next month at the Chicago District Epworth League Convention. Westergreen made favorable remarks about her speech and a paper read by another woman. Meyer, who educated women and trained them for social work and missions, was largely responsible for reviving the order of Methodist deaconesses, approved by the Methodist Episcopal Church in 1888. These women worked in Chicago's poorest communities: a religious counterpart to Jane Addams and Hull House, which was "humanitarian, social non-conversionist and explicitly earth centered . . .

31. Gustafson, *Swedish Chicago*, 85.
32. Westergreen, *Journals*, May 15, 1902.

a non-evangelical approach to social regeneration."[33] Mary McDowell, director of the University of Chicago Settlement, was another proponent of the non-religious approach. There is no record of Westergreen hearing her speak, though she was active in Progressive Era Chicago, and worked with Jane Addams to establish the National Federation of Settlements.[34] In the latter decades of his ministry, Westergreen heard more women preachers and speakers. While the Swedish Methodists did not have any deaconesses, Westergreen took no issue with women engaging in various ministries; his only criticism was that sometimes they spoke too softly, and he had difficulty hearing them.

These years were marked with loss of several people who were significant in Westergreen's life. In September, 1901 Victor Witting's wife died. The following month S. B. Newman had a stroke. Sister Newman wrote a letter to Westergreen for him, but his signature was an illegible scrawl. Early in the following year, Westergreen visited his colleague and friend Nels Eagle (1857–1902) in Brooklyn. Eagle became ill before he left, and within a week the man was dead, possibly from typhoid. In his journal Westergreen wrote, "Brother Eagle was one of our strongest men both physically and mentally. The last words he said when I took leave of him last Wednesday were, 'My prospects towards eternity is [sic] clear.' My God comfort his bereaved family."[35]

The same month that Eagle died, Westergreen went to visit Brother Newman. His old mentor was glad to see him, but was failing physically and mentally. He did not know his young wife until Westergreen reminded him, but his mind seemed clearer when the two men prayed together. He died in October 1902, ninety years old, and was buried at Rosehill Cemetery. A greater shock was the unexpected death of his longtime colleague A. J. Anderson, who was only a year older than Westergreen, and who was ordained with him in the Central Illinois Conference. The Lakeview church was full for his funeral, and there were between twenty and thirty preachers present: Swedes, Norwegians, and Americans. Westergreen later wrote this about him: "Few men, if any among us, were more favored both with natural gifts and success in his pastorate than he was, and we have none yet in sight among us like him."[36]

33. Kostlevy, *Holy Jumpers*, 45.
34. Pope-Levison, *Building the Old Time Religion*, 156.
35. Westergreen, *Journals*, February 11, 1902.
36. Westergreen, *Journals*, December 19, 1903.

The greatest loss, however, was yet to come. His brother Andrew had been appointed to the South Chicago Church at 91st and Exchange Avenue. At the beginning of December, his depression having returned, Andrew asked for a leave of absence of at least two months. A week later Westergreen received a letter from Selma, telling him that Andrew's mind had been so severely affected that he had been taken to a detention hospital. They were afraid he would be put in an asylum. Westergreen went to visit him the following day, and was shocked by the change in his condition. Andrew was strapped in a chair and did not seem to notice his brother's presence. His eyes were bloodshot, and he had bitten himself on the wrist, leaving a large, open sore. Coherent conversation proved impossible. Westergreen knelt by his brother and prayed. Selma was naturally anxious and distressed; her husband had never before been so severely disabled, and she and Nels believed he was receiving mediocre care in the detention hospital. The day before Christmas Eve, a judge ordered that Andrew be transferred to Garfield Park Sanitarium, a small psychiatric facility at the corner of Hamlin and Washington Streets. Andrew and Selma's son Wesley accompanied him there. In the week between Christmas and New Year's Eve, Andrew was restless and weak. He seemed to be in pain, but his nurse told them he was better than he had been, and his family was relieved to have him in a place where they believed he could receive proper care and treatment. Westergreen visited him almost daily. On January 6, Westergreen received a call to come to the sanitarium right away, because Andrew was dying. When he arrived, he found him in his death struggle, which the nurse told him had started that morning. He died around 9:30 p.m., and Westergreen said the last word he spoke was "Mama." He was six months shy of his sixty-first birthday. The death certificate states the cause was "valvular insufficiency of the heart," which could cause heart failure. No mention is made of severe depression as a contributing factor.

Westergreen felt his brother's death keenly. He wrote in his journal, "I miss my brother Andrew very much. He stood me nearest of my brothers as he was in the same work as I am engaged in. God's ways are wonderful and we believe he does all well and has done so even in this case."[37] Some of his actions following Andrew's death seem out of character and perhaps even bizarre. First, he met with fellow clergy Isaac Anderson, John Wigren, and Martin Hess to plan the funeral service. There is no mention

37. Westergreen, *Journals*, January 13, 1903.

of Selma or Wesley being in on the decision-making, nor waiting for his brother Swan and niece Nellie, who arrived later on the day the plans were made. At least Wesley and Swan went with him to buy grave plots at Oak Woods Cemetery in the Grand Crossing neighborhood of the south side. The funeral service took place at the South Chicago church, with a large congregation and at least twenty ministers present. Karl Herman Elmström preached the funeral sermon, John Wigren read the obituary, and Martin Hess and another minister named LaFountain spoke.

Five days after the burial, Westergreen and nephew Wesley returned to the cemetery and, according to his journal, found out that the box (presumably the casket) had not been fixed before the grave was filled in. How did they know this? Was the box already damaged at the time of the funeral? Did they inquire at the cemetery office? The journal does not explain. They went to an office in the city and got an order to have the grave reopened and the box fixed two days later. Westergreen returned for the exhumation and found that part of the top of the casket was "crushed in by the pressure of the earth because it was too low." He had the workers open the casket so he could look at Andrew's face once more, and noted, "It was little changed since we put him down."[38] A week later, he went to South Chicago and reported to Selma what had been done at Oak Woods. He also gave her instructions in regard to the property, and told her she would be receiving a widow's dole from the Conference: one hundred dollars that first year. She gave him Andrew's fur cap as a remembrance of him.

William Henschen, who was editor of *Sändebudet* at the time, wrote Andrew's obituary for the paper. It was glowing, yet surprisingly candid for the time. Henschen praised Andrew for his fine mind and business acumen, and identified him as one of the foremost leaders in Swedish Methodism. He mentioned his stately appearance, friendly and honest manner, and the ease with which he made friends. Then Henschen added, "He was known to have a sunny temperament and described himself as an optimist, yet behind this hid a depression that few knew about, which first appeared after the death of his eldest son, and manifested itself again in his final illness."[39] All mention of his depression was deleted from the version of the obituary that appeared in the Conference *Journal*, published later that year.

38. Westergreen, *Journals*, January 16, 1903.
39. Henschen, "Obituary of Andrew Theodor Westergreen," 1.

Westergreen certainly missed his younger brother, but his journal for 1903 does not have the frequent repeated laments that followed the death of his mother. As he looked forward to Annual Conference, he wrote that he would be keenly aware of his brother's absence at that event, though he missed him everywhere. One curious journal entry was written on the day of his July quarterly conference: "I think of the fourth quarterly conference in Lakeview last year, which gave such a blow to my brother who is now gone to the other and I believe, through Christ, to a better world."[40] One can only guess that Andrew wished to stay at Lakeview but the congregation and/or presiding elder wished to move him to South Chicago.

Selma continued to live in the parsonage for a few months. Westergreen kept in touch with her, and noted in April that she seemed to feel her loneliness and loss more at that point than she did immediately after Andrew's death. He also implied that Wesley was not as dutiful toward his mother as he should have been. In May of that year, Selma moved to rented rooms on Humboldt Street. Her son Wesley continued to live with her for awhile after his marriage the following year.

Westergreen kept busy through the spring and summer of that year, attending the Free Methodist Conference, going to the holiness conventions at the Union Avenue and Wabash Avenue Methodist Churches, preaching on sanctification to various congregations and at tent or campmeetings at Des Plaines, Edgewater, Hickory Grove, West Pullman, Maywood, and Blue Island. In May a Swedish Holiness Association was organized, and Westergreen elected as its president. There was no hint that he would not continue in ministry as usual until he attended the Annual Conference held at Lakeview in September. There he heard that "they have no place for me and that it will be best for me to take a superannuated relation."[41] At this conference, Anders J. Löfgren replaced Alfred Anderson as presiding elder of the Chicago district until the conference of 1907, when Anderson resumed the position.[42] When his name was called the next morning, he took a superannuated relation and made a speech to the assembly, but acknowledged he felt very strange. The rest

40. Westergreen, *Journals*, July 6, 1903.

41. Westergreen, *Journals*, September 1, 1903.

42. It is curious that Westergreen was told by Anderson that there was no appointment for him, but at conference the following year, when Löfgren was presiding elder, he was given the joint charge of Austin and Moreland. Once Anderson took the reins again, those churches were given to someone else.

of his colleagues would be going to their charges once Conference closed, but he had none. John Wigren and Eric Shogren also retired, and each of them received a pension of $125. The following month he learned that the congregation at Moreland had wanted him to be their minister. He left the Melrose Park church with mixed feelings. The day before he moved back to Humboldt Park, members of the congregation helped him with packing and had a small party for him. He was given twenty dollars, and Mrs. Malmström received five. He admitted he was glad to be back in his own house, though he had to sleep on the floor his first night there. Annie's mother and another woman came and helped them set up housekeeping the following day.

Although he no longer had pastoral responsibility for a congregation, Westergreen did not cease ministry after Conference. In the last three months of the year he preached or exhorted at sixteen different churches, one town hall, and at a funeral. He continued to attend the Swedish preachers' meetings, and when he was not scheduled to preach anywhere, visited Presbyterian, Baptist, Swedish and American Methodist churches. He spent much of his free time with friends Wigren, Elmström, Reese (who was William Henschen's son-in-law), and Isaac Anderson. With no appointment to preach on Christmas Eve or Christmas Day, he and Mrs. Malmström had Selma and Wesley and Annie's mother to supper on Christmas Eve, and he went to *julotta* (an early morning service on Christmas Day) at Kedzie Avenue Norwegian Methodist Church. In the absence of his mother and closest brother, Westergreen was building a new family with whom he could celebrate Christmas.

The day before New Year's Eve 1903, disaster struck Chicago; the Iroquois Theater burned, causing over six hundred fatalities. It was the deadliest theater fire and single building fire in US history. Some of the dead were neighbors of Westergreen, and he noticed that listed among those who perished was the pastor of Asbury Methodist Episcopal Church, and other preachers and their wives. He commented, "What a warning that is if the people would only heed it." The second of January was set apart for mourning in Chicago. He wrote, "Business has been suspended and the church bells were tolling at noon. It is thought that about two hundred funerals have been held today on the victims of the fire. What a lesson of warning for theater-going church members."[43]

---

43. Westergreen, *Journals*, December 30, 1903, and January 2, 1904.

It is just as well that Westergreen was not responsible for a particular church now, since he took another extended trip early in the year. His travels did not take him as far as the West Coast, but he left for Stromsburg, Nebraska, in early March and did not return until two months later, only to turn around and return to Davey, Nebraska, for a district meeting in late May. In contrast to his long trip three years earlier, which occurred at the invitation of Brother Falk, no single host or invitation was identified for the Nebraska sojourn. It may be that his prior conversation with Anders Gustaf Milton, concerning the number in the Kansas-Nebraska district who had attained entire sanctification, piqued his interest in visiting there. If this was motivation for his trip, he met with some disappointment; after spending an afternoon with a minister named Granberg, he wrote, "He is a great talker and a good scholar, but I fear he is not so spiritual as he ought to be. But how is it with myself in this matter? Lord, help me."[44] Westergreen stayed with Frank J. Swanson in Omaha, and with Brother Hanson in Stromsburg, but other area ministers seemed to be entertaining him as well. This was no vacation, however. He preached about seventy times in the two months he was away, mainly in Swedish Methodist churches, but also the Swedish Baptist church. He seemed to spend more time mingling with Seventh Day Adventists than he had previously, attending one of their worship services and sharing the pulpit with an Adventist preacher at a temperance meeting.

One of his sermons from the sojourn in Nebraska demonstrated his continued commitment to entire sanctification as a second work of grace. It was based on 1 John 4:17: "Love has been perfected among us in this: that we may have boldness on the day of judgment, because as he is, so are we in this world." The sermon begins with the introductory statement, "Perfect love is the highest experience of grace," followed by two explicative clauses: it is highest because it takes away all bondage and painful fear, and it is highest because in this we come most to be like Christ. The theme is stated next: "a) How can we come to be like Christ in this world, and b) of what does this likeness consist?"[45] The two main sections of the sermon are simply elaborations of the theme's two questions, though the second point comprises two-thirds of the sermon. Westergreen attempts to outline the means by which one is sanctified, i.e., through conviction of its possibility, belief in its necessity, coming to Christ and believing

44. Westergreen, *Journals*, April 16, 1904.
45. Westergreen, "Deruti är Kärlek Fullkomnad" [In this is love perfected], 1.

him solely for salvation, and total withdrawal from worldly things. The second part of the sermon appears to be an attempt to facilitate a further numinous experience for the congregation through recognition of what Christ has already done. The "application" is an invitation to consider what has been accomplished through the Spirit at work within a person, rather than exhorting listeners about what should be done next.

In addition to keeping a rigorous preaching schedule, Westergreen took some time for sightseeing: he thought Omaha was a beautiful city, complained about the wind and cold in Stromsburg, and on his way home visited Central Park in Davenport, Iowa, stopped at Government Island (now called Arsenal Island) in the Quad Cities and admired its attractiveness and order. He also visited with his brother Swan's family. Swan's son Henry had bought a farm three miles north of Swede Plain, Nebraska, and Westergreen wrote that it was fine land with the exception of a couple of sloughs in it. He also spent time with the Mobergs, Swan's wife Betsy's family of origin.

Once back in Chicago, he resumed his usual activities and interests. He preached a total of 215 times at nineteen different Methodist churches in Chicago and western Illinois, in addition to preaching at three protracted or campmeetings in Illinois. He attended the Holiness Convention at Clark Street Church, but went to hear Farson and Harvey only twice during the summer. They were holding their meetings in a large tent on Franklin Boulevard. Westergreen commented dryly that Farson preached a rambling discourse, but there was nothing especially objectionable in their speech, and they did not attack the churches as they generally did. During this year he did not publish any writing under his own name, but he composed a speech about the pioneer preachers of Swedish Methodism, which John Wigren gave as a Jubilee lecture when Annual Conference met in Beaver/Donovan that September. They were marking the fiftieth anniversary of the organization of the Beaver church. He acknowledged that Wigren would have to revise it to put it in his own style, but he was glad to supply him with historical data. Westergreen praised Bishop Thomas B. Neely, who presided that year, and remarked that it was one of the most pleasant conference sessions he had attended. The 1904 *Conference Journal* lists the Austin and Moreland churches as *att tillsättas* (to be appointed), but in fact Westergreen took pastoral charge of both congregations. He was no doubt glad to be back in regular service, since in July he wrote in his journal that he was bored and didn't have enough to do.

There were a few changes in his family and household, which suggest that Westergreen was now *de facto* regarded as the patriarch. Andrew and Selma's son Wesley wrote to him in March, telling his uncle that the company he worked for had been liquidated, and thus he was now unemployed. Westergreen wrote him a long letter of advice in return. In June, he and Isaac Anderson officiated at the ceremony marrying Wesley to Jenny Peterson, held at the home of the bride's parents. There were a total of four clergy present. The newlyweds went to the World's Fair in St. Louis for their honeymoon, and temporarily lived with Selma upon their return. In September Westergreen wrote a long letter to his nephew Henry, expressing his sorrow that Henry planned to move to his farm in Nebraska in the spring, instead of remaining at the family farm in Copley Township, "when his parents were old and feeble and needed his presence and help."[46] In this instance, he was meddling rather than helping, for Henry's own family understood the need to work his farm. Swan's younger son, Thomas, wrote the following to Henry:

> We think we understand your circumstances, Henry, and know that it would mean a sacrifice in personal property and many other things. It is perfectly natural for us to want you near, for you may be sure we all love you. I know we are unreasonable to try to make you to make a change and lose some of your hard earnings and money. Do just as you see fit and you may be sure we won't begrudge.[47]

One wonders if Westergreen's letters and advice were a reflection of anxiety about who might care for *him* in his final years. He visited the newlyweds and Selma, and was disturbed that the young folks were moving to their own flat. He wondered what Selma would do, for she could not afford her fairly large apartment without Wesley's contribution to household expenses. And a few weeks before Christmas, when his trusty and valued housekeeper, Mrs. Malmström, left for Los Angeles, he wrote, "It was not without feelings we parted." Westergreen corresponded with her, and occasionally sent money to her in California. A new housekeeper, Miss Christine Grainman, was immediately engaged to take her place. That Christmas was similar to the previous one, with Selma, Mrs. Black, and Miss Grainman keeping the feast with him.

---

46. Westergreen, *Journals*, September 2, 1904.
47. (Thomas) Westergreen, letter to Henry Westergreen, October 27, 1904.

The Austin church, which he began serving in the autumn of 1904, fit a profile similar to that of his other appointments in the years leading up to official retirement. It was a relatively new church, organized in 1893 and helped along by members of the Moreland church, which had eighty members by 1905. Austin was smaller, with thirty-four members in full connection at the time of the 1905 Conference. Until they purchased a building in 1904 that had previously been owned by an American Congregational church, they had met in various rented locations. Westergreen held protracted meetings at Austin in January and February, with his friend John Wigren often serving as exhorter.

On Palm Sunday, he tallied up the number of times he had preached, and by his count it was ten thousand at the end of that day. The number is probably accurate, given that twenty years earlier, another Swedish Methodist guessed that Westergreen had preached at least five thousand times. He preached 166 times in 1905, at eighteen Methodist churches, as well as three campmeetings: Des Plaines, a tent-meeting in Ravenswood, and another tent at North Avenue and Kedzie. It is true that he would preach a given sermon more than once, but in tallying his sermon texts for various years, there were rarely more than 20 percent repeats. For example, in 1905 he repeated sermons thirty-four times: almost exactly 20 percent. It is also true that Westergreen would occasionally take an old sermon and revise or recopy it. The Northern Illinois Conference Archives at Garrett-Evangelical Theological Seminary, which houses the Westergreen collection, includes approximately 650 sermons, lectures, hymn translations, poetry, and other documents, as well as his journals and autobiography. Only a handful include a date of composition, but from comparing his journal records with the manuscripts, it is possible to prove the oldest was written in 1858 and the newest in 1918, because the texts were preached *only* in those years. For the majority of texts, any number of dates is possible, because he preached from the text multiple times across the decades. Of the extant manuscripts, there are more sermons from Psalms, Isaiah, Matthew and John than from any other biblical books. There are no sermons drawn from Ruth, 1 Chronicles, Ezra, Nehemiah, Esther, Song of Solomon, Obadiah, Jonah, Haggai, Philemon, or 2 John. This is not to say he never preached from these books; for example, he regularly used Job 1:21 as his text when preaching at the funeral of a child. However, no manuscript based on that text is in the collection.

Westergreen did not follow a lectionary, except for using the texts recommended by the Evangelical Alliance during the Week of Prayer in

January of each year. He did normally work with seasonally appropriate texts for Christmas, Easter, and Pentecost. And he naturally gravitated toward texts having to do with conversion, consecration, and sanctification when preaching at campmeetings, protracted meetings, tent-meetings, and revivals. In 1905, those texts included Ps 30:7–13; Ezek 18:31–32; Matt 3:11; and John 3:16.

Westergreen did not lose his evangelistic zeal, as is evident from the number of times he preached, but he was aware that he did not have the same energy he possessed in his earlier years of ministry. He turned seventy-one in 1905. In addition to the inevitable changes as a person ages, his journal hints that he may have feared he was developing the same depression that haunted his mother and brothers. In March he was troubled by persistent nervousness and a feeling of unease. He had difficulty concentrating, forgot some appointments, and wrote in his journal, "I am feeling continually bad and not able to read or do anything. Have laid down a good deal on the lounge today. I am so nervous and have lost the appetite and am yet troubled with the cough. I am sick to my body and depressed in my mind. May the Lord for Christ's sake help me."[48]

The problems were not merely psychosomatic. The following year he admitted he had to shorten a sermon because of bladder urgency, and acknowledged the problem was not new. He developed trouble with his eyes shortly thereafter. He did not disclose the diagnosis, but had to wear dark glasses for awhile, and for several months in 1907 he received treatments from an ophthalmologist almost daily. The problem made it difficult for him to do as much reading as he had in years past. He later underwent cataract surgery, but eventually he lost most of the vision in his right eye. In photographs of Westergreen taken during the last decade of his life, his pupils are not completely aligned, suggesting that he was partially blind. The various symptoms he described suggest that he may have developed adult-onset diabetes in addition to an enlarged prostate.

His continuing interest in current events would not have done much to lift his spirits. His journal made note of fires at Chicago's Union Stockyards and Cook County Courthouse in January, and the Russo-Japanese War of 1904–1905. He went into more detail about the teamsters' strike, in which twenty-one were killed and over four hundred injured. In May, the cyclones in Kansas and Oklahoma and a train wreck in Pennsylvania evoked almost ghoulish comment; of the former, he wrote that hundreds

---

48. Westergreen, *Journals*, March 25, 1905.

were killed or wounded, and of the latter, "Many were killed either by being crushed or roasted to death, for the ruins [of the train] took fire last night."[49] His response to Norway's declaration of independence from Sweden was more moderate; he said he did not know what the results would be, but thought they would not be very serious.

Meanwhile, his pursuits outside of regular parish duties were unabated. He gave temperance lectures, took an active interest in emigrant welfare, wrote to Mayor Dunne in 1906 to oppose the pushing of two liquor ordinances that were to come before the city council. At the ministers' meeting, he participated in a discussion of the injustice and suffering of people in the Belgian Congo under King Leopold's rule. His friendship with the Mission Friends continued; as noted earlier, in September 1905 he went to hear Paul Peter Waldenström speak at North Park College about the separation of Sweden and Norway. Westergreen was seated on the platform close to the lecturer: a sign of the regard the Mission Friends had for him. In addition, Westergreen continued to visit churches outside his denomination whenever he had the opportunity: Baptist, Lutheran, Swedenborgian, and Russian Orthodox, as well as nondenominational Protestant churches. He attended the Holiness Convention in January 1905, as well as holiness meetings at various churches around the city. After attending his own Swedish Methodist Annual Conference, he went to the Norwegian-Danish Methodist Conference in Moreland, the Rock River Conference in the Park Avenue Church, and the Swedish Baptist Conference.

Westergreen continued to care for his extended family. Selma and Andrew had owned some lots on Summerdale Avenue, which were now sold to pay various debts. Nothing was said in his journals about the degree to which Wesley assisted his mother, but Westergreen noted there would be very little left for her to live on. Her widow's pension from the Conference was never more than $125 per year. Since Wesley and Jenny were buying a house on Belden Avenue, a little north of where Westergreen lived, it seems unlikely they had much money to spare for her. Westergreen visited Swan and his family after attending Annual Conference in Moline and visiting Bishop Hill with John Wigren. At Bishop Hill he enjoyed the memories evoked as he walked around the parsonage and church, both of which he regarded as monuments to his brother Andrew's work in that place. From there he made his way to the farm in Copley Township. He learned that Swan's son Thomas was out in Nebraska with

49. Westergreen, *Journals*, May 11, 1905.

Henry, but was sick of it and wanted to return home: an idea Westergreen heartily endorsed. Back in Chicago, Mother Black, Annie's mother, came to Westergreen's home for dinner regularly. In November, she injured one knee on a nail, and the doctor was called. There was, of course, the danger of tetanus or infection setting in, given that the first tetanus vaccine was not developed until 1924. Westergreen visited her frequently while she was laid up, and about a week after her injury, she told him of a vision she had. She had seen her daughter Annie kneeling at her bedside. She reached out and caught Annie's hand, which was warm, and then her daughter vanished. She insisted it was not a dream, because she was awake and saw things about her.[50] Westergreen, perhaps recalling the paranormal experiences in John Wesley's family and ministry, neither believed nor disbelieved Mother Black's report, but simply commented that it was strange.[51] Another possibly paranormal event in 1912 was met with the same equanimity; it happened when Selma was living with him in the house on Richmond. She reported that the upstairs neighbors said they had heard a dog wail outside the house for three nights along, and they believed it portended the imminent death of someone in the house. His laconic comment was, "What then, if we are prepared?"[52]

He maintained a lively correspondence with his extended family as well as with colleagues in ministry. In August of 1906 he received a letter from his brother Alex, who said he had been ill for about a month. For part of the time he was at home all alone with no one to take care of him. His daughter, who taught school near Boston, could not get away to tend to him. Westergreen invited his brother to come for an extended visit. Alex came the following February and stayed about two months. It was the last time the brothers were together. During his stay, they visited Selma and her family, and were entertained by number of clergy colleagues. Other excursions included Lincoln Park Zoo and a museum, the North Side Pentecostal Mission, Douglas and Garfield Parks, and the insane asylum and county poorhouse in Dunning. This last was part of

50. Westergreen, *Journals*, November 22, 1905.

51. Wesley scholars will be familiar with stories about "Old Jeffrey," a poltergeist manifested at Epworth rectory for about eight weeks beginning in December 1716. In *The Supernatural Occurrences of John Wesley*, Daniel R. Jennings catalogs numerous types of paranormal occurrences and gifts of the Spirit recorded in John Wesley's journal, including spiritual warfare, visions and dreams, miracles, holy laughter, angelic manifestations, and being slain in the Spirit.

52. Westergreen, *Journals*, March 22, 1912.

a ministers' outing. Westergreen noted that they were given an excellent free dinner as part of the tour, before acknowledging that all those who were sane and well had much reason to thank God.

During 1906 and 1907 his commitments to sanctification theology and temperance continued unabated. The former was manifested in his attendance at holiness meetings and holiness churches, as well as preaching at some campmeetings and attending others. In addition, he wrote a long letter to J. O. Nelson, a colleague in ministry, correcting what he believed was Nelson's misinterpretation of the Bible on the subject of sanctification, and his journal contains critical reflection on a Pentecostal mission on North Avenue, led by someone named Durham. He heard William J. Seymour of the Azusa Street Mission preach. Westergreen thought they put too much emphasis on speaking in tongues: something Westergreen never experienced or at least never recorded in his journals. He said Durham was a monotonous speaker, going over the same thing repeatedly. He enjoyed the testimonies, but looked askance at a young girl sitting near him and shaking violently and stamping her feet, as well as a young man who claimed that his glossolalia was actually Chinese.[53]

Westergreen's involvement in ministerial education increased during this period. He was on the Annual Conference education committee, but in 1906 he met with the school board and also lectured at the seminary's exams and closing exercises. In December he helped lead the groundbreaking for their new building, and nine months later attended the dedication of the completed structure.

It was also another season of loss. Eric Shogren, one of the patriarchs of Swedish Methodism, died in January of 1906 at age eighty-two, and his friend Victor Witting died in July, a year younger than Shogren. Westergreen wrote the lengthy memorial for Shogren in the conference journal, enumerating some of his friend's noteworthy gifts for ministry; first, that like Henry Ward Beecher, he was always on the lookout for experiences and scenes that could be used as sermon illustrations. Second, he was unusually imaginative and had a gift for painting word pictures. He was praised for his remarkable and expressive voice and a theologically systematic mind, steadfastly holding to the old Methodist teaching on sanctification.[54] In his personal journal Westergreen recorded, "Thus has passed away one of the greatest preachers that Swedish Methodism ever

---

53. Westergreen, *Journals*, May 24–31, 1907.
54. See Westergreen, "Obituary for Eric Shogren," 52–54.

produced. What solemn memories have crowded upon me since I heard it."[55] At a memorial service held at annual conference, Westergreen was one of three speakers to pay tribute to Shogren. He did not make similar comments when Witting died, perhaps because the death occurred in Worcester, Massachusetts, and Westergreen did not attend the funeral. His esteem, however, cannot be doubted; as coauthor of *Svenska Metodismen i Amerika*, written some years before Witting's death, Westergreen wrote the following:

> By nature endowed with a lively temperament and in possession of more than the usual gifts as a speaker, Witting has always been one of our most successful preachers. For the teaching of Methodist doctrine, which he on every occasion proclaimed plainly, he has done with the greatest love and, when necessary, with both courage and skill come to its defense.[56]

Yet another loss was the death of Bro. J. W. Hanner, a minister had come to the United States in 1868, at the age of twenty-two. He was converted in 1871, and served congregations in Iowa and Michigan before transferring to the Northern Swedish Methodist Conference. Later he moved to the Ravenswood neighborhood, and assisted in ministry at the Bethany Home. Unfortunately, he lost his mind (Westergreen's words) and died in the insane asylum in Kankakee. Nevertheless, Westergreen valued Hanner as a colleague and considered him a good man. His circle of close colleagues was diminishing.

There was a subtle change in Westergreen's journal in 1907. He still wrote faithfully every day, but the entries say much less about pastoral calls and programs at his own churches, and more about meetings he attended with colleagues and services he attended in other churches. He preached 138 times during the year, at twenty different Swedish, Norwegian-Danish, and American Methodist churches, at least three non-Methodist churches and as many as six campmeetings or urban tent-meetings. At the Des Plaines campmeeting, a group photo of ministers was taken for Old People's Day, and Westergreen can be seen in the front row of the picture, looking like a prophet with his piercing eyes and long, white beard. He continued to attend meetings held by the Metropolitan Church Association, but was more critical of what he called "the Farson-Harvey element" for their continual attacks upon the church. In

55. Westergreen, *Journals*, January 4, 1907.
56. Liljegren et al., *Svenska Metodismen I Amerika*, 187–88.

pastoral calls made in late August, he encountered people he described as taken up by the tongues movement. At Durham's Mission, he and Brother Wickman noted that "it is the same thing over and over again and very little to learn."[57] They thought it would have been a better meeting if not for the occasional interruptions of tongue-speaking.

Annual Conference was held at the Union Avenue Church in early September. Westergreen was invited to preach his semi-centennial sermon to a large congregation after they had election of delegates to General Conference. On the last day of Conference, he wrote, "When the appointments were read there were many changes made. I was left without an appointment."[58] Strangely enough, he wrote no immediate reaction to the fact. More than ten days later, he simply noted that it was strange not to have a charge to go to on Sundays. Westergreen preached his farewell sermon to his congregation on September 15, and Isaac Anderson was appointed to replace him at Austin.

Westergreen did continue to serve as supply preacher for other ministers, but did not preach nearly as often during the last three months of the year. Austin was his last appointment, official or unofficial. It marked his real retirement and the start of measurable physical decline.

57. Westergreen, *Journals*, August 21 and 27, 1907.
58. Westergreen, *Journals*, September 9, 1907.

9

The Final Years

1908 to 1919

My soul shall then, like thine, abhor the thing unclean,
And sanctified by love divine, forever cease from sin.[1]

THE RETIREMENT SERVICE IS a regular feature at Methodist Annual
Conference meetings. It is part worship and in larger part valedictions
from each clergy member ending his or her years under appointment.
Family and friends of the retirees attend, humorous anecdotes are shared,
and occasionally the brief speeches exhort or inspire the listeners. When
Nels Westergreen officially retired in 1903, it was because they had no
appointment for him, and the presiding elders suggested that he take superannuated status. His diary suggests he had not anticipated retiring at
that time. He made a speech, but there were no family members with him
to mark the occasion, and as we have seen, retirement only meant that he
did not have a pastoral charge for the next twelve months. He preached
215 times in 1904, and after Conference that year he took charge of the
Austin and Moreland congregations. He preached at least 150 times per
year until 1907, when the number dropped to 138, and at least ninety
times per year the following three years. He clearly did not want to cease
active ministry until age and infirmity forced him to do so.

---

1. See Charles Wesley, "The Thing My God Doth Hate," 547.

As was the case since he returned to the Chicago District in 1879, Westergreen relied on public transportation to get to his preaching appointments when the distance was too great to go on foot. He never owned an automobile, nor is there record of him hiring a livery cab to take him anywhere. This is worth noting, because at the end of the first decade of the twentieth century, although he was preaching to more than two dozen different congregations per year, the geographical range of Westergreen's ministry diminished. With the exception of one trip to Des Moines in 1910, he went as far east as Chesterton, Indiana, and as far west as Moline, and north to Milwaukee, but no farther. He could reach these by rail. The majority of his preaching, however, took place on the north and west sides of Chicago, where he could rely on the city's streetcars and elevated trains.

Westergreen's final years may be divided into three periods, corresponding to his ministerial activity and physical health. For most of the first period, 1908 to 1911, he was preaching about ninety times per year. In the second period, from 1912 to 1914, both the number of sermons and the number of churches where he preached dropped significantly to forty-five sermons at nineteen locations. In the final period, 1915 to 1919, he preached an average of twenty-three times in eleven different churches. These figures do not include preaching, exhorting, or giving a testimony at campmeetings and urban tent-meetings.

During the first period, there was a gradual change in Westergreen's preaching and journal reflection regarding theological issues he addressed. In the years immediately prior to this, holiness spirituality and in particular the urban perfectionist mission movement were center stage for him and his colleagues in ministry. Westergreen was president of the Swedish Holiness Association organized in 1903. Individual congregations had their own holiness meetings in addition to other worship. The controversy over "come-outers" and the Metropolitan Methodist Mission resulted in the formation of breakaway sects and independent churches. But beginning in 1908, holiness as a topic for reflection in his journals was eclipsed by what he called tongue-speaking. One may assert that this followed a trajectory similar to that of Wesleyan branches of North American Protestantism at the time. The shift took place somewhat later in Swedish Methodism, probably because the immigrants' initial exposure to Wesleyan theology occurred subsequent to mass emigration from Sweden, which began in the mid-1840s. In Westergreen's case, the first encounter with explicitly Wesleyan theology was reading and distributing the tract "Christian Perfection."

Speaking in tongues did not seem as controversial or divisive to Westergreen as the excesses of the "holy jumpers" in the Burning Bush Movement. For example, on Easter Sunday of 1908, he wrote in his journal, "I preached in the forenoon in Kedzie Avenue Norwegian M.E. Church from Romans 4:23–25. Had very good liberty and feeling. Was at the tongue speakers in the afternoon, and heard Brother Reese preach in the evening."[2] In August, he attended a tent-meeting at the corner of North and Homan Avenues, and heard a speaker in favor of the tongues movement. A few days later, a woman he met on the street came up to him and asked if he was ready to meet Christ. He simply commented, "The good woman belonged to the tongue speakers."[3] The following year he continued to visit services where glossolalia was featured, but this time his reflection was more critical; "I went to the tongue speakers meeting in the evening but it is nothing there to learn. It is the same thing over and over again, and yet I believe there are many good and honest people among them."[4] In the summer of 1910 he went to Riverside Park for the State Holiness Campmeeting and described the preaching as excellent, but he wrote nothing to suggest that tongue-speaking occurred there. There were sometimes pentecostal meetings held during the Swedes' annual campmeetings at Des Plaines, and Westergreen did attend them, but he reported these with the same relative detachment that he noted having visited a Swedenborgian, Free Methodist, or Nazarite [sic] service. There is no sermon or diary entry to suggest that he himself ever spoke in tongues or thought it a necessary component of Christian experience, though he was open about asserting the importance of a fresh/new baptism of the Holy Spirit. The religious manifestations respected by Westergreen and his colleagues were described in terms of "a melting time," "a solemn feeling manifested'" or all-night prayer meetings and hymn-sings: all of which were reflected in holy living following the experience. He continued to preach and reflect on Christian perfection/sanctification as something to which every disciple of Christ should aspire. As was the case in earlier periods of his life, campmeetings and protracted meetings were the settings in which Westergreen most frequently had religious peak experiences. He continued to attend and sometimes preached at the Des Plaines campmeeting, though now he was not invited to be on the

2. Westergreen, *Journals*, April 19, 1908.

3. Westergreen, *Journals*, August 22 and 31, 1908.

4. Westergreen, *Journals*, May 28, 1909.

planning committee for the annual gathering. He was a regular attendee at the Free Methodist campmeeting at Glen Ellyn and tent-meetings sponsored by different churches in the city. However, a powerful sense of the Spirit's blessing also happened in other places. In May of 1909, he wrote:

> Today while I was visiting, my soul was blessed, and it seemed I could lay hold on Christ with simple faith more than I have been able for some time, and I felt a joy that I could not but praise the Lord. O, that this might continue, but anyhow, bless the Lord.[5]

Another aspect of his vocation that continued without interruption from 1908 to 1911 was his commitment to ministerial education. In 1909 he noted that their school now had twenty-nine students, including eight new candidates. Westergreen was one of the better-educated clergy in the Central Swedish Conference, which may have been why the Annual Conference of 1910 placed him on its education committee once again. The former professor took a keen interest in the life of the seminary in Evanston, attending alumni meetings, student examinations, and opening and closing exercises. When, after a long term as seminary president, Albert Ericson was not reelected in 1909 and was replaced by C. G. Wallenius, Westergreen sympathized, and wrote, "This must have been a hard blow for Bro. Ericson who has held this place for a quarter of a century."[6] The poignancy of the situation was only magnified when Ericson died one year later.

Several colleagues who had been close friends with Westergreen died before his "second retirement" after Conference in 1907: A. J. Anderson, Eric Shogren, Victor Witting, S. B. Newman, Peter Challman, Nels Eagle, and his brother Andrew. Evidence of his enjoyment of the company of fellow clergy is given in his continued attendance after retirement at monthly meetings of the Swedish clergy, weekly clergy meetings at Clark Street Church, district meetings, and at a variety of annual conferences. His memorial in the *1920 Conference Journal* described him as "a good pastor, a jovial companion, a faithful friend, [who] entered into the joys and sorrows of his many friends . . . a man of great personality."[7] The jovial aspect of his personality is shown infrequently in his journal, but a humorous remark about C. G. Wallenius in 1913 gives evidence

5. Westergreen, *Journals*, May 29, 1909.
6. Westergreen, *Journals*, June 11, 1910.
7. See Gordon et al., "In Memoriam: The Rev. Nels O. Westergreen," 50.

of his sense of humor: "I found [out] that Brother Wallenius has lately received the title of Doctor of Divinity from the Northwestern University. We are now four bearing this title, but I don't think we are preaching any better than we did formerly."[8] Given his gregarious nature and lacking a family of his own, it is not surprising that Westergreen deepened older friendships and developed new ones during the final stages of his life.

The first of these friendships was with Isaac Anderson (1845–1927), who was almost a member of the family. Born in Sweden, he emigrated to the United States in 1867. He was converted after hearing Albert Ericson preach, joined the Methodist church, and soon began theological studies. His first ministerial appointment was Keokuk, Iowa, where he met and married Jenny Hanson, the sister of Selma (nee Hanson) Westergreen. This led to a relationship with Nels and Isaac Anderson that was beyond simply colleagues in ministry. A further bond was the fact Anderson served some of the same appointments as the Westergreen brothers: Swedona, Beaver, Geneva and Batavia, Englewood and South Chicago. He retired in 1909. There was no shortage of memories to share and topics to discuss when the two men met, although the absence of publications by Anderson, either in *Sändebudet* or monographs, suggests that Anderson was perhaps not Westergreen's intellectual peer. Isaac Anderson was one of the close friends who helped plan Andrew's funeral service in 1903, and in the final years of Westergreen's life, Christmas Eve was nearly always celebrated with Anderson and his family.

John Wigren (1826–1916) was the second friend with whom Westergreen spent much time during these years. He was eight years Westergreen's senior, and trained as a stonemason in Sweden before emigrating from Göteborg a week before the Westergreen family in 1852. Converted under the preaching of S. B. Newman in Attica, Indiana, he soon became a Methodist class leader, and in 1858 was licensed as a local preacher and appointed to the Indiana Swedish Mission. Westergreen followed him on that circuit two years later. Like Isaac Anderson, Wigren served several other charges to which the Westergreens had been appointed during the course of their ministries: Moline, Swedona, Rockford, Geneseo, Fifth Avenue, Bishop Hill, Forest Glen and Lakeview, as well as being presiding elder of the Chicago district. Wigren's three eldest sons followed him in the ministry. Westergreen regarded him as a mentor as well as a friend; when Nels and Andrew were disturbed about the appointments Alfred

---

8. Westergreen, *Journals*, June 10, 1913.

Anderson assigned them, they went to Wigren for advice and counsel. Like Isaac Anderson, Wigren helped plan Andrew's funeral. Because he retired in 1903, at the same time as Westergreen's official retirement, the two men were at leisure to visit each other's homes frequently, without ministerial responsibilities calling them away.

A third friend was Andrew G. Johnson (1857–1924), who came to America in 1873 and joined the Methodist church in Chicago in 1874. He was one of the first students after the Swedish Methodist seminary moved to Evanston. After serving in Minnesota and New York, he was appointed to the Galesburg church for two years, and then was moved to Ravenswood and agent for both the Bethany Home and the Swedish Methodist Book Concern. The genesis of the friendship between Westergreen and Johnson is not evident in the journals, but like the Isaac Anderson family, Johnson often joined the Westergreens for Christmas and other celebrations.

Three other clergy were not in the first circle of friends during the final decade of Westergreen's life, but their names appeared regularly in his journal, and he did socialize with them after retirement. Two were related to each other; Andrew Reese (1860–1947) was married to William Henschen's daughter. Henschen's biography has already been given, so there is no need to repeat it here, but it should be remembered that Henschen was the colleague Westergreen visited immediately after Swan's medical crisis early in 1899. Henschen was the peer with whom Westergreen has the greatest intellectual rapport; they both edited *Sändebudet* and served as seminary professors. Reese arrived in America in 1880. He was converted as a child but was not actively Christian as a young man. While working factory jobs in New Jersey and New York, he came under the influence of a Presbyterian evangelist in 1884. In 1886 he moved to Evanston to study at the Swedish seminary and was ordained a deacon by Bishop Andrews. His ministerial appointments that were also served by the Westergreens included Melrose, Oak Park, South Chicago, Humboldt Park, and Donovan.[9] The third friend, Karl Herman Elmström (1850–1921) became a Methodist in Sweden, although he was educated for ministry in the state church. He served several congregations before emigrating to the United States in 1882. He served Donovan, May Street, First/Market Street, and Evanston churches, as well as a stint as editor of *Sändebudet*. Moreover, for several years he conducted the examinations in church history and Methodist doctrine at the theological seminary. It

9. The Donovan appointment was also known as Beaver, and was originally part of the Indiana Mission Circuit.

is no wonder that he and Westergreen became friends, given how much they had in common, and Westergreen held his colleague's preaching in high esteem, praising Elmström as well as Reese in his journals.

During the years 1908–1911, Westergreen's notations about current events continued intermittently, but he less often used such occasions to moralize or comment on the necessity of preparing for eternity. Perhaps this was because the events noted (usually disasters in which people were killed) were mostly accidents beyond human control, in contrast to the Iroquois Theater fire of 1903. In 1908 he mentioned the earthquakes in Mexico and Sicily, and forest fires in Wisconsin and Minnesota. However, it is rather surprising he made no solemn pronouncement after a Chicago water intake crib in Lake Michigan burned in January 1909. The fire was caused by a small powder explosion in a temporary crib a little more than a mile off 71st Street. At least fifty-three men died; some were burned, and others drowned or died of exposure when they jumped into the lake. He also listed only the estimated number of casualties after the mine disaster on November 13, 1909, in Cherry, Illinois: the third most deadly mine disaster in United States history. In 1910 he voted against the annexation of Oak Park, Edison Park, and Morgan Park to the city of Chicago. Of the three, Edison Park *was* annexed in 1910. Morgan Park followed, four years later. In 1911 there was little mention of current events, possibly because with his failing eyesight, Westergreen could no longer read the newspaper.

His investment in social causes and commentary on political issues narrowed and decreased during this period. The Emigrant Aid Society is not mentioned at all in his diary, nor is there commentary on labor strikes, though he did attend a meeting at the YMCA for the suppression of vice and human trafficking.[10] One cause in which he consistently remained invested was temperance. He voted for any candidate put forward by the Prohibition Party, heard Bishop Matthews speak at a meeting of the Anti-Saloon League, attended temperance meetings at local churches, and participated in a temperance march/parade in September 1909. Beyond that, he simply noted issues brought up at clergy meetings, such as a collection being taken up for the Halsted Street Mission/Methodist Church in 1909, and hearing Amanda Berry Smith speak at a local church to raise funds for the orphanage and industrial home she founded "for abandoned and destitute colored children" in suburban Harvey, Illinois. His writing did not acknowledge growing tensions between Austria-Hungary and Serbia, the

10. Westergreen, *Journals*, February 8, 1910.

massacre of thousands of Armenians by the Turks, or the terrible working conditions that preceded the 1911 Triangle Shirtwaist Factory Fire.

Early in 1908 Westergreen may have had some intimation of his brother Alex's decline in health. While the journals never described any particular illness, Alex had written about being sick early in 1906, and letters between the brothers became longer and more frequent than in previous years. On May 25, after returning from a visit to Knox County to visit brother Swan and his family, the following letter arrived from Alex's daughter Annie, who lived in Boston, not far from her father:

> Dear Uncle Nels,
>
> Father has been called to his heavenly home. I can hardly realize that he has left me, for it has all been so sudden. I will try to tell you about it as much as I am able, but the strain of the past few days has made me feel that I am not quite sure about the way I say things. I am saying over and over, it must be all for the best, and I am sure that according to our belief, his faith in Christ his Savior has given him entrance into his eternal home to be forever with his Lord. . . . Saturday I received a letter saying that he had blackened his eye by a fall from a chair and he would not come up this week. On Monday I had a telephone message from the doctor that father was very sick, and to come at once. I got permission to leave school, and got to Hingham about 1:30. I found father in considerable pain from pleurisy. I went to the doctor and he advised taking him to the hospital here in the city. . . . He came up in an easy carriage that afternoon. . . . [On Thursday morning] there came a call on the telephone for me. They said father was much worse and I went at once. . . . I went in and realized that it must soon be all over for this life. I was alone with him when he died, but I don't think he recognized me or distinguished me from the others. . . . The doctor said that he had pneumonia badly in the left lung but they did not understand the sudden change for the worse. They feel that there must have been some other trouble that they did not know about. He will be buried in Hingham beside mother, and the funeral will be from the church there on Saturday at 3:00 p.m. . . . Will you let Uncle Swan know and also Aunt Selma, and any of the others in Galesburg. I do not feel that I can write more at the present.
>
> With love from your niece,
> Annie[11]

11. Olsson, letter to Nels O. Westergreen, May 25, 1908. According to Hingham

The loss of Alex evoked a different sort of grief from Westergreen's other bereavements, and it was the only funeral of an immediate family member that he did not attend. He wrote in his journal, "I am feeling somewhat lonesome after brother Alex's death," but it had been two years since he had last seen the brother closest to him in age. For the most part, Alex had lived over eight hundred miles from the rest of the family since they came to America in 1852. It was inevitable that the sense of loss would be less keen and immediate than after Andrew's death.

There were further changes in the life of his extended family. When Westergreen went to Knox County to visit his brother Swan and wife, Betsy, the reunion included their daughter Nellie, who was probably named after him. He also noted visiting with Swan's son Thomas, his wife, and their baby. In 1909 he baptized Thomas's toddler son, Arthur. The child was sickly, possibly with tuberculosis, and ended up being separated from his parents and siblings and raised largely by Nellie. She was a spinster who taught in several rural schools in the county, and lived nearby in Victoria at the time. With the exception of Henry, who was farming in Nebraska, Swan and Betsy's other children remained in the area, and some of their descendants live in Knox and Henry Counties to this day. Swan's health was precarious by 1909. Years of hard farm labor had taken their toll, and Nellie's letters to her uncle described her father's weakness and swelling in his legs and feet. He was in Galesburg Cottage Hospital for a period before returning to the farm. A day or two before Christmas, Swan consented to come to Chicago for an operation. Nellie brought him to Augustana Hospital on December 26. She, Nels, and his housekeeper, Miss Grainmann, kept vigil at his bedside. He appeared to improve slightly on January 4, but was nevertheless weaker and in pain. A few days later the journal entry was as follows:

> I got a telephone [call] last night after I came home that Brother Swan was sinking. We started immediately for the hospital. He was then in his death struggle which lasted till about 3:00 in the morning, when he quietly and peacefully passed away. Wonderfully, it is the same night that Brother Andrew passed away in Garfield Park Sanatorium, and now they are both in a better world.[12]

Cemetery records, Alex died on May 20, 1908.

12. Westergreen, *Journals*, January 7, 1910.

Swan's daughter and elder brother traveled by train with the coffin to Oneida, and then the two of them went the last nine miles to Swan and Betsy's home in a sleigh. They met the sorrowing widow and four of his children, and wept together. The funeral was held the following morning in the nearby Victoria church, with three ministers officiating. He was buried in the afternoon in Westfall Cemetery, not far from the family homestead. His obituary in the local newspaper included the following:

> Of the Swedish Methodist church in Victoria, [Swan] Wester-green has been a good and faithful member for about fifty-two years. He was a local preacher forty years and a local deacon of the Methodist church since the 8th of September 1895. A good preacher and a strong man in character and in prayer has gone to his reward in heaven. He was well-known in this community and everybody feels the loss very keenly of this good man.[13]

The obituary for *Sändebudet* was written by Nels. A few days later he wrote in his journal, "I feel so lonely now, when I am all alone of our family left."[14] His words bring to mind an incident from the life of John Wesley, two weeks after his brother Charles died. In a worship service at the chapel in Bolton, Lancashire, there was no explicit reference made to the death, but the second hymn was Charles's "Wrestling Jacob," which begins:

> Come, O Thou Traveler unknown,
> Whom still I hold but cannot see,
> My company before is gone,
> And I am left alone with Thee;[15]

John Wesley broke down and sobbed, and the congregation also began to weep over the loss of the beloved brother.[16] There is no record of Wester-green shedding tears in worship immediately following Swan's death, although he was seemingly comfortable with weeping and groaning during after-meetings, as part of seeking conversion and sanctification.

Two other people close to Westergreen died around this time. His former housekeeper, Mrs. Malmström, had been in failing health since her return from California. She died in December of 1910. And "Mother Black," Annie Westergreen's mother, died in April of 1911. One positive family-related development was that Selma, Andrew's widow, moved in

13. "Mr. Westergreen Died in Chicago," January 11, 1910, n.p.

14. Westergreen, *Journals*, January 21, 1910.

15. See Charles Wesley, "Come, O Thou Traveler Unknown," 386.

16. Brailsford, *Tale of Two Brothers*, 281.

with him and became his paid housekeeper in September of that year. A few years earlier he had written of her difficult financial circumstances, but the journals contain no discussion of why she moved in at that particular time. Miss Grainman remained a good friend who visited them often, and stayed with Westergreen when Selma made a trip back to Keokuk. There were several advantages to the new arrangement; it provided Selma with a home and some income besides her widow's pension. For Westergreen, it meant that for the first time since his mother's death, he was sharing his home with someone who was equally invested in the life of the church, and who would accompany him to social gatherings. It also meant that as his own health began to break down, both Selma and Miss Grainman were on hand to tend to his physical needs.

He had always been something of a hypochondriac, making mention of every chill and fever, and how much "slime" he coughed up during periodic colds, but now he was faced with the onset of significant health problems along with the less serious chronic ailments. The major issue was his vision. He resumed frequent treatments for his eyes in January 1908, sometimes as many as three in a day. These seem to have been eye drops plus something else that required him to go to his doctor's office. By March he wrote that he could not read for long because his eyes were weak. He had to wear "colored glasses" beginning in 1909, and was receiving daily treatments on the eyes in January. His doctor told him there was nothing to be done for his right eye until his cataract ripened, and reduced the treatments to three times per week. This was an ordeal for Westergreen, who lamented that his eyesight had become so bad he could no longer read the Bible. The handwriting in the latter part of the 1910 journal is difficult to read because he could not see what his was writing. Unable to study theology at home, as he had always done in leisure hours, and hesitant to be out and about without someone to guide him, he sat at home and wrote letters. It sometimes took him days to complete a letter in a form that would be legible to the recipient. His partial blindness caused him to stumble and fall down a flight of stairs and hit his head. Finally, on October 11, 1911, he was admitted to Lakeside Hospital in Chicago and a surgeon named Harper removed the cataract. He remained there for just over six weeks, and aside from a two-sentence entry, ostensibly written two days after surgery, he did not resume writing in his journal until the third week of November. A portion of his summary of the experience is as follows:

Now, as I was in the hospital six weeks and one day was very much like the other, I shall not try to specify anything more, only that I was visited several times by brethren and friends who brought me flowers and sweet-meats and who prayed for me in my room. I also had some new religious experiences in the hospital which I don't think I have had before and which may perhaps be of some use to me in my teaching others when I come out from here. I also made some promises which I intend with God's help to fulfill. . . . After I got home I had to get two pair of glasses, one stronger to read and to see at a distance and walk with, and O, how happy I felt when on the morning of Wednesday the 13th December I could again read my Bible, which I have not been able to do for over two years. . . . Even since I have got the glasses I have to be careful and in crossing the streets I have not only to look on all sides to avoid danger, but when I go down steps as the glasses magnify the objects then I don't take [*sic*] a mistake and fall.[17]

Failing eyesight was not the only physical problem Westergreen faced, though it had the most significant impact on his life and ministry at the time. He also wrote of suffering a pain under his breast on the left side. His regular physician, Dr. Roan, said it was neuralgia and gave him some unspecified medicine. Westergreen took it, but also put on a mustard plaster, a home remedy that generated heat and was thought to "sweat out" whatever was ailing a person. (It could also cause the skin to blister.) He reported it gave him only temporary relief, so he next took three spoons of castor oil for the soreness. After a few days he returned to his doctor, who gave him a new medicine and recommended he put on an Allcock's Plaster whenever the pain was bad. Allcock's Plaster and similar patent medicines were advertised on the back pages of *Sånde-budet*, promising amazing cures when they were just as likely to cause serious harm. First marketed by a chemist named Thomas Allcock in 1854, the plaster was made from shredded India rubber dissolved in turpentine and put through a sieve before adding cayenne pepper, ground litharge (lead monoxide, which is poisonous), balsam, and pine gum. A cloth soaked in this mixture was applied to the affected area. It was claimed that Allcock's Plaster could treat lumbago, diabetes, quinsy, epilepsy, dyspepsia, diarrhea, paralysis, kidney trouble, tuberculosis, and more.[18] Westergreen also applied turpentine-soaked cloths to his chest.

17. Westergreen, *Journals*, November 22, 1911.
18. "Allcock's Plaster," n.p.

Eventually his symptoms diminished, though whether this was due to the prescription medicine or simply the passing of time is impossible to determine.

He was less anxious about the periodic constipation he suffered, though he nevertheless consulted his doctor about it. There were plenty of over-the-counter remedies available, and he may have used them, but he also made his own tonic. He gave the recipe to Nellie in a 1909 letter, in response to her description of her father's health problems:

> Now we become more or less costive when we get old. I am troubled with the same besides being troubled with piles, which makes it more difficult to carry it off. . . . It is well to have a house medicine at hand to take it when we need it, and that is the reason I write to you and give you a prescription of a very simple one that we use with effect when we need it. It is this: take one pound of figs, then one pint of the best molasses, and then five cents' worth of sennate tea; then cut the figs in small pieces, and also cut the leaves of the sennate tea, of course you can get sennate powder and then you don't need the cutting of the leaves; but they say the leaves are better than the powder. Then you cook the molasses and after that put the cut figs and the cut sennate leaves in, and let it cool and the medicine is ready. Then put [it] in a jar and it stiffens and becomes elastic. When you use it, you may take a teaspoon topped or about as much as a half thumb, and under ordinary circumstances it may have its effect. It has, for the most part, for me.[19]

Here Westergreen was on safer ground, since both senna and figs are known to be natural laxatives. However, the remedy did not prove to be useful for his brother Swan, whose death certificate listed "pyloric obstruction—inflammatory" as the cause.

Two other afflictions, each serious in its own way, came to Westergreen during these years. The first he described as "trouble with his water." He experienced both bladder urgency and difficulty passing his urine. Often he would be up several times in the night, trying to empty his bladder. Dr. Roan was consulted repeatedly, but nothing resolved the problem. Given his age, it is likely Westergreen had an enlarged prostate, but perhaps he already had prostate cancer, not detected until much later. The second difficulty was psychological, which he most commonly described as feeling nervous. There were hints of it as early as 1905, but

19. Westergreen, letter to Nellie Westergreen, October 26, 1909.

now it was manifested with greater frequency. In one journal entry, for example, he wrote, "I am not feeling well. I am so nervous and don't seem to have any strength. . . . I don't feel inclined to either write or do anything but rather to be down on the lounge. I hope if it is God's will I may not be sick and that the present feeling of nervousness may pass away."[20] In his autobiography, Westergreen mentioned an unspecified childhood illness that left him with weak nerves. Knowing that his brother Andrew died in a mental hospital, and his mother was given to fits of weeping in her final years, he might have wondered if he, too, suffered from the familial affliction. In earlier journal entries about emotional or spiritual distress, Westergreen usually identified the cause, whether it was longing for a deeper or new religious experience, yielding to temptation, or something else. Beginning in 1909, whatever precipitated his anxiety or depression was not as apparent. In the remaining years of his life, he became increasingly dependent on sleeping powders to help him rest at night, wrote that he dreaded the nights, and confessed that a few times he became disoriented when traveling to preaching appointments. He consulted someone else—not identified as a doctor—about his periodic bouts of insomnia. The person gave him a tonic containing cannabis, and Westergreen wrote that it improved his appetite as well as helping him sleep at night.[21] He later became dependent on a non-specified sleeping powder to help him rest. Despite his emotional distress, there were moments of mystic communion with God that brought him joy: "Had a blessed time last night on my bed and did not go to sleep before after midnight. I got such a clear sight of Christ and his atonement that I could not but praise God, and though I do not feel the same joy today, yet I have a sweet rest."[22]

One might expect that following the successful cataract operation, Westergreen would resume his prior ministry and lifestyle as much as age would permit. He did go on preaching, but the operation in 1911 seemed to be a turning point in his life. Near the beginning of 1912, when he was seventy-seven years old, he recorded a candid self-assessment of his gifts and limitations:

> I wrote an article for *Sändebudet*, but will rewrite it again and
> see if there is anything that needs to be changed. I find I can-
> not think or write so fast as I did formerly, but I have reason to

20. Westergreen, *Journals*, October 8, 1909.

21. Westergreen, *Journals*, September 24, 1914.

22. Westergreen, *Journals*, October 20, 1909.

thank God that my mind is as clear as it is. May God help me use
the powers I have in his service.[23]

He did continue to participate in the life of the larger denomination
as much as possible, regularly attending the Monday clergy meetings at
Clark Street Methodist Church, district meetings, and the monthly meetings of the Swedish Methodist clergy until 1914, when ill health kept him
housebound for much of the year. He made it to Annual Conference held
in Moline in 1912, at the Market Street/First Church in 1913, and at the
Galesburg Church in 1914, though he had some difficulties in Galesburg.
Brother Theodore Peterson met him at the depot and carried his bag to
his boarding place at Brother Lindquist's. Westergreen's prostate problems flared up, and he was up fifteen or twenty times in the night, trying
to empty his bladder. Nevertheless, he led the Love Feast at Conference
on the closing day, and preached from Num 6:24–26, the Aaronic bene-
diction. It was a fitting text for the last time he addressed the Conference,
though he attended in 1915 and, surprisingly, a little more than a month
before his death in 1919. He also continued to attend non-Methodist
gatherings, such as a conference on prophecy held at Moody Bible Institute in February 1914 and the General Assembly of the Presbyterian
Church in May of the same year.

Westergreen's body was slowing down, but he was determined to
remain intellectually active. Between 1912 and 1914 he wrote an article
explaining justification by faith for *The Epworth Star*, plus a historical
sketch on the beginnings of Methodism among the Swedish immigrants
until the Swedish Conference was organized in 1877. That article, presented as a lecture, is now housed in the Northern Illinois Conference
Archives. He also wrote an essay about the life of Eric Shogren and a
history of the earliest Swedish meetings at Des Plaines Campground,
and periodically produced articles for *Sändebudet*, probably including
his 1912 translation into Swedish of Mathetes's *Epistle to Diognetes*.[24] He
read voraciously, once his vision improved. His bibliography for this period included extensive reading of the Ante-Nicene Fathers, particularly
the writings of Clement of Alexandria, Hippolytus of Rome, Tatian, and
Origen. He also studied the sermons of Puritan preacher Thomas Watson (1620–686), Victor Witting's and S. B. Newman's autobiographies,

---

23. Westergreen, *Journals*, February 16, 1912.

24. Westergreen, *Journals*, July 1, 1912. *Sändebudet* included "wholesome fiction"
of the day, published in serial form.

Phoebe Palmer's works, and Daniel Steele's *Milestone Papers*. Steele was a Methodist minister and biblical scholar, as well as a leader of the Holiness Movement who zealously promoted the doctrine of entire sanctification. The reading list also included less scholarly religious works of the time, such as *Sprinkles from the River of Life*. He had some ongoing difficulties with his eyes even after the cataract removal. He asked his doctor to prescribe new glasses, and his less than perfect vision may have been responsible for his being knocked down by a motorcycle near a tent-meeting in August of that year.

He did not spend all his waking hours in scholarly pursuits, but had a busy social life with three groups that sometimes overlapped: extended family, fellowship groups within the local church, and colleagues who were fairly close to him in age. For example, in January of 1912 he participated in no fewer than ten social gatherings. In a few cases, he was host of the occasion, but more often he was out enjoying himself with friends. He mentioned writing eight long letters, mostly to other clergy, during the same month. In addition to socializing, he was making pastoral calls on the sick, and went to the county courthouse with John Wigren to testify that S. B. Newman's will was written *before* his marriage to young Anna Ohman. More often than not, Selma accompanied him to the church-related gatherings. Members of Selma's family were also regular visitors or hosts; these included her son Wesley and his wife, Jenny, their two sons, Donald and Edward, Selma's brother Joseph, visiting from Keokuk, her sister Jenny (wife of Isaac Anderson) and nieces Edna and Libby. Miss Grainman was also a frequent visitor or substitute housekeeper when Selma was away. Most of the above-named, plus Andrew Johnson and K. H. Elmström, came to celebrate Westergreen's birthday each July. They were the people with whom he went on excursions or discussed religion and current events. He seemed to be energized and happy when he was with others, or engaged in ministry of some sort. He wrote about his desire to continue pastoral work in September 1913:

> Have stayed in the whole day writing and answering letters. It seems to me so monotonous and I almost wish I had a small charge where I could preach on Sundays and do a little extra work, not so much for the pay as to be busy in my calling, and I think I would be more blessed and perhaps have less temptations. It is hard to be laid aside in this way before we really need it. . . . I have a sermon ready if I get a chance.[25]

25. Westergreen, *Journals*, September 9, 15, 16, 1913.

A contrasting pattern gradually emerges in the journals; when he did not otherwise state a cause, spiritual and emotional depression seemed to strike when he was separated from others by illness or lacking opportunities to live out his calling. In addition to the face-to-face fellowship that sustained him, Westergreen corresponded with his nieces, Nellie in western Illinois and Annie in Boston, but there is no mention him spending time with Annie during these years. When he attended Conference in Galesburg in 1914, he did not have the stamina for an additional side trip to Victoria or the family farm in Copley Township.

He continued to record and comment on current events and social issues in his journal. The sinking of the *Titanic* was described over the course of several days, capturing the disbelief and horror it engendered at the time:

> We read in the evening paper of a terrible disaster at sea. The greatest and finest steamer in the world, the new *Titanic*, with over two thousand aboard had struck an iceberg and gone down. How many were saved is not yet fully known. . . . The papers are full of descriptions of the *Titanic* disaster. It is now concluded that over 1300 lost their lives in it and found a watery grave. . . . We now get through the papers more defined reports of the great *Titanic* disaster, in which only 745 are reported saved, while 1591 were lost and went down with the gigantic bulk of the world's greatest steamer to a depth of about 2,000 fathoms or about 12,000 feet, and there were great men and millionaires among the lost, but here they were all alike, and so it will be at the Judgment.[26]

The language and phrasing here suggest Westergreen may have copied newspaper accounts verbatim for part of the journal entries. He made note of other current events, and, as was the case in earlier years, focused chiefly on disasters and body counts. In early July of 1912, he wrote about an accident on the Delaware and Lackawanna Railroad when "a fast express at a high speed ran into the rear end of an excursion train, in which forty-one were killed and over fifty wounded."[27] A few weeks later he wrote of another train accident in Western Springs, Illinois, in which thirteen were killed. In October he noted that former President Theodore Roosevelt was shot by an anarchist or lunatic, and expressed the hope that the wound would not prove fatal, saying, "We need such men as Roosevelt

26. Westergreen, *Journals*, April 15, 17, 19, 1912.
27. Westergreen, *Journals*, July 5, 1912.

in our time."[28] His vote for Roosevelt in the 1912 national election was a departure from his usual habit of preference for Prohibition Party candidates when one was running for office, and otherwise voting Republican. Roosevelt was identified as a Progressive at the time, having split off from the more conservative mainstream Republican party. Perhaps it was Roosevelt's pro-labor and reform platform than won Westergreen's support. He also voted for women's suffrage that year.

The Great War and events leading up to it did not evoke as much commentary as one might expect. Westergreen did write briefly about the First Balkan War, and expressed hope that the Turks would be driven out and peace restored. He mentioned in passing the Chinese Revolution of 1911 and 1912. Though he did not mention the assassination of Archduke Ferdinand at the end of June, 1914, a few weeks before war was officially declared at the end of July, he wrote:

> There is war in Europe between Austria and Serbia, but it seems to threaten the whole of Europe and involve it in war. Germany mobilizes her troops and so does Russia, and there seem to be a threatening also in the money world, as some of the large business houses in New York are making failures. What the end will be God only knows, but it looks dark.[29]

As the summer progressed, he continued to note briefly developments in the conflict, blaming the pope's death in part to his grief over the war. In late August he observed that the Germans appeared to be winning, though with great loss. He lamented the continuation of the war, and prayed frequently that God would put an end to it. In October President Wilson ordered a Sunday of prayers for peace, but Westergreen made no mention of that happening in the churches he attended.

His involvement in social issues was now limited to attending local temperance meetings, helping the poor when he personally encountered them, and supporting issues that were brought up at the weekly clergy meetings and monthly Swedish Methodist clergy meetings. Foreign missions were a particular concern, given the turmoil of the Great War. Westergreen no longer mentioned the Emigrant Aid Society, but in fairness to him, immigration from Sweden reached its peak more than twenty-five years earlier, in 1887.[30]

28. Westergreen, *Journals*, October 15, 1912.

29. Westergreen, *Journals*, July 31, 1914.

30. Blanck, "Swedish Immigration to North America," n.p.

The theological seminary was still of interest to him, but his participation in its life was minimal. He attended the closing exercises and graduation, and in June of 1914 went to a convention in Evanston that included the dedication of the memorial table for Albert Ericson.[31] Bishop McDowell was there and gave a talk, and then speeches were made by Alfred Anderson, J. E. Hillberg, and C. G. Wallenius. Westergreen led a noonday meeting on the last day of the convention and spoke from Luke 11:13 on the necessity of a special outpouring of God's Spirit in that age and the manifestation of it. Unfortunately, the manuscript for that sermon has not been preserved.

As mentioned earlier, although there are about 680 extant sermons by Westergreen in the Northern Illinois Conference archives, only a handful have dates on them: usually from the "Week of Prayer" held in January each year. Matching texts with dates noted in his journals demonstrates that he preached some of the sermons between 1912 and 1914. However, there is no sermon text/manuscript that was preached *only* in one of those years, making it impossible to determine whether and how his theology and method changed during this period. It was necessary for him to make fresh copies of old sermons, because some of them were used periodically across the sixty years of his ministry. For example, there are sermon manuscripts in English and Swedish on one his favorite texts, Matt 11:28–30: "Come to me, all you that are weary and are carrying heavy burdens, and I will give you rest. Take my yoke upon you, and learn from me; for I am gentle and humble in heart, and you will find rest for your souls. For my yoke is easy, and my burden is light." Westergreen preached that text in at least twenty-five different years between 1858 and 1910, often multiple times within a single year.

Westergreen's health took a downturn in 1914, affecting his involvement in Annual Conference, but more noticeably in the number of times he preached. From fifty-two times in 1913, his preaching appointments dropped to twenty-nine in 1914, and never rose above thirty-five times per year for the remainder of his life. In September he revised his will, naming John Wigren's son James (1854–1941) as his executor, with Francis and Lydia Logren as witnesses. The decline in health should not be attributed to his eyesight; with few exceptions, his handwriting was clear and fine in the final journals. His physical problems were rather due to the usual infirmities that come with age, plus increasing bladder troubles. He complained of

31. The tablet is now housed in the archives of the Northern Illinois Conference.

insomnia and overall weakness, and, acknowledging that he was unsteady on his feet, began using a cane in 1916. When William Henschen invited him to a district meeting in Chesterton, Indiana, he wrote that he could not come because of his health. In spite of these limitations and fewer opportunities to preach and lead worship, his day to day life did not change dramatically in 1915. He usually went to the weekly clergy meetings, monthly meetings of Swedish clergy, and attended Annual Conference, held that year at the First/Market Street Church. He preached at Chicago area churches and sometimes visited the nearby Swedish and Norwegian Lutheran churches, preferring the Norwegian pastor's sermons, though he considered the liturgy "stiff." He probably felt more at home at the Free Methodist church, various Mission Friends' churches, the Adventist Church, the Salem Evangelical Free Church, and the Free Church near 113th and Indiana Avenue: all non-MEC places he visited.[32]

Westergreen's ability to get around to see friends and worship with various congregations appeared to contribute to a general (though not total) lifting of the depression that plagued him a few years earlier. He had at least two spiritual "high points" during the year. Unlike most of the "melting times" he enjoyed at campmeetings and after-meetings over the years, these occurred when he was engaged in solitary meditation:

> Went to Kedzie Boulevard Norwegian Methodist in the forenoon and heard a very good sermon of the pastor, Bro. Hanson. Have read a great deal in the afternoon in some old sermons until I felt my own heart warmed. I think we sometimes fail now to make things so clear as they did in the olden times. Perhaps our own experience is not so clear as it was then, and we have not the chance to sharpen it with earnest seekers as they had then.[33] I was blessed while I had laid [*sic*] awake by thinking upon Isaiah 53 and other scriptural promises, and I had a sweet rest that I have not felt for some time. Thank God.[34]

He still reveled in protracted and campmeetings and their convicting, converting, and sanctifying potential. In January of that year, he described protracted meetings at the Humboldt Park Church:

32. The Salem Church was located on California Avenue south of Armitage Avenue. The original name was First Scandinavian Congregational Church of Chicago.

33. Westergreen, *Journals*, January 3, 1915.

34. Westergreen, *Journals*, March 17, 1915.

Brother William Swenson (1863–1936) preached a very strong sermon to the professing Christians and asked them if they really had the feeling against sin that we should have, and then the feeling for the sinner by seeing his great danger that we should have, and it was a heart-searching and solemn meeting. . . . [After another service] they had testimonies after Swenson preached, and prayers at the altar, and then a lunch and a little social talk.[35]

He made similar favorable remarks while attending the campmeeting at Des Plaines, singling out Dr. Paul Rader, who was then the pastor of Moody Church, for particular praise. In 1915 and 1916 he made the rounds of the Free Methodist and Salvation Army campmeetings in Glen Ellyn, plus urban tent-meetings at Armitage and Kimball and Hirsch and California: both tent-meetings were within reasonable walking distance of his home.

He was too old to travel alone to visit Swan's family in Knox County, but they came to him. Betsy, Nellie, and little Arthur, now eight years old, stayed with him and Selma for a week in 1915. Unlike earlier visits from extended family, during which Westergreen took them to Lincoln Park Zoo, the Columbian Exhibition, and other tourist attractions, he now took his visitors to take meals with clergy colleagues, and to local parks. Seventy years later, when Arthur Westergreen recalled his great uncle, he described him as a kind and scholarly man rather than as someone who took a little boy to exciting places in the city! For the most part, time spent with extended family meant entertaining Selma's son Wesley and his family, going to their home in the Austin neighborhood of Chicago, visiting the graves of Andrew or John, and attending church-related social events. They gathered for birthdays, usually joined by Isaac Anderson's family, Andrew Johnson, and sometimes the Wigrens, although the Wigrens' age and infirmity placed limits on their participation. When Selma's brother suddenly died of a heart attack in July 1916, she traveled to Keokuk alone for the funeral, and when Betsy Westergreen died in November of that year, Westergreen sent a telegram to the family saying he was not well enough to go to the funeral service at the Methodist Church in Victoria.

When the weather was good and he had the energy, Westergreen was out calling on both active clergy and retired colleagues, often staying for a meal. Isaac Anderson and John Wigren were the two with whom he spent the most time. Wigren was now eighty-nine years old and

35. Westergreen, *Journals*, February 2 and 7, 1915.

possibly suffering from osteonecrosis brought on by diabetes. In early April 1915 Westergreen called on him and found him walking on two crutches. Wigren told him he was being admitted to Augustana Hospital the following day to have his right foot amputated. When Westergreen visited him about a week later, the amputation had not taken place, and some of the swelling had subsided. Wigren was in the hospital more than fourteen weeks. By October he was able to get up and preach, leaning on one crutch, and Westergreen exhorted after him. However, this was a temporary reprieve, not a cure. The following April he was taken to the hospital again, and this time the amputation was done. About ten days later Westergreen wrote in his journal:

> I walked over to Isaac Anderson's. He was not at home when I came, but had gone to the hospital, but came while I waited and he said Brother Wigren was doing well. When I walked out [from] Brother Anderson's I felt very happy and I could not but praise the Lord. It is a long time since I felt so happy. Went to church in the evening and we had a good meeting.[36]

He and Anderson continued to visit Wigren at the hospital and later at home. Near the end of June, he wrote that Wigren's leg was healing and he hoped he could soon use an artificial foot. Then in mid-August Wigren developed trouble with his urinary tract and returned to the hospital, in great pain and scarcely able to talk. He died eleven days later. The cause of death given was hypertrophic prostate cystitis. There were two funeral services. Westergreen preached at the first one, held in the Wigrens' home, taking Rev 14:13 as his text: "And I heard a voice from heaven saying, 'Write this: Blessed are the dead who from now on die in the Lord.' 'Yes,' says the Spirit, 'they will rest from their labors, for their deeds follow them.'" The principal theme of the sermon was the present and future blessedness of those who die in the Lord. Some characteristics of the present blessedness were as follows:

- They rest from our earthly and bodily labors.
- They rest from any temptation, for nothing unclean can exist there.
- They rest from sorrow and misery, for there are no more tears there.
- They rest from troubles and mourning, for there shall be no more pain. Rev 21:4.[37]

36. Westergreen, *Journals*, May 3, 1916.
37. Westergreen, "Funeral Sermon on Revelation 14:13," 3.

As was the case in other funeral sermons Westergreen preached, this was an exploration of a text, and there was no explicit mention of the deceased. This may have been because there were several speakers at the funeral. Others would give eulogies or relate the particulars of the deceased person's life, while the sermon was intended to convey biblical promises and the faith that sustained the deceased. This is borne out in the final or application section of the sermon, in which Westergreen exhorted listeners to have a childlike trust, without which no one can enter the kingdom of heaven, and then offered comfort by reminding them they could have the assurance of knowing where their deceased loved one had gone. After the service at the Wigren home, the main funeral took place at church. William Swenson opened with prayers, K. H. Elström preached the funeral sermon, and then both Theodore Moberg, who was the pastor at Humboldt Park, and C. G. Wallenius spoke. Westergreen described it as a fine funeral, but he and Isaac Anderson keenly felt the loss of this longtime friend.

The death of John Wigren evoked a personal grief, but the years 1915 and 1916 also brought occasions of large-scale mourning and fears about the future. In May of 1915 Westergreen wrote in his journal:

> There is a kind of sadness on account of the fate of *Lusitania*, in which so many Americans perished, and there is also considerable of feeling of excitement aroused. I hope, however, that we may not be drawn into this terrible war. We ought to pray more for our president in these critical times for surely he needs them. May God be with us is my prayer.[38]

He did not write specifically about the *Lusitania* again, but the journal periodically mentioned the war and his fear that the United States would be drawn into it. A few months later, he was unable to resist moralizing over a more local calamity in which 844 people died. It was the largest loss of life from a single shipwreck on the Great Lakes:

> Heard in the morning of a terrible accident that had happened in the city. The steamer *Eastland*, which was going out to a picnic with between two and three thousand on board, capsized in the river, and it is thought about one thousand were drowned. . . . This has been a day of mourning in so many churches on account of the many funerals of those who lost their lives on the *Eastland*. I saw in the paper that there were twenty-nine coffins

---

38. Westergreen, *Journals*, May 10, 1915.

in one Catholic church and thirteen in another, and there will be
funerals of others during the week. I see there are three in one
family on the boulevard not far from us. What a warning this is
if men would only heed.[39]

Westergreen's notes on the disaster were mostly accurate. St. Mary of
Czestochowa Church in suburban Cicero did lose twenty-nine members,
but the priest conducted a total of forty-one funerals. Another church,
Grace Lutheran at 25th and Karlov, lost twenty-five members. The accident occurred during an outing organized for employees of the Western
Electric Company's Hawthorne Works in Cicero, and perhaps because
many of the dead were Czech immigrants, more *Eastland* victims were
buried at Bohemian National Cemetery on the Chicago's northwest side
than anywhere else.

Westergreen's fears were confirmed when the United States did enter the war on April 6, 1917. He did not comment on the event that day,
but he acknowledged in February of that year that it seemed likely. In
January his colleague Gustaf Gordon had been offered the opportunity to
take a long journey with several other Swedish ministers in the Russian
Missionary Service. They were to travel to Japan, then through Russia
to Petrograd, and finally through Scandinavia before returning home.
All their expenses would be paid. Westergreen acknowledged it was a
great offer, but he nevertheless wrote to Gordon and advised him "not
to travel in these warlike times, unless it was a necessity and he had a
special call of God for it." He wrote periodically about developments in
the war, bought liberty bonds, and mentioned that two of his ministerial colleagues' sons were drafted in February of 1918. They reported to
Camp Grant near Rockford. Westergreen supported President Wilson's
call for a day of fasting and prayer for God's help in the war, a few months
later. The president called for a second day of prayer for a speedy and
successful end of the war on Sunday, August 4; Westergreen underscored
the theme by preaching on 2 Sam 5: 23–25, which is about a battle. On
November 7, 1918, he wrote in his journal: "We had a long whistle at
noon. I wondered what it meant. Heard that the long whistling meant
that peace had been declared. Thank God if it is so."[40] Four days later he
wrote that he and Selma got very little sleep on account of the continual

39. Westergreen, *Journals*, July 24 and 28, 1915.
40. Westergreen, *Journals*, November 7, 1918.

whistling and noise-making that started around midnight and continued all day in celebration of the armistice.

At the outset of 1917, Westergreen had appeared to be remarkably vigorous for his age, in spite of claiming to have a cold and cough in January. He preached at seven church services and one funeral in the two months, exhorted three other times, and was otherwise regular in his church attendance. In March, health problems returned. It was more than another cold; he experienced pain "in his loins" and his breast. Dr. Roan, his physician, came to the house several times, and gave him medicines for his cough, his kidneys, and something to counteract the foul odor of his chamber pot. During one visit, the doctor took Selma aside and had a long talk with her: an ominous sign. Westergreen wrote that his urine was nearly red as blood, and a few entries in April are nearly incoherent. He could not attend church on Easter. When he managed to go to Humboldt Park the following Sunday, people told him he looked so pale he should not have made the attempt. His nephew Wesley and Theodore Moberg, who was then pastor at Humboldt Park, came to visit regularly. The symptoms gradually subsided. He and Selma were able to attend the closing exercises of the theological seminary near the end of May. He began writing articles again for *Sändebudet*, dealt with difficulties with his tenants, and spent several days at the Des Plaines campmeeting at the end of July. He gave his testimony there and reported there were sermons and speeches from Bishop Nicholson, Dr. Wedderspoon, N. M. Liljegren, and a missionary to the Philippines named Farmer. On his eighty-third birthday, Westergreen assisted Theodore Moberg in conducting a funeral. For the remainder of the summer he resumed guest preaching, attending tent-meetings, and going to social events alone or with Selma. A visit with Isaac Anderson was likely the high point of the season. He wrote, "I went in the afternoon to Brother Isaac Anderson's, walking both there and back. It was a pleasant and I think profitable visit for us, for we talked mostly on religious subjects and answers to prayer as well personal experience, until I felt my heart was becoming somewhat warmed, thank God.[41] But such leisurely conversations with Isaac Anderson were going to become less frequent. Isaac had retired in 1907, after serving his last appointment at the Austin Church. Two weeks after the conversation noted above, the Andersons moved to Norwood Park, northwest of the city. It was possible but not convenient to get there on

41. Westergreen, *Journals*, September 3, 1917.

public transportation, and certainly much too far for Westergreen to walk there. The Andersons and Westergreens remained friends and continued to see each other on special occasions. When Selma celebrated her sixty-third birthday in November, the entire Anderson family came, along with Selma's son Wesley and his family, plus several others. The Andersons came again to celebrate Christmas Eve; nevertheless, the two longtime colleagues must have missed each other's regular company.

At Annual Conference in 1917, Theodore Moberg was replaced by Peter Magnus Alfvin as the minister at the Humboldt Park Church. He was there for only a year before William Swenson (1863–1936) was appointed. Westergreen was on friendly terms with all three men. When he went out walking, he regularly dropped in at the parsonage to rest before walking back home, and they made him welcome. Alfvin frequently invited Westergreen to assist in conducting funerals or leading other worship, and Swenson occasionally did the same. Westergreen considered Alfvin the better preacher. He assessed Swenson's inaugural sermon at Humboldt Park as tolerably good. Several months later he wrote, "Brother Swenson is earnest, but has a lack of unction." However, a few weeks later he wrote that Swenson was doing his best not only in the pulpit, but also in his pastoral work.[42] Swenson was the minister at a challenging time of transition. It appears that the Humboldt Park Church was holding at least half its services in English rather than Swedish, and it ultimately transferred out of the Swedish Conference to affiliate with the Chicago Home Missionary and Church Extension Society of the Rock River Conference.[43] While Swenson did not come under personal attack, both the ministerial and lay sessions of Conference voted resolutions deploring the actions of the Humboldt Park congregation, and the clergy contemplated legal action against the church.

With Isaac Anderson no longer living close by, Westergreen socialized more with the Alfvins and Henschens, and also developed a friendship with Pastor Hanson of nearby Trinity Norwegian Lutheran Church. It was closer than Humboldt Park Methodist, and he liked Hanson's preaching. Selma's son and grandsons were frequent visitors, along with his former housekeeper, Miss Grainman.

Aside from two lingering colds, one starting in February and the other in September, Westergreen's health seemed much better than the

42. Westergreen, *Journals*, March 16 and April 7, 1919.

43. *Protokoll för vid Svenska Centrala Konferensens* [Minutes of the Swedish Methodist Conference], 17–18.

previous year. He was able to participate in the monthly Swedish preachers' meetings, and in June did a week-long preaching tour in Milwaukee,
Racine, and Rockford. Although he did not go to the Swedish Methodist
Annual Conference in Donovan, he attended both the Rock River and
Norwegian-Danish Methodist Conferences, closer to home. He also went
to a Mission Friends church to hear Dr. David Nyvall, whose sermon he
rated excellent, and the Norwegian Methodist church on Kedzie Avenue.
In July he and Selma went to the Des Plaines campmeeting for several
days. He preached there for what proved to be the last time, taking Acts
20:17–21 as his text. Though he noted in his journal that he preached
in the Swedish tabernacle to a large congregation, the only extant sermon manuscript for this text seemed to be directed mainly to his fellow
preachers. It is possible that the sermon was composed and delivered
at least once before, perhaps to a district meeting of Swedish Methodist ministers. However, the absence of an application at the end of the
manuscript is characteristic of sermons preached at campmeetings and
protracted meetings, where a separate exhorter followed the sermon
proper. In addition, many of the points in the sermon could be applied to
Christian laity as well as clergy, and Westergreen could have departed as
needed from what he had written, to tailor the message to the Des Plaines
congregation. The theme of the message is an examination of Paul as a
model of faithfulness in his work as an evangelist. The first half of Acts
20 is a narrative describing Paul's ministry in Macedonia and Greece,
and his decision to bypass Ephesus in order to be in Jerusalem on the
day of Pentecost. He made a stop at Miletus and sent for the elders from
Ephesus to meet him there. Westergreen does some amplification of the
text, imputing motives that may or may not have been the case:

> Paul could have wished to stay at Ephesus. There he could see
> how things were going with the church where he had enjoyed
> some glorious times. He could have stayed awhile and encour-
> aged them, and enjoyed the love they had for him in return.
> He could have wanted to report to the brothers about his work
> among the Gentiles. He could have preached the Gospel to more
> people. But duty called him to Jerusalem, and to bring the alms
> he had collected (Galatians 2:10). He had been there on such an
> errand about four years earlier. Having decided not to stop at
> Ephesus, he did the next best thing and called the leaders of the

Ephesian church to him. . . . What was of greatest importance
for Paul should be of greatest importance for us as well.[44]

Westergreen then went on to describe aspects of Paul's character and witness that should serve as a model for his listeners: earnestness in piety
and holiness in relationship to others, laboring without ulterior motives
and seeking God's glory rather than worldly fame, counting one's own life
as loss (v. 24), etc. All the characteristics named by the preacher may be
found in Paul's words to the elders of Ephesus. In the course of the sermon, trustworthiness, transparency and holiness of life, and zealousness
for Christ were emphasized. There was a poignant irony in Westergreen's
choice of text, for the scene at Miletus ends with Paul and the elders praying, following by weeping and grieving because they would not see Paul
again. There is no record of the congregation's reaction to Westergreen's
message, though presumably they prayed together, but this was the last
time they saw him in the pulpit of the Swedish Tabernacle.

Spending time at the Des Plaines campmeeting was always a
spiritual high point for Westergreen, and in 1918 he mentioned hearing Arvid Sörlin preach a good sermon, and then going to the American
(Waldorf) tabernacle to hear Bishop Quayle. However, he did not report
anything out of the ordinary this year, or claim that it was one of the
best campmeetings they had held. Perhaps it was eclipsed by the Billy
Sunday campaign. A curious aspect of the campaign was that local clergy
organized, prayed, and otherwise helped prepare for it, just as many Protestant clergy did for the Billy Graham crusades in Chicago in 1962 and
1971. Westergreen wrote that Brother Alfvin was working out a schedule
of prayer meetings in members' homes prior to Billy Sunday's arrival. A
large tabernacle, built at the corner of Chicago Avenue and Lake Shore
Drive, was dedicated on Sunday, March 3. Beginning the campaign during Lent was not an issue for Billy Sunday, any more than crusades during
Lent were an issue for Billy Graham. In fact, Billy Sunday held a special
service for men only on Easter Sunday afternoon. Westergreen attended
the tent-meetings between twenty and thirty times, sometimes accompanied by Selma. He enjoyed the singing and was generally approving of the
sermon content, but less enthusiastic about Sunday's style of delivery and
the behavior of the crowds that came to hear him. Some of his remarks
were as follows:

---

44. Westergreen, "Sermon on Acts 20:17–22."

I heard him talk but I cannot say preach, for I could not hear him take a text. He may have done it and I [did] not hear it for I hear poorly and he speaks very rapidly. He spoke about spiritual power and said, among other things, that the church, although it was more numerous in membership, more wealthy and more generally educated, she had lost a great deal of the power that she once had. When I went home I felt much moved to prayer. . . . There was grand music and singing and [Sunday] spoke well, but there was too much of handclapping and laughing occasionally that I did not have the use of it. . . . I got a good seat so I could hear him and see his manners and gestures, and over he jumped right up on the pulpit. . . . Went to hear Mr. Sunday's famous sermon on the second coming of Christ. He spoke both long and loud today and it was a more serious feeling so there was not so much of laughter or hand-clapping. . . . Large crowd, and his text was Galatians 6:9 and it was strong, for he made fearless attacks upon the sins that are prevailing, not only among the worldly people, but even among some who profess themselves to be Christians.[45]

The campaign ran from the first week in March until nearly the end of May. Westergreen arrived there early enough to sit on the ministers' platform at least once: another indication of the widespread support for Billy Sunday among evangelical clergy and churches. On other occasions, the tabernacle was so overcrowded he could not get in at all.

At the end of 1918 and throughout 1919 there was a strange reticence about the Spanish flu pandemic in Westergreen's journal. The pandemic lasted from February 1918 to April 1920. Yet influenza was mentioned only twice by Westergreen; in the autumn of 1918 he wrote that he was miserable with cough and flu. Five days later he went and saw Dr. Roan, who gave him a prescription "and some powder for to sleep." Westergreen was sufficiently recovered that he attended the Rock River Conference exactly one week after writing that he had flu. The second mention occurred in January of 1919, when he noted that Selma had gone to visit the wife of the sexton, who had influenza. Given Westergreen's tendency to hypochondria and habit of including details of epidemics—after all, he was counting coffins on a train during the 1866 cholera outbreak—one can only speculate about reasons for silence about one of the deadliest epidemics in modern history. First, it is possible he himself had a mild case of Spanish flu in September 1918, making further discussion less

45. Westergreen, *Journals*, March 16, 19, 31, April 11, May 3, 1918.

important to him. A second possibility is that during the final year of his life, Westergreen was less aware of current events around him. There are fewer comments in general about the world and national situation than in previous years. A third possibility is that the pandemic simply did not directly affect Westergreen and his circle of friends as it did the larger population. For example, in October 1918, Chicago closed theaters, movie houses, and night schools, and prohibited general public gatherings in an attempt to avoid contagion.[46] Pious Methodists like Westergreen never went to movie houses or theaters, and there was no ban on religious gatherings. It should also be remembered that Westergreen was eighty-four years old at the start of 1919. His housekeeper, Selma, was sixty-five. Isaac Anderson and William Henschen were in their seventies, and Pastors Alfvin and Swenson were nearly sixty. In other words, the people closest to Westergreen were not young adults, the age group in which the mortality rate was around 50 percent.[47] And since Westergreen was not serving a church and conducting funerals, he would have had less direct involvement with those affected by Spanish flu.

Westergreen admitted that by now he only glanced at the daily newspaper, but read the *Christian Advocate* and *Sändebudet* more carefully. This may account for his less frequent mention of current events, and when he did, he reflected on them less. He made brief notes of Theodore Roosevelt's death in January 1919, the danger to missionaries in Korea in March, and the Chicago race riots and "car strike" in July of that year. Illness kept him close to home much of the time. In December 1918 he had written again about having "trouble with his water," and speculated that perhaps he had diabetes after reading about its symptoms. Dr. Roan was consulted frequently, making house calls when Westergreen was too feeble to go to his office. He relied on what he called sleeping powders to get rest at night, and during the day spent much time lying on the couch, reading and meditating.

His choice of reading material expanded beyond the Ante-Nicene Fathers now, though he did enjoy rereading Clement's epistles to the Corinthians, Polycarp, Irenaeus, Tatian, The Shepherd of Hermas, and others. Now he also studied the journal of John Wesley, *The Works of the Rev. John Fletcher*, Ridpath's *History of the United States*, Finney's *Lectures on Revival*, W. D. Conybeare's lectures, and Phoebe Palmer's *The*

46. "Pandemic Resources 1918," n.p.
47. "Spanish Flu," https://en.wikipedia.org/wiki/Spanish_flu.

Economy of Salvation. After reading Robert Hall's *Help to Zion's Traveler*, he remarked,

> "It certainly is a remarkable book and seems to correct some errors and pretty well describe the state of our hearts and feelings, yet I cannot agree with him in all, for as a Methodist I hold more to Wesley's views on entire sanctification in this life."[48]

Westergreen's health improved with warmer weather, as it usually did. Not only did he attend some of the preachers' meetings and the annual preachers' picnic in Lincoln Park, but he also took the train to attend Annual Conference in September, and took local transportation to visit Isaac Anderson in Norwood Park. A fellow minister took him by car to the Des Plaines campmeeting, where he heard C. G. Wallenius give a lecture on the Holy Spirit. He and Selma attended the closing exercises at the seminary. He composed a historical paper to be read at the fifty years' festival of the dedication of the Victoria church. He celebrated his eight-fifth birthday with William Swenson and his wife, Wesley Westergreen's family, Selma, and a number of guests from the Bethany Home, and described it as a festivity with good things to eat and pleasant company. There was even a brief article about the celebration in *Sändebudet*:

> Last Friday afternoon, July 25, several Christians gathered in Dr. Westergreen's home to enjoy fellowship with our venerable brother as he marked the eighty-fifth milestone in his long and interesting life journey, and to wish him well in his pilgrimage. . . . Mrs. A. T. Westergreen, who for some years now has been his faithful housekeeper, offered refreshments, and the Christian social gathering closed with prayer. . . . Brother Westergreen is now the only one left among the ground-breakers of Swedish Methodism, and is believed to be the oldest Swedish Methodist preacher in the world. . . . When he is not filling the pulpit on Sundays, he attends our Humboldt Park Church.[49]

Early in the year, Westergreen wrote that he was looking over sermon outlines to see if there was one he could use if called on to preach the following Sunday. His love for pulpit ministry did not weaken even as his body was failing. He was able to preach, exhort after the sermon, assist with Holy Communion, or give testimony more than a dozen times at seven different churches and a tent-meeting on Fullerton Avenue. He

48. Westergreen, *Journals*, March 6, 1919.
49. Swenson, "Dr. N. O. Westergreen Fyller 85 År," 5.

described the tent-meeting, led by J. R. Andrews, a fellow Swedish Methodist, as glorious, and attended other tent-meetings in Norwegian and English with Selma. Of the ten sermons he preached, only one was based on a text that could logically be used to speak about sanctification: Phil 3:7–11. Unfortunately, the manuscript for this sermon was not preserved. His last sermon was preached at the Austin church on August 24: a fitting setting, given that it was the last church he served. He spoke on Heb 13:8: "Jesus Christ is the same yesterday and today and forever."

It can be demonstrated that Westergreen preached on this text in 1870, 1879, 1902, 1909, and 1919, though naturally he may also have preached on it in other years. The 1909 sermon was preached in English at Moreland. The Swedish manuscript seems so uncharacteristic of his homiletical method that one is tempted to double-check the handwriting and ask whether Westergreen was actually the author, or if perhaps some other Swedish minister's sermon was slipped into the files. Although the sermon begins with the usual format of setting the theme and enumerating main points, there is no conclusion or indication that an exhorter followed the preacher. There are only three other texts cited in the seven-page manuscript: Gal 3:28; 2 Cor 3:18; and Eccl 12. By contrast, his sermon for John Wigren's funeral cited other texts twenty-four times, and the six-page manuscript of a 1918 sermon on 1 Tim 1:5 had fifty text citations. Finally, the sermon content, while orthodox enough, draws more from the field of psychology than Christian theology. The thesis of the sermon is that Christ is the eternal fountain of youth. He is the same for all believers without regard to their education, degree of enlightenment, or any other circumstances, and if two saints—one from the first century and the other from the twentieth—were to meet, they would immediately recognize Christ as the same Lord. Westergreen then abruptly shifts to the observation that for us, youth is the most hopeful time of life, and also the time when a person makes decisions that will shape the rest of life. Drawing on Hippocrates's four temperament theory, he asserts that the choleric temperament is characteristic of childhood, the sanguine temperament of you, the phlegmatic temperament of middle age, and the melancholic temperament of old age. Westergreen places greatest emphasis on the youthful *Christian* temperament, because the majority of conversions are among the young, and habits, whether holy or unholy, are established during this period. The conclusion invites listeners of all ages to receive the original apostolic Spirit, becoming one in heart and soul, so that they are able to set aside thoughts of earthly differences and discover Christ as the fountain of eternal youth truly among them.[50]

The respite from illness that he enjoyed during the summer did not last. Even during the months when he was engaging in ministry and interacting with family and friends, his body was failing. At the end of May he wrote in his journal, "I am a sick man." He frequently called out to Selma during the night to come and administer his liquid medicine, because he was unable to do it for himself. His diet became mostly liquid and sparse as his bladder and bowels failed. In addition to the occasional laments about his spiritual state, a leitmotif running through all his journals, he began to suffer from some confusion. He was troubled sometimes with doubts and distressing thoughts, and was afraid of the night. Beginning in February, there were entries such as, "I engaged in reflection on my life and in earnest prayer for I don't understand myself . . . I feel so strange. Lord, help me . . . I am deeply moved to pray for myself and others, but I am bewildered sometimes, that I hardly know how to pray. Lord, help me, and grant me thy Spirit to help my infirmities, but leave me not alone."[51] A few journal entries switch back and forth from English to Swedish for no apparent reason. Dr. Roan visited, and told Westergreen his heart was weak, and that caused "hard breathing." His handwriting changed for the worse in mid-September. Nevertheless, in the midst of these difficulties, there were moments of religious consolation and refreshment:

> I had a very pleasant dream last night and I wish it would come out true about myself, for it seemed that my faith in Christ had been suddenly strengthened, and I had received the full assurance of faith and the peace and joy of salvation, and [though] the road was rough, I was running and shouting, and I wanted to tell others. This set me a-praying, Lord help me.[52]

> In the afternoon I was left alone, and it began to shadow for my faith, but I was engaged in earnest prayer for awhile until the shadows fled and light broke in, and I can rest more firmly on the rock of ages.[53]

> I talked with Brother Nelson [probably Charles J. Nelson] about different periods of my life, which had been so very checkered,

50. Westergreen, "Sermon on Hebrews 13:8," 4, 7.

51. Westergreen, *Journals*, February 25, March 19, October 3, 1919.

52. Westergreen, *Journals*, January 4, 1919.

53. Westergreen, *Journals*, September 14, 1919.

but showing that God in his providence had undoubtedly ordered it all.[54]

William Swenson came frequently to pray with him, and was there
twice on October 21. Westergreen no doubt appreciated his spiritual support, but noted with regret that during their worship together he had to
do it in a sitting position, being too weak to kneel. A Methodist deaconess
was sent to the house to assist Selma, who needed help with caregiving.
According to his final journal entry, Selma went to Augustana Hospital
that day to inquire about having her brother-in-law admitted. He was
taken there on the Wednesday, October 22, and died at 4:40 p.m. the
following day. The cause of death given on the certificate was primary
carcinoma of prostate gland, with an ascending urinary infection as the
secondary cause. The bill from the hospital was $2.50.

There were two funerals for Westergreen, just as there had been for
his mother and for John Wigren. The first was at the First / Market Street
Church in Chicago: the charge conference with which Westergreen was
affiliated. No record remains of what was said or sung, but probate records show that William Swenson, his pastor, officiated. He was probably
assisted by C. J. Erickson, who was the minister at Market Street Church,
and his friend Isaac Anderson. It is also likely that C. G. Wallenius, who
wrote his obituary for *Sändebudet*, and/or his friends K. H. Elmström
and William Henschen had roles in the service. Westergreen's body, like
his brother Swan's nine years earlier, was taken by train to Galesburg,
where the second funeral was held on Tuesday afternoon in the Swedish Methodist Church (later called Emmanuel). Eric P. Swan, the pastor,
officiated. A photograph was taken from the balcony during the service.
Though somewhat blurred, it shows the casket draped with a wide garland of flowers. At least five clergymen are seen in the chancel behind the
casket, with a trio of ministers performing a song to one side. After the
service, Westergreen was buried next to his parents at Hope Cemetery in
Galesburg. He was the only one of the five brothers to be interred there.

The first obituary to appear was in *Sändebudet*, a few days after his
death. It gave no information about the obsequies, probably because it
was published the same day as the Galesburg funeral. It was a lengthy
memorial, taking up two broadsheet columns. Both this memorial and
the one that appeared in the 1920 Central Swedish Conference *Minutes/
Journal* manifest typical Victorian linguistic devices such as metaphors,

54. Westergreen, *Journals*, October 14, 1919.

metonymies, and hyperbole rarely found in contemporary church publications.[55] The memorial begins this way:

> Last Friday morning word reached us that the previous day the
> elderly veteran had laid down the traveling staff and exchanged
> the pilgrim's attire for the heavenly garments. With Dr. Wester-
> green's death, the last of the earliest group of Swedish-American
> preachers has left us, and likewise a remarkable man.... His real
> life's work has always been carried out as a preacher, for which
> he possessed a number of qualities that made his a renowned
> speaker. His passion and enthusiasm in the days of his strength
> gave him a reputation as one who could hold a listener's atten-
> tion. He could wield the Word as a two-edged sword to awaken
> others to decide for the right. He understood, as few others did,
> the art of pouring the Gospel's soothing balm into the broken-
> hearted. He knew the Bible in the original languages and could
> communicate unusually well in both Swedish and English. He
> was also well-acquainted with theology and church history,
> which made his sermons intellectually rich as well as inspired.
> Furthermore, he was always a noble champion for sound Meth-
> odist doctrine.[56]

Portions were paraphrased the following year for the memorial in
the *Minutes/Journal*. It also employed its own similes and hyperbole to
praise Westergreen:

> His declining years were full of peace and sunshine.... He now
> rests from his labor and we miss the patriarchal solemn counte-
> nance in our gatherings. Having been a man of a great personal-
> ity and an inestimable life-work, he, like a fallen tree, "leaves a
> lonesome place against the sky." Many have been led to Christ
> and kept from falling by the power of his influence. Walking
> humbly in the Master's footsteps he was a worthy example in
> faith and good works, diligence, purity and faithfulness.[57]

In *A Short Story of the Swedish Methodism in America*, C. G. Wallenius and E. D. Olson, the authors, wrote, "Westergreen was reputed
among his brethren to be a profound scholar and a good speaker.... His
ability as a scholar and preacher has been recognized by the Abingdon

---

55. Crespo-Fernandez, *Linguistic Devices*, abstract.

56. Wallenius, "Dr. N. O. Westergreen Ingången I Vilan" [Dr. N. O. Westergreen
enters into rest], 1.

57. See Gordon et al., "In Memoriam: The Rev. Nels O. Westergreen," 50.

College, his Alma Mater, which conferred upon him the degree of Doctor of Divinity, *honoris causa*."[58] Strangely enough, the book does not mention his death, though it does note the deaths of Alfred Anderson, K. H. Elmström, and William Henschen in the 1920s.

His estate was worth just under ten thousand dollars. Of this, he made bequests of four hundred dollars each to the Swedish Methodist Theological Seminary and the Bethany Home. Three hundred dollars were bequeathed to the superannuated ministers' fund of the Central Swedish Conference, and one hundred dollars to Miss Grainman, his former housekeeper. After various funeral and estate-related expenses were paid, the remainder of the estate was distributed as 40 percent to Selma, 40 percent to be divided in equal shares among Swan and Betsy's children, and 20 percent to Annie, his brother Alex's only child. Each beneficiary agreed to have three dollars per month deducted from their share for Selma's maintenance until July 1, 1921, and which time they were receive the remainder of their share. Nothing was left to Selma and Andrew's surviving son, Edwin Wesley Westergreen. Westergreen explained his reasons for this distribution as follows:

> [Regarding Annie:] The reason I make this distinction is not from any disrespect to her, for I regard her as a good Christian lady and a worker in the church, but as she was the only heir after my deceased brother, she has some means of her own. In the division left to my sister-in-law, Selma Westergreen, I further order and decree that she retain this for her own personal use and benefit. But if she wants to leave anything to her son Edwin Wesley Westergreen, she must not leave any more than one fourth of her share to him, but that she shall retain the rest for her own personal use and benefit during her lifetime. The reason is not ill feeling to or disregard for Wesley Westergreen, whom I regard and respect as a man of good character, and without bad habits, but I did not like the manner in which he took advantage of his mother in the division of the property after my deceased brother Andrew Theodor Westergreen, who died intestate.[59]

According to the terms of the will, Selma was allowed to live in the house on Richmond until 1921, at which time it was sold for fifty-eight hundred dollars. She then moved into an apartment at 2904 Warsaw

58. Wallenius and Olson, *Short Story*, 45–46.
59. Westergreen, *Last Will and Testament.*

Street before a final move to the Bethany Home in 1927.[60] She died there of leukemia complicated by pneumonia on January 23, 1930, and is buried at Oak Woods Cemetery by her husband, Andrew. Their stillborn child is buried in another section of the cemetery, with no marker.

60. The street name was later changed to W. Nelson Street.

10

Epilogue

1919 to 1942 and Beyond

Now let me gain perfection's height, Now let me into nothing fall,
Be less than nothing in Thy sight, And feel that Christ is all in all.[1]

AT ITS PEAK, THE Swedish Methodist Church had about twenty thousand
full members, not counting probationary members or Sunday School attendees.[2] It was the largest foreign language group within American
Methodism, and it had the highest concentration of churches in the
Chicago area and western Illinois: the places where Westergreen was in
ministry.

The nature, location, and needs of the Scandinavian immigrant
community changed during the years of Westergreen's ministry, and
church life evolved as well. Some who were close friends and colleagues
at the time of his death in 1919 did not survive him by many years: K. H.
Elmström died in 1921, William Henschen in 1925, and Isaac Anderson
in 1927. One year after Westergreen's death, all the Swedish Conference
Journals were entirely in English for the first time, and continued in English until the Swedish Conferences merged with the larger denomination in 1942. The Norwegian-Danish Methodist Conferences followed
a similar trajectory; in their 1919 Conference Journal two reports were

1. See Charles Wesley, "Holy, and True, and Righteous Lord," 570.
2. Norwood, *Story of American Methodism*, 289.

given in English, with the rest in Norwegian or Danish.[3] The Augustana Swedish Lutheran Synod substituted English for Swedish for the first time in 1924.[4]

Sändebudet, the newspaper Victor Witting started in 1862, had run both Swedish and English articles since at least 1904. Advertisements in English began even earlier. From the late 1880s it had been published by the Swedish Methodist Book Concern, but in 1921 that went out of business, and the American Book Concern took ownership. It ran at a considerable loss until 1934, when the Book Concern withdrew support from all its foreign language publications. Various Conferences then set up a publication committee to continue producing the paper, reducing it to two issues per month, each with eight pages.[5] In 1925, the paper had grown to sixteen broadsheet pages. The percentage of English language articles increased, and the English content was interspersed throughout the paper rather than being a separate section. By the time of the Diamond Jubilee Issue in 1937, the paper had changed formats again. The pages were much smaller in size, with the first eight pages in English and most of the remaining pages (as many as twenty-four) in Swedish, with letters to the editor in either language. When the final issue was published in December 1969, even the name had been changed to the English translation: *The Messenger*. Aside from a list of living clergy who came out of and/or had served in the Swedish Methodist Church, plus a story about an event at the Bethany Home, it was a generic, mainly Midwestern regional Methodist magazine, published monthly and only eight pages long. It listed over seventy pastors still living, from all over the United States, who had served or were from former Swedish Methodist churches.

The Norwegian-Danish Methodist newspapers, *Den Kristelige Talsmand* (The Christian advocate) and *Evangelisk Tidende* (Gospel tidings) followed a similar trajectory. They changed from Teutonic to Roman type in 1919, and the "young people's column" was printed in English the same year, in hopes of appealing to the younger generation.[6] By 1935,

3. The presentation of reports at Scandinavian Conferences had always been cumbersome. Until the end of World War I, Conference reports were usually presented orally in English for the sake of the non-Scandinavian bishop, then translated in the appropriate Scandinavian language for publication.

4. Nylin, "History of Swedish Methodism in Chicago," 48.

5. Wallenius, "Story of Sändebudet," 3.

6. Andersen, *Salt of the Earth*, 262.

the paper was equally divided between Norwegian and English, and the following year, at the recommendation of the publishing committee, gave prominence to the English section, with a front page usually in English.

The gradual shift from Swedish to English in publications was also reflected in the church's hymnody. The Swedish immigrants who arrived in New York and found aid at O. G. Hedstrom's Bethel Ship worshiped using *Den Svenska Psalmboken* (The Swedish hymnbook), edited by Archbishop Johan Olof Wallin, plus whatever Wesley hymns had been put into Swedish.[7] In addition, dozens of independently written or collected songbooks were published for use by Swedish immigrants, beginning with T. N. Hasselquist's compilation, *Femtio Andeliga Sånger* (Fifty spiritual songs), published in 1856. These little books, compact enough that a circuit rider could carry a stack of them from one place to another for leading a congregation in song, had two notable characteristics; first, both their theological emphases and musical structure reflected primarily the American campmeeting culture, and second, a substantial percentage were translations into Swedish of songs by American or British evangelicals, such as Ira Sankey, Fanny Crosby, P. P. Bliss, etc. In 1880 the General Conference approved the publication of an official Swedish Methodist Hymnbook. It was not simply a translation of the MEC hymnal into Swedish; instead, a committee that included Nels Westergreen and Victor Witting met for over two years to assemble and edit a collection of 662 hymns that reflected at least three distinct religious cultures: the hymnody of the American Methodist Episcopal Church, the evangelical/holiness orientation of Swedish Methodism in America, and the 1819 *Psalmboken*. Only about 5 percent of the collection were not strophic hymns. All the hymns were in Swedish. When the next official Swedish Methodist hymnal was published in 1904, six hundred selections were in Swedish and fifteen in English. By the time the Methodist Book Concern published *Evangeliska Sånger för Söndagsskolan, Hemmet och Evangeliska Möten* (Evangelistic songs for the Sunday School, home, and evangelistic meetings) in 1916, the Americanization of immigrants was even more evident; it had 325 selections in Swedish and 196 in English, with responsive readings in both languages. Even without all the authors and composers being identified, it is obvious that about half the Swedish

7. Williams, "America's First Hymnals," 149. In 1770, Andreas Rudman had published two hymnals in Swedish for use in two immigrant congregations in Philadelphia and Christina (Wilmington), but these were no longer in use. We cannot be sure O. G. Hedstrom even knew of their existence.

selections are simply translations of English language hymns and songs. The second generation and third generations were assimilating into the Methodist Episcopal Church.

In their brief history of Swedish Methodism, Wallenius and Olson noted that at the beginning of the twentieth century, the Swedish population began to move away from the areas where they first settled, and migrated to other parts of the city and suburbs. The process accelerated during and after World War I. First Swedish Methodist Church, at Market (Orleans) and Oak Streets, held its last services at that location in 1918, and relocated to the corner of Paulina and Highland Avenues in the Edgewater neighborhood. However, the Methodist presence at the original address continued when the congregation of St. Matthew's Methodist Church, which was established in 1915, purchased the Swedes' building. This African American congregation was part of the Lexington Conference, but eventually became part of the Rock River/Northern Illinois Conference. The Highland Avenue location eventually became home to an Eritrean Orthodox congregation. The May Street/Second Church moved in 1911 and eventually erected a new building on Irving Park Road at Avers Avenue, on the northwest side of Chicago. After the congregation merged with another nearby Methodist church and the property sold in 1956, the building housed a variety of communities, including Free Methodist, nondenominational, and Korean congregations. The population in the area around the Fifth Avenue congregation changed dramatically as a result of the Great Migration from the south, and in 1917 the building was sold. The money was turned over to Auburn Park Methodist Church at 78th and Loomis Avenue, and most of the dwindling congregation joined that church. Eventually the name was changed to Grace Methodist Church. The Englewood congregation also merged with Auburn Park in 1920. Both Emanuel Church and Moreland merged with Austin in 1922.

It is interesting to compare the Swedish Methodist church's pattern of relocation and primary language for communication with that of more recent ethnic minority United Methodist congregations in the Northern Illinois Conference, formerly known as the Rock River Conference. In 2020 there were about thirty congregations whose primary language for worship was not English. In Hispanic congregations, there is a greater likelihood of bilingual services than in Korean, and Hispanic congregations are apt to continue in their first language longer than the Korean. A probable reason for this is immigration from Korea is less than it was a generation ago, while immigration from Spanish-speaking countries is not.[8] The children and grandchildren of immigrants are more comfortable with English than with their parents' first language. The Korean congregations, like the Swedes in the early twentieth century, are likely to move to another location when church members themselves relocate.

In addition to the migration of Chicago-area Swedes away from the city center, there was also a plateau in the development of new congregations and construction of new buildings. This correlates with the gradual slowing of immigration from Sweden after its peak in 1880 and the Americanization of the second generation. After 1900, only three Swedish Methodist buildings were erected in the metropolitan Chicago area. The first, Humboldt Park, was built in 1906, though the congregation was organized twenty years earlier. The second, Austin, was organized as a congregation in 1893, bought its first building in 1904, and replaced it with a new building in 1923. The third church, constructed in 1920, was the new home of the Second Swedish Methodist congregation. In 2021, there is only one building that was home to a Swedish Methodist congregation that is still Methodist: Emmanuel United Methodist Church in Evanston, which now worships primarily in Hindi and Gujarati.

Several Swedish Methodist church buildings in Chicago where Westergreen preached are still standing, though the Elim/Lakeview building has been turned into condominiums. The others, which house independent or otherwise affiliated congregations, are the Second Church (later renamed Parkview) on Irving Park Road, the Salem Church on Wabansia Avenue, the South Shore / Cheltenham Church on 79th Street, the Union Avenue Church, Hermosa Church on Tripp Avenue, the Roseland/Pullman Church on Indiana Avenue, and the Humboldt Park Church on Fairfield Avenue.

In western Illinois, the fate of Swedish Methodist congregations where Westergreen preached and/or was appointed has been somewhat different. Many of them are still functioning as Methodist congregations, though their Swedish ancestry is evident only in the surnames of some members, and possibly manifested on occasions when they celebrate their history. Such churches include Abingdon, Altona, Bishop Hill, Galva, Geneseo, and Victoria. With the exceptions of Bishop Hill and Victoria, their current buildings were erected after Westergreen's death. Other Swedish congregations were eventually absorbed into larger,

8. Conversation with the Reverend Arlene Christopherson, Assistant to the Bishop, Northern Illinois Conference of the United Methodist Church, August 10, 2020.

English language Methodist Episcopal churches which, in turn, became United Methodist in 1968. These include Moline and Galesburg. One can speculate that the churches in small rural communities, such as Victoria and Bishop Hill, were established very early in the community's existence, and the general population has remained too small to sustain additional churches. In the cities of Moline and Galesburg, on the other hand, there were multiple churches, both Methodist and other denominations, along with changing racial/ethnic demographics. This increased the likelihood that smaller congregations would merge with each other or be absorbed into larger, stronger congregations as religious affiliations shifted or diminished.

Westergreen's other appointments from early in his ministry outside metropolitan Chicago are also worth noting. He preached multiple places in the Fox River Valley, and there are extant Methodist churches today in both Leland and Norway. The Indiana Mission, which included classes or congregations in both Indiana and Illinois, yielded mixed results. The Beaver church, not far from Donovan, Illinois, and was established in the 1850s by S. B. Newman. The American Methodist Church in Donovan was more than twenty years older. For much of the twentieth century, the churches shared a pastor. The Beaver church was destroyed by fire in 1964, but the Donovan church remains to this day. In Attica, missionary efforts by the Swedish Methodists were eventually abandoned, though there is a large United Methodist Church with a different history there today. In addition, Westergreen preached at Brookston, Montmorenci, Bunkum/Iroquois, Buena Vista, and Lafayette while appointed to the Indiana Mission. Of these, there are United Methodist churches today in Brookston, and Lafayette, but no buildings or congregations established by the Swedes.

The Swedish Methodist Theological Seminary, founded in 1870, also evolved over the years, as has been explicated in earlier chapters. In 1925 the name was changed to Wesley Academy and Theological Seminary, because a four-year academy course had been added. The Norwegian-Danish Methodists organized their own seminary in Evanston in 1886 for the training of pastors for their churches. They added a program of high school level courses in 1920. Like the Swedish Seminary, the Norwegian-Danish school was designated as a department of Garrett Biblical Institute. Garrett faculty conducted courses in which Scandinavian students were enrolled, and Garrett's president signed the diplomas of its graduates. Both the Americanizing process and the Great Depression took a toll on the schools. An excerpt from *The Salt of the Earth* explains:

> A Bible School, operating concurrently with the [Norwegian-Danish] seminary, was announced in 1932. While no new students had been admitted for the past two years, and only one class of seminarians remained to be graduated, the full four-year course of studies still appeared in the year book of 1932. Very noticeable was the scarcity of Norwegian book titles (eight) and the larger number in English (twenty-nine).[9]

The two Scandinavian institutions merged in 1934 to become the Evanston Collegiate Institute, a three-year training school and two-year junior college. It opened its doors to thirty-four students, and an equal number of Swedish and Norwegian-Danish Methodists on its board of trustees. In the new junior college, German was a required course, but Swedish and Norwegian were elective courses. The 1942 *Journal* of the Central Northwest Conference described the evolution of the institution's identity:

> The Evanston Collegiate Institute is a child of circumstance. For some sixty years the Swedish Methodist Episcopal Theological Seminary trained bi-lingual preachers for our churches. When the need for that kind of service ceased we had a property without a purpose. For a few years the Wesley Academy made some use of it. But it was in the midst of the Depression after the first World War, when thousands of young people walked our streets and could neither find work nor money to go to school that some far-sighted men in our midst and in the Norwegian-Danish Conference, where they also had a property without a purpose, conceived the idea of a self-help Junior College in the two properties. . . . The E.C.I. has just closed its eighth year with twenty-five graduates. Through these eight years it has graduated some over five hundred students, of which some eighty or more per cent have earned their own way. Which means that four hundred young men and woman, most of whom have continued their further education, found there an open door to a larger life and service than otherwise might have been possible for them. The school has served as a fruitful recruiting place for Christian service. A large percentage of its students have been directed into the ministry.[10]

9. Andersen, *Salt of the Earth*, 268.
10. See "Evanston Collegiate Institute," 207–8.

The school's name was changed to Kendall College in 1950, to honor the late son of a major benefactor. The institution's president, Wesley Westerberg, was the son of a pioneer in Swedish Methodism, but the college's immigrant roots were withering. Business programs were launched in the 1970, and in 1985 the School of Culinary Arts was founded. In 2005, with its focus on hospitality management, Kendall College moved from Evanston to Goose Island, an area closer to downtown Chicago. It was incorporated into National Louis University in 2018.

One institution that underwent fewer changes is the Bethany Home, located in the Ravenswood neighborhood of Chicago. Though founded for the widows of Swedish Methodist clergy and indigent women, over the years the campus grew both in size and racial/ethnic diversity. It retained its Methodist identity, though the focus of its ministry changed from independent and assisted living to independent living only. Private nursing and physical therapy can be arranged through the Methodist Hospital, located on the same block. Two other Methodist-administered homes for the elderly are nearby: Wesley Place, for long-term skilled nursing, and Covenant Home of Chicago, for assisted living. The Swedish Methodist church on the same block as the Bethany Home, which Westergreen served in the 1890s, changed from being entirely Swedish to predominantly Spanish-speaking before it closed and was then demolished in the 1990s. The land is now a small park between the Bethany Home and Methodist Hospital.

On the West Coast, the first Swedish Methodist congregation became an autonomous church in 1875. In the years that followed, congregations were established in Kingsburg, Berkeley, Los Angeles, Pasadena, Spokane, Tacoma, Seattle, Portland, Salem, and Venersborg. They organized as the Pacific Swedish Mission Conference in 1908, but dissolved in 1928 and amalgamated with the surrounding English speaking conferences. At one point, this conference had fourteen pastors, over thirteen hundred members, sixteen churches and eleven parsonages.[11] The East Coast churches, mainly in Massachusetts and New York, had never been in a semiautonomous Swedish conference, but had existed as foreign language churches within their respective American Methodist conferences. In this way they were similar to the Italian, French, and Bohemian Methodist congregations in Chicago.

11. See "Statistical Report," 54.

In Texas, the Swedish congregations were organized into the Southern Swedish Mission Conference in 1912. In 1926 it merged with an MEC South conference, but remained a Swedish district within the Conference. As an autonomous conference, it had ten pastors, over eighteen hundred members, fourteen churches and thirteen parsonages. It appears this merger did not go as well as hoped. In 1931 the Central Northwest Conference drafted a resolution to be presented at General Conference the following year. It asked that the boundaries of the Central Northwest Conference be extended to include the former Southern Mission Conference, and that the work in Texas be organized into a district of the expanded conference. The reasons given for this included the following:

- The effort to fuse the groups (the Gulf Conference, Southern German Conference, and Swedish Mission Conference) into one strong unit utterly failed as far as the Swedish work was concerned, causing a process of disintegration instead.

- The Texas Swedes had much in common with Swedish American work elsewhere, such as *Sändebudet*, the aid society, and the Susanna Wesley Home.

- Language, national traits, traditions, and Swedish American history were things of real value not easily sacrificed, and ties that could not be severed without the work sustaining a loss.[12]

However, the General Conference did not approve this resolution, and the Swedish churches in Texas remained part of the English-speaking MEC South Conference.

As the resolution to the 1932 General Conference demonstrates, language, piety, and identity are inextricably linked, and the assimilation of the Scandinavian conferences into the larger Methodist Church was not without controversy. This was true more than a decade earlier.

In 1918 A. J. Löfgren wrote an essay published in *Sändebudet* that strongly opposed dissolving the Swedish Conferences. He claimed it would be a "great loss for our beloved church" for a number of reasons:

- It would result in the absorption of many of the smaller Swedish congregations into larger English-speaking ones, where the Swedish members would never feel at home. They would be likely to drop out.

12. See "General Conference Memorial," 334.

- The character of Swedish Methodist piety, which he described as genuine, deep, and serious, would gradually be displaced.

- The Swedish Methodists were unlikely to be represented sufficiently at General Conference.[13]

- The future of the Swedish seminary, publications, Bethany Home, etc., might be jeopardized.[14]

There was an analogous debate over merger in the Norwegian-Danish Methodist Church during the same period. In *The Salt of the Earth*, Arlow Andersen summarized arguments for and against a merger that appeared in *Den Kristelige Talsmand* in 1919. The pro-merger argument was presented by Jonas A. Jacobsen, a pastor serving as financial agent for the Elim Home for the Aged in Minnesota. It included the following points:

- The overlap of foreign-language conferences with American wasted resources.

- Decline had already set in because of decreasing immigration and the transfer of members to American congregations.

- Eastern Norwegian-Danish congregations and pastors already existed without impediment within American conferences, while continuing to use the Scandinavian languages.

- The larger American conferences could provide higher salaries and pensions for pastors.[15]

- There would be few institutional losses.

13. This fear was well-grounded. Swedish Methodists did have less representation at General Conference after the 1928 merger. Until that year, the Western, Central, and Northern Conferences had *each* sent one clergy and one lay delegate, plus their alternates. Once they combined to become the Central Northwest Conference, they had only one clergy and one lay delegate, i.e., their representation was a third of what it had been previously.

14. Löfgren, "Inlägg i frågor på dagordningen" [Inserting a question about the agenda], 2.

15. The daughter of an Augustana Synod Lutheran minister told me she believed salary and pension funding were important factors in the Swedish synod merging with the Lutheran Church in America (now Evangelical Lutheran Church in America). While he was pastor of a congregation in Peoria, Illinois, in the 1930s, her father moonlighted as a stock boy in a local grocery store to support his family.

- Younger English-speaking pastors would have better opportunities in American conferences.[16]

The arguments in opposition to dissolution and merger with the American church were somewhat different from those presented by the Swedish Methodists. While they echoed the fear of feeling scattered and disenfranchised within the American church, the Norwegian-Danish opponents conveyed a more oppositional attitude toward the larger denomination, saying that the American Methodist leadership regarded their work as completed and unnecessary, even though Scandinavian immigrants were still arriving. Furthermore, American patriotism should not be substituted for or equated with Christianity, and salvation of souls was more important than conservation of financial resources. They were also skeptical about the survival of their institutions and publications if a merger took place.

One catalyst for the merging of foreign-language conferences with the larger denomination, noted by J. Gordon Melton, was anti-German feeling as a result of World War I.[17] A second factor was the quota system on immigration to the United States that was instituted in 1924. The era of mass emigration from Scandinavia was over; the second and third generations in America spoke English, and wanted to worship in English. In 1925, a report from A. W. Carlson, superintendent of the Eastern District of the Western Swedish Conference, noted:

> The transition from Swedish-speaking to English-speaking congregations has been safely passed by almost all of our churches and the way is open for a normal development for them as English-speaking churches serving the communities where they are located.[18]

The Midwestern German Conferences began the process of merger at the 1924 General Conference, and culminated within the Rock River Conference in 1933.[19] The Swedish Conferences began the process of merging with one another in 1927, presenting a recommendation and memorial to the General Conference in May 1928. They favored an amalgamation of the Northern, Central, and Western Conferences for several

16. Andersen, *Salt of the Earth*, 259.
17. Melton, *Log Cabins to Steeples*, 150.
18. See Carlson, "Report on the Eastern District," 281.
19. Melton, *Log Cabins to Steeples*, 350.

reasons: it would make appointments easier, serve the common interests of education, publication, and benevolences, and promote the interests of retired ministers. The General Conference approved the merger, and called the newly united conferences the Central Northwest Conference, taking effect at the start of the 1928 conference year. It now comprised four districts: Chicago, Galesburg-Iowa, St. Paul, and Superior. The resulting Conference had 97 ministers, over 12,250 members, 118 church buildings, and 87 parsonages.[20]

Change and assimilation seemed to escalate in the Swedish Methodist Church after the 1928 amalgamation of conferences. The Central Northwest Conference drew new district boundaries by 1935: Chicago, Galesburg, Jamestown, Omaha, and St. Paul. The statistical report from the 1935 *Conference Journal* presented an ominous picture: the total membership had declined to about 10,750 members, and the number of churches had decreased by fourteen. More alarming, however, was the fact that only thirteen churches had a membership of more than two hundred. Forty-nine churches had fewer than one hundred, and seventeen had a membership of less than twenty-four.[21] It is likely such churches would have to become two or three-point charges in order to pay even modest clergy stipends, much less contribute to the ministers' pension fund.

By 1940 the Central Northwest Conference had about eighty-four churches, of which eleven were two- or three-point charges. Jamestown was not truly a district but consisted of two churches in Cleveland and Akron, served by one minister. Sixteen churches, from Colorado to Jamestown, New York, transferred to other jurisdictions, i.e., they affiliated with American Methodist Episcopal conferences. Total church membership in the Central Northwest Conference was about ninety-three hundred, which speaks well of their tenacity and evangelistic zeal, given that nineteen hundred members were in the churches that transferred to other jurisdictions. They had forty-one churches with a membership of between fifty-one and one hundred, ten with twenty-five to fifty, fourteen with ten to twenty-five members, and six with few than ten. One disadvantage for Swedish Methodists during the period of the Central Northwest Conference was they had eight different bishops presiding between 1928 and 1942: Ernest G. Richardson, William F. Anderson,

20. Wallenius and Olson, *Short Story of Swedish Methodism*, 53.
21. See Chindberg, "Special Statistical Report," 324.

Wallace E. Brown, Edwin Holt Hughes, Ernest L. Waldorf, J. Ralph Magee, Raymond J. Wade, and Adna Wright Leonard. With the exception of Waldorf, who twice presided at three consecutive sessions of the Conference, this meant no other bishop became well versed in the particular mission and possible idiosyncrasies of the Swedish immigrant church. In the Rock River Conference sessions during the same period, five different bishops presided, but Waldorf presided over ten of the fifteen years, which would have facilitated greater stability and continuity.

The sixty-sixth and final session of the Central Northwest Conference was held at Elim (Lakeview) Methodist Church June 20–23, 1942. Among the business items taken up were the sale of two churches in Minnesota and Michigan, the closure of a third one in Illinois, and the transfer of one Minnesota building to become a cemetery chapel.[22] The remaining charges in the Central Northwest Conference were assigned to eleven different annual conferences in the Midwest.

It was a time of celebration as well as sadness. A banquet was held on the first evening, and Sunday morning worship was a Wesleyan Love Feast. On the second day of Conference, greetings from two bishops were read. Bishop Nicholson, who had presided at five Central Swedish Conference sessions, but never a Central Northwest Conference session, wrote c/o Swan W. Mattson, the Conference secretary:

> I had a close and personal contact with you brethren. I found a most loyal and capable group of men and it was a delight to work with them. Though it was inevitable, it was with a pang of regret that I saw these conferences dissolve and lose some of their individuality. I felt toward them a sense of real brotherhood and as long as I live I shall be remembering the great work which your men did, often at great sacrifice to themselves.[23]

The Superintendents' Historical Report at the final meeting of the Central Northwest Conference reminded readers of multiple factors leading to the decision to merge, and acknowledged the mixed sentiments about dissolution into various English-speaking conferences:

> In 1844 he [Hedström] was appointed Swedish Missionary to sailors and immigrants in New York harbor and fitted out with a house-boat for a meeting place. In that boat, the Bethelship

---

22. It was actually the fifteenth session as the Central Northwest Conference, but they were counting from 1877, when the Northwest Conference was organized.

23. See Nicholson, "Historical Edition," 198.

John Wesley, was organized the first Swedish speaking Methodist Church in this nation. . . . From that small beginning this foreign speaking mission grew. With the increasing immigration from the Scandinavian countries after the Civil War, Conferences were organized, institutions started, schools and publishing ventures begun, so that by the turn of the century there were six Conferences, a seminary for training bi-lingual preachers, a book concern, several weekly papers, three old people's homes, a preachers' aid society, a general aid association, and some over 20,000 active members in our churches.

This growth continued for about two thirds of a century. But with restricted immigration, and our church membership largely second and third generation born, and the church language becoming predominantly English, a reversal set in. In the last third of the century of our existence we have been retracing our steps, until now we are about to dissolve the last of our Swedish speaking Conferences and return the churches and pastors to the English speaking Conferences where they originally began.

It is not without a keen feeling of regret that we see the end of our Conference organizations. We have enjoyed an autonomy in the work that can no longer be ours. We must surrender leadership in much of our planning for the congregations, a thing that in the past has inspired confidence and satisfaction among our people. And our fellowship in the service has been exceptionally sweet and enriching. Our Conference sessions and summer assemblies have been veritable love feasts for our people.

But coming to an English speaking land to be a part of it, we have anticipated this throughout our separated existence. We have had no desire to build a nation within the nation. We have learned long ago to say with John the Baptizer, "I must decrease, he must increase." And to preserve our happiness we must learn to say with the colored [sic] man who was always in a cheerful mood, that we "cooperate with the inevitable."

We thank God for the century of Swedish speaking Methodism in this land. Our record of the years justifies the organizations that have been. And we believe that the Mother Church is amply rewarded for such nurturing care as she has given to this branch of her missionary outreach. And it is with a sincere word of thanks to American Methodism for the opportunity and encouragement she has given to it that we now bid farewell to our period of separate existence. And it is likewise with a hopeful

anticipation of continued usefulness in the future that we turn
our eyes forward to a closer fellowship in Conference relations.[24]

The penultimate page of the *Journal* has a photograph taken during the Rock River Conference session, showing Bishop Waldorf shaking
hands with Dr. E. P. Swan, representing the Swedish Methodists as they
joined the Rock River Conference. Dr. C. B. Newham and Dr. Ernest Fre-
mont Tittle of First Methodist Church of Evanston (the host church) are
also pictured in this symbolic welcome.[25]

The Rock River Conference convened the day after the Central
Northwest Conference concluded. There was much less fanfare at this
meeting, though during the morning session of the first day, Dr. Newham
again welcomed E. P. Swan into the body, and Swan made a response
on behalf of the Swedes. Bishop Waldorf then called for a vote on the
merger, and the Conference voted unanimously to certify the actions of
the committee.

What happened to the Chicago area Swedish churches immediately
after the merger? It appears they did not initially experience a great change
at the local level, although their representation at General Conference diminished, as noted earlier. The majority of their pastors and lay delegates
to the Rock River Conference had Scandinavian surnames. By the end
of the 1940s, with various new appointments, eleven of the Chicago area
churches were led by ministers with no apparent Swedish connection.
Membership in these churches held steady or enjoyed modest growth for
the next decade, with the exception of Austin/Trinity Church.[26] Change
and consolidation were inevitable with the passing of time, due to the end
of the postwar baby boom, shifting demographics, and further redundan-
cy resulting from the union of the Evangelical United Brethren with the
United Methodist Church in 1968. In the Roseland/Pullman neighborhood, for example, the Pullman and West Pullman churches had already

24. See "Superintendents' Report," 205–6.

25. The *Journal* also contains a photograph of Westergreen, allegedly taken in
1920—which would have been a year after he died—proving that even official records
sometimes contain errors.

26. Hahn, "Church Lacks Racial Diversity." After World War II, black people
moved into the Austin neighborhood of Chicago, and the former Swedish Methodist
Church was located in South Austin, the first area to turn black. In 1970, 32 percent of
the population was black, and in 1980 it was 73 percent. A demographic study of the
United Methodist Church done in 2008 showed that only 5.8 percent of the denomination's membership was black. Therefore, it is not surprising that membership in the
Austin church went from 262 in 1942 to 164 in 1956.

consolidated in 1913, keeping the building on Indiana Avenue. This church was about a block away from the much larger and better-equipped Pullman Methodist Church. Both the Humboldt Park and Union Avenue Swedish Methodist Churches added or substituted "Community" to their names, so as to distinguish them from nearby American Methodist Churches bearing the same name.[27] In Rockford just prior to the 1942 merger, there were already six other Methodist churches. The number increased to eight by 1956, and fourteen by 1970. Of these, only three had a smaller membership than Bethany, the Swedish church founded more than century earlier by S. B. Newman. In addition, much of the neighborhood around Bethany was subject to demolition and urban decay. The result for Bethany and churches like it was first an attrition of Swedish immigrant identity in the congregation, gradually followed by assimilation into other local and usually stronger churches.

Westergreen would have almost certainly supported institutional evolution and consolidation of resources. Throughout the years of his ministry he was an advocate for churches working together cooperatively in mission. The majority of his ten thousand preaching opportunities were in Swedish, but that was a reflection of the needs of his constituency at the time rather than a commitment to the preservation of immigrant identity or culture. Furthermore, he never expressed any longing to see the land of his birth again. Midsummer Day was the only Swedish holiday mentioned in Westergreen's journals, while American holidays were noted on an annual basis. After becoming a United States citizen in 1864, he considered himself American to the point of promising God he would go anywhere to proclaim the gospel, even if it meant going back to his ancestral land, if God would save his brother John's soul.[28] The "even if" is evidence of his identification with America rather than Sweden.

While Westergreen would have regarded the Americanization of the immigrant community and church as a natural progression, I suspect he would have been less happy about the theological trajectory of the Methodist Church by the time of the 1942 merger and beyond. The trajectory can be inferred from the lives and writings of the second and third generations of Swedish Methodism. As has been demonstrated, Wesley's teaching on Christian Perfection was of paramount importance to Westergreen and most of his peers in the first generation of the

27. The Humboldt Park Church was a former Evangelical United Brethren congregation until 1968.

28. Westergreen, *Uppteckningar*, 110.

immigrant church. This can be attributed in part to the early contact and conflict between the Eric Janssonists and the Hedstrom brothers, as Henry C. Whyman notes in his 1992 biography of the Hedstroms. Other shaping influences were the congenial holiness/revival/campmeeting culture of the 1850s and beyond, and, of course, the *läsare* upbringing many of them had in Sweden. The fact Westergreen was made president of the Swedish Holiness Association, founded in 1903, speaks to his life-long commitment to pursue entire sanctification.

But Christian perfection as a central theological marker was fading in both Swedish and American Methodism in the twentieth century. When John Vincent, former editor of the *Sunday School Journal*, was elected bishop in 1890, he was a major voice in marginalizing or silencing those who believed in the holiness movement's view of sanctification as a work of grace subsequent to justification/conversion.[29] John L. Peters has described the controversies and polarization inside and outside American Methodism over the doctrine in the last years of the nineteenth century.[30] He notes there was a moratorium on publishing articles on the subject of holiness in the *Methodist Review* from 1896 to 1900, and a statement by the church to the effect that while it maintained the distinctiveness of the doctrine, "it is not vital that we hold the work done instantaneously" and "it is not essential that a man [*sic*] make a specific profession of the experience."[31] The Swedes had publications in their own language, and may not have paid attention to the *Methodist Review*. But they must have been aware that as the Methodist Church gained middle-class respectability, it largely shed and/or shunned liturgical practices associated with lower class or frontier religion. This is demonstrated in the strophic hymns found in the denomination's official hymnal, used for Sunday morning worship, versus the first-person narrative theology prevalent in Gospel songs and choruses. The latter music was to be found in supplemental and self-published books. It should also be recalled that the Azusa Street Revival and rise of the Pentecostal movement in 1901 shifted many evangelicals' attention from the Holy Spirit as sanctifier to the Holy Spirit as baptizer, the proof of which was speaking in tongues and exercising other spiritual gifts. Theologian Paul Rademacher asserted that empirical experiential theology in Western spirituality found

29. Haynes, "Methodism," n.p.
30. Peters, *Christian Perfection in American Methodism*, 177.
31. Peters, *Christian Perfection in American Methodism*, 179.

expression in Wesleyan sanctification theology in the eighteenth century, shifted to the Holiness movement in the nineteenth, and was then followed by Pentecostalism in the twentieth.[32] Westergreen was aware of the shifting theological emphasis in the denomination. In a 1918 letter to his niece, he wrote:

> And of the doctrine of entire sanctification, we don't hear much now, even among the Methodists with perhaps a few exceptions. And yet deep in our hearts there is feeling moving us to prayer and separation from the world, and this must be from the Holy Spirit, let us therefore follow it, and may it not then lead us to a higher life and a more blessed state, where we can run our race with joy and sing praises to the Lord. I have prayed for this more than for anything else of late.[33]

The diminution of sanctification theology is shown in the 1942 *Central Northwest Conference Journal* as well as other publications of the Swedish Methodists. In the superintendents' historical report, there is no mention of perfectionist theology as part of their heritage—or indeed, any other theological markers, excepting a brief biblical quote. The authors, Carl A. Holmgren, Thor J. Westerberg, Carl Linden, and George A. Schugren, all entered the ministry more than a half century after Jonas Hedstrom debated Eric Jansson. Only Holmgren had served any of the early Swedish Methodist congregations in western Illinois, where a significant number of church members were former Janssonists or their descendants.

Carl G. Wallenius, an elder statesman in the church at the time of the merger, gave a historical retrospect of Swedish Methodism at the meeting of the Central Northwest Annual Conference in 1942. His presentation focused primarily on the organization of the church in Victoria, Illinois, in 1846 as its beginning, rather than on O. G. Hedstrom's ministry on the Bethel Ship *John Wesley*. The *Conference Journal* for that year praised him for his "ability to present facts in a living way, [he] thrilled us with his panorama of the past ninety-six years."[34] Wallenius had a different personal history from the superintendents named above. Born in Sweden in 1865, he became a Methodist and served as an assistant to a minister in Jönköping before emigrating to the United States in 1888. Therefore, his sense of Methodist identity was formed in a different culture, many

32. Rademacher, "Methodist Bicentennial Lecture," January 1984.
33. Westergreen, letter to Nellie Westergreen, August 5, 1918.
34. "Inspirational Hours," 208.

years after Eric Jansson and his followers had left the country. This seems to have led to his silence about or relative indifference to sanctification theology and the holiness movement in America. In the brief history of Swedish Methodism that Wallenius and E. D. Olson published in 1931, he acknowledged the existence of Eric Jansson, but said nothing comparing Jansson's perfectionist theology with Wesleyan doctrine. Instead, this history placed early Swedish Methodism in contrast to the Reverend L. P. Esbjörn, the Lutheran minister who arrived in western Illinois in 1849. The sometimes-acrimonious rivalry between the Methodists and Lutherans was worth noting, of course; Westergreen also wrote about it. Yet it can be argued that Lutheran theology *influenced* Swedish Methodism in America less that than Janssonism, which inadvertently shone a spotlight on Wesley's distinctive teaching. Wallenius served as president of the Swedish Methodist Theological Seminary and later Wesley Academy from 1924 to 1936. After retiring in 1936, he served for years as editor of *Sändebudet*. One might say no one in his generation had greater opportunity to shape the corporate memory and consciousness of ministers and laity. The May 21, 1945, issue of *Sändebudet* commemorated one hundred years of Swedish Methodism, including the work of the Hedstrom brothers. There were historical essays by Wallenius, B. W. Selin, Henry C. Whyman, and others. Conversion was mentioned, but not sanctification. In other issues of *Sändebudet*, there was similarly scant attention to the subject. Wallenius did include a sermon titled "A Sanctified Life" by the Reverend Adolph Lindskog. The language in the sermon suggests the preacher was speaking to the already converted: a reasonable assumption, given that it was published in a denominational periodical. The dominant theme was an exhortation for Christians to live a sanctified life rather than describing sanctification as a religious experience or work of the Holy Spirit. Listeners were encouraged to use whatever gifts and abilities they had to serve others humbly, not reserving their energy for supposedly great achievements. A second piece Wallenius published was a sermon outline titled "Sanctification." This outline sounds more like Wesley, with statements such as "not freedom from sin, but free from the necessity of sinning." However, Jesus Christ and the Holy Spirit are not mentioned at all.

In 1948 Thor J. Westerberg gave a lecture, "Address on a Century of Swedish Methodism," which was then published in *Sändebudet*.[35] He

---

35. Westerberg, "Address on a Century of Swedish Methodism," 1.

divided the previous century into three periods. The first fifty years, starting with the Bethel Ship in New York Harbor and the first Swedish Methodist class-meeting in Victoria, Illinois, constituted the immigration period. The preachers of this era, which was the major period of Westergreen's ministry, frequently had meager education but tremendous zeal for the spiritual and physical welfare of their fellow immigrants. Next came the transition period, lasting about twenty-five years. Immigration diminished, worship and publications were often bilingual, and new immigrants were greeted by fraternal lodges and secular organizations as often as by churches. Swedish Methodism changed from a foreign national church to a community and family church. The final period, from about 1925 to 1950, was the assimilation period, when Swedish Methodists met their goal of being in union with the American church.

Westerberg's taxonomy is primarily sociological rather than theological, and yet one can see theological undertones in each of the periods proposed. It assumes one aspect of the preacher's role during the earliest years of Swedish Methodism was to be the creator of community and religious identity among a disenfranchised people: people who left their homeland largely for socioeconomic or religious reasons. During the transition period, when the language of preaching and worship was increasingly bilingual, one of the preacher's tasks would be to mediate between the dominant religious culture and the immigrant community. One place this happened was at the Des Plaines Campground, where people had opportunity to hear preaching and testimonies in a variety of languages and from preachers of different traditions and backgrounds, and where the sponsoring organization had been invested in the Holiness movement. For Swedish Methodist preachers in the assimilation period, the movement into the mainstream of American Methodism must have involved conscious and unconscious adoption of the denominational *Zeitgeist*. Peters has described this era as a time when scientific humanism was beginning to assert its omnipotence, and a rather naïve liberalism was in vogue.[36] Neither of these was a bedfellow of the National Holiness Movement nor of the sanctification theology received and proclaimed by Westergreen and his peers in the middle of the nineteenth century. If Westergreen's aim was "future perfect," by the 1942 merger such an aspiration was relegated to "past perfect."

---

36. Peters, *Christian Perfection*, 177.

A hundred years after Westergreen's death, candidates for ordination in the United Methodist Church must still respond to a list of questions outlined in *The Book of Discipline*. Two of the nineteen questions are:

1. Are you going on to perfection?

2. Do you expect to be made perfect in love in this life?[37]

It is common for contemporary candidates, some of whom have not studied biblical languages, to chuckle at what sounds preposterous to them. Their idea of perfection comes from the Latin *perfectus*, which sounds more like the English word. It means ideal or flawless, rather than the New Testament Greek τελείος, which has connotations of maturity and completeness, and is the term used in Matt 5:48.

The sanctification theology articulated by Westergreen finds expression in twenty-first-century United Methodism in those Wesleyan hymns included in the 1989 *United Methodist Hymnal*, rather than in sermons preached in local churches. There are a number of lyrics by Charles Wesley in the sections on "Sanctifying and Perfecting Grace" and "Personal Holiness." Of these, two employ the most explicit vocabulary about perfection/sanctification as a work of the Holy Spirit within the Christian: "O For a Heart to Praise My God," and "Jesus, Thine All-Victorious Love." In my own experience, the hymns in these and the "Social Holiness" sections that focus on human rather than divine action are generally more widely known and sung by contemporary United Methodists.

Within the family tree of institutions and denominations that trace their roots to Wesley, it is probably the Wesleyan Church whose expression of sanctification theology most nearly resembles Westergreen's, though their Articles of Religion speak of the culmination/perfection as a distinct crisis religious experience: something that is not prominent in Westergreen's preaching.[38] The Wesleyan Church was founded in 1968 when the Wesleyan Methodist and Pilgrim Holiness Churches merged. The latter split from the Methodist Episcopal Church in 1897 through

37. *Book of Discipline of the United Methodist Church*, para. 330.

38. Westergreen did speculate as to how many were converted or sanctified at campmeetings and protracted meetings, but his sermons in themselves focused more on clarifying what genuine sanctification/holiness *is* and living a life of holiness, rather than exhorting listeners to seek and then testify to a cathartic experience. Of course, at campmeetings an exhorter usually followed the preacher, and the exhorter may have encouraged such an experience. Because the exhorter's "application" was extemporaneous, however, we cannot know for certain.

the efforts of Martin Wells Knapp, and its president was the same Seth C. Rees whose preaching Westergreen heard at the Metropolitan Church Association. Another institution that has maintained a focus on Christian perfection is Asbury Theological Seminary, founded in 1923. Its history is clearly Wesleyan, but it is not affiliated with a particular Methodist body, and various presidents of the seminary have come from different churches in the Wesleyan family.

Nels Westergreen believed and taught what he understood to be John Wesley's theology of sanctification/perfect holiness, but in reality both men were part of a much longer and deeper tradition. The New Testament testifies that sanctification is God's gift, using passive verbs to emphasize divine rather than human agency (1 Cor 6:11).[39] During the Middle Ages, the Western Church spoke of the real change wrought in the individual following justification: a growth in grace, as described by Paul in Phil 1:6. The Council of Trent described it as an increase in justification which amounted to a growth in sanctification. The idea of "growing in grace," reflected in the text cited above and in Phil 3:12–14, underlies the long history of sanctification theology in the larger church. It can be found today in any Christian body with a focus on evangelism,[40] a belief in the ongoing work of the Holy Spirit to transform the individual believer into the knowledge and likeness of Christ, and a commitment to continual openness to the Spirit's work. It is evidenced by loving obedience to God's revealed will in everyday life, both individually and communally. In this respect, Westergreen was part of a legacy that lives on in Christian tradition.

39. Wainwright, "Sanctification," 521.

40. By evangelism, I mean sharing the gospel with others through word and action and, with God's help, leading them to faith in Jesus Christ as Savior and Lord.

Churches and Preaching Places
of the Central Swedish
Methodist Conference

WESTERGREEN WORKED WITHIN WHAT became the Central Swedish Conference his entire ministry. In some instances, the dates listed in *Svenska Metodismen I Amerika* do not agree with those given in conference journals. Westergreen preached multiple places that are not part of this list, including Leland, Norway, and Bunkum/Iroquois, Illinois; possible reasons are that these chose to affiliate early on with the Norwegian-Danish Methodists or the Methodist Episcopal Church, or the ministry of Swedish Methodists did not result in the establishment of a permanent church. It should also be remembered that conference and district names and boundaries changed multiple times over the years. For a listing of churches and preaching places in the Northern, Western, Eastern, Pacific, and Southern Conferences at the time of the merger with the larger Methodist Church, see the *Official Yearbook and Journal of the Central Northwest Conference* (1942).

Church or Place	Work Began
Abingdon, IL	1850
Akron, OH	1914
Aldine/Knox, IN	1911
Alliance, OH	1914
Andover, IL	1849
Ashtabula, OH	1914
Attica, IN	1855
Aurora, IL	1884
Battleground, IN	1863
Batavia, IL	1876[1]
Beaver, IL	1853
Belleview, PA	1915

1. The congregation was established in 1870, according to *Svenska Metodismen i Amerika*.

Bishop Hill, IL	1855[2]	South Shore/Cheltenham	1881
Bloomington, IL	1884	Union Avenue	1893
Braddock, PA	1887	Wellington Park	1926[4]
Buffalo, NY	1853	West Pullman	1909
Buena Vista, IN	1855	Chicago Heights	1903
Canal Dover, OH	1915	Cleveland, OH	1885
Canton, OH	1915	Corning, NY	1914
Center Prairie, IL	1850	Donovan, IL	1854
Chandler's Valley, NY	1851	Downers Grove, IL	1894
Chesterton, IN	1879	East Chicago, IN	1890
Chicago, IL:		Erie, PA	1914
Atlantic	1887	Evanston, IL	1870
Auburn Park	1913	Falconer, NY	1894
Austin	1893	Frewsbury, NY	1853
Bethany	1891	Galesburg, IL	1849
Bethel (Mt. Greenwood)	1921	Galva, IL	1867
Bethel (Eastside)	1911	Gary/Chesterton, IN	1909
Carmel	1906	Geneseo, IL	1853
Elim/Lakeview	1882	Geneva, IL	1870
Emanuel	1892	Harvey, IL	1902
Englewood	1883	Highland Park, IL	1895
Fifth Avenue/Third	1873	Hinsdale, IL	1894
First/Market Street	1852	Highwood, IL	1894
Forest Glen	1856	Hobart, IN	1884
Humboldt Park	1886[3]	Jackson Center, IN	1934
Hyde Park	1890	Jamestown, NY	1851
May Street/Second	1852	Joliet, IL	1890
McKinley Park	1891	Kennedy, NY	1853
Moreland	1890	Kewanee, IL	1859
Roseland	1881	Knox, IN	1911
Salem	1900	Knoxville, IL	1850

2. The first sermon by a Swedish Methodist preacher may have been given in 1855, but the first pastor appointed there was Nels O. Westergreen in 1864.

3. Joined with the Rock River Conference in 1919.

4. Joined with the Rock River Conference in 1919.

Lafayette, IL	1859	Racine, WI	1883
Lafayette, IN	1855	Randolph, PA	1887
La Grange, IL	1894	Riverside, IL	1894
Lake Forest, IL	1894	Rochester, NY	1914
Maywood, IL	1888	Rockford, IL	1854
McKeesport, PA	1887	Rock Island, IL	1851
Melrose Park, IL	1888	Ross Mills, PA	_____
Michigan City, IN	1913	St. Charles, IL	_____
Milwaukee, WI	1895	Sugar Grove, NY	1853
Moline, IL	1849	Swedona, IL	1854
Monessen, PA	1909	Tipton, IN	1863
Monmouth, IL	1850	Victoria, IL	1846
New Aldine, NY	1853	Warren, PA	1887
New Windsor, IL	1883	Wataga, IL	1857
Oak Park, IL	1888	Watertown, IL	1853
Opheim, IL	1854	Washington, PA	1914
Orion, IL	1854	Waukegan, IL	1892
Ottawa, IL	1892	Western Springs, IL	1877
Oquawka, IL	1850	Worksbury, NY	1853
Peoria, IL	1858	Weightsville, NY	1853
Pittsburg, PA	1887	Youngstown, OH	1914
Poolsville, IN	1855	Yorktown, IN	1854
Quaker Hill, PA	1851		

Glossary

After-meeting	an informal and spontaneous time of prayer, singing, and testimony following a campmeeting or protracted meeting. It may last a few minutes or many hours.
Application	the final part of a sermon, in which the preacher brings the ideas already presented to bear on the congregation. In a campmeeting or protracted meeting, the application was often done by an exhorter, and included an invitation to come to faith in Christ, reconsecrate oneself to Christ, and/or pray for the sanctifying power of the Holy Spirit.
Appointment	In the MEC and Swedish Conferences, the bishop, assisted by presiding elders/superintendents, decided annually where a minister would serve the church. This is in contrast to congregational governance, in which an individual congregation could call or fire a minister without approval from a denominational leader, such as a bishop or president.
Azusa Street Revival	a revival meeting in Los Angeles that ran from 1906 to approximately 1915. It is considered the genesis of the modern Pentecostal movement, emphasizing the necessity of baptism in the Holy Spirit and exercising various spiritual gifts, especially speaking in tongues.
Book of Discipline	A book published every four years that states the beliefs and policies of the Methodist

Church. The *Book of Discipline* may be amended or altered as the result of legislative action by the General Conference.

Burning Bush

a periodical published by the Metropolitan Church Association, also known as the Burning Bush Movement.

Campmeeting

an annual summer gathering of believers and seekers for several days of worship, Bible study, and fellowship. Early campmeetings took place in the open air or large tents; later, amenities such as cottages, dining facilities, and tabernacles were built. A campmeeting was usually led by multiple ordained and lay preachers/ministers, with an exhorter immediately following the preacher. In the Methodist tradition, this was a time when new classes or congregations might be organized, and quarterly conferences might also take place.

Chautauqua

an adult education and social movement originating in Chautauqua, New York. It was organized in 1874 by John Heyl Vincent, a Methodist minister, for the purpose of training Sunday School teachers in an outdoor summer school. The focus gradually became less religious. In outward appearance, the original Chautauqua resembles established religious campgrounds, with individual cottages and large auditoriums in an attractive wooded setting.

Circuit / circuit rider

a geographical area in which an itinerant preacher (circuit rider) traveled, usually on horseback, leading worship, attempting to establish new congregations, and ministering to Christians already organized into classes or congregations.

Class-meetings

small groups within the Methodist system that met regularly for prayer, mutual support, and accountability. Each class had lay leadership.

Conference	In Methodist parlance, conference refers both to the churches within a geographical area and the annual meeting of clergy and lay delegates from that area. A bishop is the administrative, pastoral, and liturgical leader of a conference. The bishop is assisted by superintendents/presiding elders, each with responsibility for one region within the conference. At an annual conference meeting, there will be worship, committee reports, legislative action, and ordination of new ministers.
Consecration	to set aside or dedicate for sacred purposes. In the sacrament of Holy Communion, the bread and the cup are consecrated. In some traditions, the liturgical rite for making someone a bishop is called consecration. In individual religious experience, a person dedicates oneself anew to holy living or some other change in the name of his/her faith.
Conventicle	In Sweden, a meeting of pious Christians for Bible study, prayer, the singing of religious songs, and/or testimony, often without the permission or leadership of clergy.
Conversion	a gradual or crisis experience of putting one's trust in Jesus Christ as Savior and Lord, and committing oneself to be his disciple.
Course of study	a series of courses in Bible, theology, history, and ministry, offered for those who wish to become local pastors and who, for various reasons, do not enroll in a master of divinity or equivalent degree program.
Deacon	in Methodist polity, a (transitional) deacon is a probationary minister who may be ordained an elder/presbyter and member of the Conference in full connection after a period under supervision.
Elder	synonymous with presbyter, an elder has been ordained by a bishop and is a clergy member in full connection. Elders may preside at Holy

Communion and vote on all matters that come before the conference.

Evangeliske Tidende	*Gospel Tidings*, a newspaper of the Norwegian-Danish Methodist Church.
Exhorter	someone who speaks after the preacher, usually in an evangelistic worship service, bringing the message proclaimed to bear on the listeners' particular circumstances and issuing an invitation to come forward for prayer. In the Methodist tradition, this was sometimes a lay preacher, licensed by the ordained minister or conference, who also led prayer and class-meetings. An exhorter's license was often the first step toward ordination. Today, it is called a license to preach, and is one step in becoming a local pastor.
General Conference	a quadrennial meeting of clergy and lay delegates from all the conferences, at which there is worship, common concerns are addressed, and legislation may be passed to amend or change the *Book of Discipline*.
Glossalalia	from the Greek word meaning "tongue talking," i.e., speaking in tongues. It is most often a private prayer language, as enabled by the Holy Spirit. In a public religious gathering, another person may interpret what has been said in tongues for the edification of others present.
Gospel song	a type of congregational song used in informal settings. It is often narrative theology about the singer's pilgrimage of faith, and has a repeated refrain after each stanza.
Holiness	the state of being filled with and directed by the Holy Spirit, evidenced in godly speech and action that reflect the grace of the Lord Jesus Christ.
Holy jumpers	a name given to people given to dancing, jumping, and other demonstrations in worship when under the power of the Holy Spirit. The name was particularly applied to members of the

	Metropolitan Church Association in Chicago, also known as the Burning Bush Movement.
Justification	an expression for salvation, i.e., being made just or righteous before God by grace through faith in the merits and atoning work of Jesus Christ, rather than through one's own works.
Kristelige Talsmand	*Christian Advocate*, a newspaper of the Norwegian-Danish Methodist Church in America
Läsare	"readers." It was a name given to Pietists in Sweden who met together in small, house groups called conventicles for Bible study and prayer.
Local pastor	a person who has been granted a license to preach and attended the ministerial course of study at an approved seminary, and is authorized by the bishop to ministry of Word and Sacrament only at the church/es to which he/she is appointed.
MEC	The Methodist Episcopal Church, which, along with the MEC South, were the largest Methodist groups in the United States in the nineteenth and early twentieth centuries.
Mission Friends	one of the names of the Swedish Evangelical Lutheran Mission Synod, which became a separate denomination in 1885 and is now known as the Evangelical Covenant Church.
Perfection	completion or maturity. Christian perfection, a moment by moment attainment subsequent to justification, is a state of being entirely filled through the Holy Spirit with love for God and for neighbor, so that the heart is purified from original sin, one is delivered from the necessity of sin, and grows into the likeness of Christ. Irreversible perfection does not happen in this mortal life but is completed at the final judgment.

Pietist/Pietism   a religious movement originating in the 17th-century German Lutheran Church, started by Philip Jakob Spener, which emphasizes individual and group Bible study, devotional experiences, and practice rather than dogmatic orthodoxy or fixed liturgical forms.

Platform   the portion of a religious assembly space where the preacher, other speakers, and possibly musicians are during worship. In evangelistic services there is not likely to be a formal altar in this space, though the entire are below/in front of the platform may be referred to as the altar.

Presiding elder   a minister assigned by the bishop to oversee other ministers and congregations within a geographical portion of a conference. They are now called district superintendents.

Protracted meeting   a series of evangelistic services, akin to a camp-meeting but held indoors. Protracted meetings might run for one week or for several week depending on the level of participation and response.

Psalmbok   the hymnbook of the Swedish (Lutheran) Church and other denominational hymnbooks containing primarily strophic hymns.

Quarterly conference   In Methodist tradition, a congregational meeting and/or report on membership statistics, stewardship, and ministries, which took place every three months. The report was given to the district superintendent/presiding elder, who shared it with the bishop to guide them in making appointments and providing guidance for the congregation and minister(s).

Sanctification   the ongoing work of the Holy Spirit in an individual after justification (coming to faith in Christ): the process of being made holy. Sanctification enables the believer grow in grace and in the likeness of Christ, and may culminate in Christian perfection.

Sändebudet	(*The Messenger*) the main newspaper of the Swedish Methodist Episcopal Church. It was started in 1862 by Victor Witting.
Tabernacle	a building used for summer campmeetings, often with open or screen sides. It normally has a raised platform the speaker(s) and seats may be arranged in a semicircle. Traditionally, the floor was covered with sawdust, hence " walking the sawdust trail" was a metaphor for going forward when an invitation was issued to be converted.
Temperance	An attitude toward the consumption or production of beverage alcohol. Originally it meant refraining from distilled spirits and moderation in the consumption of beer and wine, but in American culture it came to mean total abstinence.

Bibliography

Abraham, William J., and James E. Kirby, eds. *The Oxford Handbook of Methodist Studies*. Oxford: Oxford University Press, 2009.

Advertisement for "Maltos Cannabis." *Sändebudet*, September 5, 1895.

"Allcock's Plaster." October 16, 2009. www.thequackdoctor.com/index.php/allcocks-porous-plasters/.

Altenburg, Johann Michael, and Johan Olof Wallin. "Förfäras ej, du lilla hop" [Be not dismayed, thou little flock]. In *Den Svenska Psalmboken av konungen gillad och stadfäst år 1819 och nya psalmer år 1921 medgivna att användas tillsammans med 1819 års psalmbok* [The Swedish Hymnbook approved by the king and ratified in 1819 and new hymns 1921 granted for use together with the 1819 hymnal], 378. Göteborg, Sweden: Melins, 1921.

Ancestry.com. *The Westergreen Name in History*. Print book. Provo, UT: Generations Network, 2007.

Ander, Oscar Fritiof. *T. N. Hasselquist: The Career and Influence of a Swedish-American Clergyman, Journalist and Educator*. Rock Island, IL: Augustana, 1931.

Andersen, Arlow W. *The Salt of the Earth: History of Norwegian Danish Methodism in America*. Nashville: Parthenon, 1962.

———. "*Sändebudet* and American Public Affairs 1862–1872." *Augustana Quarterly* (October 1945) 1–10.

Anderson, Alfred. *Historiskt föredrag vid 50-årsfesten den 26 maj 1920 i Metodistkyrkans Svenska Teologiska Seminarium* [A historical lecture on the fiftieth anniversary of the Swedish Methodist Theological Seminary]. Chicago: Svenska Metodist Episkopal, 1920.

Anderson, Philip J., et al., eds. *Scandinavians in Old and New Lands: Essays in Honor of H. Arnold Barton*. Chicago: Swedish American Historical Society, 2004.

Anderson, Philip J., and Dag Blanck, eds. *Swedish-American Life in Chicago: Cultural and Urban Aspects of an Immigrant People, 1850–1930*. Urbana: University of Illinois Press, 1992.

Andersson, Ingvar, and Jörgen Weibull. *Swedish History in Brief*. Stockholm: Swedish Institute, 1980.

Andreas, A. T. *History of Cook County*. Chicago: Andreas, 1884.

Arden, G. Everett. *Augustana Heritage*. Rock Island, IL: Augustana, 1963.

Armstrong, Chris. "Wrestling Jacob: The Central Struggle and Emotional Scripts of Camp-Meeting Holiness Hymnody." In *Singing the Lord's Song in a Strange Land: Hymnody in the History of North American Protestantism*, 175. Tuscaloosa: University of Alabama Press, 2004.

"Arrival of Swedish Immigrants." *Fall River Monitor*, September 27, 1852.

Arthur, William. *The Tongue of Fire; or, the True Power of Christianity*. New York: Harper, 1870.

Atterling, Henry. *Henric Schartau och John Wesley: En Jämförande Studie* [Henric Schartau and John Wesley: A comparative study]. Stockholm: Svenska Kyrkans Dialonistyrelses, 1938.

Bachin, Robin F. *Building the South Side: Urban Space and Civic Culture in Chicago*. Chicago: University of Chicago Press, 2004.

Beijbom, Ulf. *Swedes in Chicago: A Demographic and Social Study of the 1846–1880 Immigration*. Translated by Donald Brown. Växjö, Sweden: Davidsons, 1971.

Blake, William O. *The History of Slavery and the Slave Trade*. Columbus, OH: Miller, 1857.

Blanck, Dag. "Swedish Immigration to North America." 2009. https://www.augustana.edu/swenson/academic/history.

Book of Discipline of the United Methodist Church. Nashville: United Methodist, 2004.

Bowman, C. V. *The Mission Covenant of America*. Chicago: Covenant, 1925.

Brailsford, Mabel Richmond. *A Tale of Two Brothers: John and Charles Wesley*. New York: Oxford University Press, 1954.

Brochure from Swedish Theological Seminary, 1889. Northern Illinois Conference Archives, Garrett-Evangelical Theological Seminary, Evanston, IL.

Brown, Kenneth O. "Finding America's Oldest Camp Meeting." *Methodist History* 28 (July 1990) 252–54.

Brown-Lawson, Albert. *John Wesley and the Christian Ministry: The Sources and Development of His Opinions and Practice*. London: SPCK, 1963.

Butler-Wall, Brita. "Anna Sophia: Memoir of a Prophet's Wife." *Swedish-American Historical Quarterly* 66 (July 2015) 151–76.

Carbaugh, Harvey C., ed. *Human Welfare Work in Chicago*. Chicago: McClurg, 1917.

Carlson, John A. "Report on the Eastern District." In *Year Book: Western Swedish Annual Conference, Methodist Episcopal Church 1925*, 281–82. Swede Plain, NE: Committee on Conference Journal, 1925.

Case, Riley. "United Methodism: Upper Grade Clergy." August 2019. https://www.facebook.com/confessing/movement/posts/ 3267424956602842.

CDC. "1918 Pandemic." https://www.cdc.gov/flu/pandemic-resources/1918-pandemic-h1n1.html.

Central Swedish Methodist Conference Journal. Chicago: Methodist, 1906.

Chapman, Charles C., et al. *History of Knox County, Illinois*. Chicago: Blakely, Brown & Marsh, 1878.

Chindberg, O. J. "Special Statistical Report." In *Official Journal of the Eighth Annual Session, Central Northwest Conference of the Methodist Episcopal Church*, 324. Chicago: Methodist, 1935.

Church Messenger: Bishop Hill Community Methodist Church. Marceline, MO: Walsworth, 1951.

"Course List for Swedish Methodist Theological Seminary." *Sändebudet*, January 25, 1886.

Crespo-Fernandez, Eliecer. *Linguistic Devices for Coping with Death in Victorian Obituaries*. Master's thesis, University of Castilla-La Mancha (Spain), 2007.

Crook, Richard J. *Jesse Walker, Pioneer Preacher*. Plainfield, IL: Crook, 1976.

Dahlhielm, Erik. *A Burning Heart: A Biography of Erik August Skogsbergh*. Chicago: Covenant, 1951.

———. *On the High Tide of Faith: A Sketch of the Life of Erik August Skogsbergh.* Chicago: Covenant Historical Commission, 1940.

Dayton, Donald, ed. *Late Nineteenth Century Revivalist Teaching on the Holy Spirit.* New York: Garland, 1985.

Den Svenska Psalmboken av konungen gillad och stadfäst år 1819 och nya psalmer år 1921 medgivna att användas tillsammans med 1819 års psalmbok [The Swedish Hymnbook approved by the king and ratified in 1819 and new hymns 1921 granted for use together with the 1819 hymnal]. Göteborg, Sweden: Melins, 1921.

Dieter, Melvin E. *The Holiness Revival of the Nineteenth Century.* Lanham, MD: Scarecrow, 1996.

Dowie, James Iverne. *Prairie Grass Dividing.* Rock Island, IL: Augustana, 1959.

Dru, Alexander. *The Journals of Soren Kierkegaard.* London: Oxford University Press, 1938.

Edgren, Adolf. *Kantat vid Jubelfestem: till firande af Svenska M. E. Kyrkans Femtio-åriga tillvaro i Amerika* [Cantata for jubilee festival celebrating fifty years of the Swedish Methodist Church's presence in America]. Chicago: Adolf Edgren and A. J. Anderson, May 30, 1895. Northern Illinois Conference Archives, Garrett-Evangelical Theological Seminary, Evanston, IL.

Elmen, Paul. Letter to Carol Norén. November 1980.

———. *Wheat Flour Messiah: Erik Jansson of Bishop Hill.* Carbondale: Southern Illinois University Press, 1976.

Elmström, et al. "En Värdeful Bok" [A valuable book]. *Sändebudet*, June 29, 1885.

Empereur, Raymond W. *The Development of Public Health in Rockford and Winnebago County, Illinois from 1854 to 2004.* Rockford, IL: Winnebago County Health Department, 2004.

Erickson, Scott E. *David Nyvall and the Shape of an Immigrant Church: Ethnic, Denominational, and Educational Priorities Among Swedes in America.* PhD diss., University of Uppsala, 1996.

Erikson, Erik. *Childhood and Society.* New York: Norton, 1950, 1963.

"Evanston Collegiate Institute." In *Official Journal and Year Book of the Central Northwest Conference, Sixty-Sixth Annual Session, June 20–23, 1942*, 207–8. Chicago: Methodist, 1942.

Froman, B. R. "An Interior View of the Camp Douglas Conspiracy." *Southern Bivouac*, October 1882.

Fuener, Cynthia A. "Religion Under the Stars: The Des Plaines Methodist Campground." *Historic Illinois*, April 2010.

Fyrlund, Björn. *Tro och Helgelse. En Analys av Johan Olof Wallins Moraluppfattning* [Faith and holiness: An analysis of Johan Olof Wallin's moral understanding]. PhD diss., University of Uppsala, 1999.

"General Conference Memorial." In *Year Book: Central Northwest Conference, Methodist Episcopal Church Fourth Annual Session, 1931.* Milwaukee, Wisconsin: Swan W. Mattson, 1931.

Giffords, Carolyn DeSwarte, ed. *Writing Out My Heart: Selections from the Journal of Frances E. Willard, 1855–96.* Urbana: University of Illinois Press, 1995.

Gordon, G. E., et al. "In Memoriam: The Rev. Nels O. Westergreen." In *Minutes of the Twenty-seventh Session, Central Swedish Annual Conference of the Methodist Episcopal Church.* Chicago: Methodist, 1920.

Granquist, Mark A., ed. *Scandinavian Pietists: Spiritual Writings from 19th Century Norway, Denmark, Sweden, and Finland.* New York: Paulist, 2015.

Greenwall, Robert. "What Was Schartauan Pietism." *Pietisten* 16 (Spring 2001) n.p.

Gustafson, Anita Olson. *Swedish Chicago: The Shaping of an Immigrant Community 1880–1920.* Dekalb: Northern Illinois University Press, 2018.

Hacker, Ruth Michaelsen. *Precious Memories: Kedzie Avenue Methodist Church.* Chicago, 2000. Northern Illinois Conference Archives, Garrett-Evangelical Theological Seminary, Evanston, IL.

Hagelin, Gösta. *Den Som Skrev Våra Psalmer* [Those who wrote our hymns]. Stockholm: Verbum, 1969.

Hägglund, Henrik. *Notes on Henric Schartau and the Order of Grace.* Rock Island, IL: Augustana, 1928.

Hahn, Heather. "Church Lacks Racial Diversity." September 20, 2010. https://www.umnews.org/en/news/church-lacks-racial-diversity-officials-say.

Hartwell, Joseph. "Chapters from Memory." *Prattville District Register*, December 1885.

Hasselmo, Nils, ed. *Perspectives on Swedish Immigration.* Chicago: Swedish Pioneer Historical Society, in association with University of Minnesota, Duluth, 1978.

Haynes, Donald W. "Methodism: How We Went Wrong." October 2020. https://firebrandmag.com/article/methodism-how-we-went-wrong.

Henricson, Ingvar, and Hans Lindblad. *Tur och Retur Amerika: Utvandrare som Förändrade Sverige* [To America and back: Emigrants who transformed Sweden]. Stockholm: Fischer, 1995.

Henschen, William. "Är Du Ett Helgon?" [Are you a saint]. *Sändebudet*, March 28, 1876.

———. Obituary of Andrew Theodor Westergreen. *Sändebudet*, January 14, 1903.

History of First Lutheran Church of Attica, Indiana. Swenson Swedish Immigration Center Microfilm Archives, Augustana College, Rock Island, IL.

"History of Garrett-Evangelical Theological Seminary." http://www.garrett.edu/history.

Hodsdon, Lucille Hemon, and Noella Hemond. *Homesteads/Homes of Minot: Schools, Granges, Churches.* Norway, ME: Hodson, 2004.

Hurtig, Mansfield, ed. *Metodistkyrkan i Sverige 100 År 1868–1968* [The Methodist Church in Sweden: One hundred years 1868–1968]. Stockholm: Nya Bokförlags Aktiebolaget, 1968.

Hymnal of the Evangelical Covenant Church of America. Chicago: Covenant, 1950.

Hymnal of the Evangelical Covenant Church of America. Chicago: Covenant, 1973.

Hynson, Leon O., ed. *The Development of Wesleyan Holiness Theology.* Wesleyan Theological Journal 13. Marion, IN: Wesleyan Theological Society, 1978.

"Inspirational Hours." In *Official Journal and Year Book of the Central Northwest Conference, Sixty-Sixth Annual Session, June 20–23, 1942*, 208. Chicago: Methodist, 1942.

Isaksson, Olov, and Sören Hallgren. *Bishop Hill, Illinois: A Utopia on the Prairie.* Translated by Albert Read. Stockholm: LT, 1969.

Janes, Edmond S. "Sker Helgelsen Ögonblickligen eller Småningom?" [Does sanctification happen instantly or gradually]. *Sändebudet*, March 9, 1885.

Jansson, Eric. *Cateches* [Catechism]. Söderhamn, Sweden: n.p., 1846.

Jennings, Daniel R. *The Supernatural Occurrences of John Wesley.* Oklahoma City: Sean Multimedia, 2005.

Johannsen, Robert W. *Letters of Stephen A. Douglas.* Urbana: University of Illinois Press, 1961.

Jones, Charles Edwin. *Perfectionist Persuasion: The Holiness Movement and American Methodism, 1867–1936.* Metuchen, NJ: Scarecrow, 1974.

Johnson, Charles A. *The Frontier Camp Meeting.* Dallas: Southern Methodist University Press, 1955.

The Journal of the General Conference of the Methodist Episcopal Church. Nashville: Methodist, 1896.

Kingo, Thomas. "Nu Skall Ej Synden Mera" [No longer shall sin hold me]. In *Den Svenska Psalmboken av konungen gillad och stadfäst år 1819 och nya psalmer år 1921 medgivna att användas aillsammans med 1819 års psalmbok* [The Swedish Hymnbook approved by the king and ratified in 1819 and new hymns 1921 granted for use together with the 1819 hymnal], 209. Göteborg, Sweden: Melins, 1921.

Kostlevy, William. *Holy Jumpers: Evangelicals and Radicals in Progressive Era America.* New York: Oxford University Press, 2010.

Leman, Kevin. *The Birth Order Book: Why You Are the Way You Are.* Old Tappan, NJ: Revell, 1985.

Levy, George. *To Die in Chicago: Confederate Prisoners at Camp Douglas, 1862–1865.* Evanston, IL: Evanston, 1994.

Lewis, Rob. *Images of America: Fall River.* Charleston, SC: Arcadia, 1997.

Liljegren, N. M., et al. *Historik över Svenska Metodismen i Amerika från 1877 till 1903* [History of Swedish Methodism in America from 1877 to 1903]. Chicago: Svenska Metodist Episkopal, 1903.

———. *Svenska Metodismen i Amerika* [Swedish Methodism in America]. Chicago: Svenska Metodist Episkopal, 1895.

Lippy, Charles. "The Camp Meeting in Transition: The Character and Legacy of the Late Nineteenth Century." *Methodist History* 34 (1995) 3–15.

Ljungmark, Lars. *Swedish Exodus.* Translated by Kermit B. Westerberg. Carbondale: Southern Illinois University Press, 1979.

Löfgren, Anders J. "Inlägg i frågor på dagordningen: Ännu ett ord i frågan om de svensktalade metodistkonferenseras upplösning" [Inserting a question about the agenda: Yet another word about the dissolving of the Swedish-speaking conferences]. *Sändebudet,* August 20, 1918.

Lorenz, Ellen Jane. *Glory, Hallelujah! The Story of the Campmeeting Spiritual.* Nashville: Parthenon, 1978.

Lövgren, Oscar. *Den Segrande Sången* [The song of victory]. Falköping, Sweden: Gummessons, 1967.

Marsden, George M. *The Soul of the American University.* New York: Oxford University Press, 1994.

Maser, Frederick E., and Howard T. Maag, eds. *The Journal of Joseph Pilmore: Methodist Itinerant, for the Years August 1, 1769 to January 2, 1774.* Philadelphia: Message, for Historical Society of Philadelphia Annual Conference of the United Methodist Church, 1969.

Melton, J. Gordon. *Log Cabins to Steeples: The United Methodist Way in Illinois, 1824–1974.* Nashville: Parthenon, 1974.

The Methodist Hymnbook with Tunes. London: Methodist Conference Office, 1933.

Metodist Episkopal Kyrkans Svenska Psalmbok [Methodist Episcopal Church's Swedish hymnal]. Chicago: Svenska Metodist Episkopal, 1884.

Moran, George E. *Moran's Dictionary of Chicago and Its Vicinity.* Chicago: Moran, 1910.

"Mr. Westergreen Died in Chicago." *Galesburg Republican-Register,* January 11, 1910.

Nausner, Michael. "Swedish Methodists in America and Their Quest for Identity: An Identity Struggle as Mirrored by the Magazine *Sändebudet* in the 1860s." *Methodist History* 39 (October 2000) 4–14.

Nelson, Edward O. *Hallelujah! Recollections of Salvation Army Scandinavian Work in the U.S.A.* Chicago: Salvation Army, 1987.

Newman, S. B. *Pastor S. B. Newmans Sjelfbiografi: Den Äldste Svenske Metodistpredikanten* [S. B. Newman's autobiography: The oldest Swedish Methodist preacher]. Chicago: Svenska Metodist Episkopal, 1890.

Nicholson, Thomas. "Historical Edition." In *Official Journal and Year Book of the Central Northwest Conference, Sixty-Sixth Annual Session, 1942*, 198. Chicago: Methodist, 1942.

Norén, Carol M. "A Study of Wesley's Doctrine of Christian Perfection in the Theology and Method of Nineteenth Century Swedish Methodist Preachers in Northern Illinois, with Particular Emphasis on the Writings of Nels O. Westergreen." PhD diss., Princeton Theological Seminary, 1986.

Norwood, Frederick. *From Dawn to Midday at Garrett*. Evanston, IL: Garrett-Evangelical Theological Seminary, 1978.

———. *The Story of American Methodism*. Nashville: Abingdon, 1974.

Nylin, Henry G. *The History of Swedish Methodism in Chicago*. Master's thesis, Northwestern University, 1925.

Odegaard, R. Arlo. *With Singleness of Heart: Pioneers and Pioneering for Christ in Home Mission Fields*. Minneapolis: Free Church, 1971.

Official Church Record: Historical Record of Permanent Data for Bethany United Methodist Church, Rockford Illinois. Northern Illinois Conference Archives, Garrett-Evangelical Theological Seminary, Evanston, IL.

Official Journal of the Eighth Annual Session, Central Northwest Conference of the Methodist Episcopal Church. Chicago: Methodist, 1935.

Official Journal and Year Book of the Central Northwest Conference, Sixty-Sixth Annual Session, June 20–23, 1942. Chicago: Methodist, 1942.

Official Records of the War of the Rebellion. Washington: US Government Printing Office, series 2, no. 3, 1901.

Olson, Ernst W., et al. *History of The Swedes of Illinois, Part I*. Chicago: Engberg-Holmberg, 1908.

———. *The Illinois Conference 1853–1928 Jubilee Album Published in Commemoration of the Seventy-Fifth Anniversary of the Illinois Conference of the Evangelical Lutheran Augustana Synod*. Rock Island, IL: Augustana, 1928.

Olson, Oscar N. *The Augustana Lutheran Church in America: Pioneer Period 1846–1860*. Rock Island, IL: Augustana, 1950.

Olsson, Annie S. Letter to Nels O. Westergreen, May 25, 1908. Private collection of the late Arthur Westergreen.

Olsson, Karl A. *By One Spirit*. Chicago: Covenant, 1962.

Olsson, Mats, and Patrick Svensson. "Explaining Agricultural Growth: The Case of Sweden 1700–1850." Paper presented at the Social Science History Association Conference, Miami, October 23–26, 2008.

Olsson, Nils William, ed. *A Pioneer in Northwest America 1841–1858: The Memoirs of Gustaf Unonius*. Translated by Jonas Oscar Backlund. Minneapolis: University of Minnesota Press, 1960.

———. "St. Ansgarius and the Immigrant Community." In *Swedish-American Life in Chicago: Cultural and Urban Aspects of an Immigrant People, 1850–1930*, edited by

Philip J. Anderson and Dag Blanck, 39–47. Urbana: University of Illinois Press, 1992.

Original Parish Register of Immanuel Lutheran Church. Evanston, Illinois, 1888.

Ottander, Otto A. "Trust in the Savior, O Precious Soul" [Håll dig vid klippan]. In *The Covenant Hymnal*, 402. Chicago: Covenant 1973.

"Pandemic Resources 1918." http://www.CDC.gov/flu/pandemic-resources/1918.

Pennewell, Albert M. *The Methodist Movement in Northern Illinois.* Sycamore, IL: Sycamore Tribune, 1941.

Perry, Albert J. *The History of Knox County Illinois: Its Cities, Towns and People.* Vol. 1. Chicago: Clarke, 1912.

Pethrus, Levy. "Löftena kunna ej svika" [The promises cannot fail]. In *Psalmer och Sänger* [Hymns and songs], 254. Stockholm: Verbum, 1987.

Peters, John Leland. *Christian Perfection and American Methodism.* Nashville: Abingdon, 1956.

Pope-Levison, Priscilla. *Building the Old Time Religion: Women Evangelists in the Progressive Era.* New York: New York University Press, 2014.

"Prospectus for Swedish Methodist Theological School." *Sändebudet*, October 16, 1882.

Protokoll fört vid Svenska Centrala Konferensens av Metodist Episkopal Kyrkans Tjugofemte Sammanträde Hållet i Svenska Metodistkyrkan, Donovan, Illinois, den 19 till den 22 September 1918 [Minutes of the Swedish Central Conference of the Methodist Episcopal Church, twenty-fifth meeting in the Swedish Methodist Church, Donovan, Illinois, September 19–22, 1918]. Chicago: Methodist, 1918.

Rademacher, Paul. "Methodist Bicentennial Lecture." Lecture presented at Garrett-Evangelical Theological Seminary, Evanston, Illinois, January 1984.

Rees, Seth Cook. *Miracles in the Slums.* New York: Garland, 1885.

Richey, Russell E. "Shady Grove, Garden, and Wilderness: Methodism and the American Woodland." *Methodist History* 51 (2013) 258–74.

Ryden, E. E. *The Story of Our Hymns.* Rock Island, IL: Augustana, 1955.

Saliers, Daniel R. *The Des Plaines Campground: 125 Years of Methodist History.* Brochure. 1984.

Sandell, Lina. "Jesus, in Stillness Longing I Wait" [Herre, mitt hjärta]. In *The Covenant Hymnal*, 327. Chicago: Covenant, 1973.

"Scandinavian-Americans in the American Civil War." http://www.civilwarhome.com/scandinavian.htm.

Schalk, Carl, ed. *Key Words in Church Music: Definition Essays on Concepts, Practices, and Movements of Thought in Church Music.* St. Louis: Concordia, 1978.

Scott, Franklin D. *Sweden: The Nation's History.* Minneapolis: University of Minnesota, 1977.

Shaw, S. B., ed. *Echoes of the General Holiness Assembly: Chicago May 3–13, 1901.* New York: Garland, 1984.

Shelley, Bruce. "The Seminaries' Identity Crisis." *Christianity Today*, May 17, 1993.

Shetler, Brian, compiler. "Regarding Old Jeffrey: The Wesley Family and Its Paranormal Disturbances." *Methodist History* 59 (2020) 51–56.

Smith, Charles Howard. *The Hymnody of the Free Churches of Scandinavia: Its Background and Development.* PhD diss., University of Minnesota, 1968.

———. *Scandinavian Hymnody from the Reformation to the Present.* Metuchen, NJ: Scarecrow, 1987.

Sörlin, Daniel Salomon. "Ännu Rum" [There is yet room]. In *Davids Harpa* [David's harp], 10. Chicago: Williamson, 1883.

"Statistical Report." *Official Journal and Year Book of the Central Northwest Conference, Sixty-Sixth Annual Session, June 20–23, 1942*, 54. Chicago: Methodist, 1942.

Stein, K. James. *Philipp Jakob Spener: Pietist Patriarch.* Chicago: Covenant, 1986.

Stephenson, George M. *The Religious Aspects of Swedish Immigration: A Study of Immigrant Churches.* Minneapolis: University of Minnesota Press, 1932.

Stoeffler, F. Ernest. *Continental Pietism and Early American Christianity.* Grand Rapids: Eerdmans, 1976.

Stoneberg, Philip J. "Swedish Campmeetings." In *History of Henry County.* Vol. 1. Carrollton, MS: Pioneer, 1910.

Strom, Carl G., et al. *Nils Frykman, J. A. Hultman, A. L. Skoog: Biographical Sketches.* Chicago: Covenant, 1943.

"Superintendents' Report." In *Official Journal and Year Book of the Central Northwest Conference, Sixty-Sixth Annual Session, 1942*, 205–6. Chicago: Methodist, 1942.

Svedberg, Jesper. "Av Dig Förordnand, Store Gud" [By thee, ordained, great God]. In *Den Svenska Psalmboken av konungen gillad och stadfäst år 1819 och nya psalmer år 1921 medgivna att användas tillsammans med 1819 års psalmbok* [The Swedish Hymnbook approved by the king and ratified in 1819 and new hymns 1921 granted for use together with the 1819 hymnal], 316. Göteborg, Sweden: Melins, 1921.

Svensson, Patrick. "Peasants and Entrepreneurship in the Nineteenth-Century Agricultural Transformation of Sweden." *Social Science History* 30 (2006) 387–429.

Swanson, Alan. "Där Ute: Moberg's Predecessors." In *Perspectives on Swedish Immigration: Proceedings of the International Conference on the Swedish Heritage in the Upper Midwest, April 1–3, 1976*, edited by Nils Hasselmo, 279–90. Chicago: Swedish Pioneer Historical Society, in association with University of Minnesota, Duluth, 1978.

Sweet, William Warren. *Methodism in American History.* New York: Abingdon, 1961.

Swenson, William. "Dr. N. O. Westergreen Fyller 85 År" [Dr. N. O. Westergreen celebrates eighty-five years]. *Sändebudet*, July 29, 1919.

Syllabus Brochure of Swedish Methodist Theological Seminary, 1905. Northern Illinois Conference Archives, Garrett-Evangelical Theological Seminary, Evanston, IL.

Thirty-Fifth Anniversary 1892–1927: South Avenue—First Swedish Methodist Episcopal Church, Waukegan, Illinois. Northern Illinois Conference Archives, Garrett-Evangelical Theological Seminary, Evanston, IL.

Tredway, Thomas. "Two Anniversaries and Five Historians." *Swedish American Historical Quarterly* 63 (2012) 61–83.

Tucker, Karen B. Westerfield. *American Methodist Worship.* New York: Oxford University Press, 2001.

The United Methodist Hymnal. Nashville: United Methodist, 1989.

Wainwright, Geoffrey. "Sanctification." In *The Westminster Dictionary of Christian Theology.* Philadelphia: Westminster, 1983.

Wallenius, C. G. "Dr. N. O. Westergreen Ingången I Vilan" [Dr. N. O. Westergreen enters into rest]. *Sändebudet*, October 28, 1919.

———. *Historik över Fifth Avenue Svenska Metodist Församling i Chicago 1875–1917* [History of Fifth Avenue Swedish Methodist Church in Chicago 1875–1917].

Northern Illinois Conference Archives, Garrett-Evangelical Theological Seminary, Evanston, IL.

———. "Några uppgifter om tidnings utgivare, redaktion och sätteri" [Some statements about the paper's publishing, editing and composing room]. *Sändebudet, Diamond Jubilee Issue*, July 18, 1922.

———. "The Story of Sändebudet." *Sändebudet*, July 19, 1937.

Wallenius, C. G., and E. D. Olson. *A Short Story of the Swedish Methodism in America.* Reprint from vol. 2 of *The Swedish Element in America.* Chicago: Methodist, 1931.

Wallin, Johan Olof. "Ho är den för Herren träder" [Who shall come before the Lord]. In *Den Svenska Psalmboken av konungen gillad och stadfäst år 1819 och nya psalmer år 1921 medgivna att användas tillsammans med 1819 års psalmbok* [The Swedish Hymnbook approved by the king and ratified in 1819 and new hymns 1921 granted for use together with the 1819 hymnal], 294. Göteborg, Sweden: Melins, 1921.

———. "Jag Tror På Gud och Vet, att Han" [I believe in God, and know]. In *Den Svenska Psalmboken av konungen gillad och stadfäst år 1819 och nya psalmer år 1921 medgivna att användas tillsammans med 1819 års psalmbok* [The Swedish Hymnbook approved by the king and ratified in 1819 and new hymns 1921 granted for use together with the 1819 hymnal], 380. Göteborg, Sweden: Melins, 1921.

Wesley, Charles. "Come, O Thou Traveler Unknown." In *The Methodist Hymnbook with Tunes*, 339. London: Methodist Conference Office, 1933.

———. "God of All Power, and Truth, and Grace." In *The Methodist Hymnbook with Tunes*, 562. London: Methodist Conference Office, 1933.

———. "Holy, and True, and Righteous Lord." In *The Methodist Hymnbook with Tunes*, 570. London: Methodist Conference Office, 1933.

———. "The Thing My God Doth Hate." In *The Methodist Hymnbook with Tunes*, 547. London: Methodist Conference Office, 1933.

Wesley, John. "On Sin in Believers." In *Sermons on Several Occasions*, first series, published in 4 vols., 1771. London: Wesleyan Methodist Book Room, 1872.

———. "The Scripture Way of Salvation." In *John Wesley's Fifty-Three Sermons*, edited by Edward H. Sugden, 721–33. Nashville: Abingdon, 1983.

———. *Works of John Wesley.* Vol. 1, *Journals.* London: Wesleyan Methodist, 1872.

Westerberg, Thor J. "Address on a Century of Swedish Methodism." *Sändebudet*, November 15, 1948.

Westergreen, Henry. Unpublished essay about emigration journey of his father, Swan. Private collection of the late Arthur Westergreen, 1959.

Westergreen, Nels O. "Allmänna Helighets Principer" [General principles regarding holiness]. *Sändebudet*, July 20, 1885.

———. "Deruti är Kärlek Fullkomnad" [In this is love perfected]. Sermon on I John 4:17. Westergreen Papers. Northern Illinois Conference Archives, Garrett-Evangelical Theological Seminary, Evanston, IL.

———. "Funeral Sermon on Revelation 14:13." Westergreen Papers. Northern Illinois Conference Archives, Garrett-Evangelical Theological Seminary, Evanston, IL.

———. "Helgelsen Såsom ett Särskildt Nådeswerk" [Sanctification as a particular work of grace]. Sermon on Hebrews 12:14–15. Westergreen Papers. Northern Illinois Conference Archives, Garrett-Evangelical Theological Seminary, Evanston, IL.

————. "Hvar är Klagan, Hvar är Jemmer" [where are misery and groaning]. In *Metodist Episkopal Kyrkans Svenska Psalmbok* [Swedish hymnal of the Methodist Episcopal Church], 579. Chicago: Svenska Metodist Episkopal, 1884.

————. "Hwarje Kristen Bör Likna Kristus" [Every Christian should be like Christ]. Sermon on Philippians 2:5.Westergreen Papers. Northern Illinois Conference Archives, Garrett-Evangelical Theological Seminary, Evanston, IL.

————. "Icke Att Jag Allredan Hafver Det Fattat" [Not as though I had already attained]. Sermon on Philippians 3:12. Westergreen Papers. Northern Illinois Conference Archives, Garrett-Evangelical Theological Seminary, Evanston, IL.

————. *Journals from 1856 to 1919.* Westergreen Papers. Northern Illinois Conference Archives, Garrett-Evangelical Theological Seminary, Evanston, IL.

————. *Last Will and Testament.* Chicago: Cook County Archives, September 14, 1914.

————. *Lefnads Anteckning Från Min Barndom* [Life memorandum from my childhood]. Westergreen Papers. Northern Illinois Conference Archives, Garrett-Evangelical Theological Seminary, Evanston, IL.

————. Letter to Nellie Westergreen, October 26, 1909. Private collection of the late Arthur Westergreen.

————. Letter to Nellie Westergreen, October 15, 1914. Private collection of the late Arthur Westergreen.

————. Letter to Nellie Westergreen, August 5, 1918. Private collection of the late Arthur Westergreen.

————. "Men Fridens Gud Sjelf Helga Eder Till Hela Eder Warelse" [May the God of peace sanctify you wholly]. Sermon on 1 Thessalonians 5:23. Westergreen Papers. Northern Illinois Conference Archives, Garrett-Evangelical Theological Seminary, Evanston, IL.

————. "Minnen af Min Werksamhet som Predikant för Emellan 50 och 60 År" [Memories of my work as a preacher for between fifty and sixty years]. Westergreen Papers. Northern Illinois Conference Archives, Garrett-Evangelical Theological Seminary, Evanston, IL.

————. "Obituary for Eric Shogren." In *Central Swedish Methodist Conference Journal*, 52–54 Chicago: Methodist, 1906.

————. Postcard and letter to Swan Westergreen, December 18 and 19, 1898. Private collection of the late Arthur Westergreen.

————. "Sermon on Acts 20:17–22." Westergreen Papers. Northern Illinois Conference Archives, Garrett-Evangelical Theological Seminary, Evanston, IL.

————. "Sermon on Hebrews 13:8." Westergreen Papers. Northern Illinois Conference Archives, Garrett-Evangelical Theological Seminary, Evanston, IL.

————. "Sermon on John 7:37–39." Westergreen Papers. Northern Illinois Conference Archives, Garrett-Evangelical Theological Seminary, Evanston, IL.

————. *Skillnaden på Sann Helighet och Religiöst Svärmeri* [The difference between true holiness and religious fanaticism]. Chicago: Williamson, 1885.

————. *Uppteckningar af Mötande Omständigheter* [Notes on circumstances encountered]. Westergreen Papers. Northern Illinois Conference Archives, Garrett-Evangelical Theological Seminary, Evanston, IL.

————. "What Attitude Should We Assume toward Those Who Spread Error among Us." Westergreen Papers. Northern Illinois Conference Archives, Garrett-Evangelical Theological Seminary, Evanston, IL.

Westergreen, Thomas. Letter to Henry Westergreen, October 27, 1904. Private collection of Louise Mosher, Victoria, Illinois.

Westin, Gunnar. "The Background of Swedish Immigration." In *The Swedish Immigrant Community in Transition: Essays in Honor of Dr. Conrad Bergendoff.* Rock Island, IL: Augustana Historical Society, 1963.

———. *Ur Den Svenska Folkväckelsens Historia och Tankevärld* [From the Swedish revival and world of ideas]. Stockholm: Evangeliska Fosterlands Stiftelsen, 1930.

Whyman, Henry C. *The Hedstroms and the Bethel Ship Saga: Methodist Influence on Swedish Religious Life.* Carbondale, IL: Southern Illinois University Press, 1992.

Williams, Kim Eric. "America's First Hymnals by Andreas Rudman, Pastor, Gloria Dei (Old Swedes') Church, Philadelphia, Pennsylvania, 1697–1702." *Swedish-American Historical Quarterly* 69 (July 2018) 149–209.

Witting, Victor, ed. *Andeliga Sånger för Böne, Klass, och Förlängda Möten* [Spiritual songs for prayer, class, and protracted meetings]. Chicago: Hitchcock and Walden, 1870.

———. *Minnen Från mit lif som Sjöman, Immigrant och Predikant, Samt en Historisk Afhandling af Metodismens Uppkomst, Utveckling, Utbredning bland Svenskarne i Amerika och Sverige* [Memories of my life as a sailor, immigrant, and preacher, together with a historical treatise on Methodism's beginning, growth, and spread among Swedes in America and Sweden]. Worcester, MA: Burbank, 1902.

Year Book: Central Northwest Conference, Methodist Episcopal Church Fourth Annual Session, 1931. Chicago: Methodist, 1931.

Index

www.ingramcontent.com/pod-product-compliance
Lightning Source LLC
Chambersburg PA
CBHW070909100426
42814CB00003B/115